# ENGAGING WITH STRANGERS

## ASAO Studies in Pacific Anthropology

General Editor: Rupert Stasch, Department of Archaeology and Anthropology, University of Cambridge

The Association for Social Anthropology in Oceania (ASAO) is an international organization dedicated to studies of Pacific cultures, societies, and histories. This series publishes monographs and thematic collections on topics of global and comparative significance, grounded in anthropological fieldwork in Pacific locations.

Volume 1
*The Anthropology of Empathy: Experiencing the Lives of Others in Pacific Societies*
Edited by Douglas W. Hollan and C. Jason Throop

Volume 2
*Christian Politics in Oceania*
Edited by Matt Tomlinson and Debra McDougall

Volume 3
*The Death of the Big Men and the Rise of the Big Shots: Custom and Conflict in East New Britain*
Keir Martin

Volume 4
*Creating a Nation with Cloth: Women, Wealth, and Tradition in the Tongan Diaspora*
Ping-Ann Addo

Volume 5
*The Polynesian Iconoclasm: Religious Revolution and the Seasonality of Power*
Jeffrey Sissons

Volume 6
*Engaging with Strangers: Love and Violence in the Rural Solomon Islands*
Debra McDougall

# Engaging with Strangers

*Love and Violence in the Rural Solomon Islands*

Debra McDougall

berghahn
NEW YORK • OXFORD
www.berghahnbooks.com

First published in 2016 by
Berghahn Books
www.berghahnbooks.com

©2016, 2020 Debra McDougall
First paperback edition published in 2020

All rights reserved. Except for the quotation of short passages
for the purposes of criticism and review, no part of this book
may be reproduced in any form or by any means, electronic or
mechanical, including photocopying, recording, or any information
storage and retrieval system now known or to be invented,
without written permission of the publisher.

**Library of Congress Cataloging-in-Publication Data**
A C.I.P. cataloging record is available from the Library of Congress

**British Library Cataloguing in Publication Data**
A catalogue record for this book is available from the British Library

ISBN: 978-1-78533-020-9 (hardback)
ISBN: 978-1-78920-761-3 (paperback)
ISBN: 978-1-78533-021-6 (ebook)

For my parents

# Contents

| | |
|---|---|
| List of Figures | viii |
| Acknowledgments | x |
| Notes on Language, Orthography, and Names | xiv |
| Maps | xviii |
| Introduction: On Being a Stranger in a Hospitable Land | 1 |
| 1 Ethnicity, Insularity, and Hospitality | 17 |
| 2 Ranongga's Shifting Ground | 34 |
| 3 Incorporating Others in Violent Times | 64 |
| 4 Bringing the Gospel Ashore | 91 |
| 5 No Love? Dilemmas of Possession | 124 |
| 6 Estranging Kin: The Tribalization of Land Ownership | 160 |
| 7 Losing Passports: Mobility, Urbanization, Ethnicity | 188 |
| 8 Amity and Enmity in an Unreliable State | 219 |
| Glossary | 245 |
| References | 247 |
| Index | 275 |

# *Figures*

| | | |
|---|---|---|
| 0.1 | Map of Solomon Islands | xviii |
| 0.2 | Map of New Georgia Group | xix |
| 0.3 | Map of Ranongga Island, circa 2000 | xx |
| 0.4 | View from the gardens above Pienuna | 5 |
| 0.5 | "We Germans are buying and taking this woman from America" | 8 |
| 2.1 | Bleached coral south of Pienuna village | 35 |
| 2.2 | John Pavukera in a coconut grove | 49 |
| 2.3 | Community work in the garden of Liza Ekera | 51 |
| 2.4 | Loading a market canoe | 52 |
| 3.1 | An ancestral shrine | 74 |
| 3.2 | A large cache of intact shell valuables | 80 |
| 4.1 | Costas Paleo leads the mock attack on an arriving canoe | 92 |
| 4.2 | Bishop David Havea and Marama Havea arrive at Pienuna | 92 |
| 4.3 | Sera Wesley with her daughters Hazel Piqebakia Paleo and Grace Nose Sasapitu | 93 |
| 4.4 | United Church ministers are welcomed by the community | 94 |
| 4.5 | James Paleo and Grace Nosequla with an unidentified soldier | 104 |
| 4.6 | Monument to the memory of Joyce Dunateko Panakera | 118 |

5.1  Rosie Ekera gathering *Canarium* nuts (*ngari*) in a grove above Pienuna                                             129

5.2  John Wesley Paleo and Simion Beto with a canoe          132

5.3  An *ivata* (feast laid out on banana leaves)                  134

5.4  The grave of Lokasasa, with a painted cross and a *bakia* embedded in the cement                                       147

5.5  Helena Enaduri speaking in front of baskets (*topa*) at a grave cementing ceremony                                       148

6.1  Baniata after the completion of logging operations       161

8.1  "Freestyle" dancing in a peri-urban neighborhood of Honiara   229

All photographs taken by the author except as noted in captions.

# Acknowledgments

My biggest thanks go to the generous people of Ranongga. I hope that this book does some justice to their experiences and struggles and that it will be useful to future generations of Ranonggans and other Solomon Islanders trying to understand their own history. In order to acknowledge the contributions that many people have made to this study, I change names only in cases where the information presented is sensitive or controversial. I thank Pienuna village chief John Pavukera and the late Samuel Samata, as well as Giblin Lapo and Pastor Willie Sasala, for inviting me to live in Pienuna in 1998. Rosie Ekera and Hazel Piqe took me under their care when I arrived and became constant companions. I am grateful for their friendship, wisdom, humor, and compassion. Matiu Matepitu probably spent more hours with me than anyone else, helping me to learn the Kubokota language, working on transcriptions with me, sharing news, and answering my constant stream of questions. I learned a great deal from countless conversations with Jebede Toribule, the late Samuel Samata, and the late Geoffrey Panakera about the challenges facing village leaders today, and I learned even more by watching and listening as they settled conflicts that arose within the community. The late John Wesley Paleo taught me a great deal about the history of Christianity and many other things. Marina Alepio, Luida Edi, the late Helena Enaduri, Ziosi Luke, Hazel Jioni, the late Jenny Kamdao, Mezi Mikolo, Vezi, Hakaness Samata, Sera Wesley and many other senior women joyfully welcomed me into the United Church Women's Fellowship and the lives of their families. Miranda Vozaqula and the late Philip Piukera taught me much about the forest, about customary ways, and about language. Alaria Medosi and Lovelyn Luke were travel companions, and Emarine Guavoja helped me to make a garden. Joseph Sasapitu and Grace Nose took me to visit their family in Sepa, Choiseul, a trip that broadened my vision of the region. For much of my time in Pienuna, I stayed in the hamlet of Liza Ekera with her daughters Rosie, Zirolyn, and Luvalyn and in a house built by Rocky Panakera: I am grateful to them all, as well as Geoffrey Panakera and Lea, Marina and Alepio, and Margaret Besa and their families in Jericho. I also lived in a house belonging to the Pienuna Primary School; I thank teachers, principles, and the School Committee for allowing me to reside there and am particularly grateful to Dixon Paleo and Newlene Dixon who helped to look after me during that time.

There is not a family in Pienuna who did not welcome me into their homes, offer me hospitality, and share their experiences and stories with me; I regret that I cannot name them all. I would like to mention in particular David Alepitu, Philip Boazi, Dina Henry, Luke Irapio, Marion Jebede, the late James Jioni, Mary Gina Jioni, Thelma Jioni, the late Ruben Kiapio, John Kadesi, Morris Kadesi, the late Doresi Kiapio, Lovelyn Luke, Gladys Luke, Manrose Medosi, Eunice Nisa, the late Paul Mumapitu, Ezi Mumapitu, Joyce Paul, Costas Paleo and Rosie Costas, the late Henry Putamata, the late Kent Roga, Rose Sagopio, Evalyn Qago, Jeffrey Sem, Manakera Samata, Helena Tolavido, Edi Ukebule, the late Izikeili Vaikera, Mavin Vaikera, the late Seito Vaikera, Paul Vavira, Edi Ziro. I was hospitably welcomed in every village around Ranongga. I would mention in particular the families of the late John and Zimah Roga and Cherry and Veronica Tanito in Vonga; Derek Alekera Jiru in Poro; John and Betsy Lampule in Obobulu; Neri Poselini, Timoli, and Grace in Suava; Panakolo at Baniata; Oqoro, Vania, Aeda, and Kebu and families in Paqe; Eddie Aleqeto and Elinta, the late Eroni Kumana, Vavini Maqara, Reverend Abraham Toribule and Marama Stella, Rev. David Garunu and Marama Violet in Koqu; the late John Wesley and Iqadao, and the late John and Voerini Aqolo in Lale; John Tengana in Saevuke; Esme Ida, Pita Minu, and the late Lila Laena in Keara; Dalesi, Lavenda, Ale, Ken Pili and the late Voerini Ken in Kudu; the late Ellen and Ian Lopa in Suvuru; the late Simion Beto, Amos Kaidi, and Toqe in Sabala; the late John Matepitu and Edo and the community in Modo; Diamali and family, and Herrick Ragoso in Keikoro; the late Bruce Ragoso and Esau and Kulu in Buri; Gouza and Enoch Pina in Koriovuku; Medosi Tivikera and Jillian in Kolomali; Gago Rove in Patu; the late Hilda Nikolo and family in Rava; Den Maka and Peter Dimei in Varovo; Elena Pikesa and family in New Bare. I thank Nason Beikera and Eloma for taking me on a memorable trip to north New Georgia in March 2007. I thank the Hon. Francis Billy Hilly for meeting with me in July 2010.

Many other people have offered hospitality and assistance in Gizo, elsewhere in the western Solomons, and Honiara. I thank Rev. David Havea, Vaoline Hite, Seri Hite, Claudine Lilo, Pat McMakin, Moderator Philemon Riti, Kenneth Roga, His Grace the late Rev. Ikan Rove of the Christian Fellowship Church, Ian Scales, Lorimer Tuke, Tonga of Duvaha village, and Eda Wesley. I thank Jolene Stritecky for welcoming me to visit her in Gilbert Camp in 1998. Niumali and Adrian Tutuo welcomed me into their home in both Honiara and Gizo. Simon Foale became a dear friend in the scary days of mid-2000. Inia Barry and Jillian hosted me in the peri-urban Honiara settlement of Adaliwa in 2006/7. I thank Christine Dureau for hosting me in Auckland and Charlie Panakera for hosting me in both Canberra and Waikato in 1999/2000. In 2006/7 field research, I had the good fortune to spend time with Sarah Krose, who carried out anthropological research on Vella Lavella, and Mary Raymond, who carried out linguistic research on Kubokota language in Obobulu. Alphaeus Zobule welcomed me to workshops on vernacular language in Ranongga, and has been generous with his time and insights.

My research was undertaken with permission from the Ministry of Education and Human Resource Development of the Solomon Islands national government. Field research in Ranongga in 1998/9 was funded by an International Dissertation Research Fellowship from the Social Science Research Council; additional research in 2000/1 was funded by a Small Grant from the Wenner-Gren Foundation for Anthropological Research. Between 2006 and 2010, postdoctoral research has been supported by an Australian Research Council Discovery Project Grant (#0666652), with additional funds from the University of Western Australia. I am grateful to all of these organizations for their support.

This book has taken a long time to write, and I am grateful to many people who have contributed intellectually and practically to the process. The work originated as part of doctoral study at the University of Chicago and I would like to acknowledge the contribution of my committee chair John D. Kelly, as well as Danilyn Rutherford, Beth Povinelli, and Michael Silverstein. In different ways, they all pushed me to think about big questions about socioeconomic and religious transformation through rigorous ethnographic analysis. David Akin initially pointed me to the Solomons and has been generous with his knowledge and time ever since. Edvard Hviding encouraged me to work on Ranongga; I thank him for many stimulating conversations about the western Solomons, a letter of introduction to the Christian Fellowship Church, and for generous hospitality during a visit to Bergen in 2011. Michael Scott has also been engaged with this project since the beginning and I thank him for hosting me during a visit to London in 2011 when I presented some of the ideas in this book. Among those who read or commented on versions of chapters in this book over the years are Greg Acciaioli, Ira Bashkow, Cato Berg, Kyunjin Cho, Greg Downey, Mark Edele, Simon Foale, Ilana Gershon, Alex Golub, Courtney Handman, Edvard Hviding, Jessica Jerome, Martha Kaplan, Anne Lorimer, Kathleen Lowrey, Marston Morgan, James Rizzo, and Daniel Rosenblatt, as well as attendees at seminars at the University of Chicago, the University of Notre Dame, the University of Michigan, LSE, the British Museum, and the University of Western Australia. David Akin, Rupert Stasch, and Holly Wardlow read the manuscript in its entirety and provided extraordinarily helpful critical feedback. I thank Mary Murphy for assistance in creating the maps. Staff at Berghahn Books, especially Molly Mosher and Charlotte Mosedale, have been a pleasure to work with. I thank Victoria Burbank for opening her home to me as a writing retreat so that I could carry out the focused work at a critical stage in writing.

I have discussed some of the material in this book in previous publications. An early version of one section of Chapter 3 appeared in "Paths of

*Pinauzu*: Captivity and Social Reproduction in Ranongga," published in 2000 in *Journal of the Polynesian Society* 109 (1): 99–113. Some material from Chapters 5 and 6 is also discussed in "The Unintended Consequences of Clarification: Development, Disputing, and the Dynamics of Community in Ranongga, Solomon Islands," in 2005 in *Ethnohistory* 52 (1): 81–109. Brief passages from Chapter 6 appeared in "Church, Company, Committee, Chief: Emergent Collectivities in Rural Solomon Islands" in Mary Patterson and Martha Macintyre's edited volume *Managing Modernity in the Western Pacific*, published in 2011 in St Lucia by the University of Queensland Press. I thank the publishers of these pieces for permission to include this material here.

No one is happier to see this book completed than Mark Edele and I thank him for supporting me in many ways, pragmatic and intellectual, as I have worked on it. Our daughter has a middle name that links her to one of the great modern heroes of Ranongga; her presence in the world reminds me of what is really important in life. Finally, I thank my parents Carol and David McDougall, to whom I have dedicated the book. The path that took me to Solomon Islands led to a career that has taken me far from home. They have offered their unstinting support over these many years, and have also moved beyond their comfort zone to share my life.

# Notes on Language, Orthography, and Names

People of Ranongga speak two closely related languages that are part of the North West Solomonic branch of Western Oceanic within the broader Austronesian language family: Luqa (or Lungga) and Kubokota or Ganoqa (or Ghanoga or Ghanongga) (Lanyon-Orgill 1969; Tryon and Hackman 1983; Kettle 2000; Chambers 2009). Ranonggans are also fluent in Solomon Islands Pijin, the English-based creole that is the lingua franca of Solomon Islands (Jourdan 2002), and many are proficient in English, the national language. The names of vernacular languages are homologous with the territories with which they are associated: Luqa in the south, Kubokota in the northeast, Ganoqa in the northwest (Figure 0.3).

Linguists and local people alike treat Kubokota and Ganoqa as a single language, but many local people say that Ganoqa was once a distinct language spoken in the northwest quarter of the island. Today, people of Kubokota who are adherents of the United Church (formerly Methodist Mission) tend refer to their language as Kubokota, while people of Ganoqa and Kubokota who are Seventh-day Adventists tend to refer to their language as Ganoqa. There are significant dialectical differences between these two speech communities, but they seem to have resulted from engagement with different mission lingua francas and different attitudes toward vernacular language and English within the different missions and churches (cf. Watson-Gegeo and Gegeo 1991), rather than any underlying linguistic differences. Throughout this book, for simplicity's sake, I refer to the language referred to variously as Ganoqa and Kubokota as "Kubokota."

Vernacular terms are italicized and, unless otherwise indicated, are in Kubokota. Though similar gramatically, Luqa and Kubokota have significant lexical differences, with Kubokota borrowing a number of words from the non-Austronesian language Bilua of Vella Lavella (Chambers 2009). Differences include phonemic changes (e.g. /z/ in Kubokota is /s/ in Luqa) and systematic omission of sounds and syllables in Luqa (e.g. the reciprocal prefix *vari-* in Kubokota is *vai-* in Luqa; the word for group or clan, *butubutu* in Kubokota, is *bubutu* in Luqa). In translations of vernacular language texts, English or Pijin words in the original are underlined in the translated text. In quoted speech or local expressions where it is not clear whether the code was English or Pijin, I spell in standard English.

In the early twentieth century, Methodist and Seventh-day Adventist missions introduced competing orthographies for the regional mission lingua francas (the Roviana language for the Methodist Mission, the Marovo language for the Adventist Mission). Older Ranonggans apply these orthographies consistently to Ranonggan languages, but few people born after around 1975 have learned to write vernacular languages consistently. Throughout this text, I have adopted the modified Methodist orthography used in the Luqa New Testament (*Na Vinaego Korega* 2002), which is also used in associated vernacular language training workshops that local Bible translators have established (McDougall 2012). It builds on earlier Methodist orthographic traditions. Within this orthography, vowels are as follows:

| | |
|---|---|
| *a* | pronounced as in spa |
| *e* | as in bet |
| *i* | as in machine |
| *o* | as in boat |
| *u* | as in rule |
| *ei* | as in fate |
| *au* | as in cow |
| *ae* | as in buy |
| *ai* | as in nice |

Pronunciation of consonants denoted by the letters *k, l, m, n, p, r, s, t, v,* and *z* is similar to English equivalents. The palatal nasal is represented by *ny* and is pronounced as in "Tanya" (or as the Spanish /ñ/); *r* is slightly trilled. In Luqa, *z* is often pronounced as /j/. All voiced stops are pre-nasalized in New Georgian languages.

| | |
|---|---|
| *b* | pronounced as "mb," as in member |
| *d* | pronounced as "nd," as in pond |
| *j* | pronounced as "nj," as in banjo |
| *q* | pronounced as "ngg," as in finger |

Velar consonants have been represented differently in the competing mission orthographies and are the source of confusion for contemporary Ranonggans.

| | |
|---|---|
| *q* | voiced velar stop, pronounced as "ngg," as in finger; "g" in Adventist orthography |
| *g* | voiced velar fricative, sometimes called a "soft g" or "Melanesian g"; "gh" in Adventist orthography |
| *ng* | velar nasal, pronounced "ng," as in sing; "ng" in Adventist orthography, n̠ in older Methodist orthography |

The island name "Ranongga" requires some comment. It is derived from a European mispronunciation of the northwest region Ganoqa, and I have considered writing the island's name according to the older indigenous pronunciation. However, many local people today pronounce the name of the island with an "r" not a "g." Moreover, referring to the island as a whole as "Ganoqa" might obscure the degree of socio-geographic transformation that has occurred in the past 150 years. It seems plausible that at the end of the nineteenth century, Kubokota, Luqa, and Ganoqa were distinct regions and were not integrated into any larger island whole that was called "Ganoqa" by locals or their regional neighbors. In 1908, on the eve of European hegemony, A.M. Hocart carried out research on neighboring Simbo, then known as Eddystone Island by Europeans or Madegusu by local people. He wrote of Ganongga and Lungga as distinct districts (Hocart 1922: 101–2), describing Kubokota as an ally of Simbo (Hocart 1931: 303); "Vesu Gogoto" (which means "eight hundred"), a reference to the number of warriors that could be summoned from the area, was also used in reference to the island, but it is not clear if this referred to the island as a whole or the district of the northwest. In light of such questions, I use Ganoqa to refer to the northwest of the island, and Ranongga to refer to the island as a whole.

Because many stories make little sense when removed from their spatial context, I have found it necessary to mention many places throughout the book. I hope that the accompanying maps (Figures 0.1, 0.2, 0.3) will assist readers in following this topographic detail. I have written most Ranonggan place names according to the orthography above. However, some islands and towns have official spellings that differ from this orthography, often including additional "m"s or "n"s to indicate the nasalization of voiced stops. In some cases, these spellings have an official weight (the member of parliament is elected from Ranongga/Simbo not Ganoqa/Sibo).

Like place names, personal names are not consistently used or consistently spelled. Names often consist of an English language or Biblical name combined with a vernacular language "custom" name. A person may be called by one or the other of these names. Women and children sometimes add their husband or father's given name to their own names, but sometimes they do not. In cases where I know how a person writes their own name, I use that spelling; otherwise, I spell phonetically according to the standard orthography. Except where indicated, I have used real names of people, places, and kin groups rather than pseudonyms.

In the PhD dissertation (McDougall 2004) that contained some of the material incorporated into this book, I consistently concealed my interlocutors' identities except in well-known events of public significance like narratives of Christian conversion. On return visits, when I discussed that work with friends in Ranongga, most expressed disappointment with this approach. I subsequently gained explicit permission to use the names of most people mentioned. I continue to use pseudonyms or to avoid naming people when the discussion might reflect badly upon them personally. With regard to case studies of land transactions and land disputes, I have named actors involved when transactions became a matter of public record, as was the case in the disputes around logging or in cases where organizers hoped that my presence would create a public record of the events they directed. I avoid naming groups or individuals who have told me controversial details concerning histories of named kin groups. Many narratives and genealogical accounts in this book are disputed in ways that I indicate in the text; none should be taken as definitive or used as evidence in legal disputes over land.

# Maps

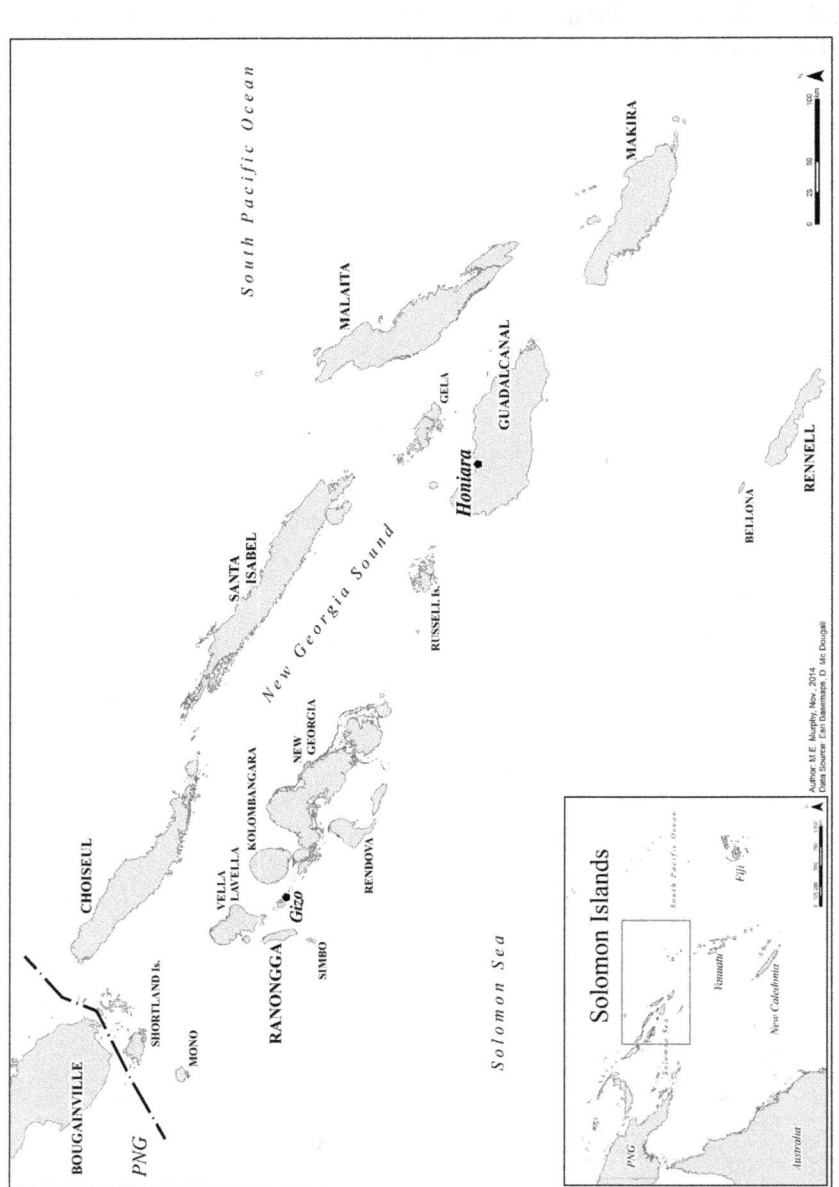

**Figure 0.1.** Solomon Islands. The main map shows only the main islands in the double chain of volcanic islands; the inset map shows the full extent of Solomon Islands, including distant Temotu Province.

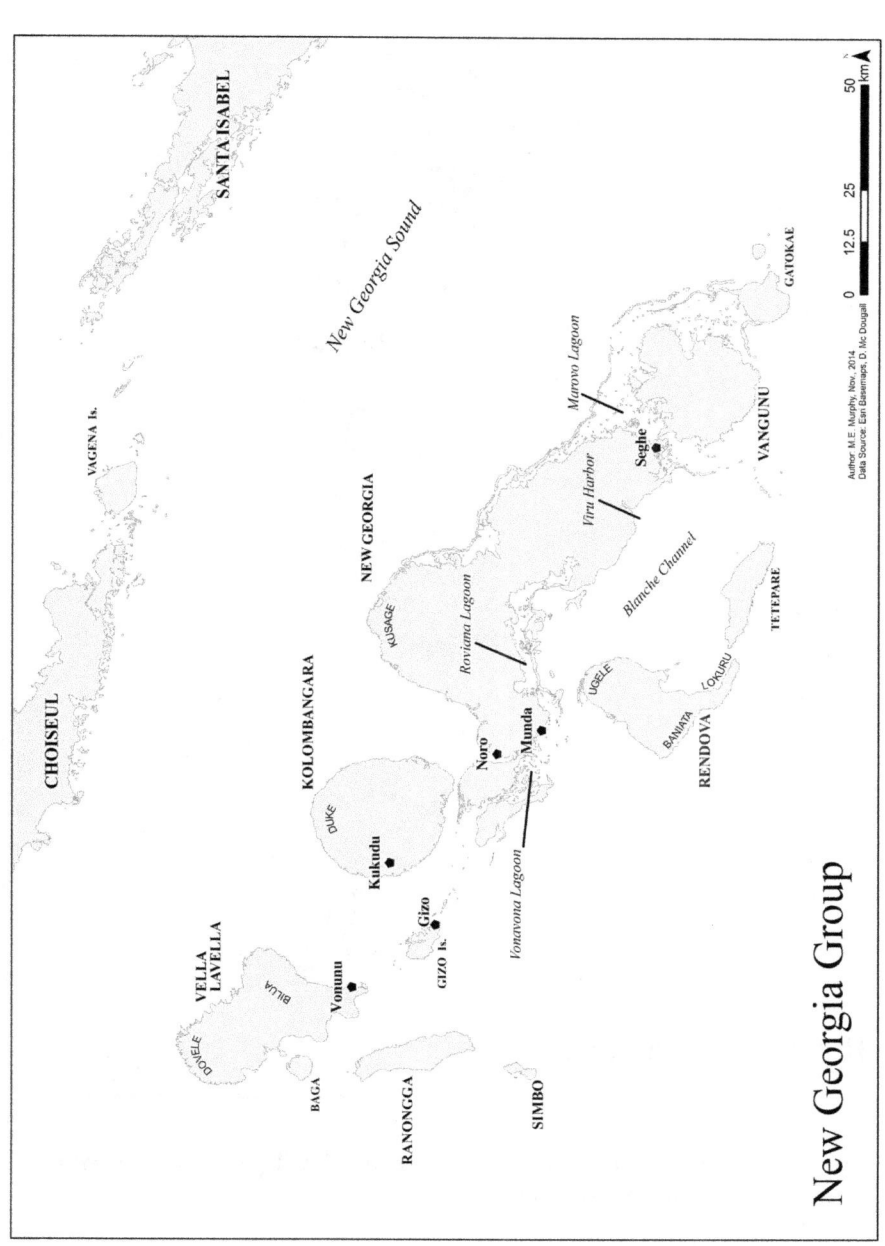

**Figure 0.2.** New Georgia Group.

xx  *Maps*

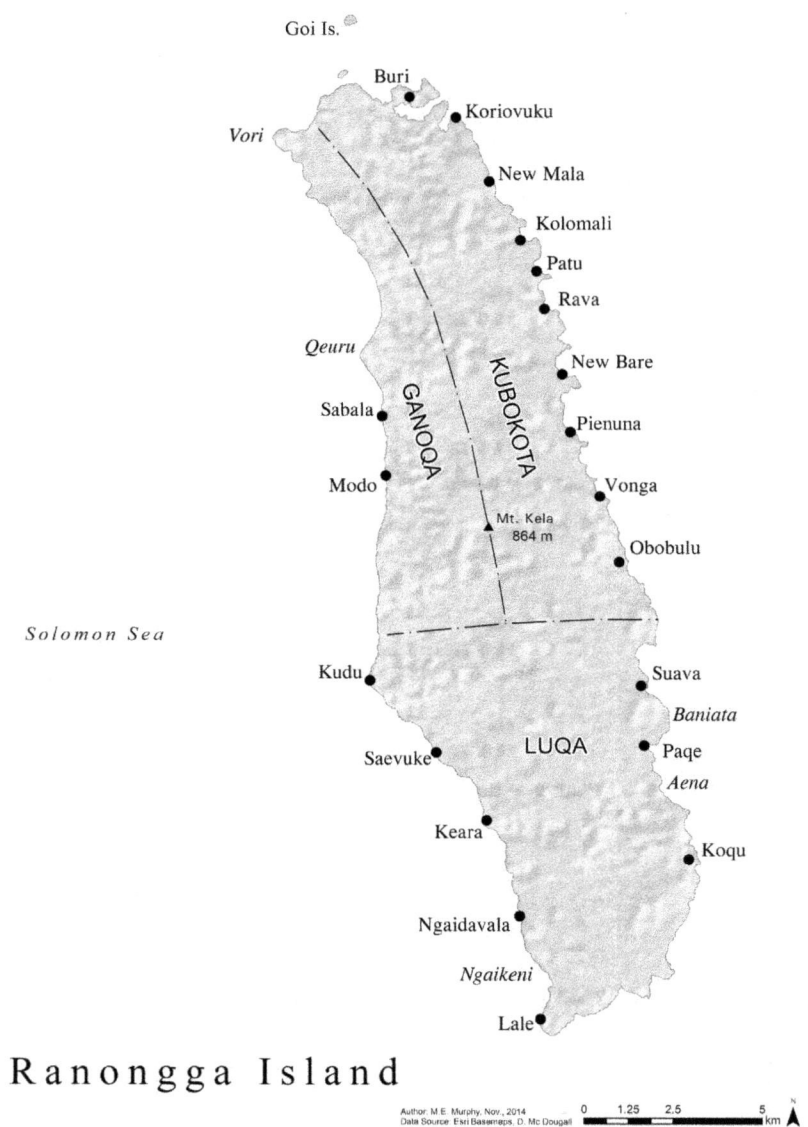

Figure 0.3. Ranongga Island, circa 2000. Major church villages are shown, with other places named in the text in italics.

*Introduction*

# On Being a Stranger in a Hospitable Land

Standing on the rugged coast and gazing from the cliffs westward to the vast open sea, the island of Ranongga feels a bit like the end of the earth. At the far western edge of the New Georgia Group of the Western Province of Solomon Islands (Figures 0.1, 0.2), this narrow mountainous island has long served as a last refuge for people fleeing trouble. Yet Ranonggan communities have long been integrated into a larger regional world, and residents have long traveled across the sea and welcomed ashore foreign things, ideas, and persons.

The following chapters track Ranonggan engagements with a wide range of strangers: captives taken in nineteenth-century warfare, men and women from other islands living with Ranonggan spouses, Christian missions and their foreign god, conservation projects and multinational logging companies, migrant laborers, and others. By way of introduction and to provide a sense of the context in which the research for this book was carried out, I begin with my own experience of being welcomed ashore to the village of Pienuna, the place I lived for much of my research on Ranongga. Although it has now been several years since I have returned, this book is not based on a snapshot of local life taken from a single period; my engagement has stretched over nearly two decades. Over the years, I have watched as friends moved from early adulthood into middle age; I have seen kids turn into young adults; I have mourned the deaths of people I came to know and love. Yet, despite those long-term relationships, I have not really fully taken up the welcome that has been extended to me. Like many anthropologists, I have remained "stranger and friend" rather than really becoming a person of the place in the way that my hosts have invited me to be.[1]

## Arrival

I arrived in Pienuna in October 1998, hoping that this large village on the populous eastern shores of Ranongga would be a good base for research (Figure 0.3). I lived there until November 1999; after a short trip home to the United States and to New Zealand and Australia for archival work, I returned to Ranongga for a second period of research lasting from April

2000 to February 2001. In the nearly two years I spent living in Pienuna, I traveled extensively around the island and stayed in most major settlements for at least a few days. After completing my doctorate, I returned to Pienuna in 2005, 2006/7, and 2010 as part of four visits ranging from three weeks to four months. During these later research trips, I have also interviewed Ranonggans and non-Ranonggans in Gizo and Honiara, coming to urban research like many Solomon Islanders come to town—with the sense of having a rural home to which I might return.

In 1996, two years before settling in Pienuna to begin research, I had visited Guadalcanal and Western Province to find a site for research I planned on local courts. Since the late 1980s, local courts (informal courts with limited jurisdiction) and local area councils (the third tier of government) had been overwhelmed by disputes arising from logging on customary land. By the mid-1990s, national politicians were in the process of dismantling these institutions. Area councils were defunded in 1993 and disbanded in 1996–97; local courts continued to exist and were minimally funded, but heard cases only when logging companies funded hearings (see Allen et al. 2013; McDougall 2014a). After this initial trip, I reformulated my project to focus more broadly on the gendered dynamics of land tenure in the western Solomons, a region with matrilineal kinship but with a male-dominated political economy. I decided to focus on Ranongga because it was on the margins of the logging economy, and thus seemed like the sort of place where an outsider could learn something about land without stumbling into the middle of bitter disputes. By 1998, WWF (World Wide Fund for Nature) had begun a conservation and development project in Kubokota. The WWF project raised many of the issues that concerned me, so I decided to try to work in a community involved in the project.

As the site of a school, clinic, and frequent canoe journeys between Gizo and Ranongga, Pienuna was a hub of activity and seemed like a good place to be based. By the time I began research, the dismantling of local government had led to a breakdown of formal processes for negotiating access and permissions for research and other activities undertaken in rural areas. I had received permission to undertake research in Ranongga and had paid research fees to the Ministry of Education and Human Resource Development in Honiara before I traveled to Western Province. I was also in touch with some individuals on Ranongga, but no local representative body had approved my research because no such body existed. Kenneth Roga, officer for the Western Province Culture Office, as well as Cherry and Veronica Tanito, field officers for the WWF project, helped me to organize visits to villages within the WWF project in Ranongga. I was invited to live in Pienuna by village chief John Pavukera, Nulu clan chief Samuel Samata, and United Church catechist Giblin Lapo. Later, I would explain my research and seek permission from the community at large during announcements following a church service, something I did whenever I visited new places over the years.

A few weeks after my initial visit, I was deposited at the beachfront hamlet of Pienuna that gives the contemporary village its name (in the past, the settlement was called Kubokota and was located inland, while Pienuna referred only to the site where canoes were landed and housed). Pienuna was home to the family most accustomed to hosting foreigners: the children and grandchildren of postwar leader Simion Panakera and his wife Joyce Dunateko, whose lives are discussed in Chapters 2 and 4. I lived with Rosie Ekera, her mother Liza Ekera, Liza's other daughters and their families, and Liza's cousin Matiu Matepitu. A few months later, in February 1999, I moved into an unused teacher's house located near the Pienuna Primary School and the United Church building next to a hamlet known as Zion. Living semi-independently on the school compound meant that many people of Pienuna, not just the children of Panakera and Dunateko, took responsibility for me. They gave me food and assistance, took me along as they visited relatives and traveled to church, helped me make a garden, and shared their lives with me. In my second year of research, when the house was reoccupied by a teacher, I returned to stay with Rosie and her family in Pienuna, and I have stayed there on subsequent visits.

During the initial months of fieldwork, I spent a lot of time learning the local language, Kubokota. I carried out a village census that helped me understand basic social patterns. I participated in most activities of the church and school, and attended meetings for the WWF project. In Pienuna and villages around the island, I interviewed older people about their lives, often with the assistance of Rosie and other young women who traveled with me. I quickly learned that the best interviews were ones in which I said little and let people talk about what interested them. Later in 1999 and in 2000/1, I began to systematically visit villages around the island, tracing out webs of genealogical relationship that stretched across the island and recording histories of local places. Wherever I could, I followed Samuel Samata, John Pavukera, Jebede Toribule (John Pavukera's mother's brother's son and "spokesman"), Geoffrey Panakera and other leaders as they undertook the work of solving local disputes, mostly focused on sexual offenses and land (McDougall 2014b, 2015). Using what anthropologists call an "extended case study" method, I recorded information about disputes, especially those related to land, to see how they were solved and how histories of clans and people were narrated in such contexts. It proved impossible to understand any aspect of community life, not even issues around resource development or land use, without serious attention to Christianity. Local histories of Christianity, and changing forms of Christian faith, became a central focus of my PhD dissertation and subsequent postdoctoral research.

As I was settling into fieldwork on Ranongga in late 1998, news arrived of violent attacks on settlers in northern Guadalcanal. A troubled period of civil conflict that is known locally as "the Ethnic Tension" had begun. By the time I finished my second period of fieldwork, Solomon Islands was on the path to becoming what some observers called the Pacific's first "failed state." The only time I feared for my own safety was during trips to Gizo, when armed men from Bougainville arrived, ostensibly providing "security" to the people of Western Province. Yet, the crisis was a constant background to daily life. It curtailed my mobility and the mobility of the people I lived with. Few people traveled to Honiara. Fuel shortages made travel by motorized canoe around the island and up to Gizo difficult. The crisis inflected the ways that people told stories; it inspired church leaders to pray for the unity of the country; it increased the sense of insecurity experienced by migrants on the island. Over the years, I have struggled to make sense of how the research I conducted on Ranongga was related to these broader national events. The focus on relations with strangers in this book emerges from my dialogue with my hosts on Ranongga during this transformative period in Solomon Islands history.

## *Crying for Merika*

Despite the warm welcome that I was accorded, during my first months of research I was intensely lonely and full of doubt. Sticking to the tried and true methods of the discipline, though, I continued to tag along as people went about their lives. So, one day, I accompanied Rosie and the village's United Church youth group to their collective garden, which had been planted the previous month. (Youth in the Solomons is defined not by age but by marital status; anyone unmarried is "young" and the group was mainly men and women in their twenties like me at that time.) The group planned to sell produce from the garden at the market in Gizo to raise funds to attend a regional youth rally later in the year.

As we walked up the steeply sloped path that leads from the coastal village to hillside gardens, the young men climbed trees for drinking coconuts and the young women ducked off to their gardens along the path to gather cassava and greens to steam in bamboo containers for lunch. My friends were enjoying themselves, but I found myself growing increasingly homesick. I could communicate in rudimentary Solomon Islands Pijin and English with my companions, but I did not understand what they were saying to one other in Kubokota. I wondered why I had come here, and kept wishing that I was at my cousin's wedding that day in far-away Pennsylvania. When we finally arrived at the garden, I wandered off from the group a bit, sat on the trunk of a felled tree, and looked out across the mirror-like sea toward Gizo, the wide hills of Vella Lavella, the steep craters of Kolombangara, and the dark line of distant

**Figure 0.4.** View from the gardens above Pienuna, looking out toward small Inuzauru Island and Vella Lavella. On clear days, Choiseul is visible on the horizon. The main clearing of Pienuna village is just inland from Leva Point on the shore on the right-hand side of the photo. Rai Mikolo cuts sugarcane in foreground. October 2007.

Choiseul on the horizon. I had a quiet little cry. I pulled myself together then joined in the work, feeling a bit silly that I had been so despondent.

That night, Rosie and others who were becoming close friends—Hazel Piqe, Mavin Vaikera, and Alaria Medosi—came by to keep me company and to help me learn Kubokota language. I turned on my tape recorder and Hazel narrated the events of the day, describing all of the places that we passed on the path to the garden, what we ate and how it was cooked . . . and how I went off and wept. We all laughed a bit about that. A couple of weeks later, I went with Rosie to her own garden, which is on the side of a valley and does not have a view of the ocean. As we rested, she reminded me of my tears up at the youth's garden. She said that she was glad that her own garden had no view across the sea, because looking out into the distance makes her think of the people who are absent. Views over the ocean on fine days, she told me, make her weep for her deceased father.

My feelings of melancholy did not last. Quite suddenly, in the fourth month of research, I began to enjoy myself. I am not exactly sure what triggered the change. I had taken a trip to the village of Keara on the west coast of Ranongga and found myself homesick not for Pennsylvania, but for Pienuna. And—I am not sure if it was a coincidence or not—I got my first, and worst, episode of malaria. I felt like I was going to die, not only from the malaria, but also because in my delirium I had taken additional chloroquine thinking that it was paracetamol. Rosie and Hazel nursed me through both the malaria and the chloroquine overdose. When my fever broke, I felt better than I had for months. My language capability was improving and I was even starting to understand jokes. Some jokes were about the possibility of me staying on as an in-law rather than an anthropologist; women of my mother's generation grabbed me and pinched me, saying that they had better do this now before I became their daughter-in-law, when such intimate contact would be taboo.

My original arrival in Pienuna in 1998 was muddling and uncertain. When my parents came for a visit in 1999, however, we were all welcomed ashore in a dramatic fashion. Pienuna was the final stop in a tour of Ranongga and Simbo undertaken with Dr Michael, a Gizo-based dentist. (My father was then a practicing dentist and assisted Dr Michael, who expertly extracted scores of teeth at each rural clinic. Dental tours were supposed to happen yearly but lack of funds meant that they had not been undertaken for years; my parents brought dental supplies and purchased fuel for the tour.) As we approached Pienuna, the beach was uncharacteristically quiet. Suddenly, dozens of young men sprang from behind bushes and dropped down from trees; dressed in leaves, decorated with war paint, and brandishing axes and spears, they told us to go away from the shore. Village chief John Pavukera stepped forward, holding a shell valuable, and told the warriors to let us ashore. By this time, most of the other villagers had appeared and everyone lined up to welcome us and to shake hands with my parents before we sat down for a large feast. It was the first time I had witnessed a warrior welcome, which I would see in many different versions over the coming years, and which I have come to see as a key symbol of Ranonggan engagements with strangers.

I left Ranongga in November 1999 and returned in April 2000. In my absence, Edi Ziro had started to call the place of the youth garden Kabo Merika: *kabo* means "cry" in the language of Roviana, where Edi is from, and Merika is a local rendering of America. That year, Samata gave me permission to make a garden there, and so I went to Kabo Merika many times during this second stint of field research, with Emarine Guavoja who was 15 at the time. Our gardening was not very productive, but I loved being in that place.

The story of Kabo Merika reveals something about how experiences and events become embedded in the landscape. Places have layers of names: old ones are sometimes forgotten and new ones do not always stick. To take another example, a hamlet just to the north of Pienuna was named Kana Tapo, a phrase meaning "enemy of the sun," by old man Meka who cleared the area in the 1970s. His wife Liso, a devout Christian, did not like the idea that they were enemies of something that God himself created. She called their new hamlet New Silas. But most people continued to call it by its older name, Kilisie. Like Kabo Merika, many place names point across the sea, named for home places of people who migrated to Ranongga or for places that people born and raised on the island have visited or read about. As early as the 1890s, there was a place on the west coast called Iqiladi (England), named by a local man Sadeboko who had worked for European sailors and reportedly visited England. Today, Ranonggan hamlets are named for settlements in Honiara and suburbs of Australia, as well as places all around the Western Solomons. Foreign places are thus present in the landscape, as are the traces of the people who have lived here, looked across the sea, and longed for distant homes and absent relatives.

## *Joy and Sadness*

In 2006/7, I returned to Ranongga for another extended period of postdoctoral research. This time, my husband Mark Edele came to visit for a month in January 2007. Like my parents, he was greeted by spear-thrusting warriors as our canoe attempted to land. Before we disembarked, other villagers rushed out and threw both of us into the sea, the usual procedure for a newly married couple. Mark arrived in the middle of a week of New Year's celebrations, with soccer and netball competitions, running and swimming races, debates, and other activities. I had purchased a large pig, fuel for a fishing trip, a few bags of rice, and other store-bought food to contribute to a feast that would close the New Year's celebration, say farewell the village pastor who was moving to another post, and welcome Mark. My friends in Pienuna transformed the New Year's feast into a mock wedding, dividing the village into America and Germany (Mark is German). Each side constructed a platform in the shape of a ship to carry food and the two of us. My ship was the MV *MGPie* (an acronym of my three places, Merika, Germany, Pienuna). To his bemusement, Mark's ship was the MV *Nazi* (quite innocently taken as a nickname for Germany), decorated with balloons, flowers, and swastikas. Disembarking from these ships, we sat with our ersatz parents for the marriage exchange. Samuel Samata, as spokesman for Mark's side, put down a pile of cash and three shell valuables (one each for my head, torso, and legs). He declared that he was buying this American woman for Germany. John Kadesi stood up for my side, put down another shell valuable and more cash, and said that while America allowed Germany to take their woman, they did not want her to be stuck there, so this money would open the path for us to travel back and forth. It was a mock exchange, and shell valuables and cash were returned to the original owners. Some visitors from other villages, however, thought that

**8** *Engaging with Strangers*

**Figure 0.5.** "We Germans are buying and taking this woman from America." Samuel Samata has placed three *bakia* (traditional shell valuables), along with cash, on the ground in front of us: one each for my head, torso, and legs. I am seated between Paul and Joyce Vavira; John Pavukera and his wife Eloqula are seated to the right. Mark was standing behind Samata, out of the frame. January 2007.

the event marked my adoption into Kubongava, the clan of Simion Panakera whose children had been my hosts over many years.

Returning just a few months later, those happy times seemed a distant memory. Soon after I had departed in March 2007, a massive earthquake struck Western Province. Elsewhere the earthquake caused a devastating tsunami, but the wave did not hit Ranongga because the entire island had been lifted a further 2 to 3 meters above sea level. While mercifully few people were killed in the earthquake and landslides that followed, children and adults alike were traumatized, and the destruction of houses and disruption of health services had longer-term effects. A number of older people died in quick succession. My friends later said that there was one death after another (*uke varitoto*); mourning had only finished for one person when the wailing for the next began.

The most recent loss had been Samuel Samata. I heard about his death as I was finalizing plans to visit Ranongga after the earthquake. Not yet seventy,

Samata was vigorous and apparently immune to the malaria that plagued everyone else. He fell ill in late September and died quickly without passing on his knowledge of land and genealogy, or indicating who should replace him. Though Samata had been buried by the time I arrived, his siblings and families were still sleeping in a large room with Samata's widow Hakaness. On the evening I arrived, I slept there as well to mourn Samata with them.

In the morning, Samata's brother Luke Irapio called the family together to talk to me. Earlier that year, it seems, Samata told Luke and others that I had acted like a daughter and sister, not a stranger; I left the island but always returned and, in recent years, brought my family with me. Luke said that although Samata had not had time to make any plans, they had all decided to give me a little place (*ia*) in an area called Mokeru, just to the south of the main village and slightly inland. The small hamlet where they now lived was becoming too crowded as the children began founding their own households; the tsunami provided the extra impetus to establish a settlement on higher ground. Luke's children and the other cousins, young men and women of my generation, were planning to found a new hamlet there over the coming years.

Later in the week, Ziosi and Luke took me to the area for the new hamlet. As we walked up from the beach, it began to lightly rain. I started to dig around for plastic to cover my camera, remarking that it had not looked as though it would rain. The sky was clear blue and cloudless. "It isn't rain," Ziosi corrected me, "it is *resana*." *Resana* is a light mist mixed with sun, a sign that the ancestral dead are satisfied. "Samata is crying," she said. Sure enough, the rain lasted for a few seconds and stopped.

When I next returned to Pienuna three years later in 2010, I brought not only Mark but also our eighteen-month-old daughter, whom we had named Anna Dunateko after Joyce Dunateko, whose life is discussed in Chapter 4, and after my friend Rosie's daughter Virginia Dunateko, who was four years old on our previous visit and had charmed Mark. Mark and I went with Luke, Ziosi, and Luke's sister Mezi to Mokeru, where Mezi's son had been the first to build a house in the new settlement. Luke felled several trees and we all cleared the underbrush to plant fruit trees ("for Anna to eat"): pomelo, guava, star fruit, and rambutan. Ziosi planted crotons that would mark the boundary between our settlement and that of the family who was already living on the coast in a separate hamlet. A few people at the time suggested that we should *pajuku* the area, a transaction sometimes understood as a land purchase and that I discuss in Chapter 5. In my understanding, though, Luke and his family were not giving away land, but trying to attach me to the land. Having a place of my own could transform me from a guest into a person of the place, someone who can welcome others ashore.

It has been several years since we visited Pienuna. We live a sea and a continent away, and, with family on two other continents, much of our travel is not to the Solomons. We have not yet built a house on the land that was cleared in 2010. In this tropical climate, it does not take long for a thicket of vegetation to erase the effort expended in clearing the land. After our last visit, Ziosi's daughter Gladys was going to make her garden there, look after our seedlings, and hold the area for us. By now, she will have planted several cycles of crops, and it is past time for the garden land to be left fallow or for a proper house to be built.

I lament my life is not more closely connected to this place and these people who are important to me. The expansion of the internet and mobile communication bridges some gaps, but globalization is uneven. At my last visit, Ranonggans could only get mobile phone reception if they climbed high into the hills. A few friends in town keep me informed via Facebook about deaths and other big events, but I no longer receive letters from my closest friends in the way that I did a decade ago. Even requests for money come infrequently. Yet, experience leads me to trust that one way or another, when we return, we will once again be welcomed ashore.

## The Chapters

From the dramatic tales of the past to the routine work of the present, the history of Ranongga can be envisioned as a series of arrivals. On the one hand, strangers who arrive from distant lands are at the mercy of their local hosts who may welcome them as friends or repel them as enemies. On the other hand, strangers are often powerful and their arrival can radically transform the socio-spatial order. Engagements with strangers is a theme in stories told throughout Solomon Islands about foreigners who bring something essential to human thriving (such as ritual knowledge, shell valuables, military power, reproductive ability, or moral sense) to a local group that had previously lacked it. Foreigners and foreign institutions become attached to local land even as their foreign origins are continually remembered and emphasized.

This chapter has provided an introduction to Ranongga and some insight into my position as a researcher and guest in Pienuna village. In Chapter 1, I outline the ways that an ethnographic study of Ranongga may contribute to our understanding of what was a transformative period in Solomon Islands history. Ranongga was far from the violence on Guadalcanal, but residents shared many frustrations about uneven development and internal migration that motivated some Guadalcanal people to take up arms in 1998. The same political-economic transformations that set landowners and migrants against one another on Guadalcanal have also driven conflict on Ranongga, albeit in less dramatic form. Most studies of the Tension period in Solomon Islands have attempted to explain why violence erupted. This study seeks to answer a different question: why was the violence so limited? Tens of thousands of people were displaced in the Tension and thousands feared for their lives, but only hundreds were killed; the mass violence that characterized other post-Cold War ethnic conflicts did not occur in Solomon Islands. The war was sometimes represented as the result of ancient tribal difference, but the fact is that people of Guadalcanal and Malaita, like the Ranonggans I write about here, have long engaged with people from distant places who speak different languages and do things in slightly different ways. In this book, I seek to call attention to understandings of the moral obligations of hospitality that are broadly shared by the diverse peoples of Solomon Islands. Even in situations where broader political and economic structures make it difficult to fulfill those obligations, Solomon Islanders often strive to act toward one another as good guests and good hosts.

Chapter 1 also begins to sketch out my approach to Ranonggan sociality. An analysis of stranger sociality in rural villages runs against dominant tendencies in Western social theory to depict small-scale or non-state societies as held together through face-to-face relationships among kin and neighbors. Yet my analysis resonates with tropes common throughout the Austronesian-speaking world and in many other places that figure power and value as arriving from outside of a local social world. Moreover, strangers are a focus of moral reflection in all societies and, as anthropologist Andrew Shryock (2012) has observed, this makes the idea of hospitality a compelling focus for comparison across scales of organization, ranging from the household to the nation-state. From Kant onward, Western political theory and international law conceives of the cosmopolitan right of strangers as existing in a neutral space where all citizens are equal in front of the law. Yet for people like Ranonggans, who live and work on land inherited from ancestors, there is no neutral space of mere tolerance. Strangers may be repelled as enemies or welcomed as friends, but they cannot remain merely strangers for long.

Chapter 2 tracks socio-spatial and political-economic transformations of the twentieth century. Throughout the geologically active Pacific Islands region, physical terrain is not a mere backdrop to social life, but has actively shaped possibilities of settlement and engagement in regional political and economic networks—a point that was driven home in 2007, when a massive earthquake lifted the entire island meters out of the water and transformed the physical and social terrain of the island. Settlement patterns changed markedly with pacification, Christianization, and incorporation into a plantation economy in the first decades of the twentieth century. Like others in the relatively commercially developed western Solomons, Ranonggans were heavily engaged in the production of copra, the main export of the Solomons until the 1970s. From the 1980s onward, the explosion of logging on customary land brought many residents of Western Province into more intensive connections with agents of multinational capitalism, but it increased a sense of marginality among Ranonggans, whose narrow mountainous island was unattractive to logging companies. By the 1990s, market gardening was the major source of income for most families in Pienuna and surrounding villages, who traveled regularly to Gizo to sell their produce.

Despite all of these changes, people of Ranongga—like their counterparts all around the country—have a powerful sense of continuity because they live and work on land inherited from ancestors who lived and worked on the land before them. This sense of continuity is encapsulated in the idea of *kastom*, a neo-Melanesian Pijin word that evokes ways of doing things that adhere to indigenous rather than exogenous values. The core of *kastom* in Ranongga is the idea that land is vested in *butubutu*, a term I gloss as clan, and that both *butubutu* identity and landownership is inherited through matrilineal ties. This emphasis on continuity can divert attention from significant changes in land tenure and social organization that occurred during the twentieth century. Prior to the expansion of the colonial state, *butubutu* identities linked people to places of origin, but there is little evidence that they were corporate descent groups in the way anthropologists since the 1960s have described them. Drawing on Ian Scales's (2004) analysis of frontier-era New Georgia, I suggest that pre-colonial polities were centered on canoe houses and ancestral shrines, not descent groups per se. Arguably, this spatially focused orientation continues, for even today, the most important collectivities in modern New Georgia are not descent-based clans but church-centered communities.

Chapter 3 steps back to an era Ranonggans and other Solomon islanders speak of as "the time before" or "the time of darkness" that preceded conversion to Christianity. In a range of genres—folk tales, myths, and accounts of the movements of *butubutu* ancestors—quasi-human ancestral beings are depicted as stupid or crazy. They gained sense and true humanity only through engagements with foreigners. People today also speak of their closer ancestors in similar terms when they describe the crazy or stupid violence of nineteenth-century headhunting. Their great-grandparents were ignorant of Christianity and its message of universal peace and harmony. In speaking of the pre-pacification past, my Ranonggan interlocutors had little to say about victims of warfare who were killed, but they recounted the stories of their own ancestors who were taken as captives and adopted by local clans. Like folk tales and myths of origin, these tales of pre-pacification warfare reveal an oscillation between brutality and kindness that is characteristic of engagements with strangers more broadly.

Government pacification preceded Christian missionization by a decade or more, and involved the violent destruction of canoes, canoe houses, villages, and gardens. In explaining the transition from war to peace, however, people of the western Solomons today focus less on the aggressive campaign of the government than on the moral and spiritual transformation of their own ancestors who embraced Christianity. In Chapter 4, I recount the dramas of conversion that are performed annually and function as the mythical charter for the contemporary social order. I also trace more subtle transformations of the landscape that occurred in the following decades. Missionary literature focuses on resistant human souls, but oral history from Ranongga tends to focus on the adventures of warrior-pastors who did battle with a recalcitrant landscape that reacted violently to foreign incursions. People today say that Christianity has made them free—free from threats of violence from human enemies, free from affliction from ancestral spirits, free to travel widely. Many describe this freedom as particularly significant for women because they were more constrained by ancestral taboos than men. The final section of the chapter tracks the arrival of women's Christian fellowship on Ranongga, drawing out parallels with earlier narratives about the arrival of Christianity and tracking the paradoxical effects of Christianization on gender relationships.

In celebrating their conversion to Christianity, Ranonggans denigrate the past as a time of violence and ignorance, but in other contexts they are nostalgic for a time when people truly loved and cared for one another. Many lament that the rise of market relations have meant that even family members no longer share property. Chapter 5 tracks the ways that Ranonggans seek to assert individualized rights to property without alienating all of the relatives and neighbors who really ought to be living together as a single unified collectivity. Because people often live and work on land that does not belong to their own matrilineal *butubutu*, they may try to affirm rights to property through a range of ceremonial transactions in which they present food, money, and shell valuables to their father, their father's clan, or to people of the original landholding clan. Yet these ritual transactions do not simply serve to delineate property rights. On the one hand, these transactions function like a purchase: money and food are exchanged for rights to landed property. On the other, when such transactions are done well, the givers also make speeches denying that they are buying anything: the gifts are described as sharing amongst kinspeople who should remember their relations to one another and their shared ancestral connections to the place. The process is paradoxical and ambivalent: many people feel they must assert property rights, but also feel that such assertions are antithetical to customary and Christian ethics of landownership.

Such careful attempts to assert differential rights without alienating relatives prove difficult in the contexts of outsider-driven development projects that require what I call the "tribalization" of land tenure. "Tribe" is a term rarely used by anthropologists, but it dominates popular and legal discourse about social organization and land tenure in Melanesia. When I use the term in this book, it is in the context of these dominant discourses. In analyzing Ranonggan social organization, I seek to pay attention to different (but often overlapping) social formations, which include families linked together through networks of relationships, communities comprised of people living together or engaging in collective projects, and clan identities defined by shared descent from a putative ancestor. The term "tribe" refers primarily to clan identities. When local sociality or territoriality is described as tribal, other kinds of social formations like families or communities often fall out of view.

Chapter 6 juxtaposes two contrasting forms of development occurring in the 1990s and 2000s in Ranongga: large-scale logging undertaken by a multinational corporation, and community conservation undertaken by a large non-governmental organization. Despite their diametrically opposed aims, both projects assumed that local people belonged to tribes and that tribes owned the land, leading people to downplay broader community membership or family connections that crosscut matrilineal clan identities. In the case of logging, the opponents of the operations attempted initially to speak for a broader public interest, but were pushed by the High Court to define themselves as tribal landowners contesting the rights of their kinspeople who had contracted the company. In the case of the community conservation and development project, the conservation organization initially assumed that the "community" it was engaging with was really a tribe; inquiries into tribal leadership precipitated a dispute over chiefly succession that threatened to undermine the project until leaders subsumed activities within the broader civic structures of participating communities. These cases reveal both the pervasiveness of the tribal frame in contemporary development, but also the ways that this framing is subverted or at least challenged when people come together not as landowning clans but as neighbors and kinspeople managing the shared affairs of the village.

In Chapter 7, I turn to interethnic relationships in rural Ranongga and in urban and peri-urban locales in Solomon Islands. From the beginning of commercial development in the western Solomons, local people expressed hostility toward laborers from Malaita, the island that was home to the largest number of indentured laborers throughout the colonial period. Colonial stereotypes continue to color interethnic engagements in rural areas and on the national stage, and real cultural differences can make the resolution of ordinary conflicts more difficult. Yet, in rural Ranongga, relationships between local people and migrants from Malaita have usually been amicable—a point echoed in literature about Guadalcanal and peri-urban Honiara. In rural and in urban situations, migrants seek to attach themselves to local land and people, but such attachment may be more difficult to achieve in urban areas. In rural villages, migrants become local by living on local land, caring for local people, bearing children, clearing land, planting trees, or even dying and being buried on their adoptive land. In urban areas, where people may be less dependent on local land and people than in rural areas, fluid and emergent place-based identities are likely to calcify into ethnic identity, understood as a fixed and unchanging quality of the person.

The civil conflict in Solomon Islands between 1998 and 2003 began when an indigenous militant movement on the island of Guadalcanal sought to evict settlers from the island of Malaita, many who had lived on Guadalcanal for decades or generations often at the invitation of local Guales (as people indigenous to Guadalcanal are sometimes called). Influential explanations attribute the conflict to a weak colonial and postcolonial state that failed to bring fragmented and small-scale polities into a unified nation. In Chapter 8, I argue that the violence had little to do with the failure of local people to transcend local bonds of kith and kin to embrace a more cosmopolitan national identity. Rather, it arose from a broadly shared frustration with a state that consistently failed to serve the common good, and political elites who seem more responsive to the agendas of diverse transnational actors than to the needs of the ordinary citizens they are supposed to serve. Studies of ordinary people's experiences of and involvement in Ethnic Tension-era violence reveal not incommensurable difference, but a shared set of understandings and commonly held grievances. Even Malaitan victims of Guadalcanal violence did not contest the moral right of Guales to ask them to leave. In his study of ex-militant perspectives on the conflict, Matthew Allen (2013a) found that most ordinary Guales and Malaitans who took up arms saw the government—not the ethnic "other"—as the ultimate target of their campaigns. When the Regional Assistance Mission to Solomon Islands (RAMSI) put an end to the violence in 2003, the Australian government and Solomon Islanders alike hoped that the arrival of these new foreigners would open up the space for a radical transformation of political structures, a transformation that many Solomon Islanders seem to have conceived of in moral and spiritual terms that were at odds with the secular neoliberal state-building frameworks that guided RAMSI. When RAMSI concluded after a decade of operation, it is clear that the external intervention was aimed at stabilization and did little to foster the transformation that many people desired.

Throughout most of the history of modern Solomon Islands, the expansion of the state has drawn people together in situations where they were more likely to see one another as enemies and competitors than friends and allies. This study highlights what may be lost with the expansion of a state that has not historically been aimed at ensuring and enhancing the well being of its citizens. Solomon Islanders desire and deserve a better functioning state, but this study suggests that state building should be undertaken cautiously, lest it thwart the cosmopolitan impulses of ordinary people like my friends in Ranongga who have long welcomed strangers to their shore.

## Note

1. "Stranger and friend" is how anthropologist Hortense Powdermaker (1966) characterized the position of an anthropologist. Virtually ignored by critics of anthropology who stereotyped the discipline for focusing exclusively on villages (see Chapter 1), Powdermaker worked in a village community in New Ireland (now Papua New Guinea) just a decade after Malinowski's famous Trobriand fieldwork, but then conducted fieldwork in racially divided agrarian and urban societies in the American South and Southern Africa, as well as the Hollywood film industry.

# 1
# Ethnicity, Insularity, and Hospitality

The clearest omen that I experienced of the conflict that would shatter the peace of a country then known as the "Happy Isles" came in late September 1998, a few days after I arrived in Solomon Islands' national capital of Honiara on the northern coast of Guadalcanal. I was staying with fellow PhD researcher Jolene Stritecky in Gilbert Camp, a peri-urban settlement of about 2,000 people, most of them from the nearby island of Malaita. From the back of her leaf-thatched house, we could look out onto the grassy slopes where residents grew cassava and sweet potatoes, with the dark mountains of central Guadalcanal looming in the distance (Stritecky 2001b: 253–73). Women of Gilbert Camp sometimes walked to a stream beyond the settlement to do their washing. One day at the stream, a woman who described herself as "from this island" explained to me that she and her family had been told to come down from a village further inland to "sit down on our land."

A few months later, I was settling into life in Pienuna village on Ranongga Island, hundreds of kilometers away from Honiara, when news of a violent insurgency arrived by radio and in the newspapers. An indigenous insurgency movement calling themselves the Guadalcanal Revolutionary Army (GRA) had begun to evict settlers from Malaita from areas to the east and west of the capital along the Guadalcanal coastal plain. Malaitan residents of Gilbert Camp were aware of Guale discontent, but according to Stritecky, news of the first violent attacks "seemed to come from nowhere," and residents responded "with sad bewilderment and no identification with ethnically-driven hatred for Guale people in general" (ibid.: 101, 102; see also Kwa'ioloa and Burt 2012). Early victims of the Guale militancy streamed into Honiara in the first half of 1999, seeking refuge in temporary shelters. In May and June, the Guale insurgents, by then identifying themselves as the Isatabu Freedom Movement (IFM), intensified their attacks. Malaitan patrols formed in self-defense, and some mounted counter-attacks, but mostly Malaitans simply left. Some twenty thousand returned to Malaita.

This largely peaceful mass departure did not end what came to be known as "the Ethnic Tension" or just "the Tension."[1] In late 1999, a militia known as the Malaita Eagle Force (MEF) formed and established control over Honiara. On 5 June 2000, the MEF and some elements of the Royal Solomon Islands Police undertook a "joint operation" to force a de facto government coup. Malaitan and Guale forces engaged in battles on the perimeters of Honiara. In October 2000, the Townsville Peace Agreement put an end to the confrontation between the rival ethnic militias without ending the violence or re-establishing order. The Weather Coast conflict that resulted from a schism between Guale militants led to some of the worst brutality of the war, mostly committed by Guale militants against Guale villagers. Meanwhile, ex-Malaitan militants in Honiara pressured the government to pay compensation and intimidated national leaders. The government was beholden to increasingly chaotic militant forces. After an abrupt policy change, in July 2003, Australia initiated the Regional Assistance Mission to Solomon Islands (RAMSI), a decade-long policing and state-building operation.

Ranongga Island, where most of the research for this study was carried out, was far from the violence on Guadalcanal. The unfolding conflict did not radically disrupt the lives of ordinary people. Gordon Nanau has argued that it is important to "recognize that 'failed states' are not the same as 'failed communities.' It was government apparatus that failed during the period of social unrest. Communities remained and indeed succeeded in acting as buffers providing the needs of their people in the absence of government services" (Nanau 2008: 159–60). As the situation worsened in Guadalcanal, many people originally from Ranongga returned to their natal villages or to Western Province towns like Gizo or Noro. One skilled professional who had left behind a good paying job and considerable property in Honiara noted wryly that at least his family could return to his own land and "eat potatoes." Rural communities were remarkably effective in sustaining residents in the absence of a functional state, but it is important to recognize the hardship that rural citizens endured. By late 2000, the collapse of state services had restricted mobility, decreased the availability of cash income, and limited educational opportunities for young people. And effects of the conflict were much more significant in places like northern Malaita, where large numbers of people had been living and working in Honiara and Guadalcanal.

Many ethnic conflicts of the postcolonial and post-Cold War era have been popularly depicted as the result of ancient and deep-seated animosity between culturally, religiously, even racially different communities. If there is one consistent theme that has emerged from scholarly studies of such conflicts, it is that cultural difference alone has little to do with violence. Ethnic violence often arises when interlinked communities come to see one another as rivals and enemies, a process that Stanley Tambiah referred to as "ethnic fratricide" in his analysis of ethno-religious conflict in Sri Lanka (Tambiah 1986). Simon Harrison describes ethnic conflict as "cultural dishomogenization, the deliberate, systematic, and effortful production of dissimilarities" among communities "deeply imbricated in one another" (Harrison 2003: 349; see also Harrison 2006). Colonial rule was often instrumental in producing difference in this way. Writing of the 1994 Rwandan genocide, Mahmood Mamdani has argued that although polarized Tutsi and Hutu identities had been consolidated in the pre-colonial Rwandan state, the racialized political identities that figured the former as "settlers" and the latter as "natives" emerged in the context of colonial rule. He argues, "the failure to transcend these identities is at the heart of the crisis of citizenship in postcolonial Africa" (Mamdani 2001: 14). As in Africa, in the Western Pacific, postcolonial conflicts have pitted indigenous landowners against migrant laborers, but perhaps because such divisions are comparatively recent, dating back only to the early twentieth century and the formation of the colonial state, violence here has been more limited than in similar conflicts elsewhere in the postcolonial and postsocialist world.

The Solomon Islands conflict emerged against the backdrop of the long-standing crises of post-independence Fiji. In May 2000, just a month before the coup in the Solomons, indigenous Fijian nationalist George Speight led the country's third military coup and unseated the elected government of the first Indo-Fijian prime minister (the first two coups were in 1987; the fourth would occur in 2006), an event that incited racially motivated civilian violence against Indo-Fijians (Trnka 2008). In contrast to the opposed ethnic sides in the Solomon Islands conflict, indigenous Fijian and Indo-Fijian populations were significantly different in terms of religion, language, and culture. Yet such underlying differences alone tell us little about why Fiji has been plagued by anti-immigrant coups, which requires attention to the different ways that indigenous Fijians and Indo-Fijians were incorporated into the colonial economy and represented within the colonial state. As John Kelly (1989, 1991) has highlighted, Indigenous Fijians were "protected" through legislation discouraging labor mobility, while Indo-Fijians were treated as nothing more than a labor force; indigenous Fijian culture was reified and structured into a hierarchy, while Indo-Fijian culture was ignored and disregarded. As Fiji moved toward democratic forms of representation, the British administration sought to ensure that voting would be according to ethnically defined communities, and that indigenous Fijians would retain sovereignty (Kelly and Kaplan 2001; Lal 1992, 2000). The fact that ethnic identities have modern histories hardly makes them less powerful or real, but it does mean that they cannot be understood as the legacy of supposedly customary forms of sociality.

From the beginning of the fighting on Guadalcanal, scholars contested the ethnic framing of the conflict, and emphasized historical, political, and economic causes for the unrest. Political scientist Tarcisius Tara Kabutaulaka (2001), originally from Guadalcanal's Weather Coast, was among the first to argue that the origins of the conflict were "beyond ethnicity," and were instead to be found in histories of uneven commercial development and administrative neglect, coupled with more recent forms of political corruption. Historian Judith Bennett (2002), as well as Clive Moore (2004, 2007), described the colonial roots of the conflict as a class conflict between residents of resource-rich and commercially developed areas who could grow and sell copra and other goods, and the others who had minimal access to commodity markets and could sell only their labor. Moore, along with Jon Fraenkel (2004) and Sinclair Dinnen (2002), argued patronage politics and the crony capitalism of the 1980s and 1990s created a situation in which political elites could benefit from civil unrest. In a study based on interviews with former militants, Matthew Allen suggests that if one had to choose a single most important reason that men took up arms in the conflict, it was "the perception among some Solomon Islanders of their social and economic deprivation relative to other Solomon Islanders and relative to people in other parts of the world" (Allen 2013a: 188). Long-time Honiara resident Michael Kwa'ioloa said it more simply: "[the] rich have got richer and the poor have got poorer, and as a rule a deprived man is an angry man" (Kwa'ioloa and Burt 2012: 270).

The Solomon Islands was labeled the Pacific Islands' first "failed state" in 2002. Analysis that blamed the conflict on the country's weak or failed state became influential in the decade that followed because it helped to justify and guide RAMSI, the ten-year multi-billion dollar mission that commenced in 2003.[2] Although cultural diversity is not directly blamed for the conflict, the "weak state" paradigm does depict both cultural diversity and political fragmentation as problematic because they undermine the legitimacy and power of the national state. Such an argument is evident in a report by the Australian Strategic Policy Institute, which made the case for international intervention in the form of RAMSI. According to lead author Elsina Wainwright, the problems began when "disparate ethnic and language groups" (Wainwright 2003: 18) were artificially thrown together by a colonial administration that failed to invest in the infrastructure that would bring these isolated polities together into a coherent nation-state. The postcolonial government lacked revenue and struggled for legitimacy "against older, more deeply rooted political and social traditions" (ibid.: 18). Modern institutions were "overlaid on top of a multiplicity of indigenous political structures," and the "resilience" of these underlying institutions constitutes the "broader basis for the continuing weakness of the state" (ibid.: 27). The conflict was almost inevitable with "tribal differences sparking violence on a level that challenges the capacity and authority of the state"; the rule of law collapsed, leading to "the descent into corruption and criminality" (ibid.: 18). This analysis emphasized internal drivers of the conflict, and takes "tribal differences" as pre-existing and problematic.

As a study of how some Solomon Islanders conceptualize and engage with people from other lands, this book thus offers a corrective to several influential misunderstandings of the way that Solomon Islanders have engaged with one another and with outside forces like the colonial and postcolonial state. First, colonial and postcolonial processes of state expansion are viewed as essentially benign, problematic only insofar as they did not go far enough in penetrating the resistant structures of isolated and disparate local polities. Second, ethnonationalist identities and contemporary indigenous structures are depicted as disconnected from modern processes of state formation; they are seen as the unchanging core upon which the veneer of the modern state has been laid. Finally, the failure of the state is attributed to a lack of nationalist sentiment among citizens who have not been able to transcend their particularistic commitments to localized traditional collectivities, like villages, clans, or kinspeople. Such assumptions are both inaccurate and insidious because they allow analysts, policy makers, and sometimes ordinary citizens to blame the crisis of the modern state on Solomon Island cultures and peoples, rather than broader transnational processes of capitalist expansion and state formation.

The rural forms of sociality I discuss throughout this book are nothing like the "disparate tribal and ethnic groups" described by Wainwright in her report. Far from being "resilient," indigenous social and political institutions have been dramatically transformed since the early twentieth century; far from being conservative, local people have often eagerly embraced such transformations (McDougall 2015). The rural villages I lived in and visited were full of people from elsewhere, and villagers traveled as far as their finances, local infrastructure, and stringent migration laws in neighboring metropolitan nations like Australia allowed. This mobility is often limited, and many Solomon Islanders today feel themselves neglected by the nation-state and excluded from distant sources of power and wealth. Frustration about this exclusion and limitation—not inherent political fragmentation, conservatism, or insularity—must be seen as a core cause for the recent conflict.

This ethnography demonstrates that intense attachment to place is not incompatible with radical openness to others. Like most other Solomon Islanders, residents of Ranongga work on land held and transmitted through ties of kinship. Yet, the result is not a set of neatly bounded, genealogically defined, tribal groups, but a translocal network of relationships connecting disparate people and places. Solomon Islands is often depicted as a conglomeration of externally bounded but internally coherent entities, variously called cultures, ethnic groups, tribes, clans, or villages; this is a vision of the world as "a global pool hall in which the entities spin off each other like so many hard and round billiard balls" that has been critiqued within anthropology for more than three decades (Wolf 1982: 6; see also Bashkow 2004). Arguably, few anthropologists really viewed cultures or societies as bounded in such a simplistic way, but such a vision is perpetuated in scholarly work that relies upon caricature of simple, homogeneous, face to face, non-metropolitan, premodern societies to evoke the fluid, flexible, dynamic social worlds of late modernity. Solomon Islands is not a conglomeration of disparate and disconnected cultural groups; as is the case in most human communities, Solomon Islanders' lives are irreducibly "intercultural," a term used by Francesca Merlan (1998, 2005) to explore relations between Aboriginal and white residents of a town in Australia's Northern Territory. The notion of the intercultural, Merlan suggests, allows us to explore "the implications of engagement across forms of difference that nevertheless do not imply complete boundedness" (Merlan 2005: 180). From such a perspective, all social engagement involves cultural difference; what varies is the degree of difference and whether or not actors must pay attention to one another's expectations.

This study is highly localized, and some of my analysis points to the unique situation of Ranongga. But my broader argument—that cultural difference is present at all levels of society, that rural villagers are constantly engaging with strangers, and that those engagements with others are moments when local structures may be profoundly transformed—is valid far beyond Ranongga. Many salient features of social life I discuss, such as an emphasis on narratives of arrival and migration and a concern with precedence and hierarchy, are shared throughout the Austronesian world. Other island Melanesians have experienced processes of capitalist expansion, colonial state formation, and missionization that are similar to those I describe for Ranongga and the western Solomons. Most importantly, this ethnography speaks to situations beyond Ranongga precisely because this island is full of people who come from, or have lived in, other places within Solomon Islands. Significant cultural differences exist, but there is no evidence of incommensurable cultural difference of the sort that we might expect from commonplace depictions of the highly fragmented nature of Solomon Islands society. The conflicts that arise in the course of ordinary social life in Ranongga, as well as those that arose in a violent form on Guadalcanal between 1998 and 2003, are always arguments in shared terms. This book seeks to illuminate both the specific arguments and the shared terms of these intercultural engagements.

Because the civil conflict in Solomon Islands had little to do with indigenous modes of engaging across cultural difference and much to do with inequitable forms of modern development, a study of indigenous modes of engaging with others has little to contribute to discussions of why violence occurred. Indeed, given the robust correlations between postcolonial economies dominated by resource extraction and civil conflict, the outbreak of violence is hardly surprising (Allen 2013b). What is really puzzling about the Solomon Islands conflict is not the fact that it occurred, but that it was not worse. In five years of violence, tens of thousands of people were displaced, but only 150 to 200 people were killed, with 430 to 460 non-fatal arms-related injuries (Braithwaite et al. 2010: 20). Why were only hundreds, not thousands or tens of thousands, of people killed? Why were so few ordinary citizens complicit in acts of ethnic hatred? How did so many find the courage to mediate between the opposed sides? Why did armed men give up weapons so quickly in 2003 when international military forces finally arrived? How could apparently hardened militants embrace and forgive their former enemies? We may not need socio-cultural analysis to explain the outbreak of war, but we do require a better understanding of intercultural relationships in the Solomon Islands to understand this remarkable capacity for peace.[3]

## Myths of Insularity and Oceanic Diversity

Analysis of the weak state in Solomon Islands tends to envision the country as comprised of small self-contained homogeneous communities bound together by kinship, clanship, and shared language and culture. The challenge for policy makers and donors is drawing people out of these insular and conservative social worlds and into a broader institutions, processes, and structures. Thoughtful advocates of neoliberal state building often acknowledge that the process is violent and that the transformation of customary land into modern property usually involves "coercion and fraud" (Fukuyama 2008: 22). Yet few imagine that people might continue to live in relatively autonomous self-governed communities with control over their own territory. The disruption of state building is seen as inevitable.

In its broad outlines, such a view of small-scale communities goes far beyond literature on Solomon Islands or other developing countries. In various forms, it pervades social-scientific and philosophical writing about globalization and the linked notion of cosmopolitanism, a term that has gained traction in philosophy, sociology, and anthropology since the early 2000s (see Chapter 8). Scholars of globalization and cosmopolitanism often admit that no social worlds are completely closed, but nevertheless invoke the specter of closed non-modern social worlds as a foil to the openness and mobility characteristic of late modernity. Sociologist Ulrich Beck and his coauthors, for example, note that "cosmopolitan dynamics" have existed in the past, but then declare that it is only now in the "second modernity" are we experiencing a cosmopolitan age requiring cosmopolitan social theory (see e.g. Beck 2002; Beck and Sznaider 2006; Delanty 2006). Similarly, while eschewing a "tribal fantasy" of culturally homogeneous communities (Appiah 1997: 618), well-known liberal philosopher Kwame Anthony Appiah nevertheless argues that in order to live peaceably in a cosmopolitan "world of strangers" we must "take minds and hearts formed over the long millennia of living in local troops and equip them with ideas and institutions that will allow us to live together as the global tribe we have become" (Appiah 2006: xiii). Such proclamations implicitly create a divide between those of us who presumably are already integrated into the cosmopolitan global "tribe" and local people who seem to require our help in transcending the bounds of their parochial local "troops."

Such a vision of insular non-modern societies is a myth: both an inadequate description of reality and a validation of a particular worldview. In a powerful ethnographic challenge to the idea that social unity in non-modern societies is derived from "pure mutual identification," similarity, and co-presence, Rupert Stasch (2009) characterizes Korowai speakers of West Papua (people who are often taken to epitomize primitivity) as a "society of others," arguing that Korowai understand their most intimate social relationships to be an engagement across a gap of radical social otherness and spatial distance. According to Stasch, foundational thinkers like Henry Maine, Ferdinand Tönnies, and Emile Durkheim all assumed that small-scale societies were held together by shared identity, and these scholars contrasted this homogeneity to their own internally complex urbanizing industrial society. Such myths of insularity are also to be found in Marxian theory. For all of the injustice and human suffering caused by industrialization and urbanization, Karl Marx did not lament the passing of agrarian forms of existence, famously praising the capitalist bourgeoisie for liberating peasants from the "idiocy of rural life" (Marx 1978a: 477). In the *Eighteenth Brumaire of Louis Bonaparte*, Marx argued that in order for peasants to emerge as self-conscious collective actors, they would first have to be extricated from bonds to territoriality:

> The small holding, the peasant and his family; alongside them another small holding, another peasant and another family. A few score of these make up a village, and a few score of villages make up a Department. In this way, the great mass of the French nation is formed by simple addition of homonymous magnitudes, much as potatoes in a sack form a sackful of potatoes. (Marx 1978b: 608)

Interestingly, Marx's "sack of potatoes" depiction of sub-national units resonates with Benedict Anderson's famous description of the modular nature of the modern nation. Contrary to popular misreadings, Anderson did not argue that the modern nation-state was distinctive because its members had imagined relations rather than face-to-face relations. Connections in older forms of polity were also imagined, but in a different way: not as clearly bounded and formally equivalent units, but as "indefinitely stretchable nets of kinship and clientship" stemming outward from nodal centers (Anderson 1991: 6). The modern order of nation-states, not premodern or sub-national units, takes the form of Marx's "homologous magnitudes."

As Marx's reflections on French peasants suggests, assumptions about homogeneity and insularity have been applied to non-elite or rural populations within the West as well as to colonized societies like Solomon Islands. In his classic study, Raymond Williams explored the powerful polarity between representations of the country and the city in English literature during the modern era. The literary stereotypes played on powerful and generalized emotions about the country, but the "real history" of rural life has been "astonishingly varied" and profoundly caught up in Britain's transition to industrial capitalism (Williams 1973: 1). Denigrated as backward, the country is simultaneously idealized as a place of uncomplicated and harmonious solidarity, the opposite of modern urban life, increasingly experienced as alienating and anonymous. Yet as Ching and Creed (1997) point out, rural societies are very often positioned low on social hierarchies. Rural subjects may experience an intense attachment to place, at the same time that they eagerly seek to move beyond those local worlds; they are, importantly, subject to outsiders' expectations that they remain in those fixed and designated locales.

Theories of solidarity derived from Maine, Durkheim, and other late-nineteenth-century theorists clearly shaped British social anthropology. A core research question within emerging paradigms of structural-functionalism in the 1930s centered on how societies were held together in the absence of a state. One of the most powerful answers to the question of social solidarity in stateless societies was descent theory: an approach that sought to identify the genealogical principles that defined bounded corporate groups. Beyond anthropology, descent theory remains influential: in Solomon Islands and other areas of island Melanesia, local people and outsiders alike are quick to describe local forms of socio-territorial organization in terms derived from early-twentieth-century descent theory and incorporated into the legal structures and processes of the state (Tiffany 1983). Within anthropology, however, descent theory was challenged and revised in the decades after it was formulated. In the 1950s and later, the most prominent theoretical challenge came from Lévi-Strauss's theories of alliance (Lévi-Strauss 1969), a paradigm that turned many anthropologists' attention away from the genealogical constitution of groups and toward exchanges that linked those groups. Empirical challenges to descent theory came from anthropological research in the Pacific Islands after World War II. Kinship systems in Oceania were described as cognatic, meaning that children could affiliate to either their mothers' or fathers' sides in ways that did not lead to the creation of neatly bounded corporate groups.[4] This Oceanic research led to a proliferation of descent types, but also helped to bring into question the basic assumption that genealogy was always the core principle of social organization in stateless societies (see e.g. Barnes 1962: 6; Wagner 1974). Anthropologists like David Schneider (1965, 1984) and many others began to argue for approaches that took seriously the ways that subjects of research understood and categorized their relationships.

Ethnographic studies of Melanesian societies provided the starting point for an influential theoretical challenge to the core paradigm of British social anthropology: rather than assuming that corporate groups are the building blocks of society and identifying the anthropological task as delineating the principles according to which individuals are recruited into these groups, influential scholars of Melanesia approached both groups and persons as the product of social processes such as gift exchange. In an important early work within the paradigm sometimes known as "Melanesian relationality," Roy Wagner (1967) sought to understand the social organization of Daribi speakers of Papua New Guinea through "native symbolic categories." Daribi people represented themselves as inherently bound to all cognatic kin, not only through social relations but also through shared substances like blood, semen, and food. Ceremonial exchange was not understood as a way of connecting already-bounded corporate groups in the way that alliance theory suggested. Instead, exchange effectively cut off bonds among relatives in ways that created delimited social groups; the groups were not linked by exchange, they were constituted in the process of exchange. Marilyn Strathern's seminal work *The Gender of the Gift* (1988) generalized such insights in a broad comparativist project focused on the contrasting ways that Melanesians and Westerners understand personhood and gender. Rather than asking how individuals are recruited into groups, Strathern saw persons as always and already constituted through relationships with others. The question was not how persons are recruited into groups, but how they cut off myriad relationships to a wide range of kinspeople in order to act either as autonomous individuals or as part of bounded corporate units.[5]

Over the last few decades, critiques of anthropology have focused on the way in which the discipline as a whole has assumed a sort of boundedness to cultures and societies, but they often gloss over work within anthropology that has challenged these assumptions. Gupta and Ferguson (1997), for example, argued that anthropologists have often assumed that cultures are localized and people are territorially bounded. By viewing the world as comprised of territorially distinct cultures, anthropologists often unwitting adopted a nationalist view of the world (see, e.g., Malkki 1994). Instead of assuming that cultures are bounded and locatable in space, the anthropological task ought to be exploring how locality is produced (Appadurai 1995).[6] While such critiques opened up new kinds of questions and new methods of fieldwork, they have also redirected attention away from the rural non-Western societies on the margins of the global system that have been the traditional focus of anthropological research. Eeva Berglund suggests that the "the historical legacy of the modern anthropologist studying the nonmodern Other" is "carried along as if it were the original sin to be confessed at suitable intervals" (Berglund 2006: 188). Alan Rumsey remarked that field projects in "remote" locales, once considered a professional rite of passage, "have come to be regarded as antediluvian: embarrassing reminders of anthropology's original identification with the 'savage slot' among the social science disciplines" (Rumsey 2004: 581–82). This change in disciplinary fashion "has had the unfortunate consequence of tacitly affirming the very proposition that we as anthropologists should aim to combat: that there is such a place *in the world* as 'the savage slot,' which we can and should avoid by directing our research elsewhere" (ibid.: 582).[7] In a world marked by growing inequality, and in an academy where the social worlds of the privileged are given far more attention than those of the underprivileged, this refocusing of disciplinary attention may inadvertently narrow the scope of our understanding. Moreover, the shift of anthropological attention has helped to leave the myth of insularity firmly intact, especially beyond anthropology.

Nowhere is the myth of insularity more prevalent, or misleading, than in descriptions of Oceania and, especially, of island Melanesia. The very word "insular" reveals the prejudices of non-islanders, equating life on islands with the state of being limited, parochial, self-contained. Tongan historian Epeli Hau'ofa's memorably critiqued this view, pointing out that only outsiders see the Pacific as tiny specks of land in the vast emptiness of water. For islanders, Oceania is a "sea of islands" (Hau'ofa 1993) linked by webs of interaction and engagement, where water is not a barrier but a highway. With its very small language and culture groups, Melanesia seems to epitomize the state of being insular. Yet far from being a product of long isolation, diversity is greatest in precisely those coastal and island regions where there have been the most intense engagements with strangers. Already populated millennia prior to the remarkable expansion of Austronesian speaking people through insular Southeast Asia to the farthest reaches of the eastern Pacific, the ancestors of contemporary residents have long engaged with distinctively foreign modes of living (Spriggs 1997). Facts of geography and migration help to explain the diversity of the area, but so too do indigenous attitudes toward linguistic and cultural differentiation (Laycock 1982: 34–35; Besnier 2004: 114). Diversity is not the automatic result of historical isolation from interactions with other people. Diversity is valued, cultivated, and made possible by translocal relationships and ongoing engagements with strangers.

## Strangers and Hospitality

On Ranongga, as in most societies, the moral obligations of kinship are often articulated with reference to the figure of the stranger—there is no worse admonition than being accused of treating your closest relatives as strangers. Ranonggans constantly exhort one another to remember that they are "just one people" (*maka tinoni gu*) and they should not treat another as "different people" (*goto tinoni*). The essence of kinship in Ranongga is *variroqu*, a term I translate as "love."[8] As Christine Dureau has argued for the cognate concept in Simbo (Dureau 2012), love is no mere sentiment: to speak of love is to speak of material forms of care for the loved person.[9] Kinspeople must show such love to one another, but strangers are under no such obligation; by the same logic, kindness to strangers is the first step in transforming them into kin. Conversely, kinspeople may be estranged through acts of indifference or hostility.

Stranger sociality is often taken as a feature of metropolitan social life, but strangers, and questions about the hospitality owed to strangers, are an important focus of moral reflection in all human societies, and thus a productive focus for cross-cultural analysis (Shryock 2012). And as sociologist George Simmel suggested in his famous excursus on the stranger (Simmel 1964), modern metropolitan life may actually cut off possibilities for meaningful engagements with strangers. For Simmel, people are never fully encompassed within a collectivity; they always have connections beyond the group, an externality that always has the potential for estrangement.[10] The stranger combines opposed qualities of nearness and distance, existing within a group, but defined "by the fact that he has not belonged to it from the beginning, that he imports qualities into it, which do not and cannot stem from the group itself" (ibid.: 402). A focus of both attraction and repulsion, the stranger is almost always involved in inter-group trade and never an "owner of the soil" (ibid.: 403). Simmel characterized contemporary metropolitan existence as being profoundly shaped by individuals' experiences of being surrounded by and dependent upon an unprecedented number of strangers, suggesting that increasing specialization "makes one individual incomparable to another . . . [but] more directly dependent upon the supplementary activities of all others" (ibid.: 409). In cities, the scope of engagement with strangers is expanded, but Simmel believed that the proliferation of strangers led urbanites to close themselves off from real engagement with the strangers that surrounded them. Rather than engaging with others who surround them, modern urbanites tend to exaggerate, protect, and perform their individuality.

The paradoxical role of the stranger in metropolitan societies has also been the focus of more recent critical theory. Zygmunt Bauman, for example, argued that strangers are "the waste of the state's ordering zeal" (Bauman 1995: 2), to either be excluded from the body politic or assimilated within it. In his late work, Jacques Derrida also explored the impossible position of strangers in modern nation-states, focusing especially on Kant's discussion of the cosmopolitan right of the stranger to be treated without hostility (Kant 1991).

Derrida pointed out that this Kantian hospitality is a conditional hospitality because the stranger has a right to refuge, but no right to welcome (Derrida and Dufourmantelle 2000). The host asserts sovereignty over the space of hospitality in ways that Derrida saw as violent and coercive: before welcome is granted, strangers must speak the host's language and identify themselves in ways recognized by the host. Derrida evoked the possibility of unconditional hospitality, a hospitality that would transgress "the law of right or duty" and require us to "give place" to "the absolute, unknown, anonymous other" (ibid.: 25). Yet such a total abdication of sovereignty is also no real solution to the problem, insofar as it would eliminate the condition of possibility for hospitality, namely a claim on the place into which strangers may be welcomed.

Far from being unique to metropolitan situations, such paradoxes of sovereignty are present in many societies. As Andrew Shryock has argued in work drawing on ethnohistorical research among Balga Bedouin of Jordan and readings of continental philosophy, "narratives of hospitality reveal a sense of existential danger at the heart of social life" and provide a focus for comparison across many different scales of local and national societies (Shryock 2012: S21; see also Shryock 2009). Among Bedouin, guests are honored, but subordinated; they are told to act as though they are at home, but doing so would make them the quintessential bad guests. In modern nation-states and rural Bedouin households alike, spaces of hospitality are liminal, unstable, and temporary, but among the Bedouin, there is no pretense of formal equality between host and guest of the sort prevailing in modern nation-states. For Bedouin, guests cannot remain guests for long: "'After forty days', they say, 'you become one of us'" (Shryock 2012: S31). Here, and in the Oceanic situations that are my focus, hospitality allows the transformation from stranger to kinsperson.

In Oceania, the spaces of hospitality are not houses, but beaches, memorably described by historian Greg Dening as the "marginal spaces between land and sea" where "otherness is both a new discovery and a reflection of something old" (Dening 1980: 177). The irreducible ambivalence of hospitality is on clear display in the warrior welcomes that are ubiquitous throughout Island Melanesia and the wider Pacific Islands region (see Rosenblatt 2011): strangers are first repelled as enemies before being welcomed as guests. Whether they arrive on beaches or at airports, important visitors are confronted by barechested warriors advancing upon them with spears and battle axes. After a few moments, a chief of the land steps forward, quells the warriors, and offers shell valuables to make peace and bind the visitors to the place. In pervasively Christian Oceania, such warrior welcomes simultaneously evoke an era when people were more violent and more powerful than they are today, and re-enact the moment in which local communities abandoned the violent ways of their ancestors and embraced the promise of Christian peace.

A dynamic tension between autochthons and migrants—between people of the land and people of the sea—is attested to in Solomon Islands ethnography. In studies of Marovo Lagoon, Edvard Hviding (1996, 2003a, 2011, 2014) emphasizes the expansiveness of New Georgia's marine worlds, tracing historical continuities that link the precolonial past to a postcolonial present characterized by engagements with new transnational actors like logging companies and non-governmental organizations. Even in tightly knit kin-focused communities of Marovo, Hviding observes, there is a "perennial presence of 'other people'" who have "crossed over" from other islands or come floating ashore in generations past (Hviding 2003c: 80). Geoff White's (1991, 1993, 2013) studies of Santa Isabel explore the role of the chief as the figure who mediates between the local and the foreign, especially in events leading to conversion to Christianity. Writing of Arosi people of Makira in the southeastern Solomons, Michael Scott (2007a, 2007b) has focused on cosmological and ontological imperatives to engage with others. Arosi matrilineages are autochthonous insofar as they emerged in particular places, but they also become autochthonous through engagement with ontologically distinct categories of people. The reproduction of persons and transformation of land into humanized territory requires engagement with foreign others.

Throughout Oceania, the relationship between strangers and people of the place contains the possibility for radical inversions of power and belonging. A.M. Hocart, who began his anthropological career as part of the Percy Sladen Trust Expedition to New Georgia in 1908 (see Hviding and Berg 2014a), would later write about widespread cultural patterns in which rulers come from beyond the societies that they rule (Hocart 1969, 1970). Hocart's insights provided inspiration for Marshall Sahlins's analysis of the "stranger king" in mytho-history in Fiji, Hawaii, and other Polynesian societies (Sahlins 1985: 73–103; 1992). Power does not emanate from within society; chiefs are understood as foreigners who transgress moral rules to establish their sovereignty. Described in Hawaii as "sharks who travel on land," Oceanic stranger chiefs are figured as devouring both land and people, while the quiescent people of the land retain powers of fertility and the right to ritually install these violent foreigners (see Sahlins 1985, 1992: 22; Valeri 1985; Kaplan 1995). This "stranger king" motif has been explored most directly in the context of Fiji and Polynesian societies to the east, but the ethnography of Vanuatu attests to pervasive metaphors contrasting people of the land and people of the sea as alternative and reversible forms of power (e.g. Jolly 1982; Bonnemaison 1994; Jolly and Mosko 1994; Patterson 2002; Taylor 2008). Similar themes pervade literature on Austronesian-speaking societies. As James Fox suggests, narratives from across archipelagic Southeast Asia and Oceania focus on "the 'outsider' who is received and installed inside, thus reordering precedence among an autochthonous population that has received him into their midst" (Fox 2008:

201; see also Fox 1994; Henley 2004; Caldwell and Henley 2008; Henley and Caldwell 2008; Acciaioli 2009; Vischer 2009). As Danilyn Rutherford (2003) has explored for Biak people of West Papua, the foreign is figured as a source of both value and violent power in ways that inform everything from the most intimate relations between brothers and sisters to Biak engagement with Indonesia's New Order state. Here and elsewhere, power and value are often understood as emanating from places beyond local shores.[11]

Contemporary Oceanic understandings of strangers cannot be understood without taking seriously islanders' commitment to Christian principles and worldviews. For Ranonggans and many others, the most appealing and radical promise of Christianity is a world without strangers. If all are brother and sisters in Christ, children of the same God, then there is no need to distinguish between self and other. This promise of universal peace and unity is particularly poignant when juxtaposed with a past that is constantly memorialized as a time of violence when strangers were hated and feared. Like Christians everywhere, Solomon Islander Christians find it difficult to enact the conviction that all people are kin. Beginning in the early twentieth century, denominational divisions have severed relations amongst kinspeople. While Ranongga and most rural societies in the Solomons are remarkably free of physical violence despite the absence of the coercive mechanisms of the state, land disputes are understood to violently sever relationships. Insofar as personhood is grounded in a sense of being a person of a particular place, to deny someone's connection to territory is an assault on their very person and seen as a contradiction of Christian principles of peace and harmony. Yet, despite the ongoing reality of division and conflict in a sinful world, the Christian promise of a world without strangers remains a potent force in everyday social life.

As Christians, Ranonggans envision a world in which the distinction between self and other, kin and strangers, is irrelevant. Yet everyday social life and negotiations of property rights center on the dynamic relationships between kin and strangers. Strangers can be welcomed as guests or repelled as enemies, but there is little space for neutral coexistence. The civil conflict on Guadalcanal that formed the backdrop and context to my fieldwork on Ranongga can be understood as violent resistance to a national state seeking to create such a neutral space. Ordinary Guale people and militants alike blamed the government for creating situations in which people from other islands could come to their island uninvited and unwelcomed. Perhaps the most surprising part of this conflict is that those who were the victims of violence essentially agreed that neither the government, nor commercial interests, had the right to bring others onto land without the consent of the landowners. Exploring the dialectical engagements between people of the place and strangers elsewhere in the archipelago can thus help us understand the dynamics of violence and friendship that were manifest in the civil war.

## Notes

1. Two book-length studies by political scientist Jon Fraenkel (2004) and historian Clive Moore (2004) provide detailed documentation of the unfolding of the conflict; Moore situates the conflict in the longer political and economic history of the Solomons, while Fraenkel focuses on high-level machinations of the political elite. Sinclair Dinnen provided an early analysis of the unraveling of state structures and of the way actors sought to "instrumentalise disorder" (Dinnen 2002: 285). Matthew Allen's excellent study of militant perspectives on the conflict (Allen 2013a) focuses on the grassroots-level grievances that motivated ordinary Solomon Islander men to take up arms and the micro-nationalist identities that led them to frame the conflict in ethnic terms.
2. Civil society activist John Roughan (2002) was the first to publicly describe the Solomons as the Pacific Islands' first failed state, a diagnosis echoed in "Solomon Islands: The Pacific's First Failed State?" *Economist*, 13 February 2003 (retrieved 6 January 2015 from: http://www.economist.com/node/1580220). Slightly earlier, Ben Reilly (2000) controversially argued that an "Africanisation" of the Pacific was occurring, identifying a combination of fragile states and multiethnic politics as a challenge to democracy. The "weak" or "failed state" paradigm became influential in Australian foreign policy, and has been the focus of wide-ranging critiques by political scientists and other scholars. Chapters in volumes edited by Dinnen and Firth (2008) and Fry and Kabutaulaka (2008) provide critical assessments of the paradigm and Australian foreign policy in the Pacific.
3. My argument here echoes that of Christopher Taylor (2001), who wrote of Rwanda. He suggests that political and historical accounts of the sort put forward by Mamdani (2001) are adequate to explain why violence occurred, but analysis of indigenous cultural symbols and processes are necessary to understand the form that the violence took. In the case of Rwanda, the task involves explaining why many ordinary Hutu committed genocidal violence against their neighbors and relatives. In the Solomons, the task is understanding why so few people took up arms against one another.
4. See Hviding (2003) for a discussion of the expansion of studies of non-unilineal kinship systems in the Pacific, and especially Solomon Islands; of particular note is the work of Roger Keesing on Malaita (1970, 1982b, 1987a) and Harold Scheffler on Choiseul (1965, 1985).
5. Strathern's work has been taken up in ways that suggest Melanesian persons are somehow inherently "dividual" or "relational." I have argued that this is a misreading of Strathern, whose core concern was to understand processes through which individual persons and corporate groups emerged as effective social actors, and specifically to understand why those individual and collective actors were usually gendered male (see McDougall 2009b).
6. Such critiques arguably misrepresent the anthropological tradition based on quite narrow readings of classic works. Even if presumptions of internal solidarity and external boundedness did shape early British structural-functional anthropology, Bashkow (2004) argues that Franz Boas and his students were always attentive to flows of ideas, objects, and persons across locally meaningful cultural boundaries.
7. Rumsey takes the term "savage slot" from Trouillot (1991).
8. *Variroqu* in Kubokota, or *vairoqu* in Luqa, is a reciprocal construction (*vari/vai*) of the transitive verb *roqu*, which covers all sorts of positive affective orientations to another

person. *Roqu* can mean to think of, consider, remember, have pity for, or love someone. Interestingly, its semantic domain clearly excludes what is sometimes included in the range of the English word "love": desire. Not only are lexically distinct terms used to denote "love" and "desire" (the latter is *nyoro qua*), but a distinct grammatical case (sometimes called "edible" because it is used for food as well as war victims and lovers) may be used when speaking of the object of desire, but never the object of love. Love is about responding affectively to the other; desire is about acquiring the other in the same way one might acquire any other desired thing.

9. The point struck home to me when, as I was leaving after my first extended stint of fieldwork, my hamlet "mother" Liza Ekera wept at my departure (which I found quite moving), and then lamented that there would be no one to buy sugar for tea (which made me feel that she valued me only for my money). Later, it occurred to me that I had witnessed people mourn beloved relatives in similar ways.

10. In his study of ethnic conflict as "fracturing resemblances," Simon Harrison (2006) identifies Simmel as a key figure in a tradition of social thought quite radically opposed to the dominant tradition of Durkheimian solidarity. Along with Sigmund Freud, literary theorist René Girard, anthropologist Gregory Bateson, and several others, Simmel does not assume that social order is grounded in shared values and beliefs. For these theorists, conflict is a central part of the social order, generated not by too much difference but by too much similarity.

11. Sahlins's work has made the idea of the stranger king particularly influential in studies of Pacific Islands, but Sahlins himself never saw it as uniquely Oceanic; his original formulation took inspiration from George Dumezil's work on Indo-European mythology as well as Hocart's writing on Fijian chieftainship (Sahlins 1985). More recently, he described the association of power and alterity as an "elementary structure" of kinship and politics the world over (Sahlins 2008). For work that takes Indonesia as a starting point for comparison, see articles in Caldwell and Henley (2008); on China, see Yongjia (2011). Scholars of Africa have recently engaged with notions of the stranger king that have been elaborated with reference to Oceania (Argyle 2008; Nourse 2008); Taussig-Rubbo (2012) links this notion to Evans-Pritchard's (1948) early writings on divine kingship in the Sudan (see also Graeber 2011).

# 2
# Ranongga's Shifting Ground

On the first day of the Easter holy week in 2007, worshippers had gathered for early morning devotion in Lale, a large village on the southern tip of Ranongga. Just as they sang the verse, "If you are angry with us, all of the hills will shake" in the new Luqa-language translation of the hymn "Oh God, of the Unfathomed Sea," the earth shuddered violently with a resounding boom. Around Ranongga, worshippers stumbled out of church to find the earth churning beneath them. Some later explained that it was like being on the sea in the middle of a storm. Moments later, those near the coast watched in horror as the sea rushed off the reef. Knowing what this signaled, they ran to higher ground, carrying children, the elderly, and disabled people. Around Western and Choiseul provinces, scores of coastal villages were hit by a series of tsunamis. Among the worst hit areas was northern Simbo, where two villages were effectively washed away. Just 8 kilometers north, on Ranongga, the wave itself caused no damage or loss of life because the entire island had been thrust meters out of the ocean.

The epicenter of the devastating 8.1 magnitude earthquake of 2 April 2007 was 40 kilometers to the south-southeast of the provincial capital of Gizo (see Figure 0.2).[1] It occurred along the boundary of the Pacific plate where it converges with the large Indo-Australian plate and two smaller micro-plates, the Woodlark and Solomon Sea plates; this boundary runs roughly parallel to the chain of islands making up Solomon Islands, Vanuatu, and New Caledonia. The subterranean trench between the plates lies beneath the narrow channel separating Ranongga and Simbo: it is the only place in the world where two islands so close together straddle a tectonic fault line. Southern Ranongga is on the very edge of the overriding Pacific plate, whereas Simbo is perched on the crest of a subterranean ridge of the subducting Australian plate. When the earthquake struck, the Indo-Australian, Solomon Sea, and Woodlark plates dove below the Pacific plate. Simbo dropped downwards, subsiding between 0.75 and 1 meter. At the same moment, Ranongga jolted upwards: tipping to the north, it rose between 2.5 and 3 meters in the south and 1 meter in the north.

**Figure 2.1.** Bleached coral south of Pienuna village near the new settlement of Mokeru, with Ziosi Luke, Luke Irapio, and Rosie Ekera. October 2007.

All around Ranongga, the uplift added 50 to 100 meters to the coastline. On the eastern leeward side of the island, sandy coves were replaced by fields of broken coral. On the western windward side of the island, a black sand beach suddenly appeared at the water's edge. In the days after the quake, fish floundered in exposed reefs. In the weeks that followed, the stench from rotting sea life was said to be nearly unbearable. Months later, the coral bleached white and, over the subsequent years, it has been overtaken by coastal vegetation. Continuous landslides in the months after the quake destroyed much of the western coast of the island, causing the two deaths from the earthquake on Ranongga: a woman buried in Modo village during the initial quake, and a man killed while retrieving potatoes from a garden near Keara village in the hungry months that followed. Landslides in April created dams that burst after heavy rains in June and July, unleashing floods and further landslides along both coasts. Many people believed that landslides and erosion were particularly severe because so much land had been cleared for gardening (see McDougall, Barry, and Pio 2008).

In the island Pacific, geological change can happen in moments rather than millennia. After the earthquake thrust the land upwards, I could not help but think of stories I had heard about the origins of the clan Degere that described it as the post that lifted the island out of the sea, or stories of the clan Povana that describe an underground eel moving under the earth's surface. Such myths do not "explain" geology in some straightforward way, but they depict a world in which land is not an inert background for human life, but is constantly being transformed—built by volcanoes, torn away by cyclones, thrust up and pulled down by the movement of tectonic plates, revealed and submerged by changes in sea level.[2]

Natural disasters have directly affected settlement patterns on Ranongga, and have more indirectly shaped the ways that people understand land tenure. After the 2007 earthquake, many families living in coastal villages sought to relocate to higher ground, sometimes returning to areas occupied generations earlier. Residents of one of the worst effected villages, Modo, moved en masse from the coast to an inland area previously used as garden land. The 2007 earthquake was not the first in living memory; an earlier 1952 quake had also caused massive landslides. In the years that followed, people relocated in large numbers from the steeply sloped landslide-prone western coast to the flatter areas of the north and northeast. A conversation I had in 2000 with someone whose father had refused to leave the difficult western coast after the earthquake of 1952 remained in my mind as I looked at the damage in 2007. He explained that his ancestors refused to allow anyone to *pajuku* areas from their clan territory (*pajuku* is a transaction I discuss Chapter 5 that is sometimes understood as a purchase). My interlocutor saw *pajuku* as an uncustomary individualization of land tenure and thought it was risky. If every family has its own separate block, he reflected, what happens if an earthquake comes? If your small block is destroyed, where do you go? Better to stay within the large territory of the clan, so that when your area is destroyed, you can move to other land.

This chapter introduces readers to geographic patterns and historical processes that have shaped the lives of the people who are the focus of this ethnography. Most of my research was carried out between 1998 and 2001, so I focus on years prior to the earthquake. I begin with Ranongga's geography, outlining the ways that the island's topography and orientation have shaped possibilities for settlement, subsistence, and inter-local engagements. As is the case for other areas of the Solomon Islands, pacification and missionization led to a significant reorganization of the population from defensible locations to more accessible coastal locations, and from small inland hamlets to large coastal villages. Significant portions of what was swiftly becoming the most valuable coastal land were alienated in the 1910s, and two expatriate-run plantations were established on the island. The global Great Depression of the 1930s followed by the Japanese invasion in 1942 put many small planters out of business and opened up a space for local entrepreneurs. The postwar era was a kind of golden age for Ranonggans—a time when local leaders were able to make the island a hub of commercial activity. The postcolonial era, in contrast, has been a time of disappointment. Excluded from a resource economy focused on logging, Ranonggans have watched from the margins as other areas in Western Province experienced what Edvard Hviding has aptly called "compressed globalization" (Hviding 2003a: 542–43). The eruption of conflict in Guadalcanal, and the further withdrawal of the state at the turn of the twenty-first century, caused significant hardship and a contraction of economic possibilities for Ranonggans. At the same time, national disruption also affirmed the importance of local self-sufficiency.

The twentieth century was a time of significant change in socio-political and cultural life and even in the very shape of the land itself. Yet the fact that people live and work on territory that was also held by their ancestors creates a powerful sense of continuity that is often expressed through idioms of *kastom*, a Pijin word usually glossed as "tradition" or "custom."[3] Solomon Islanders describe something as *kastom* when they want to emphasize that it is grounded in local, rather than foreign, ways of doing things. The term points to a sense of continuity with the past, but as David Akin (2013) emphasizes in his recent study of the history of Malaitan *kastom*, local people have not shared the notion held by many outsiders that only ancient and unchanged ideas and practices are truly "customary." In Malaita, and throughout the region, *kastom* became a central focus of indigenous projects of collective transformation after World War II. As Allen (2013a) has shown, *kastom* remained central to articulations of collective ethno-nationalist identities mobilized during the civil conflict of 1998 to 2003. In the western Solomons, *kastom* has not been a focus of collective movements in the same way that it has been in the eastern Solomons, yet idioms of *kastom* shape discussions of continuities with the past and possibilities for the future.

The core of local *kastom* throughout New Georgia today is the notion of the *butubutu*, now understood as a landowning descent group. Hviding (2003c) has analyzed *butubutu* in New Georgia as constituted through cumulative filiation, with people tracing membership through either patrilateral or matrilateral ties. Like people of neighboring Vella Lavella and Simbo (Berg 2008; Dureau 1994), Ranonggans trace connections to *butubutu* matrilineally. Today, local people and anthropologists alike describe *butubutu* as corporate landowning descent groups that are the cornerstone of the local socio-territorial order (e.g. Hviding 1996: 135). Yet this term is entirely missing from the otherwise empirically detailed and analytically insightful corpus of work of the pioneering anthropologists William Halse Rivers Rivers and Arthur Maurice Hocart, who were part of the 1908 Percy Sladen Trust Expedition to island Melanesia, work described by Hviding and Berg as "modern ethnographic research involving residence among and continuous interaction with the people studied, hallmarks of the advanced anthropological method later claimed by Malinowski" (Hviding and Berg 2014a: 11).[4] Either Rivers and Hocart missed the *butubutu*, or—as I believe is more likely—*butubutu* identities were not a focus of local concern in 1908 in the way that they were to become later in the century.

While there is little doubt that Solomon Islanders and other indigenous people have long defined themselves and their social relationships in connection to territory, contemporary ideologies of customary landowners are intrinsically connected to the expansion of the state and capital over the course of the twentieth century (Weiner and Glaskin 2007: 2). The late-twentieth-century expansion of resource capitalism in the form of logging and mining has put customary landownership at the center of modernist forms of prosperity and belonging (Ballard 1997). In Solomon Islands, neither colonial nor postcolonial governments have had the capacity to register customary land, despite repeated announcements of attempts to do so.[5] Although they are not fully integrated into a state legal system, local tenure practices have nevertheless been profoundly reshaped through generations of engagement with the state, and many local people have internalized the assumptions of successive government actors about the nature of customary tenure.

## A Difficult Place

Lying on a north-northwest/south-southeast axis, Ranongga is approximately 25 kilometers long and just 8 kilometers wide, with a central ridge that reaches 870 meters, dividing the island between distinct leeward and windward coasts (see Figure 0.3). As is the case elsewhere in the Solomons, the modern name of the entire island, "Ranongga," is derived from the name of one region, Ganoqa, in the northwestern quadrant of the island. The other regions are Kubokota, which comprises the eastern quadrant of the northern half of the island, and Luqa, which is the southern half. The total population of the island in the 2009 census was just over 6,000, divided almost evenly between Luqa-speaking southern Ranongga and Kubokota-speaking north and central Ranongga (SISO 2012). Until the relocation of most of Modo village inland to a new settlement called Keikoro after the 2007 earthquake, all major settlements were on the coast. Since the 1930s, the gentle slopes of the eastern, leeward side of the island have been far more densely populated than the steep cliffs of the western windward side; the northern tip of Ranongga is among the more densely settled non-urban areas of Western Province. Just under two-thirds of Ranongga's inhabitants are members of the United Church, and approximately one-third are members of the Seventh-day Adventist Church; the congregations of a number of other newer Protestant churches have been growing in recent decades.

Ranongga's geography has important implications for ordinary experience. Direction and spatial orientation is constantly present in conversation in Ranonggan and other Austronesian languages (see e.g. Senft 1997). Writing of Kubokota, Chambers (2009) shows how relationships among speakers and between speakers and referents are discursively anchored in the topography of the island (where "up" is the central mountainous ridge) and the situation of the island in New Georgia and the wider region in relation to path of the sun and prevailing winds (where "up" is to the southeast toward Gizo, Honiara, even Australia). Such constant reference to place means that movement to a new location can be disorienting. One young woman from Pienuna who had not spent much time on the western side of the island until she stayed with me in Modo for a week was almost surprised by the fact that the rising and setting of the sun and moon were reversed in relation to the island's central ridge—it was, for her, an uncanny confusion of deictic signs.

Residents of Ranongga's eastern and western coasts have markedly different degrees of access to the rest of the New Georgia Group and the commercial centers of Gizo and Noro. The eastern leeward side of the island, which includes Pienuna, the village in which I have lived for most of my research, is just a few hours on a motorized canoe from Gizo; it is within easy reach of secondary schools in Vella Lavella and Kolombangara. Terrain on the eastern coast is relatively forgiving: paths leading up to hillside gardens are not terribly steep and coastal paths run the length of the island, from Buri to Koqu then inland to Lale. The western coast, in contrast, is made up of small, rocky indentations hemmed in by sheer cliffs and lacking inland paths across the steep ridges and valleys that separate coastal villages from one another. Until the 2007 earthquake created a black sand beach at the foot of the cliffs, it was not possible to walk from one village to another along this coast. Travel between west coast villages was by canoe, sometimes a dangerous or impossible undertaking, especially in the season of the west wind (December to April). Traversing the central ridge of the island is arduous, especially across the steep valleys of the south. Travel distances (and fuel costs) for trips to Gizo from the west coast villages of Sabala, Modo, Kudu, Keara, and Saevuke are twice or three times what they are for Pienuna and neighboring settlements. The treacherous sharp coral stones of southeastern Ranongga between Koqu and Lale make landing a canoe difficult. This southern cape is regularly the site of accidents, often when overloaded canoes attempt to return from Gizo to Luqa or Simbo in rough seas.

Today, Ranongga is considered a difficult place, especially by lagoon dwellers of the eastern parts of the New Georgia Group. People of Marovo, for example, contrast their own "good life" to the "difficult life" of their Ranonggan relatives.[6] Ranonggans must travel across the open sea rather than enclosed lagoons to engage with those beyond their shores. Even before the earthquake lifted the island's fringing reef, it lacked the extensive barrier reefs that lagoon dwellers rely upon for fishing and collecting shellfish. Gardens are at some distance uphill from coastal villages and, on the west coast, they are often perched precariously on steep slopes. The Ranonggan word *tapata* means "hardship" but also "barrier" or "fortress." The same terrain that makes life difficult today is precisely what made Ranongga, especially its western coast, a good place to live in the late nineteenth century. Hemmed in by cliffs, lacking safe anchorages, inaccessible from the land, these settlements were relatively safe from attack. Populations seem to have been high. One precolonial name for the island was Vesu Gogoto ("eight hundred"), a reference to the eight hundred warriors who could be summoned for an expedition (Hocart 1922: 75).

At the turn of the twentieth century, the less difficult eastern side of the island was sparsely populated. Among the few old continuously occupied areas was the fortress at Kubokota in the hills above Pienuna, a defensible site on the edge of a small gorge located slightly above present day gardening areas. At the turn of the twentieth century, the northeast of the island was almost empty of people. A widely known myth from this area tells of how the original clan of this area engaged in senseless activities that led to their extinction; oral histories from Pienuna tell of a war raid from Vella Lavella that wiped out the population. Settlement patterns changed in the decades following government pacification in 1899/1900. People moved from the treacherous western coast to the more accessible areas of the eastern coast, as well as to the northern and southern ends of the island. They also moved from smaller hamlets into large nucleated villages centered on either a Methodist or Seventh-day Adventist church. Ranonggan population movements echo similar ones that occurred throughout the Solomon Islands archipelago in the same era. On large islands, people living in small inland hamlets came down to the coast to live in large nucleated villages; they moved from difficult to access windward coasts to easier to access leeward coasts (Hocart 1922: 76–77; Scheffler 1965: 25–28; Chapman and Pirie 1974; Bathgate 1985; Hviding 1996: 98–99; Hviding and Bayliss-Smith 2000: 145–52; Scott 2007b: 69–103; Akin 2013: 14–49). In many cases, these early-twentieth-century migrations involved people returning to land formerly occupied by their ancestors in generations prior to the intensification of warfare and the introduction of endemic diseases that occurred with European contact. Oral histories recorded in southern Ranongga suggest that residents of the west coast maintained canoe landing places and ancestral shrines on the eastern coast of the island even though no one lived in these exposed areas.

During the early Protectorate era, much accessible coastal land was alienated to Europeans or to the Protectorate government. Some 1400 acres in the north of Ranongga stretching from what is now Koriovuku to Kolomali were alienated in the 1900s and 1910s. A smaller area of 300 acres was alienated near the present-day village of Suava, and a small area appears to have been acquired by the Methodist Mission near Kudu.[7] Between the 1910s and 1930s, expatriates ran plantations on Ranongga (Bennett 1987: 235). The largest was the Emu Harbour plantation in the north of the island, which was leased by various planters, including Sydney-based multinational Burns Philp and Company. Aena plantation in Luqa was held by expatriate brothers H. and C.P. Beck, whose descendants still live in Keara and Suava. All of Ranongga's expatriate-run plantations floundered with the Great Depression and were abandoned by World War II. Since the war, this alienated land has been reoccupied and, to various extents, reclaimed by local people.[8] Here and in other areas of intensive colonial development throughout Melanesia (Martin 2013; Filer 2014), the boundary between customary and non-customary land is ambiguous.

Ranongga's once empty northeastern tip, the only area with protected harbors and an extensive reef system, is now the most densely populated part of the island. Buri, now Ranongga's largest village with nearly 1,000 inhabitants, was established on the island's northernmost peninsula in the late 1920s after a Seventh-day Adventist mission ship was nearly smashed on rocks near Modo in a storm in 1925. European missionaries instructed the people of Modo, who had collectively joined the mission in 1920, to relocate to a place with a better anchorage. There was little better ground on their own territory in Ganoqa, so Niqusasa of Modo approached leaders of Kubokota to ask for land in the depopulated north. People of the Methodist villages of Kudu and Sabala resettled alienated land in Ranongga's north in the 1950s under Luqa leader George Hilly. After the earthquake of 1952 wreaked havoc on the land of the west coast, Hilly sought permission from the Western District government to establish a new cooperative society on the land of the abandoned Emu Harbour plantation.[9] Families were expected to work a designated number of rows of coconuts for the cooperative society, and were granted a portion to work for their own benefit; Hilly also hired non-local labor to re-establish the plantation. Construction and relocation began in 1954, and Hilly attempted to force all the residents of Sabala and Kudu to relocate to the new settlement. Some residents of Kudu refused to relocate; all residents of Qeuru initially moved to Koriovuku, but some returned a decade later to re-establish the old village of Sabala. People explained to me that they left Koriovuku because they did not like the population density, the compulsion to undertake communal work, and the frequency of malaria that resulted from the swampier ground around the harbor; many also said that they missed their property, especially the groves of nut trees and old settlement sites established by their ancestors. Many families remained at Koriovuku, which grew to be the headquarters of the Methodist Church (later United Church) on Ranongga, and an important hub of commercial activity in the postwar years, with a wharf and a ship owned by Hilly.

The Kubokota coast south of Koriovuku is now dotted with growing villages that were established by people with ties to Pienuna, Sabala, and Modo. Pienuna is the site of an old canoe house and canoe-landing place, but prior to the twentieth century people appear to have resided inland at the fortress of Kubokota. Kolomali was established prior to World War II, mainly by people coming across from Sabala and Qeuru on the other side of the island. Obobulu was founded by people from Pienuna who fled to the south after the newly established colonial administration destroyed the canoe house, residences, and ancestral shrines in 1901. Rava was founded in the 1950s by a group of siblings from Pienuna fleeing family disputes. New Bare is a conglomeration of newer hamlets (New Ole, Babagea, and Retona, whose first syllables were combined to create the village name), established by Pienuna residents in the 1960s. Two major Adventist settlements were established by men who sought permission from Kubokota landowners to establish new settlements on the land. Disputes in Modo in the 1940s led Rove Ghere, Ben Levi, and Tadi to seek permission from Kubokota landowners to establish a settlement at a place called Patubolibolivi (now called Patu), now the second largest Adventist village on the island. Some of the most prominent Ranonggan Adventists had been working as missionaries in other areas of the Solomons or in Papua New Guinea at the time that Buri was established in the 1920s, and had not been able to clear (and then claim) the land in the new village. Upon retirement in the 1960s, some asked relatives in Pienuna and Obobulu for permission to found what became the village of Vonga (also known by the older name of Niami).

In Luqa, people moved from the rough western coast across to the more accessible eastern coast. Roughly speaking, people of Keara founded Suava, a village established just to the north of what was Aena plantation, in an area referred to in mission literature as Povana. To the south of Suava, Paqe was founded by people of Saevuke to the west, and Koqu was founded by people coming north from Lale. The children of those who had founded the new villages said that their parents moved to avoid social conflict and because houses and gardens were crowded onto small patches of level ground that left no room for growth. Lale became the Luqa headquarters of the Methodist Church and grew to be the second largest village on the island.

Ranongga's population today is mobile, with patterns of movement following economic opportunities. Nuclear families often move between the natal hamlets, villages, or islands of both spouses before settling on one, and children have ties to the home places of their parents, as well as their grandparents and great-grandparents before them. Old settlement sites, even those far inland, are rarely entirely abandoned, for people return to harvest nuts from groves planted by their ancestors or to plant a bush garden. Long abandoned places may be resettled in times of crisis, such as the Japanese occupation of the

Western Solomons, which caused most islanders to flee inland. In the wake of the earthquake and tsunami, and with increasing population pressure, some people today are resettling areas that their great-grandparents left a century ago.

## Colonial Transformations and Postcolonial Marginality

In the mid 1990s, when I first visited Solomon Islands, one of the slogans of the tourism bureau was "adrift in time." The phrase was featured on a series of posters depicting idyllic island scenes, smiling children, and men in customary dress—including one poster that now hangs in my office and features Dixon Paleo, Costas Paleo, and Hatakiko Muma of Pienuna village decked out in the costumes they wore to perform "custom dances" for tourists in the Gizo hotel. The slogan and images ignore historical transformations of the sort I have just discussed, but they do capture pervasive ideologies about rural life. Villages and villagers are seen to be behind the times, backwards, or "local" (the Pijin term *lokolo* is often used as a term of derision). Most tourists and some urban dwellers valorize what they see as the simple virtue of village life, but many villagers themselves are often frustrated with what they perceive as their own marginality or lack of advancement.

Prior to the twentieth century, residents of the regions of Ganoqa, Luqa, and Kubokota were at the center of their own social world, a world reaching throughout the islands that came to be known as the New Georgia Group and as far as Santa Isabel and Choiseul (see Figures 0.1, 0.2). In southern Ranongga, Luqa was closely tied to Simbo, which was linked to allies in Roviana and other areas to the east. In northern Ranongga, paths of alliance linked Ganoqa to Dovele in northwestern Vella Lavella and Kubokota to Bilua in southeastern Vella Lavella. There were also connections to the lagoon-centered polities of eastern New Georgia, Marovo and Roviana. A well-known tale in both Kubokota and Marovo tells of an encounter between two great warriors, Mekania of Kubokota and Taqitaqi of Marovo; after Mekania slaughtered a group of Roviana warriors sent to kill him at the fortress of Kubokota, a chief of Roviana hired Taqitaqi to extract revenge by killing Mekania.[10] Many scholars have depicted Roviana as a hub of precolonial networks of trade and alliance (Hviding 1996: 89–92, 2014; Dureau 1998a; Schneider 1998; Aswani and Sheppard 2003: S51). Ian Scales suggests that an observer's bias has shaped British accounts of the prehistory of the region: because Roviana Lagoon became home to resident European traders in the late nineteenth century, and to the colonial government and mission headquarters in the twentieth, British observers tended to take a Roviana-centric perspective when describing regional networks (Scales 2004: 35–54). Drawing on

German research on the northwestern Solomons, Scales argues that many regional networks did not center on the lagoon regions, and instead directly linked Bougainville, the Shortland Islands, and Choiseul with the western New Georgia Group, including Vella Lavella, Kolombangara, and Ranongga (Scales 2004: 35–54).

Archeological research suggests that Roviana and other coastal New Georgian polities were becoming more centralized in the centuries prior to sustained contact with Europeans, a centralization associated with the rise of long-distance warfare (Walter and Sheppard 2000). Tim Bayliss-Smith (2003) and Edvard Hviding (2003c) suggest that any increasing socio-political stratification on the coast was linked to the intensification of wetland taro agriculture in large areas of inland New Georgia, which was densely populated prior to demographic collapse during the late nineteenth and early twentieth centuries (Hviding and Bayliss-Smith 2000).

As elsewhere, contact with Europeans appears to have exacerbated indigenous violence (Bennett 1987: 35). The introduction of steel tools made men's work easier, and thus allowed them to dedicate more time to building war canoes; at the same time, steel axes, and later rifles, made the raids carried out on expeditions in these canoes more deadly (Jackson 1975; White 1983; Zelenietz 1983). Chiefs in Roviana, Marovo, and Simbo appear to have used connections with resident European traders to consolidate political and military power. War raids that were observed by resident Europeans in the late nineteenth century involved large expeditions with dozens or scores of large canoes carrying thirty to fifty warriors; one Roviana chief is reported to have deployed 500 men, 22 canoes, 2 English-built boats, 300 to 400 rifles, and 5,000 rounds of ammunition (Bennett 1987: 91). As Dureau (2000: 73–74) points out, European accounts of headhunting are likely to have exaggerated indigenous violence in ways that served to justify British suppression of warfare. There is little to suggest, however, that the warfare of this period was anything but devastating. Moreover, sustained contact with Europeans also had far-reaching unintended and poorly understood consequences: local populations were ravaged by epidemic diseases that contributed to depopulation caused by warfare (Bayliss-Smith 2014; Bennett 2014). The symptoms of dysentery (*pea orungunu*, "defecate blood") are still understood in Ranongga today as a sign of ancestral displeasure; trespassers on sacred ground were often said to have gone home, defecated blood, and died. Illness was also frequently understood as the result of sorcery, which suggests that common stories about groups being banished for committing sorcery or fleeing from sorcery attacks are connected to the epidemic diseases of the early contact era.

Throughout New Georgia, Europeans are known as *tio* (or *tinoni*) *vaka*, "ship people." Whalers began traversing the seas of the region in the 1820s, and traders began dealing in tortoise shell, pearl shell, and bêche-de-mer from the mid 1800s. The 1870s marked the rise of the industry that was to dominate the economy of the region for more than a century: copra. Copra is the dried kernel of the coconut, shipped to Europe where the oil was extracted and used in a wide range of products including soap, chemicals, and explosives (Bennett 1987: 47). With low population and abundant resources, the sheltered lagoons of New Georgia were the center of this emerging trade in the second half of the nineteenth century. Chiefs who established stable relationships with resident traders gained a significant strategic advantage because of their access to iron tools and trade goods (ibid.: 87–91). European ships bypassed Ranongga, deterred, no doubt, by the lack of hospitable harbors on the populated western coast. No European traders were based on the island before the twentieth century.[11] Though Ranonggans were probably involved in producing and selling copra to passing ships, no Ranonggans developed the sort of relationships with traders that chiefs of Simbo, Vella, Roviana or Marovo did.

In 1893, Britain established a protectorate over the Solomons, and in 1896 Charles Woodford arrived in Tulagi in the central Solomons as resident commissioner with a few Fijian policeman.[12] The administration claimed it necessary to protect indentured laborers from exploitation by labor recruiters; it also aimed to protect the interests of Europeans who had established commercial operations in the region. In the years prior to the establishment of the Protectorate, British warships sought to punish local people for violence against labor recruiters, resident traders, and other expatriates by shelling villages suspected of being responsible for raids, often months after the supposed offense; the HMS *Royalist* spent six months in the New Georgia group in 1891, shelling and burning villages, destroying canoes, canoe houses, and skull shrines, and looting artifacts (Lawrence 2014: 165–71). Villagers often did not know why they were targeted: a story told to me in 1999 by Apusae Bei describes the shelling of Modo by a British warship as retaliation for the misdemeanor of a cheeky young local man who stole a sailor's hat while the sailor was bathing. In 1899, Woodford posted his deputy commissioner, Arthur W. Mahaffy, to a second government station being built in Gizo. In a remarkably effective but ruthless campaign (ibid.: 111, 215), Mahaffy responded swiftly to reports of war raids, traveling to the perpetrator's homes in confiscated war canoes paddled by men of Santa Isabel whose people had often been victims of New Georgia warfare. Rather than shelling villages, he destroyed canoe houses and burned or confiscated canoes. Mahaffy raided Ranongga several times, the best documented case occurring on 10 June 1901 at Kubokota ("KumbuKotta"). Ranonggan men had reportedly undertaken a voyage with allies from Vella Lavella to Choiseul in which they had taken nine heads. Mahaffy was accompanied by Graham Officer from the Museum of Victoria, who detailed the events. According to David Lawrence:

They approached the village in two boats early in the morning but found that all the people had fled to the bush, having been warned in advance, leaving behind some large and some small canoes. Mahaffy had the boats broken up. Further along the coast they came to another larger village where they found two large *tomoko* [war canoes] on the beach. Officer took an ornamented head from a skull shine [*sic*] even though Mahaffy was much against it. This ornamented skull is now housed in Museum Victoria. Inland from the villages the gardens were damaged, coconut trees cut down and fruit trees cut and burnt. (ibid.: 229)

A man whose name was recorded as "Panangatta" (probably Padaqeto) requested the return of the skull, said to be his father's, but Officer refused the request.[13]

Long distance warfare in Kubokota, at least, appears to have ended with this raid, but Vella Lavella was not yet completely pacified. The final challenge to the colonial state's monopoly on violence in New Georgia came from the warrior Sito on Vella Lavella, who was responsible for the murder of the Malaitan wife and children of European trader Joseph Binskin in 1907 on the island of Baga. In retaliation, the colonial administration recruited a militia comprised of traders and Malaitan plantation laborers in a bloody punitive expedition that caused widespread death and destruction on Vella Lavella, and was ended through the intervention of Australian Methodist missionary R.C. Nicholson. Warfare continued for more than a decade on Choiseul, and until the 1920s, Ranonggans and Simbo people traveled on steamers to purchase Choiseul war captives.

The destruction of war canoes and canoe houses did more than end warfare; it disrupted expansive networks of travel and trade. In 1908, one of A.M. Hocart's Simbo interlocutors lamented the change: "No one is mighty now: they are all alike, they have no money; they cannot go head-hunting; they all 'stop nothing'." A woman echoed the lament: "Formerly the chiefs ordered their men to build canoes and they went forth together; that was before my time; now it is not done: the chiefs are dullards (*tuturu*) and like common folk (*tinoni homboro*)" (Hocart 1922: 79–80).

The malaise expressed by Hocart's informants was eventually replaced by enthusiastic engagement with a new source of spiritual power and social engagement (Dureau 2001: 143). Between 1902 and about 1930, virtually the entire population of New Georgia became Christian—a process I discuss in more detail in Chapter 4. The Methodist Mission was established under the Reverend John Goldie at Nusa Zonga in Roviana Lagoon in 1902; five years later, a mission station was established in Bilua, a region on the southeastern coast of Vella Lavella. A competing Seventh-day Adventist mission, under the direction of Reverend George Jones, was established at Viru Harbour in

Marovo in 1914; a few years later, an outpost was established at Dovele in northwest Vella. By the mid 1920s, the mission had become important in the lives of most Ranonggans. Integration into these new institutions linked Ranonggans to new expansive networks, but also inculcated a sense of being on the periphery, with training centers and mission headquarters located on Vella Lavella and Roviana Lagoon and Marovo Lagoon to the east.

Colonial pacification aimed at fostering the commercial development of the Protectorate. From the beginning of colonial administration in 1896, the Protectorate government was expected to be financially self-sufficient. Until the post-World War II era, it was assumed that Europeans would be responsible for commercial development, and the Protectorate administration sought to facilitate the alienation of land and recruitment of a native labor force. Land alienation of the sort I have mentioned for Ranongga occurred all around the Solomons; although alienated land was always a small percentage of the total land mass of the Protectorate, it comprised a significant percentage of the land that would become most valuable during the twentieth century. Some land was leased to small independent planters and to large multinational corporations who became powerful players in administration policy because taxes on their output alone were almost enough to cover the Protectorate's expenses. Although islanders quickly opposed land alienation, the administration acquired more land than it was ever able to effectively use. The real limiting factor in Protectorate development was not land, but labor. The closure of indenture to Queensland following the institution of the White Australia Policy of 1902 reduced demand for laborers from the resource-poor island of Malaita and elsewhere in the eastern Solomons, and many signed on for terms of labor in the Western Solomons, northern Guadalcanal, and other commercially developed areas. Yet it was never enough, and for decades the Protectorate government struggled to entice or compel islanders to work under poor conditions and for wages kept artificially low. The Great Depression of the 1930s was a disaster for many of the smaller planters or traders who had been resident in the Solomons for decades. As Bennett (1987: 241) observes, this global crisis represented an opportunity for indigenous producers, who filled the gaps left by expatriate planters. Especially after World War II, much of the land alienated at the turn of the century and leased to expatriate traders was reoccupied by local people.

The Japanese invasion of New Georgia in 1942 was a turning point in local history, dramatically changing not only Solomon Islands social life, but also its physical environment (Bennett 2009). The Japanese occupied Buri on Ranongga, and heavy fighting occurred around Vella, Kolombangara, Gizo and Marovo lagoon. At the instruction of the British administration, coastal villages were evacuated and many old inland hamlets were reoccupied as villagers tried to make themselves invisible. Young Ranonggan men, meanwhile, served as "coast watchers," reporting Japanese movements to New Zealander Rev. A.W.E. Silvester, a Methodist missionary who remained behind on Vella Lavella with Nurse Merle Farland, and District Officer Donald Kennedy in Gizo, who radioed the information to the American army. One Ranonggan, Eroni Kumana of Koqu village, was involved in the rescue of future US President John F. Kennedy east of Gizo, an act of heroism for which he was recognized only later in his life. Throughout the Pacific theater, this was a time when the sheer power of industrial civilization became evident to islanders, changing their outlook on themselves and their world in profound ways (White et al. 1988; White and Lindstrom 1989). The War helped to trigger Maasina Rule in the eastern Solomons, a political movement that sought to increase autonomy and self-government (Akin 2013). Partially as a response to Maasina Rule, and partly in response to directives from the Colonial Office in London, the Protectorate administration greatly expanded a system of indirect rule through native councils and courts in the postwar era.

After the war, commercial development on Ranongga and elsewhere in the Western Solomons occurred on a scale unmatched in later years. As Charlie Panakera recalled to me in December 2002, in the late 1950s and early 1960s, Pienuna village was a "hive of activity," with a copra shed able to store up to 1,000 copra bags: "Canoes everywhere, the goings and comings and trading was a sight to see." Much of this activity was undertaken by Charlie's father, the late Simion Panakera, one of three postwar leaders who came to prominence beginning in the 1950s. The second was George Hilly (or Gili), who I mentioned in the previous section as the leader who founded the village of Koriovuku on the alienated land of Emu Harbour plantation. The third was Niqusasa of Ganoqa, who established the Adventist village of Buri.[14] Along with other less prominent leaders, Panakera, Hilly, and Niqusasa served as village headmen and members of native councils and native courts in the Vella Lavella Sub-District of Western District.[15] In the 1950s, Panakera and Hilly set up parallel businesses focused on buying and transporting copra. As George Hilly's son, long-time member of parliament and former prime minister Francis Billy Hilly, remembered in a July 2010 conversation, his father and Panakera were simultaneously good friends and staunch rivals: "If one bought a ship, the other had to buy a ship; if one started a store, the other started a store." Like earlier European plantation managers, both Hilly and Panakera hired wage laborers from beyond Ranongga. Hilly brought men from Choiseul to clear the area around Koriovuku, build quarters for laborers and a manager's house, and provide police for the new settlement.[16] Panakera hired men from Guadalcanal and Malaita to work on his plantations, often paying them by giving them access to copra plantations that they could harvest for their own profit. Hilly and Panakera also relied upon kinspeople who worked for them without direct payment. Charlie Panakera recalled his father's ship being used

**Figure 2.2.** John Pavukera in a coconut grove on the way to Qiloe, a small hamlet south of the village of Obobulu. 17 February 2007.

to take people all around the region for church events, weddings, and funerals. While most people today remember the period fondly, there are also undercurrents of resentment—some felt that these commercially savvy mission-educated men tricked their uneducated parents into forfeiting rights to land.

By the late 1990s, few reminders of the postwar boom times remained: the large iron building that housed Panakera's trade store was rusted (it was torn down around 2005), and the sturdy wharf at Koriovuku was unused (it collapsed in the 2007 earthquake). The cooperative society at Koriovuku did not function as planned. Members of the society were supposed to work the communal holdings as well as individual plots, but most worked on their own plots and processed their own copra instead of selling it to the cooperative for higher-quality processing. Moreover, from 1956 onward, the British colonial administration provided significant support for local cooperative societies (Bennett 1987: 314). Charlie Panakera told me that these small government cooperatives initially helped to revive the Pienuna cooperative society but later created fissures as more and more individual families began to set up their own small cooperative societies, none of which lasted long. By the late 1960s and 1970s, both Panakera and Hilly became heavily indebted to Gizo-based traders of Chinese origin, and could not borrow money from banks because their enterprises were not recognized legal entities. In any case, neither the larger-scale operations led by Panakera and Hilly, nor the smaller newly formed cooperative societies, could prosper in the context of a drastic drop in global copra prices in the late 1970s (ibid.: 335; Hviding and Bayliss-Smith 2000: 153–76, 210–12).

The fall of the copra price coincided with a rise in commercial logging, an industry that has come to dominate the economy of the Solomons from the 1980s to the present. World War II was the catalyst for interest in timber in the Protectorate: the vast rainforests of the Solomons had little commercial appeal until Allied armies set up sawmills for the construction of bases (Bennett 2000: 115–41, 2009: 97–114, 119–22). Exploitation of the forests was delayed through the 1950s as the Protectorate government sought ways to centrally control exploitation and reforestation; commercial logging finally began on government-owned land in the 1960s. During this period, the Protectorate government sought to acquire more land for forest estates and reserves, and passed legislation that prevented direct negotiations between foreign commercial operations and local landowners (Bennett 1995).

Two factors changed the nature of logging in the late 1970s, creating what became a frenzy of unsustainable logging in the 1980s and 1990s: decolonization and the rise of a market for logs in Asia. Solomon Islands politicians did not share the paternalism of their colonial predecessors and, rather than retaining centralized control over logging, they devolved responsibility to provincial governments that lacked resources to regulate the industry and affirmed the rights of customary landowners to negotiate directly with companies. At the same time, Britain and Australian-based companies were increasingly replaced by Malaysian and Korean multinationals that were much more eager to deal directly with landowners. Rural people hoped that these companies would give them the schools, clinics, roads, and other infrastructure that the government was not providing, but few logging companies demonstrated any commitment to the welfare of people or the land. The court system became clogged with land disputes, and communities were riven by resource-driven conflicts.

The large, sparsely populated, gently sloped islands of New Georgia were at the heart of the late-twentieth-century logging boom, and a smaller subsidiary boom of activity by conservation NGOs. Writing of Marovo, Edvard Hviding (2003b, 2011) argues that the density of global–local connections increased dramatically over a short period of time; he emphasizes the ways people of Marovo have been able to use outsiders' projects for their own locally defined agendas. With a small land area and steeply sloped terrain, Ranongga was largely left out of this era of "compressed globalization" except as laborers. Only in 2008 did commercial logging occur on the marginal terrain of Ranongga. By that time, forest resources were virtually exhausted and a major drop in revenue was predicted (World Bank 2010).

Rather than logging royalties, wage labor and market gardening were the means through which Ranonggans earned income in the late 1990s and the following decade. As early as the late 1950s, Panakera took Ranonggan laborers to work at Viru Harbour and other areas of Marovo where he had ties by marriage. By the late 1990s, it was largely men of the remote west coast of Ranongga who undertook contract labor for logging companies, sometimes as individuals and sometimes in groups for purposes of communal fundraising. Many men and women from Luqa also worked for Solomon Taiyo, a joint-venture tuna-fishing operation and cannery based in Noro (Meltzoff 1983; Meltzoff and Lipuma 1986). In patterns echoing those prevalent throughout the Solomons over the colonial period, people living in areas easily accessible to commercial centers chose to sell their products rather than their labor. Most Kubokota men I knew who worked for logging companies were employed as salaried managers, not as contract employees.

The major focus for economic activity within Kubokota and eastern Luqa was the provincial capital, Gizo. Having learned carving techniques from Marovo relatives (whose work is described in Kupianen 2000), some men of Pienuna, Obobulu, and nearby hamlets sold carvings made of soft river stone

**Figure 2.3.** Community work in the garden of Liza Ekera. Liza paid for a day of work to extend her garden and hoe new potatoes; the group is working to raise funds for Christmas celebrations. 13 December 2006.

**Figure 2.4.** Loading a market canoe south of Pienuna. In the foreground (left to right) are Marina Alepio, Alepio, and Amon. 7 October 2000.

to tourists (Gizo is a hub of diving tourism in the Solomons). Women and men alike often complained that carving income never left the Gizo hotel, where it was immediately spent on beer; a few carvers from the Adventist village of Vonga seemed to be the exception to this trend, using their earnings to purchase items like generators and sheet-metal roofing. Carving was not nearly as important as selling garden produce in the Gizo market. It was only in the 1980s that women of Ranongga began selling produce in the Gizo market, and some remembered how embarrassed they were to be selling food; a decade later, marketing was the major source of household income in the late 1990s.

On the face of it, market gardening involved minimal transformations to existing subsistence practices, but it has had subtle but important implications for both land tenure and gender relations. Gardening is a family activity undertaken by nuclear families: men tend to clear forest and brush, while women tend to plant, weed, and harvest (Hviding 1996: 155–60, Hviding and Bayliss-Smith 2000). Yet women are generally considered to be in charge of the gardens, and the gardens of married couples are almost inevitably referred to as belonging to the woman (and men are said to "help" their wives in gardening activity).[17] Moreover, not only are women the ones who tend to sit at the market to sell their produce, but they are usually the ones who organize marketing trips, joining with two or three other women to hire a canoe to take them to Gizo. In Pienuna throughout 1998/99, one or two large canoes laden with three or four women and their produce set off from Pienuna to Gizo almost every day of the week. Before the civil conflict reached a peak in 2000, a woman might earn SI$200 to SI$300 (US$40 to US$50 at then current rates) after she had paid for her fare or for fuel for the canoe (SI$100 was considered a very poor return, and SI $500 an exceptionally good one). To a much greater degree than other earnings, this money was controlled by women who often used it for family expenses (school supplies or school fees as well as the kerosene, salt, rice and other goods now considered household necessities). Some husbands and wives worked together to invest in materials for modern houses or trade stores. Community church groups sometimes planted and harvested gardens together, or held community markets selling individually produced goods to raise money for travel and activities. Although most people believe that market gardening has contributed in positive ways to their lives, it has also become a focus for anxieties about the corrosive effects of a cash economy. Along with exponential population growth, the expansion of market gardening activities has exacerbated pressure on land. All along the central eastern coast of Ranongga, a continuous patchwork of gardens reaches nearly to the top of the ridge.

The civil crisis of 1998 to 2003 led to a contraction of formal economic activities. The Taiyo cannery in Noro eventually stopped operations and sent workers home. With fewer people earning wages in Gizo, unsold garden produce rotted in the market. It became more difficult for people to pay school fees or to buy clothing and kerosene. Especially after the coup of 2000, there was a serious shortage of fuel for the motorized canoes that are the primary form of transportation in the region. Teachers and nurses in rural schools and clinics were paid irregularly and, as the years wore on, essential medicine like malaria tablets were in short supply. While the crisis highlighted the extent to which local people were dependent upon a translocal economy and a functioning central state, it also fueled long-standing separatist sentiments in Western Province (Scales 2007). Perhaps most importantly, it highlighted the risk involved in modern urban forms of life, and the importance of maintaining connections to kin and land in rural areas. After mid 2000, many Ranonggans moved back home to their natal villages, at least for short periods of time. In 2003, the Australian-led Regional Assistance Mission to Solomon Islands (RAMSI) put a swift end to militant activity in and around Honiara. In the decade that followed, economic growth continued to be focused on Honiara and dominated by resource extraction. The RAMSI decade has left many Ranonggans feeling at least as marginal as they did before the crisis.

## Clans, Communities, and Customary Land

On an initial trip to the Western Solomons in 1996, when I was visiting different villages and islands to get a sense of where I might be able to do long-term fieldwork two years later, my guides and hosts were quick to direct me to the senior men known as experts on *kastom*. They described what they saw as the central tenets of land tenure, group membership, and leadership. "In our *kastom*, we follow women," they told me, explaining that people belong to their mother's *butubutu*, a word they glossed as "tribe." Because of this, when it comes to land, "the woman's side is strong." Men were *butubutu* chiefs, but the chieftainship passed through women, from a man to his sister's son.

The term *butubutu* can refer to almost any sort of grouping. As Hviding writes of the cognate term in Marovo, *butubutu* describes a "diverse set of groups and categories of people related through some source of 'sameness' and commonality, be it descent, filiation, or residence" (Hviding 1996: 136). A *butubutu* can be held together by citizenship (Americans are *butubutu tinoni Merika*) or belief (Christians are *butubutu tinoni Christian*). But the predominant meaning of *butubutu* in New Georgia today is what anthropologists normally refer to as "clan": a named category of people defined by descent from a common ancestor.[18] In Ranongga, *butubutu* are defined by matrilineal descent. Although *butubutu* are often understood as corporate landholding groups, I approach *butubutu* primarily as an ontological category or category of identity. Terminologically, this is the difference between being a member of a *butubutu* (a group) and being a person of a *butubutu* (an identity). The distinction is subtle and difficult to sustain because both aspects of *butubutu* are important in contemporary New Georgia. However, the distinction is important for my argument here and in Chapter 6, where I track the ways that ideas about *butubutu* have changed in the early twentieth century and identify contexts in which *butubutu* emerge as corporate landowning groups. Importantly, throughout the region, *butubutu* identities link people to their ancestral territory. The names of *butubutu* are also the names of territory. While anthropological definitions of clans tend to emphasize connection to an original ancestor, New Georgian ideas of *butubutu* point most importantly toward an ancestral land where the ancestors of the contemporary *butubutu* emerged, arrived, or experienced some transformative event.

In Ranongga, *butubutu* identities are a significant focus of everyday life. Everyone seems to know the *butubutu* identity of everyone else, and *butubutu* identities are particularly important in discussions of marriage because *butubutu* are exogamous: people of the same *butubutu* or whose fathers (or fathers' fathers) were of the same *butubutu* are not supposed to marry.[19] *Butubutu* are also important in life-cycle rituals, especially funerals. Many historical accounts focus on the exploits of people bearing the names of contemporary *butubutu* and their territories. Yet *butubutu* did not really function in the way they were initially described to me. Most of the men who explained rules of matrilineal succession to me had themselves succeeded their fathers rather than their mothers' brothers as chiefs of their *butubutu*; they often described themselves as "caretakers" (using the English word) until a suitable *butubutu* candidate could be found. And while everyone knew which *butubutu* held which territory, it was hard to see how *butubutu* owned the land in any straightforward way. Except in the contexts of legal disputes, recent histories of occupation were far more important than ancient clan histories in determining who lived and worked on what land.

The apparent gap between ideologies and practices involving land tenure is hardly surprising. For generations, Solomon Islanders have been articulating the principles of landownership in the context of colonial land inquiries and government administered courts. As Sharon Tiffany (1983) noted many years ago, although native or local courts were intended to allow islanders to adjudicate their own claims on the basis of highly localized "customs," litigants and justices alike invoked models of social organization based on ideas of patrilineal descent and primogeniture originally formulated with reference to African societies. These outdated anthropological models assumed that descent was either through the father or mother but not both; more generally, they encouraged litigants to emphasize genealogical claims over ongoing occupation, even though the latter have often been of primary significance in everyday negotiations of access to land. Through interactions with colonial institutions and ideologies, Solomon Islanders gradually came to see clan identities as the basis of landowning groups.

W.H.R. Rivers and A.M. Hocart, who visited New Georgia in 1908, made almost no reference to *butubutu* in their published and unpublished writings. The absence of *butubutu* in Hocart's and Rivers's work is notable, given the intellectual characteristics of the two men. Hocart is praised as a remarkable fieldworker who paid close attention to vernacular language terms and to the contrasting viewpoints of differently positioned informants (Dureau 2000, 2014: 50; McDougall 2000; Scales 2004; Hviding 2014); thus it seems unlikely he would miss a concept that was obvious to a novice like myself in 1998. While Rivers's empirical research has also been described as remarkably accurate (Bayliss-Smith 2014; Berg 2014), he has been criticized for forcing ethnographic information into grand theoretical frameworks whether or not it fit (Hviding and Berg 2014a; Kolshus 2014). Yet this weakness makes it even more unlikely that Rivers would have overlooked the *butubutu* in his New Georgia research. Informed by evolutionary theory, Rivers was specifically looking for matrilineally defined descent groups of the sort people of Ranongga, Simbo, and Vella Lavella today call *butubutu* and *toutou* respectively, but he was not able to find them.

Most anthropologists have followed the lead of Harold Scheffler (1962) in suggesting that Hocart and Rivers simply missed the presence of *butubutu* in New Georgia. Edvard Hviding and Cato Berg (2014a) suggest that Rivers and Hocart were insufficiently prepared to grasp the complex non-unilineality of

New Georgian kinship systems. Yet, as Berg (2014) observes, this explanation does not fully explain why Rivers did not mention the *toutou* of Vella Lavella, where he spent several weeks in 1908; today, at least, *toutou* are understood as strictly matrilineal descent groups. Arguing that *toutou* must have been a significant force in northern Vella Lavella in 1908 because the Australian missionary R.C. Nicholson described them as central in social life fourteen years later, Berg (2014) argues that Rivers's genealogical method served only to elucidate links between individuals and blinded him to corporate groups.

Yet it seems equally likely that *butubutu* were simply not as important in 1908 as they became a few decades later. This is the argument proposed by Ian Scales in an historical ethnography of Kolombangara (Nduke) that draws on a careful reading of Hocart's fieldnotes from his brief stay there (Scales 2004: 85–94). Hocart did not record the *butubutu* identities of his Nduke interlocutors, but he did record where each person came from, noting both the residential hamlet where the individual lived and the larger named territory with which they identified. These named territories correspond to what were understood as *butubutu* identities at the time of Scales's fieldwork in the late 1990s. In 1908, Hocart stayed at a coastal canoe house, and most of the men who visited him were not originally from that locale, but from other territories around Kolombangara, other islands, or from the Sabana region of Santa Isabel where they or their ancestors had been taken as captives. According to Scales, this suggests that functional groups were not defined by genealogy, but by engaging in common activities in the same place. Canoe houses were the focus for activities associated with maritime raiding and trading; ancestral shrines were the focus of ritual designed to ensure fertility and success in all realms of life. In his published writing, Hocart described chiefs (*bangara*) not as leaders of descent groups, but as leaders of territorial districts encompassing many residential hamlets (Hocart 1922; Scales 2004: 116). By most accounts, a chief led not only his own kinspeople but also a range of different people who had come together in their district. Scales suggests that social organization in frontier-era New Georgia is thus best understood as a house-based society similar to those documented for other Austronesian societies (e.g. Carsten and Hugh-Jones 1995; Joyce and Gillespie 2000; see also Sissons 2010). Beginning with the first land inquiry in the early 1920s, however, there has been "a shift in *emphasis* from a place-based concept of land control to a boundary-based concept of land ownership" (Scales 2004: 124). Although it occurred quite rapidly, the shift in understanding of land tenure and group structure was subtle enough that it was not understood by local people or outsider observers as a change (ibid.: 126).[20]

The first published anthropological description of *butubutu* is Harold Scheffler's restudy of Simbo social organization (Scheffler 1962). A critic of descent theorists who presumed unilineality was necessary for the formation of corporate groups, Scheffler nevertheless embraced the core assumption of descent theory, namely that corporate descent groups were the irreducible building blocks of any society. He argued that Rivers had misidentified the core descent group of Simbo society as the *taviti*, a term best glossed as "relative." *Taviti* were non-bounded personal kindreds that could not "form the enduring and discrete units of a social structure such as that which clearly existed on Simbo" (ibid.: 135). According to Scheffler, the real corporate groups of Simbo were *butubutu*, which he understood as corporate descent groups that owned territorial estates. Although Simbo people said that they "followed women," Scheffler disregarded these local ideologies and analyzed *butubutu* as cognatic rather than matrilineal because genealogies showed ties through both men and women and because people claimed land rights in the territory of both parents' *butubutu*. In order to argue that *butubutu* were properly corporate (that is to say, bounded) groups, Scheffler drew an analytical distinction that people of Simbo did not: *butubutu* were simultaneously non-localized and non-corporate categories of cognatic descent, and corporate localized residential groups comprised of a segment of the larger category resident on the *butubutu* territorial estate (ibid.: 139). In principle, any individual had connections to a wide range of *butubutu* through their ancestors on both sides; in practice, affiliation with one *butubutu* precluded involvement in the affairs of other *butubutu*. *Butubutu* thus functioned as bounded corporate groups.

The most detailed discussion of contemporary *butubutu* in New Georgia comes from Edvard Hviding, who has largely accepted the analytical distinctions introduced by Scheffler while emphasizing the flexibility and fluidity of *butubutu*, and the mutually constitutive relationship between a group and its territory (Hviding 1996: 136, 1993, 2003c).[21] Like Scheffler, Hviding approaches *butubutu* as both a non-localized descent category and a "corporate kin-based group, claiming and controlling a defined territory on which the core members of the group live in one or several villages" (Hviding 1996: 143). Villages are not comprised solely of people of the *butubutu* that own the territory on which they are located; people living on *butubutu* land that is not their own often have well-established entitlements, but exert "limited influence in matters of decision-making and resource allocation" (ibid.: 155; see also Hviding 2003c: 81). In Marovo, people insist that everyone is related to everyone else, and people trace connections to *butubutu* through both sides. Hviding argues that non-unilineal principles of descent do not prevent *butubutu* from existing as "viable, well-defined social groupings" with leaders (*bangara*) who "act as largely undisputed managers of clearly bounded territories of land and sea" (Hviding 2003c: 79).

One of the most fascinating aspects of Hviding's analysis of *butubutu* is his discussion of differences between those *butubutu* that identify with coastal territories and those that identify with inland "bush" territories. These differential identities endure despite the fact that today virtually all Marovo people live in coastal settlements. For both types of *butubutu*, genealogies tracing the descent of chiefs involve what Hviding calls "cumulative filiation": connections that build up through links traced either through men, women, or both, over many generations (Hviding 1996: 146–47). However, the historically coastal *butubutu* tended to emphasize patrifiliation (links through men) while historically inland *butubutu* tended to emphasize matrifiliation (links through women). Hviding suggests that these distinctions emerged out of circumstances whereby coastal groups were engaged in wide-ranging maritime exchange and warfare that gave coastal *bangara* more authority than their inland counterparts. Coastal polities were oriented around a "men-leadership-*puava* [territory]" complex, whereas inland polities were oriented around a "women-blood-*puava* [territory]" complex (ibid.: 147–50). Interestingly, people of inland groups recounted genealogical relationships not only in terms of localized *butubutu*, but also in terms of *vuluvulu*, which Hviding describes as a sort of shared lineal substance or blood that is passed through women; this shared *vuluvulu* creates "matrilineal, nonlocalized totemic clans" that are traced back to ancestral figures. These categories are embedded in land, but they are not themselves localized in the way Marovo *butubutu* are (ibid.: 148).[22]

Although Ranonggans and people of Marovo see themselves as part of a region-wide interlinked system, I have found it difficult to reconcile some aspects of Ranonggan ideologies and practices of *butubutu* with Hviding's analysis. Most obviously, Ranonggan *butubutu* identities are strictly matrilineal in a way that seems to bear more resemblance to Vella Lavella's *toutou* than to the bilateral *butubutu* of Marovo or Roviana.[23] Important social relationships are traced through both parents and a range of collateral relatives. When talking about clan identity rather than a network of kin relations, however, Ranonggans distinguish clearly between connections through the mother and all other relations. People are described as being "born of" (*vinapodo*) their father's *butubutu*; the otherwise untranslatable word *vuteri* denotes the relationship between individuals and their father's father's *butubutu*. In contrast, they simply *are* the *butubutu* of the mother. Moreover, few *butubutu* leaders in Ranongga appear to be undisputed managers of land. *Butubutu* loomed large in attempts to formalize community structures through the identification of "tribal" chiefs (and deputy chiefs), but such forms were manifestly derived from a long history of engagement with colonial categories and expectations rather than any distinctive indigenous logic (McDougall 2014, 2015). As I discuss in Chapter 6, *butubutu* emerged as corporate groups most clearly in engagements with outside actors who required people to organize themselves as "tribal" landowners, but this process of identifying *butubutu* membership seemed to create a great deal of anxiety because it involved cutting off non-members. On a day-to-day basis, authority over garden land, settlement sites, or reef areas was vested in family groups rather than *butubutu*, although most of those families acknowledged the underlying authority of the landholding *butubutu*. It was almost taboo to speak directly about *butubutu* ownership of land. Indeed, far from having less power on land that was not their own, people who had "come from elsewhere" often had gained influence and power over their adopted land.

Even if they were not understood as corporate descent groups until the early twentieth century, the named categories of identity that have now come to be called *butubutu* seem to have some historical depth. Hocart briefly noted the term *butubutu* in Simbo (Scheffler 1962: 155); German anthropologist Richard Thurnwald mentioned *toutou* for Vella Lavella in the same year (cited in Scales 2004: 114). In both cases, there is some connotation of an origin group and the idea of common descent. Yet it is anachronism to assume that *butubutu* in 1908 were corporate groups defined by their ownership of a territorial estate in an era when territory was not understood as a possession. Like the distant creator gods of ancestral religions that were of little importance until Christian missionaries began to seek equivalents of their own deity (Horton 1975), *butubutu* seems like an indigenous formation that has become more important because it "fit" the exogenous understandings of land tenure and social organization that became profoundly consequential in the decades after 1900. Even today, *butubutu* do not often function as groups. When speaking in the vernacular language and outside of legal contexts, Ranonggans never speak of "being a member of" a *butubutu*; they speak instead of being a "person of" a *butubutu*. In some ways, Ranonggan *butubutu* share many characteristics with *vuluvulu* described as translocal clans by Hviding for inland areas of Marovo. Rather than as glue that holds people in place on the territory of their ancestors, *butubutu* identities might be envisioned as strong but flexible filaments that allow people to track connections to distant places and distant people without preventing socio-spatial mobility.

## Marginality and Mobility

The previous century was a time of dramatic socio-spatial transformations in Ranongga. Seemingly traditional coastal villages were established from smaller scattered inland hamlets following pacification and Christian conversion. The population shifted from the defensible west coast to the accessible east coast and to northern harbors. The terrain of the island was transfigured when most accessible coastal land was covered in coconut plantations. Leaders of the mid twentieth century who were recognized as customary chiefs by the colonial state combined their traditional authority with mission education and the backing of the colonial state to undertake large-scale commercial projects.

More recently, the rise of market gardening had dramatically increased households' requirements for cleared garden land and increased women's engagements in the regional economy.

Arguably, the marginal position of Ranongga has made it a particularly fortuitous site for research into the changing ways that people conceptualize their relationship to territory and to one another. While conflicting claims to garden plots and settlement areas were a constant source of tension, there were few high-stakes disputes over timber rights during the period of my most extensive research between 1998 and 2001. Though everyone knew that only "tribal" landowners earned royalties, the absence of logging disputes meant that I heard stories about land and people that went against the grain of dominant narratives. Rather than describing *butubutu* as clans that owned land, people sometimes spoke of *butubutu* territories as canoes, on which many different people were traveling and whose leaders had to keep it on the proper bearing. Other metaphors emphasized the rootedness of the *butubutu*, anchored in the land by the dead and by the heavy shell money sitting in a chief's basket. Such conceptualizations of the *butubutu* and territory did and do not translate into the legally recognizable forms of customary landownership.

This chapter has examined the upheavals of the twentieth century on an island that is literally being thrust out of the sea. Far from being bound inalienably to ancestral land, Ranonggans have been highly mobile over the course of the twentieth century, moving from the defensible west to the accessible east, severing connections to some places and forging new connections to others. From a Ranonggan point of view, the changing regional political economy is only one factor that allowed this geographical reorganization; much more important was the religious transformation that allowed them to confront and overcome dangerous spirits thought to hold people on familiar ground, a transformation I consider in Chapter 4. In the next chapter, I step back from these twentieth-century transformations to try to understand something of the relationships between people of the place and the strangers they brought from across the sea in a time of terrible violence.

### Notes

1. For more on the 2007 earthquake, see Fritz and Kalligeris (2008), NDAJ (2008), Taylor et al. (2008), and USGS (2008).
2. The relative fixity of cosmic vision in Aboriginal Australia has been contrasted to the reversals, paradoxes, and transformations evident in Melanesian cosmologies, though scholars caution against over-emphasizing conservatism and underestimating creativity in Aboriginal Australia (see Rumsey and Weiner 2001).
3. *Kastom* became a major focus of research among Pacific scholars in the 1980s and 1990s, many of whom emphasized the ways that the category itself emerged in encounters with the colonial or postcolonial state (see e.g. Keesing 1982a, 1989a; Keesing and

Tonkinson 1982; Tonkinson 1982, 1993; Handler and Linnekin 1984; Hanson 1989; Jolly 1992, 1994; Trask 1991; Lindstrom and White 1993; Schwartz 1993; White 1993; Lindstrom 2008).
4. Hocart conducted several months of intensive research on the island of Simbo, then known as Eddystone, as well as survey work elsewhere in the New Georgia Group. Rivers worked on Simbo with Hocart and conducted extensive survey work elsewhere in the region, including areas of island Melanesia he traveled through on the way to and from the Solomons. The third member of the expedition was Gerald Camden Wheeler, who traveled onto the Shortlands after a brief period in New Georgia. See Scales (2004: 59–60) and Hviding and Berg (2014a).
5. Like almost all of its predecessors, the recently elected government of Manasseh Sogavare has just announced its intention to begin the long process of recording and registering tribal land in order to "unleash the economic development potential of our country" (comments broadcast on Solomon Islands Broadcasting Corporation, 28 January 2015).
6. Hviding personal communication, 24 November 2002; see also Hviding and Bayliss-Smith (2000: 76).
7. This information is drawn from a government list of alienated land outside of towns in 1959 (BSIP 13/I/1). Details of the original alienation of the area around Emu Harbour are not entirely clear, but a portion of the territory was purchased for £110 by the Crown in 1912 from individuals named Veti, Wamba, and Gatakolo (BSIP 7/I/DCW/130, no. 88).
8. Part of this land, near the present day settlement of New Mala, was held in the late 1950s and 1960s by Kitchener Wheatley, the son of one of the first European traders and planters in New Georgia. He contracted Malaitan laborers to clear and plant the area. See Chapter 7.
9. According to a "Note on Emu Harbour Cooperative Scheme" of 13 January 1954 (BSIP 7/I/DCW/130), the government had purchased Crown Leases 14 and 94, comprising 650 acres, at Emu Harbour and Kia Point, for £650 from Messrs Burns Philp Ltd. The northern tract was to be leased to Methodists (led by Hilly) and the southern reserved for Seventh-day Adventists (led by Niqusasa), but the Adventists did not take up the lease. Settlement began in January 1954, but the formalities of the lease proved problematic. A government note of February 1956 advised that the lease should have one part for individual families and one for the cooperative society as a whole (BSIP 7/I/DCW/130). On 6 May 1958, the commissioner of lands sought the attorney general's advice about how to vest rights in "a fluctuating body of persons" (BSIP 7/I/DCW/130, no. 88). The attorney general agreed with the commissioner of lands and declared that the persons living at Emu Harbour "have no legal entity" and thus cannot be granted a lease. He suggested a temporary occupation license to the identified "trustees"—a stopgap measure that was apparently adopted (BSIP 7/I/DCW/130, no. 89). The Emu Harbour settlement was denied status as an officially recognized cooperative in 1957 because, as the cooperative societies officer pointed out in a letter to the district commissioner of Western District, the society hired wage laborers who did not share in the profits of the society, which was clearly "contrary to cooperative principles" (BSIP 7/I/DCW/130, no. 68). By 1959, however, the Emu Harbour group appears to have been recognized as a cooperative society: in the 1959 list of alienated land, L.R. 214 is listed as being leased to the Emu Harbour Cooperative Society Ltd for 99 years from 1 Jan 1959 (BSIP 13/I/1).

10. I recorded a version of this story from Samuel Samata of Pienuna on 30 August 1999. I also recorded another version from Alik Hite, the brother-in-law of Vaolyn Hite (the eldest daughter of Panakera and Dunateko of Pienuna), during a visit to Nazareth village in Marovo on 8 July 2010; Vaolyn translated the story from the Marovo language into Kubokota as Alik spoke. Edvard Hviding has also recorded versions of the tale in Marovo (personal communication, 20 January 2010).
11. For the period between 1860 and 1900, Bennett (1987: 375–88) lists eight traders for Simbo, thirty for the Roviana lagoon area, six for Marovo, and none for Ranongga.
12. At the time of the initial declaration of the Protectorate, Santa Isabel, Choiseul, and the Shortland Islands were under German control but came under British control in 1899 with Germany retaining the right to recruit laborers from the islands (Bennett 1987: 435, n.30).
13. On museum collecting in this era, see also Rhys Richards (2012).
14. Niqusasa was involved in the purchase of copra: there is correspondence about a dispute between Niqusasa and Panakera when Panakera tried to purchase copra from an area under Niqusasa's buying license (BSIP 7/III/34/5, no. 9, notes by the district commissioner dated 3 September 1949). However, the story of the Adventist community is less tied up with copra and colonial government than is the story of the Methodists.
15. Niqusasa, Hilly, and Panakera are listed as members of the native council and court, first of Vella Lavella sub-district and then for Ranongga-Simbo in the 1940s (BSIP 7/III/34/5, documents dated 11 November 1948 and 9 November 1948; BSIP 7/I/DCW/124, document dated 6 June 1957).
16. Interview, Isaac Valaka, Sepa village, Choiseul, 30 June 1999; see also correspondence from district commissioner, Western Province, to chief secretary, Western Pacific High Commission, regarding the Emu Harbour scheme, 4 July 1957 (BSIP 7/I/DCW/130, no. 71).
17. The one case in which the garden was regularly referred to as the husband's (rather than the wife's) garden was that of Willie Sasala and the late Jenny Kamdao, who had been stricken by polio as a young woman and was not able to go often to the garden or carry the food back down to the village.
18. In most instances, I use the term "clan" (or "matriclan") rather than "lineage" (or "matrilineage") because *butubutu* are understood to be derived from very distant and sometimes semi-mythical founding ancestors. Anthropologists normally use the term "lineage" to refer to groups defined by descent from proximate ancestors.
19. Ranonggans take principles of exogamy to an extreme. In addition to being forbidden to marry descendent of shared great-grandparents (a relationship known as *pujuku dara*), people are forbidden to marry anyone of their own, their father's, or their grandfather's *butubutu*, no matter how distant the relationships of filiation.
20. Damon makes an analogous suggestion that island Melanesian polities might be productively analyzed in relationship to the hierarchial polities of Southeast Asia, from which Austronesian speakers emerged. He observes that the apparent ambiguity of the *butubutu* in Simbo identified by Scheffler was largely the result of the anthropological assumption that "entities have to be unambiguously defined" to be "distinct building blocks" of the social order (Damon 2000: 58, 59).
21. Arguably, there is an unresolved tension within Hviding's work on Marovo social organization. On the one hand, he emphasizes the inherent dynamism of the processes

through which Marovo people establish connections to their kin and to resources, elucidating an "indigenous theory of sociality" that centers on pan-Austronesian notions of making "sides" (*kale* in both Marovo and Ranongga) and tracing "paths" (*huana* in Marovo, *zona* or *soana* in Ranonggan languages). As Michael Scott (2007a) has observed, this emphasis on flow and flexibility is consistent with what has been called the "new Melanesian ethnography" in emphasizing emergent relationality rather than any a priori established social groupings or categories. On the other hand, like Scheffler, Hviding embraces the core premise of descent theory, analyzing *butubutu* in order to demonstrate that "it is indeed possible to form viable, discernible social groupings from such a non-orderly basis as the *butubutu* concept's seemingly endless number of meanings" (Hviding 2003c: 79). This theoretical and methodological premise—that analysis of social organization should begin with corporate groups—is precisely what theories of Melanesian relationality have called into question.

22. Rebecca Monson's (2012: 160–210) research on Vangunu suggests that *vuluvulu* is (or was) not only a sort of lineal connection, but also a status of leadership that was vested in women, one that was not recognized by colonial authorities.
23. Although Hviding (2003c, 2014) and Berg (2014) characterize Vella Lavella as uniquely matrilineal in contrast to the rest of non-unilineal New Georgia, such characterizations of *butubutu* as non-unilineal throughout New Georgia, including Simbo, seem to rely on Scheffler's (1962) quick dismissal of matrilineal idioms in Simbo. Christine Dureau (1993, 1994, 1998b) emphasizes matriliny in her discussions of Simbo kinship.

# 3

# Incorporating Others in Violent Times

"We're all from somewhere else," Matiu Matepitu mused, "we came ashore like coconuts floating on the sea." It was early in my fieldwork in 1998. I had returned after a day working on a village census and I sat down for a chat with Matepitu, who was one of my hosts in the beachfront hamlet where I was staying. Though Matepitu was born and raised in Pienuna, he explained to me that he was really from Rauru, the local name for Choiseul Island. His father Stephen Rama, the brother of post-war leader Simion Panakera, had served as a Methodist pastor in Choiseul, where he met Matepitu's mother in the 1930s. Matepitu explained to me that he and his siblings were in touch with their Choiseul relatives, who encouraged them to return home to the land of their mother. "But," he said, "we live well here and don't want to leave." Matepitu explained that his father Rama and uncle Panakera were also from Choiseul; as people of the *butubutu* (clan) named Kubongava, they were descended from a woman captured from Choiseul many generations ago. According to her descendants, this woman was not called a "captive" (*pinauzu*), but was adopted by the ancestors of Pienuna village chief John Pavukera, a man of the *butubutu* named Vitu. According to some people of both Vitu and Kubongava, the descendents of this captive Kubongava woman were supposed to replace Vitu should Vitu ever become extinct.

Matepitu was not the only life-long resident of Pienuna to describe himself as a migrant. Our conversation was prompted by discussions with other Pienuna residents that day who declared themselves to be *tio kamudi*, "people who have arrived" or *tio karovodi*, "people who have crossed the sea." Here, and all around Ranongga when I asked people about their family history, they often began by telling me of ancestors who had arrived from somewhere else. If they were descended from a woman taken captive on a war raid, they would almost invariably explain that their ancestress was not known as a *pinauzu* but as a woman of a local *butubutu* involved in the raid.

In public events, especially funeral rituals, in which *butubutu* identity is most strongly emphasized, participants would often highlight their status as people from other lands. Thus, at the 2001 funeral of his clanswoman Evelyn

Qago, John Wesley Paleo reminded his relatives that they had come from elsewhere and were welcomed ashore and adopted by village chief John Pavukera. Like Matepitu, John Wesley was not someone who was obviously a migrant. He, too, was born and raised in Kubokota, and his relatives on both sides had been long resident on Ranongga. As is common in the Pacific (Rumsey 2000), John Wesley was speaking of himself and John Pavukera as though they *were* their distant ancestors; he used the present tense to refer to a time in the quasi-mythical past when his ancestors fled sorcery and other trouble in their own territory and eventually sought refuge on Ranongga. Using the same metaphor that Matepitu did, he said, "We came here like dry coconuts floating on the sea."

Arrival narratives are politically consequential for the negotiation of land rights. Though people like Matepitu and John Wesley identified themselves as migrants, it would be terribly rude for anyone else identify them as such. Here, and elsewhere in the Solomons, reminding guests that they are not on home ground by telling them where their ancestors came from is an act entirely counter to the ethics of hospitality considered appropriate to people of the land. Guests ought to acknowledge the precedence, priority, and generosity of their hosts, but hosts cannot demand that recognition without acting inhospitably and thus undermining their authority as people of the place – a point developed by Michael Scott (2000, 2007b). Details of stories about ancestral arrivals had significance for the rights of migrants on their adopted land. If a foreign *butubutu* is said to have arrived empty handed, then it is understood that they were at the mercy of the local people who took them in; the descendents of those migrants remain subordinated to the descendents of the autochthonous hosts. If, however, migrants arrived with baskets of shell money, they are understood to have been in a better position to negotiate an alliance of equals with their would-be hosts. In many cases, indigenous *butubutu* are described as beholden to the foreigners who arrived on their shores, especially when those foreigners died on their behalf in warfare or in sacrifice. Stories about *pinauzu* are equally consequential, and therefore contested. I knew of no cases where a local *butubutu* was undisputedly replaced by the descendants of a captive woman: even if the local branch of a *butubutu* had no female descendants, *butubutu* members living elsewhere could claim to be successors on the basis of the genealogical integrity of the *butubutu*.

From one perspective, it was hardly surprising that the first stories that I heard when I began fieldwork in earnest were stories of migration. As Hviding (2014) has pointed out, at the turn of the twentieth century, A.M. Hocart documented the fundamentally "extra-local" quality of New Georgia social life; not only had many residents of Simbo come from elsewhere, but people frequently responded to the ethnographer's queries by describing regional variations in material culture and ritual practice. Then and now, genealogies, *butubutu* histories, epic tales, and material transactions extend across this maritime world. Yet by the late twentieth century, stories of ancestral migration ran against the grain of dominant representations of social organization and territorial belonging that I introduced in the previous chapter. Those dominant representations focused not on histories of movement and attachment, but on the timeless and inalienable rights of the landowning descent group to its ancestral territory.

Accounts of ancestral movements focus on a time prior to the turn of the twentieth century, an era that people today call the "time before" or the "time of darkness." Although the pre-Christian past is now represented as a time when people feared strangers and ventured away from local shores only because of warfare, stories from these violent times show that engagements with strangers were essential in local social life. Western social theory often depicts violence as the negation of social life, but ethnographies of warfare in Melanesia suggest that violence should be understood as part of the broader social processes through which persons and groups are made and unmade. Writing of Papua New Guinea's Sepik region, Simon Harrison suggests that warfare (like ceremonial exchange) is necessary in the constitution of a sociopolitical unit—it allows people to cut off relationships with intimate others and thus emerge as a bounded collectivity. In the Sepik, war enemies were always neighbors because "it is only close neighbours who *need* to be preoccupied with the maintenance of their shared boundaries" (Harrison 1993: 59). In much Western social and political theory, the social order is seen as a bulwark against the chaos that would ensue if each individual were allowed to pursue his will against every other individual; Harrison suggests that Melanesians see a different threat: "If they have an image of a disintegration of society, it would seem to be of a collapse, not into violent chaos, but of uninvolvement and detachment" (ibid.: 21; see also Scott 2005a). Precolonial warfare in New Georgia was directed against distant others, not near neighbors in the manner of Sepik warfare, but Harrison's approach to amity and enmity as entwined forms of social relationships, rather than as a presence versus absence of relationship, helps us understand otherwise puzzling reversals that occur when victims of violence are incorporated as kinspeople.

This chapter begins with myths and folk tales that depict the emergence of true humans on the land of Ranongga. Though fragmentary and disconnected, many of the stories I was told shared a common theme: proper humanity requires engagement with other people. As is the case for societies throughout the Solomons, Ranonggan stories often focus on quasi-human creatures, often larger than normal humans, who are depicted as greedy, amoral, and ignorant. They lack intelligence and moral sense, a stupidity evident in the fact that they treat their own relatives like strangers by killing them or committing incest with them. In *butubutu* origin stories, only when such beings engage with other people from other lands do they become properly human. Engagement with others marks a transition from ignorance to wisdom, from immorality to morality, from partial humanity to full humanity.

Many foreigners did not simply "float" onto Ranongga's shores; they were violently uprooted from their homes by warriors from Ranongga or their Vella Lavella allies.[1] Most ethnographic and archeological analysis of "headhunting" (referred to locally as *keni qeto*, "setting out in the war canoe") has focused on headhunting as an expression of male chiefly power, reflecting a broader tendency within the discipline to analyze warfare in terms of social control (see Knauft 1993: 116–19). Building on the analysis of Christine Dureau (1994, 2000), I focus instead on connections between warfare and social reproduction. Skulls and captives were often taken in the contexts of mortuary ritual, and these victims of violence were not simply signs of chiefly and ancestral power, but also essential in the creation of ancestors. Taking my lead from my interlocutors, I begin not with the stories of chiefs who led headhunting raids, warriors who committed violence, or the skulls of enemies who were slain, but with captives (*pinauzu*) taken on those raids who are now remembered by their living descendants.[2] In seeking to understand narratives dating from the turn of the twentieth century, I draw on the rich corpus of work by A.M. Hocart based on research he carried out in Simbo in 1908. Hocart's discussions of captives can be found in his writings on both warfare and death rituals. Only when considered as part of broader process of social reproduction, rather than the narrower frame of male chiefly leadership, do the stories of captives told on Ranongga today begin to make sense.

Contrary to colonial era and contemporary scholarly depictions of *pinauzu* as little more than "slaves" or designated victims for future sacrifices, many war victims were adopted by their captors or allies of their captors. The incorporation of war captives into local society to bolster it against the threat of depopulation is not unusual in Melanesia (Knauft 1993: 136–71), but several aspects of the incorporation of captives in Ranongga are unusual. First, none of the stories I heard depicted captive women as wives—they were always figured as potential sisters. Despite being taken on as a "sister," captive women continued to be known as people of their home place, and this foreign identity has been passed onto their children as *butubutu* identity. On the one hand, the replacement of an autochthonous *butubutu* by a foreign one appears like a dramatic break in succession; on the other hand, it may be seen as ensuring continuity in the relationship between ancestors, land, and people. Existing studies of headhunting in New Georgia suggest that enemies were dehumanized—ripped from the landscapes in which they were powerful and treated as treated as objects rather than persons (see esp. Thomas, Sheppard, and Walter 2001). I show that even the most abject victims of warfare could become rehumanized by being re-embedded in local places and reconnected with local people.

## From Stupid Isolation to Human Engagement

Ranonggans distinguish between mythical folk tales and *butubutu* histories. The former genre is *vavakato iliganigani* (ogre or giant stories), named after one of the most common characters in the stories. These ogre stories are told for the amusement of children, and are also the genre of story that most New Georgians provide when outsiders ask them to tell "custom stories."[3] Ranonggans explicitly contrast these ogre stories to what they consider real human history: the stories of how human *butubutu* originated, interacted with one another, and became attached to particular territories. Unlike ogre stories, stories about the origins and movements of *butubutu* are not told to amuse or edify. They are known by senior men, and occasionally women, who pass them on selectively to descendents or successors.[4] Though distinct, the genres of folk tales and *butubutu* histories overlap. In some cases, the fantastic non-human creatures that are the focus of folk stories are considered to be progenitors of real humans, or they interact with people of named *butubutu*. One *butubutu*, for example, was chased by their ogre "grandmother" around the archipelago of New Georgia, a journey that is taken to explain why this *butubutu* has branches on nearly every island. The omission or inclusion of a few key details, like names of people, clans, and places, determines whether a story is a folk story or a true history.

These Ranonggan folk tales and *butubutu* histories bear much in common with similar genres of tales analyzed by Michael Scott (2007b: 139–54) for Arosi on the island of Makira in the southeastern Solomons. As is the case in Ranongga, for Arosi, the first step in becoming properly human is engaging with others. The worlds depicted in Arosi myth and narratives of the distant past are polyontological: the cosmos is not understood to be made of essentially undifferentiated matter, but of fundamentally different kinds of beings. In contrast to origin myths that depict a single event in which humanity was created, like the Biblical story of Genesis or Polynesian myths of the mating of Sky and Earth, different Arosi matrilineages (and New Georgian *butubutu*) emerged at different times and places. Scott argues that this assumption of a radical, fundamental difference that is given in the nature of humans means that the "first order cosmogonic task" for any proto-human matrilineage is engagement with other such proto-lineages; through such engagement, proto-lineages become human lineages and their land becomes humanized territory, with gardens, settlements, paths, shrines, burial sites, local spirits, and named places. Yet when an autochthonous lineage brings in other lineages and allows them to engage in place-making activities (gardening, burying their dead, and so on), these outside lineages begin to forge their own independent relationship to the territory. Thus, the "second order cosmogonic task" is for autochthonous lineages to maintain their primordial connection to their ancestral territory so that they continue to anchor all other lineages on the territory. Scott identifies a fundamental, constitutive tension between the need to become entangled with other lineages and the need to maintain territorial and social boundaries. Such a tension is also evident in Ranonggan myths, narratives, and contemporary struggles over land and property.

In societies throughout island Melanesia, myths and folktales depict quasi- or proto-human creatures as physically powerful, but morally and mentally deficient and unable to reproduce themselves. Stories from Guadalcanal, Malaita, and elsewhere in the eastern Solomons focus on a set of brothers who fool and kill a stupid but terrifying ogre who often consumes the population.[5] A similar story is well known in the Trobriand Islands, where a culture hero named Tudava is credited with killing an ogre who frightened away local residents (Malinowski 1935: 68–75). In Ranonggan stories, giant, greedy, stupid ogres (*iliganigani*) are depicted as having an insatiable appetite (the term *iliganigani* incorporates the verb *gani*, the impolite term for "eat"), but never hunting, fishing, or gardening themselves. Moreover, rather than exchanging valuables for food, they either steal people's food or eat people themselves. Humans and ogres address one another as "grandparent" and "grandchild" in a perversion of proper kinship: these grandparents eat their grandchildren rather than feeding them. These kinship interactions misfire, ending in violent destruction rather than productive cooperation.

Greedy and stupid, ogres engage with humans, but not in ways that foster social reproduction. In one characteristic story (Pavukera 1989), eight ogres lived on a hill and ate anything that moved in the forest. When they discovered human gardens, they realized that they could eat not only gardens but also the humans who made the gardens. The ogres killed them one by one until there were no more humans. Deprived of their food source, one ogre was sent to investigate the empty village and was frightened by a tame dog, which chased the ogre back up the hill and trapped him and the rest of the ogres in a cave, where they starved to death.

Another story (Piukera 1991) tells of an ogre who is continually outsmarted by three young cousins. The children have caught themselves some crabs; when the ogre smells the food grilling, he lumbers over, demands some, and devours it all. When he asks how to catch crabs himself, the children trick him, saying that he should not try to get crabs on the sand but should put his fingers into the crab's hole so that it will bite it and he can pull it up. He does so, and comes up empty-handed, howling with pain, and enraged. The next day, he plans to kill the three children but completely forgets his rage when he smells roasting cuscus (a tree-dwelling marsupial). Again he demands food, eats the entire cuscus, and is tricked by the children, who tell him that good cuscus live only in the highest dead branches of a tree. He climbs up to get one and crashes to the ground, nearly killing himself. The next day, he is tricked into drinking an entire river pool to get the small fish at the bottom. The story continues in this vein until the ogre finds the children eating a giant clam. After he gobbles all of their food, the children tell him that to get this delicacy, he has to ignore the clams lying on the sand, wait until low tide, then put his testicles into a clam he finds wedged into coral rock so that he can pull it up to the surface. He follows their instructions and is drowned. I heard this story frequently in Ranongga, as well as during a visit to Sepa village in Choiseul, where I was shown the places where the ogre drank the pool, fell from the tree, and was drowned by the rising tide.[6]

Ogre stories are tall tales, not taken seriously. Stories about the origins of *butubutu*, by contrast, are considered to be "real history." The proto-humans in these stories are understood to be the ancestors of living people today, and are often depicted as attempting, but failing, to reproduce themselves sexually and socially through engagement with other beings. Like Arosi matrilineages described by Scott, Ranonggan *butubutu* emerged under diverse circumstances and in different places. The *butubutu* named Degere, for example, is said to have originated when a (female) coconut crab mated with a (male) pandanus tree and produced two human females as well as a number of non-human beings. Povana traces its origin to a woman who was born from an eel. Nulu originated when a brother and sister descended from the sky to the top of a mango tree in the central mountains of the island. Maluku is said to have descended from *tuturu*, forest spirits that cause people to lose their senses (a state also known as *tuturu*). In a state of isolation from other categories of people, the original *butubutu* of Ranongga lacked the capacity for fully human life and reproduction. One *butubutu* did not know how to cook until people of another *butubutu* showed them how to make fire. Another *butubutu* did not know how women should give birth so they cut babies out of women's wombs until people from another island explained how children could be born without sacrificing the mother. Another was engaged in acts of suicidal stupidity before they were rescued by people of another *butubutu*. Without "different people" (*goto tinoni*), these original proto-peoples would have destroyed themselves.[7]

Cooking and giving birth were not the only deficiencies of these original *butubutu*. They were also unable to speak properly. In a typed account of the origins of one Ranonggan *butubutu* held by a local custodian, two *tuturu* (who were named "Dripping Penis" and "Dripping Vagina") bore human children, but their children spoke stupid or crazy (*tuturu*) language to communicate with their parents and ancestral spirits. According to this text: "They did not speak the same way that you and I would speak, but they spoke the language of *tuturu*. Good and bad—all of it was good to them. Examples of this stupid language included, 'I'm going to pee,' 'I'm going to shit'." Ranonggans are not, categorically, prudish: it is perfectly acceptable to say something like "I'm going to pee" to a parent, child, spouse, or same-sex sibling. Yet direct reference to any bodily processes constitutes a significant offense when made in the presence of other kinds of people like a chief, an in-law, or a cross-sex sibling. What is "stupid" about the way *tuturu* and their human children speak is their failure to distinguish among categories of kin—the "bad talk" is "all good."

People of a *butubutu* descended from these *tuturu* are well known for bringing about their own extinction through suicidal stupidity (Keza 1989; Panakera 1991). In an often-told story, people of this "stupid clan" thought that it would be fun to float gently down to the ground like the large leaves of a breadfruit tree. One by one, they climbed a tall tree and jumped, expecting to float gently to the ground; one by one, they plunged to their deaths. In another adventure, they tried to cut a large sago palm to use the leaves in building a new house, but they didn't want the leaves to be crushed when the palm fell, so they stood beneath it to catch it—and were themselves crushed by the massive trunk. Another time they took their nets to the sea to catch fish, but they forgot to bring floats to hold the nets. They decided to tie it to their own legs, using them as substitutes for the floats, but when school of dolphins came into the nets, all of these stupid people drowned. In his analysis of similarly stupid proto-humans in Arosi, Scott points out that all of their ridiculous exploits were carried out without any allies or associates. They are not differentiated in terms of kinship relations, but as a "homogenous group of comically foolish people" (Scott 2007b: 140). Again, such stories of a stupid primeval race of semi-human creatures are widespread throughout the Solomons.

Unlike the ogres, who became extinct, proto-clans emerged from this primordial isolation and began to interact, exchange, intermarry, and share knowledge with other humans. (Some stories suggest that even the stupid clan was rescued from extinction through an alliance with people from other places.) They learned to cook, give birth, talk respectfully, and have sexual relations with non-relatives. In stories of these real human *butubutu*, two kinds of events are centrally important: dispersal from territory of origin and the arrival of foreigners in the territory. One of the few stories I ever heard about the mythical history of the island as a whole was told by Gago Rove of Patu village in 1999. In the beginning, there were people from four different territories living together on top of Mount Kela, the highest peak of Ranongga. When they began "doing wrong" (*varivasela*, usually a euphemism for incest) amongst themselves, each moved onto its own separate coastal territory. The incestuous state of affairs on Mount Kela was unavoidable—as long as there were only four groups living together, real exogamy was impossible because within two generations everyone would be related. Once on the coast, the autochthonous people of Ranonggan territory began to engage with people from other lands. Dispersal might look like simple processes of subdivision that became necessary as populations grew. It is significant, however, that such splits are described as moral breaches. Fragmentation and dispersal are most often attributed to some kind of wrongdoing, prototypically incest or sorcery. Sorcery is differentiated from other kinds of magic or violence because it must be used against one's own relatives before it can be used on one's enemies. Unless the breach opened by sorcery is mended by the exchange of shell money or the punishment of the offenders, the group is permanently split. In the case of both of these offenses, a person treats a relative in a way that they should only treat strangers, namely as a sexual partner or as an enemy.

Of two dozen or so named *butubutu* on Ranongga, most are said to have originated from lands across the sea. Some of these foreign *butubutu* came to the island when women were taken captive in war raids. Others came in canoes to Ranongga as refugees from persecution, whether due to persistent sorcery directed against them or punishment for some infraction they had committed. When interlocutors on opposed sides of land disputes told me of the history of their territories or *butubutu*, their accounts often diverged on two points: Who brought the strangers ashore? Did they arrive with baskets of shell valuables or empty handed? If the ancestors of living people were understood to have welcomed strangers ashore, or even sold them land, at some point in the past, then they are assumed to be the original owners today. But these encounters are also remembered to have established a special relationship of alliance between hosts and guests. In several narratives I encountered, especially from the once densely populated coast of southern Luqa, hosts and guests exchanged names or disguised identities, apparently with the explicit purpose of making it impossible for their descendants to argue among themselves about who had precedence regarding the land. The way in which strangers arrived was also significant. If they came seeking refuge, they were at the mercy of their hosts and are thus seen to be indebted to and thus "under" their hosts. If they arrived with baskets of shell valuables, then they could have established themselves independently on the land, establishing an alliance with their hosts rather than acting as dependent clients.

Today, stories of the arrival of ancestors are contested and fraught with consequences. From a broader perspective, however, they encode many broadly shared precepts of Ranonggan social life. Fantastic "ogre stories" and the stories of the origins and movements of human groups depict a transformation from ignorance to wisdom made possible though engagement with people from across the sea.

## Warfare and Mourning

When I returned to Ranongga in 2000 for a second research trip, I brought copies of A.M. Hocart's articles about warfare and mourning on Simbo.

After reading through the articles, Samuel Samata of Pienuna suggested that perhaps captives and sacrificial victims served the same purpose that cement tombstones or photos do today: they are *merumeru* (memorials) that remind people of deceased friends or relatives. Such a suggestion suggests a radically different interpretation of nineteenth-century warfare than do conventional accounts of headhunting as an expression of male chiefly control. Victims of warfare, living or dead, were not only a sign of chiefly power, collected as trophies or slaves; they were also sacrificial victims whose death was necessary for the production of ancestors and the continuity of ancestral relationships with land.

Subsequent scholars have interpreted headhunting in light of A.M. Hocart's descriptions of the reasons for headhunting in Simbo a few years after the government pacification campaign of 1899/1900:

> Heads were not caught at random, but for the definite purpose of inauguration, if we may so translate the vernacular *vapenja* . . . The word *vapenja* should therefore mean "to moisten, to wet," presumably with blood. The occasions of *vapenja* are new canoes, new communal houses (*paele, njelepande*), new skull-houses, the death of a chief, and the release from confinement of a widow. (Hocart 1931: 303)

The inauguration of houses and canoes with blood makes sense of the most widely circulated eyewitness account of the brutal murder of a war captive in the region, one that has been cited repeatedly as evidence of the fate of captives. In 1883, a European trader in Roviana witnessed the gruesome death of a young Santa Isabel boy, who was dunked repeatedly in water before his throat was slit; he was beheaded, and his body was carried around a new canoe house so that his blood splattered on it (Woodford 1890: 154–57). Although this human sacrifice appears to have been anomalous,[8] the incident helped to solidify an understanding of headhunting ritual as part of "inauguration." But the other occasions that Hocart said prompted headhunting—the death of a chief and the release of a widow from confinement—do not fit this interpretation, for it is not clear what might have been inaugurated in such situations.

The long-distance, highly organized, and devastatingly violent war raids that were a notable feature of nineteenth-century New Georgia seem to have begun in the sixteenth or seventeenth centuries as part of a broader process of political consolidation. Archeological research on Roviana documents a historical progression from simple shrine structures located inland to the elaborate shrines that are characteristic of New Georgian society in the historical era (Sheppard, Walter, and Nagaoka 2000; Thomas, Sheppard, and Walter 2001; Walter, Thomas, and Sheppard 2004; Walter and Sheppard 2006; Thomas 2014). Such changes in landscape and shrine architecture accord with oral traditions recounting a move from inland to coastal areas many generations

**Figure 3.1.** An ancestral shrine, inland from Modo village. This unusual stone structure has a human figure carved on the right side; to the left of the large stone is a smaller stone trough that was presumably used for pounding puddings in propitiation rituals. Like most ancestral shrines on territory held by Seventh-day Adventists, this one is desacrilized or, in the words of John Matepitu of Modo who took me to see it, "completely safe." No valuables remain on the shrine. Many skulls in the shrine were destroyed in the 2007 earthquake. June 2000.

ago, the establishment of a chiefly lineage linked to supernatural beings, and the beginning of long-distance warfare (Sheppard and Walter 2000; Thomas, Sheppard, and Walter 2001: 558–61; Aswani and Sheppard 2003). Richard Walter and Peter Sheppard (2000: 315) argue that local conceptions of chiefly efficacy were spatially located in the twin structures of ancestral shrines and coastal war-canoe houses, with the former taken as expressing "internal power" emanating from the ancestral shrines and the latter expressing "external power" of a military tradition.

During his Simbo fieldwork, Hocart witnessed the return of a war party with a captive (*pinausu* in Simbo) (Hocart 1922: 89, 1931: 305). The young Choiseul boy (never named by Hocart) was taken by Lembu, a Ganoqan man living in Simbo who wanted to adopt the captive as his son. This "raid" was carried out from a trade steamer, not a war canoe, because the British administration had already destroyed the sea-going plank-built canoes of the region. Lembu and a party of Simbo men traveled to Choiseul, and Lembu purchased the boy with trade goods and fossilized clamshell rings (*bakia*).

When the party returned to Simbo with their purchased captive, Lembu and his company paddled, sang, and blew a conch as they came ashore—an arrival that Hocart analyzed as the return of successful headhunters (Hocart 1931: 306). The chief asked where they had taken the slave, and Lembu listed the places he visited in his journey. The chief then "threw" an arm-ring to Lembu, and the rest of the villagers followed suit. Finally, the women who were gathered on the shore took the "little slave" and ushered him to a house. Lembu then blew a conch and went to the house of Widow Emele, whose husband had died about a week earlier. She was sitting in her confinement room when he came in, blew a conch, and removed the door of her small enclosure. In return, the widow paid him two large shell valuables. Later, Lembu repeated the procedure for another widow, Widow Gage, whose husband Iranga was a kinsman of Lembu, also from Ganoqa. When Lembu blew the conch for Widow Gage, he and the widow wept together, and Widow Gage did not pay Lembu with shell rings.

This example illustrates the intimate connection between warfare and mortuary rituals: the arrival of the captive released widows from mourning. In the past, chiefly widows sat in a crouched, sitting position that mimicked the position of the body of the deceased who was tied onto a platform to allow the flesh to rot away. They stayed in small enclosures inside of their houses, leaving their houses only to relieve themselves, and then covered themselves with a mat. They did not cut their hair (or shave if male), bathe, or eat from the same kitchen as the rest of the community (Hocart 1922: 84). Writing of a similar kind of widow confinement in Tubetube, Macintyre suggests that the confinement represents the "symbolic transformations wrought by death"; as the corpse rots beyond the bounds of the village, the bodily presence of the widow keeps the deceased metaphorically present (Macintyre 1989: 138).

Although no cases of widow suicide occurred while Hocart was on Simbo, he recounted the suicide of the wife of the last chief upon his death. The suicide (by hanging) proved difficult because of faulty ropes and breaking branches, but she persisted, apparently of her own will. Rather than mourning, she wore her finest clothes and sat beside her deceased husband; all others wailed, but she "did not cry or she could not have died, for a widow who cries cannot hang herself" (Hocart 1922: 86). I heard stories from Ranongga in which mothers hanged themselves when their sons died; there were also cases in which the widow and even children of a slain chief were killed by his own *butubutu*. John Pavukera of Pienuna explained that when the wife of a chief died to follow the chief to his death, his relatives would kill a captive if they had one, so that the captive would follow the chief's wife in death. The practice is called *borotoni*, from the terms *boro* (meaning strangle or hug) and *toni* (to lead, as one would lead a child along a path).

The mourning rituals performed at the turn of the century continue to be observed in attenuated form today, despite the fact that Christianity has changed people's understandings of the power and fate of the dead.[9] Both in the past and the present, relatives, affines, and neighbors of the deceased gather at the home of the deceased as soon as the news is heard. Work in the village ceases. A few primary mourners, usually women, stay beside the body and wail almost constantly, and others arrive to come to "help them cry." The body is buried as soon as possible after the arrival of the most important relatives. In the days following the death, the spouse of the deceased does not bathe or leave the hamlet. On the fourth day after the death, the immediate kin and affines of the deceased hold a small feast, after which those who had been sleeping in the house or hamlet of the deceased return to their own homes. Unless a chief has died, most restrictions on the village are lifted at this time. On the tenth day after the death, neighbors and relatives cover the grave with gravel. The tenth-day feast is much more elaborate than the fourth-day feast and is more clearly sponsored by the deceased's *butubutu*, with baskets of food carefully distributed to all those who helped in the work of burial and mourning. Today, the tenth-day feast sometimes ends formal mortuary rituals, although mourners may continue observing dietary or other kinds of restrictions for many months or even years after the death of a loved one. Ideally, though, the kin of the deceased sponsor elaborate celebrations when the grave is encased in cement a year or more after the death. These occasions (known as "cementing," see Chapter 5) are crucial in the disposition of the property of the deceased, particularly if the deceased was a man who cleared land for settlement, gardening, or coconut plantations.

The death rituals of past generations focused on ridding the living of the contamination of death, thought to spoil the fertility of the land and people.[10] In the past, the feasts that were held after a death symbolically sent the dead away from the village of the living. The dead in New Georgia are said to have boarded a canoe paddled by ghosts and gone to the land of the dead at Zodo, thought to be located near the Shortland Islands. The fourth day was the day when a ghost war canoe came to take the recently deceased to Zodo. The relatives put a small bit of fish or pudding into the fire as rations for the deceased to take on their journey to the land of the dead. Without such an offering, it was believed, the deceased was likely to throw a sea cucumber (thought inedible by Ranonggans) onto the gardens of their kin, causing famine. The tenth-day feast was the occasion for releasing the widow from restrictions and returning luck and fertility to the community as a whole. Until about thirty years ago, the widow and other mourners would be ritually bathed (*iru pale na bose*). The widow and all of the village were led to a nearby stream, carrying plants, tools, and fishing lines. The widow sat down in the shallow water of the stream, and the female ritual specialist "brushed down" (*iru*) the widow with a leaf to get rid of bad luck and contamination (*bose*). Then she tossed away the leaves she was holding, and the assembled people scrambled to grab them. Those who caught the leaves were blessed (a state known as *masuru*)—their gardens would thrive and they would be lucky in fishing and love endeavors thought to require strong powers of attraction. The connection between mortuary ritual, fertility, and powers of attraction is widely attested throughout island Melanesia. Among Kwaio of Malaita, for example, mortuary rituals also involve wealth-attraction magic called *mamu*, a word that also denotes fishing bait even among inland people who rarely fished (Keesing 1982b).[11]

In the past, elaborate funerals of chiefs (*bangara*) appear to have motivated war raids as well as the suicide of widows or others to travel with the dead chiefs to Zodo. People used knots on a plant fiber rope to count one hundred, three hundred, or one thousand days after the death of a very great chief. Until that time, all people living under the chief observed many restrictions known as *jiru*; they were forbidden to fish on the reefs that the chief held, to light fires, to clear gardens, or to make loud and joyous noise. Widows were in even stricter confinement. At the end of the mourning time, a great feast (*vavolo*) was organized by the chief's successor and his (or her) allies, who set out to take a sacrificial victim, referred to as the *vavuluna* of the deceased.[12] When the conch was blown to announce the arrival of a war party and a victim, people were released from the restrictions of the *jiru*. Before the 1900s, this was the occasion of headhunting, from which, if all went well, warriors would return victorious with severed heads and captives.

In the 1910s and 1920s, warfare continued unabated on Choiseul, a longstanding site of raids mounted from northern Ranongga via their allies in Vella Lavella. Like Hocart's Simbo hosts, Ranonggans continued taking *vavulu* from Choiseul by purchasing them from the groups that had violently taken them. In Pienuna, a woman named Aloteko was taken as the *vavuluna* of a great chief of the *butubutu* Vitu upon his death in 1910. Even after it became impossible to purchase captives from Choiseul, the taking of *vavuluna* continued with turtles standing in for human victims. Samuel Samata described how he and his father killed a turtle after the death of Nake, the previous chief of Nulu, whose territory encompasses Obobulu and Pienuna. The scenario he described was very much like what Hocart described: everyone assembled at the beach, including a man representing Nulu. When Samata and his father came ashore and brought the turtle, they were given food and money, but only a small amount of money because they were relatives of the deceased (Samata's father was of the *butubutu* Vuruvasu, but his mother was Nulu). If "different people" had brought the victim, Samata explained, the villagers of Obobulu would have given them a large sum of money.[13] Perhaps the most striking historical transformation of the practice of taking a *vavuluna* occurred in the context of the Christian conversion of the Ganoqan community at Modo in 1920. To conclude the death rituals of the last non-Christian chief, his successor sent warriors to capture a missionary. The Seventh-day Adventist church is thus said to be that chief's *vavuluna*.

Both in the past and the present, mortuary rituals on Ranongga have a dual purpose—they are intended to distance the dead from the living at the same time that they keep symbols of the dead present in the lives of the living.[14] Unless the dead were properly separated from the living, they would attempt to pull their loved ones along with them. The obsolete practices of widow suicide and the sacrifice of captives, as well as ongoing rituals that symbolically provide the dead with food and other goods for the journey, ensure that the deceased has company and provisions for a journey away from their living kin. At the same time, other aspects of mourning rituals ensure that the spirit of the deceased remains close to the living. This closeness was far more evident in the pre-Christian past, when ritual priests (*iama*) regularly interacted with the spirits of the local dead. Rituals of propitiation mirrored the give and take between living kinspeople as people shared with their ancestors tokens of what they would have shared in life (bits of food, broken shell rings) while pleading with the ancestors to share their blessings with them (Dureau 2000; see also Hocart 1914; Keesing 1984; Hviding 1996). If this regular interaction is no longer part of everyday life, the placement of the dead in the midst of the living represents a striking parallel with precolonial practice despite differences in the treatment of corpses. Walter and Sheppard (2000: 316) note that while gravesites are kept separate from the sites of domestic activity in many Oceanic societies, in pre-twentieth-century Roviana, ancestral shrines were sometimes concentrated in central locations but sometimes interspersed with the domestic spaces of dwelling houses (ibid.: 316). The arrangement of Christian graves on Ranongga mirrors such patterns. In Pienuna, the graves of the founders of the contemporary Christian village in the 1910s were buried together near the site of the first church.[15] In the decades following the establishment of the village, however, the dead have been buried within small family hamlets so that they remain near their relatives. Christian burial and Christian graves keep the remains of the dead geographically close to the living and serve to anchor them in the territory.

Throughout island Melanesia, mourning rituals simultaneously acknowledge the ways that persons are constituted by "different people," especially people who are not of their own clans, and seek to re-establish the integrity of the matrilineal clan as a integral whole. As Nancy Munn explains for Gawa:

> In contrast to marriage exchanges, which are concerned with the spatiotemporal extension developed in the formation of the marital whole, Gawan mortuary exchanges are concerned with factoring out the marital, paternal, and matrilineal components, which have

been amalgamated to form the deceased's holistic being, and with returning this being to a partial, detotalized state—its unamalgamated matrilineal source. (Munn 1986: 164)

Annette Weiner's (1980, 1988) discussions of mortuary rituals in the Trobriand Islands also show how the matrilineal relatives of the deceased gradually repay their debts to the clan of the deceased's father and affines who have made the person over the course of their life. This social decomposition mirrors the process of bodily decomposition of the person. The flesh, created through the nurture of fathers and spouses, dissolves; the bones, the hard core of matrilineal essence, remain. In rituals, the deceased's connections to people of affinal and patrilineal clans are stripped away, creating a pure ancestor of the clan. Engagement and indebtedness are repeated in the next generation, but mortuary exchanges allow accounts to be evened, if only temporarily.

In the context of the ethnography of matrilineal societies in island Melanesia, Ranonggan mortuary rituals are unusual: rather than being the point at which debts to others are repaid, death is the point at which the greatest of all possible debts accrue. The first part of the ritual cycle follows well-documented regional patterns. The fourth-day feast is sponsored by all who are gathered around the corpse, but the tenth-day feast is held in the name of the *butubutu* alone. It is understood as compensation to those beyond the *butubutu* who nurtured the deceased and participated in the work of mourning, including the token work of carrying gravel to the grave before the feast. In the ceremonies that occur months or years after the death, however, these debts are dramatically renewed. Today, when the grave of a man is cemented, this is often connected to *pajuku* ceremonies organized by the deceased's wife, children, and their relatives. They give pigs, baskets of food, and sometimes *bakia* to their father's *butubutu* to compensate the *butubutu* for their father's "tiredness" and "sweat," that is, the work that he put into clearing garden land, planting nut groves, or establishing settlements. Such prestations work as an implicit announcement that the children of the deceased will continue to hold the property and the area that belonged to their father.

In the pre-Christian past, the last stage of mourning for chiefs required the most radical sacrifice from those outside of the *butubutu*: the suicide of the widow or the sacrifice of a foreign victim. This act of sacrifice created a debt that could not be repaid except through the incorporation of the victims' descendants into the *butubutu* or the transfer of land to them (which seems to have amounted to the same thing). If you die for us, this logic seems to suggest, you *are* us. Sacrifice contained the potential for a radical transformation of relationships among *butubutu* and between *butubutu* and their territory—a potential that becomes evident in narratives focused on captives taken in warfare.

**Figure 3.2.** A large cache of intact shell valuables, including *bakia*, grooved valuables known as *bareke*, and carved shell figures called *barava*, in an ancestral shrine located in the midst of an old settlement site. The upright whale's tooth and the large *bakia* that it rests on were described to me as the anchor (*titi*) of the shrine. August 1999.

## Sacrifice and Succession: The Fate of War Captives

Archeological and ethnohistorical research has focused primarily on the skulls of slain victims of warfare rather than on the living captives whose descendants continue to live throughout New Georgia. Skulls were present in both ancestral shrines and canoe houses, but they were treated in strikingly different ways (Walter, Thomas, and Sheppard 2004: 149–55). Ancestral skulls were positioned in shrines. They were the end product of a careful series of mortuary rituals that physically cleaned the flesh from the bone and metaphysically transformed the dead person into a benevolent ancestor. In contrast to ancestral skulls, the skulls of enemy dead were displayed as trophies in canoe houses. They were not treated with any ritual care, nor were they considered to be powerful or dangerous (Thomas, Sheppard, Walter 2001: 570; see also Aswani 2000; Walter, Thomas, and Sheppard 2004; Thomas 2014). These skulls had been severed from the bodies that gave them life and ripped away from the contexts in which they might have been transformed into efficacious ancestors. No power seems to have come with the skulls back home with their killers. Though their skulls were taken away, these "bad dead" remained in their homelands as endo-cannibalistic spirits who consumed their own relatives. In this way, the taking of heads amplified the direct devastation of a headhunting raid on the victimized communities (Dureau 2000: 91).

In accounts of the meaning of and motivations for warfare, captives are often depicted as the living equivalents of these enemy skulls: a subordinate class of slaves forced to produce shell valuables, perform the ritually dangerous and disgusting work of cleaning corpses, and to sell sexual services on behalf of the chiefs who own them (Aswani 2000; cf. Dureau 2000; McDougall 2000). Yet, such depictions clash with contemporary observers' reports, which describe captives as well treated and "on a perfect footing of equality and familiarity with their captors" (Woodford 1890: 154; see also Goldie 1909: 27). Hocart (1931: 306) observed that most captives on Simbo married and had children in their adopted homes and used reciprocal kin terminology with their captors; Dureau (1994: 71) also notes that captives were very much like adopted children. In contrast to the skulls of victims killed in warfare, the skulls of long resident captives were enshrined beside those of people of the place. Even though living captives served the same ritual role as slain enemies in mortuary rituals that were often the impetus for war raids in the way I have suggested above, their trajectories were very different than these trophy skulls because they were not inert objects, but living human beings capable of engaging in relations with local people and local land.

Ranonggans often emphasized that some captives were called *pinauzu*, but others were adopted into the matrilineal *butubutu* that brought them ashore. Simon Beto of Sabala village explained it to me this way in August 2000:

> So, if they were to go fight in Rauru [Choiseul], and take a girl, they would come back and call her a *pinauzu*. But some weren't called *pinauzu*, but they called them "their *butubutu*." That is how it was. It was the same for those from Rauru, same for those from Bugotu [Isabel]. Those they called *pinauzu* belonged to the chiefs, they owned the *pinauzu*, he or she was their servant, the one they could order around, whether it was a woman or a man. The chiefs own him or her. But say I went to join a war raid and I took a small girl, and I were to adopt her, and I would know that no more women will be born from the branch of my *butubutu*, then I would say, "Hey, you will replace my *butubutu*. She is my *butubutu*, my branch." Say it happened like that. Then, that one is of the *butubutu*.

Interestingly, all of the women and most of the men that Beto and others have described to me as *pinauzu* were childless. Beto explained that they were barren, and speculated that this was because people of Choiseul have a kind of medicine to prevent childbearing. Perhaps this was the case. However, it seems likely that when a *pinauzu* bore children in this era of declining population, those who owned her decided to incorporate her as a kinswoman. Everyone I met who claimed descent from a captive woman insisted that she was not called *pinauzu* but was called *butubutu*.

Men who were called *pinauzu* served the chiefs by doing things like making shell money, climbing nut trees, even tending ancestral shrines. Women gardened and prepared food and some served as *tugele*, ritual prostitutes who would, at feast times, have sex with men who paid shell rings to the chief (Aswani and Sheppard 2003: S63). None of these roles were exclusively reserved for *pinauzu*, however, nor were they necessarily degrading. *Tugele*, for example, were apparently waited on hand and foot by the chief's wife and daughters. But these captives were like slaves insofar as they could be bought and sold. Beto told me about a woman named Matuseko, who was captured in Choiseul by a man of the *butubutu* named Galagala but later purchased by the chiefs of Nulu for the price of a rifle. She had no children and lived and died at a settlement just south of Pienuna. Another woman, Pupuriko, was also taken from Choiseul and lived at Puki, the now-abandoned village of Beto's father Diavara. She married but had no children and was widowed. Beto remembered her living alone far away near the head of a stream in a house made of rock instead of sago palm. She made gardens for his father's people.

I encountered far fewer stories about these *pinauzu* than I did about war captives who were said to have been incorporated into local *butubutu*. One raid that was described to me was organized by a female chief of Ganoqa to avenge the killing of her brother by people of Vella Lavella, and was carried out by four different *butubutu*, each in their own war canoe. The raid was a success and each canoe took a captive. Upon their return home, each of the leading warriors handed back the *bakia* that they had been given as payment for their service to the female chief, since each preferred to keep a captive woman as a sister whose children could replace their *butubutu* should it ever become extinct.

Some stories from the descendents of these captives focus on apparent betrayal. Speaking to me in 1999 in Suava, Timoli Neri told of a woman of Zabana in Santa Isabel who was taken in a raid; they did not call her *pinauzu*, but *butubutu*, and she had children on Ranongga. One day, this woman (or perhaps one of her descendants; the story was unclear), left her child with a young girl in the village when she went up to her garden. She came home in the evening and asked for the child so that she could nurse it, only to learn that the chief of the village had died that day and her child had been killed to accompany the chief on his journey to the land of the dead. "They called us *butubutu*, but now they are killing us!" Before dawn broke, the women and her kinspeople fled to the other side of the island.

Pize of Rava, whom I spoke to shortly before her death in 1999, was the child of two Santa Isabel captives. Her father, Kaidi, was bathing when warriors from Java (on Vella Lavella) killed his companions and captured him. Later, he traveled with his Java captors to join a feast at Qeuru on Ranongga. The bush spirits around Qeuru are notorious for disorienting strangers and he became lost and was unable to return to Java, staying behind at Qeuru. As *pinauzu* often did, Kaidi became a *iama*, a priest who kept ancestral shrines. Pize's mother, whose original name was Foru but was known in Ranongga as Kiapaku, was taken from Kokota near Maringe in Isabel by men named Oqere and Sogavaka in a canoe belonging to people of Nulu (Pize called it "Tiqi's canoe," naming a Nulu woman of her generation). Pize insisted that Kiapaku was not taken as a *pinauzu* but as a sister for the children of Sirikana, a chief of Povana. Years later, after Kiapaku married Kaidi but before Pize was born, Kezokolo of Nulu died. There were rumors that Kiapaku would be killed as his *vavuluna*, since it was his canoe that took her from Isabel. According to Pize, however, her sister Zazamule volunteered to be sacrificed in place of her mother, who had young children to nurse. She was hanged as part of Kezokolo's funeral.

The logic of sacrifice becomes particularly clear in relation to the story of Awana, also known in Ranongga as Mija, who arrived on Ranongga in the 1870s or 1880s. Awana was the great-grandmother of Ziosi Luke of Pienuna, who told me about her soon after I arrived. I learned more details from Ziosi's mother, Laela Laena of Keara village, when I visited her in February 1999 not long before she died. Warriors from Ranongga, Laela explained, set out on a war expedition, and attacked a village in Santa Isabel (I later learned it was called Lohasa). They captured Awana and her child, whom she carried in a sling. They set off to return to Ranongga, came to Vagena, an island in the Manning Straight between Isabel and Choiseul, then asked for the child:

> They asked, but she refused, she cried about her child. They asked, they begged her. She cried—cried for her child without stopping. "No, he is my child," she said. But they pleaded and pleaded there, and then . . . she gave up, took down the sling, and they killed him. Oh, this is horrible! [. . .] So they brought back the mother, but blew the conch shell when they arrived because they had the boy's head. [. . .] She cried. She was crying there, [and they said] "Don't cry. You will have, yes, you will have *aoro* [nut groves], *neni* [*Canarium salomonense*], *ngari* [*Canarium indicum*], *busabusa* [cleared land for gardening]; we'll give it to you. Don't cry."

The child's skull was carried back and put into a shrine, and Awana married Minu of *butubutu* Povana; their only surviving son was Beikera, Laela's father.

During what Laela called the "time of darkness," her father Beikera took part in at least two war expeditions, and also served as a ritual priest (*iama*) who looked after shrines, including the one that contained the skull of his older half-brother. He converted to Christianity in 1924 and became a pastor-teacher. Before Beikera died in the late 1970s, his sons recorded his version of the raid that led to Awana's capture and the fate of his mother and half-brother. In December 2000, his son Nason Beikera generously played this tape for me and helped me decipher his father's faint words. His account of the organization of the raid is far more detailed than other accounts of war raids told by people born in the twentieth century. While it is not appropriate to make public many of the details of this narrative (such as the names of people or *butubutu* involved), even its general outline is very helpful in revealing something about the socio-political structures of the late nineteenth century, the link between warfare and mortuary rituals, the organization of warfare, and the connection between sacrifice and sovereignty.

Like so many other expeditions, the one that brought Awana to Ranongga was motivated by the death of a great chief. According to Beikera, this chief was leading preparations for a feast in his west-coast village: thirteen pigs were tethered and the women were gathering greens to roast with the pigs. While the women were high above the shore in the forest looking down, they heard a *Canarium* nut tree begin to crack. They called down to the fourteen chiefs on the shore, but they refused to move out of danger, instead sitting and laughing at the women. When the tree came crashing down, all fourteen were smashed to bits, along with children of all sizes. Only the son of the great chief survived. The great chief organizing the feast was not on his own ancestral territory, which was on the other side of the island. A man on whose territory the accident occurred called for a war raid; a third man, of yet another territory, responded to the cry saying, "I'm a man, so let's go!" He took the chiefs' war canoes and the war party set off.

Here Beikera's account joins that of his daughter. The warriors went over to Choiseul, but the raid was unsuccessful; traveled southeast to Kia on Santa Isabel, but again without luck; finally, they continued along the shore to Lohasa.

> Then they fought, there were many people killed, but when they got Awana Mija and Bulepeja, her grown child, they stopped. "Let us return." They returned, they returned, the came to Babatana. This woman gave permission, "Let us take our *kokomate* [sacrificial victim]," they said. This is the *kokomate*, but this one you can't take. This woman here. You can't take her but the boy you can take. Those of [the *butubutu* of the deceased chief], they took that boy, they took him, they took him, and they killed him.

The warriors returned to Ranongga, but rather than going to the west coast where the chiefs had died, they came ashore onto the ancestral territory of the deceased chief and his successor on the east coast. There, the *iama* sent them back to the west coast to end the period of mourning for the chief. Then they circled the island again, carrying the skull of the dead chief and the boy Bulepeja to the ancestral territory of the deceased chief.

> They went down there, and they opened the shrine. "Who should we put in first?" asked people of the clan. "You can't put the chief in first; it's the boy who we will put in first. He will establish the shrine, then we will put in the chief," said the *iama* who tended the shrine. So then they put in the boy, put him in first. The shrine was thus established and the chief was put in afterwards.

The *iama* then directed the new chief—Beikera's father—to marry the woman taken from Lohasa. The *iama* said: "This *butubutu* land belongs to her, not to us, because her child established the shrine here. The land belongs to her." Awana bore a child, Beikera. In his narrative, Beikera explained that he was appointed to succeed his father as chief of the land because of the sacrifice of Awana's first child, whom he referred to as his elder brother. He reported that his father said: "I will not give any other person the land here, but only to my child, whose older brother was the *kokomate*... That is who I will give it to." According to Beikera, the announcement was public, and the chiefs and chiefly women around Luqa assented to his father's decision.

This claim of succession is not uncontested. In recounting part of his narrative, I do not mean to suggest that rights over the land, its shrines, and people were definitively transferred to the children of Awana; other narratives are equally compelling. What is of interest here is the underlying cultural logic that makes such an account plausible. That logic suggests that sacrifice transformed relations of sovereignty. The slain boy was a foreigner, but because his skull opened an ancestral shrine, his mother acquired power over the land, power that was passed down to her son, his younger brother, Beikera.

This narrative affirms the insights of archeological research focused on the role of enemy skulls. Aside from Awana, the victims of the raid on Lohasa are of little importance; they are neither named nor remembered. Perhaps their heads were displayed as trophies in war canoe houses; perhaps they were quantified in competition for status and rank. From a local perspective, it hardly matters. What matters, and what is remembered about this expedition, is the arrival of the living woman and the child who was sacrificed in order that the chief could be enshrined. The return of successful war canoes was a sign of ancestral efficacy, chiefly power, and military prowess, but it was also the moment in which the local polity became radically indebted to the very same foreigners who were violently taken from their land.

When I first heard Laela speak of her grandmother, I was shocked not only by the violence of the murder of the child but by the dramatic oscillation between brutality and compassion. Victims of headhunting raids were dehumanized, ripped unceremoniously from the territory of their ancestors and from their networks of kin. Some were killed and dismembered. Noting a tendency in literature on Melanesian relationality to focus on generative rather than destructive forms of relationship, Martha Macintyre observed that in pre-pacification Tubetube in the Milne Bay Province of Papua New Guinea, "The logic which connects people and things, which enables people to construe their products as inalienable and commemorative, also provides the basis for actions against enemies, so that people may be objectified, their humanness and their sociality denied and obliterated" (Macintyre 1995: 34). Yet, this objectification was not necessarily permanent, and a dehumanized subject could be made human again: "As a *gum* [captive], she was like a thing that could be eaten and exchanged for objects; but as an adoptive member of a Tubetube group she is constituted as a reproductive person whose value cannot be established by barter with valuables" (ibid.: 38).

In the Ranonggan narratives I recorded, this rehumanization was also a reterritorialization. Awana was not just married to a chief; she was granted property in her own right, areas that were her own and that she would pass onto her kin. Hocart, too, recorded information about rituals that seem to have been aimed at introducing foreign captives to the land and spirits of Simbo. There are strongly gendered dynamics to these stories of warfare. If male warriors were the ones who killed, dehumanized, and deterritorialized victims, women seem to have played a critical role in rehumanizing and reterritorializing captives who became local.

## Violence, Power, Perversion

Headhunting may have been tied up with the expansion of chiefly power, but it can also be seen as a perversion rather than triumph. Stories from the "time of darkness" often seem to suggest a reversion to the amoral and idiotic behavior of proto-humans of *butubutu* origin stories and the ogres of folk tales. A legend about the origins of headhunting from Roviana lends itself to such an interpretation.

> The Kaleqe Mateana [a female spirit being] from Parara had a stone war canoe (*tomoko*). She asked her son to make the canoe fit for fishing. They built a canoe made from stone. The son went to inaugurate the canoe and asked dolphins to tow the canoe. They went far away until they arrived to Lauru [Choiseul]. There he took no fish. When the Lauru people saw him they wanted to kill him, but he killed everyone. He said to himself, "Oh! I have been unlucky taking fish, but I have been able to kill many men." So he cut off their heads.

He took the heads because in burial custom they were taken and left in ancestral shrines. When the son returned the mother was angry because he had not taken fish. The boy responded that he had collected heads and that he had inaugurated the canoe. The woman was not happy, because she was worried of future enmity. The women sank the canoe in a place where today a stone resembles a canoe. (Aswani 2000: 49–50)

This tale serves to explain why heads were taken to inaugurate canoes. Yet what is striking about this excerpt is the way that it depicts headhunting as a mistake—the misinterpretation of a mother's instruction to hunt the fish that would feed them. Far from celebrating the expansion of local power, the mother laments the inauguration of a time of perpetual war.

Chiefs and warriors who when to fight were not simply strong and brave, they were also stupid, crazed, or immoral—they became *tuturu*, the same term used to describe ogres and other quasi-human beings. Violence was not a natural state, but was brought about by rituals that often involved the consumption of things that no proper human would ever consume. My Ranonggan interlocutors explained that, before setting out on headhunting expeditions, warriors would eat pieces of taro dipped into the putrid liquid that oozed out of the decaying corpse of a chief. In Roviana, warriors were fed a pudding containing the flesh of a particularly fearless lizard as well as "scraped tree bark from where women and children had previously defecated" (ibid.: 60). There were other contexts associated with chiefly installations and warfare in which people became senseless and acted in ways otherwise considered abhorrent. Alice Beikera (the second wife of Beikera, whose story is quoted above) told me that when a chief of her father's *butubutu* was installed, her father took off his loincloth and danced around naked, his genitals flopping about in all directions. "Why?" I asked, surprised at this behavior at a chiefly installation. "Why indeed!" she replied. "Because he was happy? The crazy behavior of those people before."

The death of chiefs and the violent sacrifice of foreign victims are moments where the cosmo-political order is overturned and reinvented. In his discussion of "stranger kings" in Polynesia, Marshall Sahlins argues that Fijians and Hawaiians do not view power as inherent in the nature of the world. Power is aberrant; it is figured as coming from elsewhere: "power is not represented here as an intrinsic social condition. It is a usurpation, in the double sense of a forceful seizure of sovereignty and a sovereign denial of the prevailing moral order. Rather than a normal succession, *usurpation itself is the principle of legitimacy*" (Sahlins 1985: 80, original emphasis). In Polynesia and the western Solomons, such inversions have hints of the carnivalesque as well as the gruesome; things that are shameful and horrible become permissible and laudatory. Or, in the words of the narrator of the history of the so-called "stupid clan," "good and bad—all of it was good to them."

Today, people of Ranongga and the rest of New Georgia look back to the nineteenth century and previous eras as a "time of darkness" that they have now transcended through their embrace of Christianity. Some images of this moral transformation are derived from Christian doctrine and narratives, but narratives about stupid greedy ogres and proto-human ancestors of modern humans suggest that the stories of progress from an era of ignorance and violence to an era of enlightenment and peace have a much longer history.

At the center of these stories of transformation are engagements with people considered to be radically "other": strangers, foreigners, or enemies. In the folk tales and *butubutu* histories this chapter began with, quasi- or proto-human beings are depicted as having existed in stupid isolation until they learned to properly engage with other people and distinguish between strangers and kin. The remembered ancestors who figure in stories of *pinauzu* and other accounts of warfare from the last few centuries did engage with strangers in a way those mythical beings did not. However, those "people of darkness" (*tio rodomo*) were ignorant of what is now taken to be the truth of the Christian Gospel, namely that all humans are a single family, children of one Father, and we need not kill one another. From the perspective of the present, especially as depicted in dramas of welcome and celebrations of Christian conversion, these ancestors were—like their mythical forbears—stupid, violent, crazy, and not really properly human. The present is clearly superior to the past. Yet, this progressive narrative is ambivalent. The transition from ignorance to knowledge, from violence to peace, and from worship of ancestors to the worship of God, has also led to a certain diminution of power and potency.

## Notes

1. It is possible that the metaphor of the coconut invokes a history of headhunting. In upland Sulawesi, dry coconuts were substituted for heads in rituals commemorating headhunting (George 1996: 96–99). Although Aswani (2000: 63) reports that the severed heads of enemies were carried like bundles of coconuts, there is little evidence that people of New Georgia made use of the iconicity of coconuts and heads through either metaphor or post-pacification ritual substitution. Until the 1930s, turtles, not coconuts, served as substitutes for living captives or severed heads in the mortuary rituals that were a key driver for headhunting.
2. Throughout New Georgia, captives are called *pinauzu* or *pinausu*, which is derived from the verb *pauzu*, which means "to adopt." In Kubokota and Luqa languages, there is a lexical distinction between *pinauzu*, which I am glossing as "captive," and *pauzu-na*, which could be glossed as "adoptee," and is used for adopted children, as well as pets.

3. Most translators have used "giant" rather than "ogre" to gloss *iliganigani* or corresponding terms in other vernaculars (*malivi* for Roviana and Luqa, *ruruhu* for Marovo). For examples of ogre or giant stories from Ranongga, see Aqar (1989), Pavukera (1989), Piukera (1991), and Keza (1989); from Roviana, see the collection compiled by Sister Lina Jones and Rev. E.C. Leadley in the 1930s and 1940s and edited by Jully Makini (1991: 52, 70–72); for Hoava (New Georgia), see the collection by Karen Davis (1991: 4–7, 21–31, 42–47).
4. Several of my interlocutors found it inappropriate that one man's version of such a story was published in a book of custom stories, although for different reasons: some felt that the teller had given away what he should have kept secret lest his enemies use it against him, while others were bothered by the fact that because it was published, this version would have more force than the alternative stories that they supported. If publicizing such stories is problematic, so too is failure to publicize them: many people lamented that the true history of the island was lost when the last generation of chiefs died without passing on their knowledge to their successors. In recounting these histories, I provide the broad outlines of the stories I heard and try to indicate the points at which there was disagreement amongst my informants.
5. David Akin, personal communication, June 2014.
6. These themes are found in several of the Western Solomon Islands stories in collections cited above. In a discussion of animal tales, Kirtley and Elbert (1973: 245) discuss several stories involving one character tricking another into putting a body part into a giant clam shell; in one example, from Bellona, a female ogre is tricked into putting her finger into a clam and is drowned by the rising tide.
7. Several features of these Ranonggan proto-lineages are also evident in origin myths from Arosi. One lineage is said to have arisen through the mating of two quasi-human mythical beings: *pwapwaronga* and *masi* (Scott 2007b: 139–40). *Pwapwaronga* are very short, strong, reclusive autochthons who are still understood to defend the island against trespassers (Scott 2012, 2013). In their primordial state, *pwapwaronga* did not have fire and ate uncooked food; they also did not know how to give birth properly and cut the child from the mother's womb. Only when a female *pwapwaronga* mated with a male *masi* could they reproduce without the sacrifice of the mother. In contrast to the clever *pwapwaronga*, *masi* were "remarkably stupid" in ways that caused their deaths (Scott 2007b: 14). Like Ranonggan *tuturu*, *masi* are said to have been killed by a sago palm they were trying to catch to prevent damage to the leaves; they also had the unfortunate habit of launching canoes from cliffs.
8. Hocart's informants claimed that this practice was long abandoned in Simbo and attributed it to Roviana people (Hocart 1931: 315–16).
9. There is a marked difference in funerals among United Church and Seventh-day Adventist communities. United Church members continue to carry out a series of mortuary feasts, but Adventists say they do not mourn excessively because they have faith that they will soon be reunited with loved ones when Christ returns.
10. My discussion draws on my observations of many funerals as well as recorded interviews with Muleduri of Obobulu village, Sesolo Walter of Bagu, and Vezi Vavira of Pienuna village on the occasion of the death of Evalyn Qago.
11. This point was also made to me by David Akin, personal communication, 6 June 2014.
12. Hocart wrote that taking a head or captive in honor of a chief to set the widow free is known as *teku vavolo*, translating *vavolo* as the last death feast or a great war

feast (Hocart 1922: 90). It seems likely, however, that Hocart might have mistaken *vavolo*, a term for a large feast, for *vavulu*, which my friends used to describe the people (or person substitutes like turtles) brought ashore in the context of mourning. Interestingly, *valulu-* is a term that requires the inalienable possessive suffix (normally the third person singular suffix *–na*, thus *vavuluna*) that is also used for kin terms and body parts. It would seem that the sacrificial victim always belongs to the person for whom they were sacrificed.

13. Chiefs' funerals are still more elaborate than others, but fewer and fewer of the current generation of chiefs were installed in the way that Ranonggans say is necessary—through a gathering of all of the island's *butubutu* during which the chief was seated on top of traditional valuables (*bakia*). Most are now more like heads of families; they are chosen by their own siblings as first among equals, and are not shown the elaborate respect that was accorded the chiefs of the previous generation.

14. See Munn (1986: 163–80), Battaglia (1990), and Foster (1995: 97) on other matrilineal societies of island Melanesia.

15. Founders of the Christian village who died prior to World War II were buried near an ancestral skull shrine on Leva Point, which gradually became swampy. Those who died later were buried a few hundred meters inland. Their elaborate cement gravestones are clustered in a site along the main path into the village on the first small plateau that is home to the current church. The bones of some village founders who died before the war were disinterred and reburied at this site. After this generation had died (the last to be buried there was Pankera, who died in 1996 at the age of 98), the dead have been buried not in a central locale but within smaller family hamlets.

# 4
# Bringing the Gospel Ashore

On 1 August 2005, a fleet of canoes appeared around Leva Point, approaching Pienuna village. The beach looked abandoned, but as the canoes came ashore, warriors sprang out from behind bushy undergrowth and came down from trees, brandishing spears and axes as they threatened the disembarking travelers. Dressed in bark loincloths, shell ornaments, and white body paint, they yelled, "Kill them!" and "Go away!" A few moments later, a senior woman came across the beach and pushed her way through the young men. "I am the *kalao bangara* (chiefly woman) here! This is my village! Allow them ashore!" The warriors retreated. The woman led the visitors up a path from the beach, where they were garlanded with flowers and greeted by village leaders. The local Girl's Brigade chapter, dressed smartly in blue and red, marched them to the church, where nearly one thousand attendees were assembled for speeches and music to open the synod of the central-west region of the United Church of Solomon Islands.

Such dramatic welcome ceremonies simultaneously assert ongoing ancestral sovereignty over territory and re-enact the historical moment when the first missionaries arrived on local shores. They play on what Sherry Ortner (1973) many years ago referred to as a "key scenario": a symbolic schema that cuts across otherwise disparate domains of life, that orders experience, and provides a pattern for action. That scenario is the arrival of strangers from across the sea. On one level, local people assert their ancestrally given right to either violently repel or hospitably welcome the strangers. The initial hostility of the warriors highlights the generosity of the chief of the land, whose intervention transforms strangers into guests. Within such a frame, Christianity appears as one of many other foreign ideas, goods, and people that have been welcomed onto local shores. Like the captives discussed in the previous chapter, it has been localized without ever losing its identity as something foreign. On another level, such dramas re-enact the moment when the distinction between local and foreign was made irrelevant. Unlike other good things that have arrived from across the sea, the Gospel of Jesus Christ—Methodist and Adventist missionaries alike espoused a distinctly New Testament version of the Christian faith—is understood to have eliminated differences between

92  *Engaging with Strangers*

**Figure 4.1.** Costas Paleo leads the mock attack on the arriving canoe of Bishop David Havea of the United Church. 27 May 1999.

**Figure 4.2.** Bishop David Havea and Marama Havea arrive at Pienuna village. 27 May 1999.

**Figure 4.3.** Sera Wesley with her daughters Hazel Piqebakia Paleo and Grace Nose Sasapitu. Sera is dressed as the old woman Takvoja, and the three are waiting to welcome delegates for a meeting of the central-west synod of the United Church. 1 August 2005.

Figure 4.4. United Church ministers arriving in Pienuna for the synod are welcomed by the community. 1 August 2005.

local people and strangers through a vision of the world where all are "one" in God. Modeled on old processes of incorporating others, these welcome ceremonies also dramatize the New Testament expansion of the followers of God from the Israelites to all peoples of the world. In this drama, the collectivity produced by the confrontation on the beach is a celebration of the Christian promise of universal, unbounded, community.

This 2005 welcome ceremony was clearly modeled on annual dramatizations of the arrival of the church on those same shores in 1916. According to the narrative that is the founding myth of the contemporary village order, a young man known as Paleo boarded a mission ship, and his relatives considered him lost. Years later, he reappeared, with other native evangelists, to bring the Gospel to his own people, and this arrival is celebrated in annual dramas on the anniversary of the founding of the church. The scene opens with a handful of men dressed in leaves, smeared with dirt, and decorated with white war paint, who are making burnt sacrifices to their ancestors. They see a canoe coming ashore, grasp their weapons, and rush down to chase away intruders. Paleo and his companions step ashore, dressed in spotless white shirts and black ties, carrying Bibles and staffs. They stand implacably as the warriors thrust spears and axes at them, crying "Go away!" "We will kill you!" "Do not dirty our sacred shore!" A woman, dressed in an old copra sack and her face smudged with dirt, steps between the warriors and missionaries. This is Takavoja, the *kalao bangara*, sister of the Vitu chief of Pienuna.[1] "Stop!" she says. "This is my child, Paleo. Let him ashore!" The violent warriors thus silenced, she leads Paleo away from the beach and into the heart of the village, where he holds the first Christian service.

Throughout island Melanesia, dramatic encounters between missionaries and local ancestors are replayed annually in a similar fashion (e.g. Gewertz and Errington 1993; Errington and Gewertz 1994; Young 1997). This process of memorialization has been explored in most depth by Geoffrey White (1991, 2013) for Santa Isabel, where the population joined the Anglican Melanesian Mission in the late nineteenth century. Anniversary dramas focus on the conversion of the last warrior chief, who drank the blood of a sacrificed child to mark his renunciation of his old gods, and then became the first Christian chief. In successive installation rituals for the island's paramount chief, the story of this warrior chief's conversion has been told and retold, linking past and present and situating the secular power of chiefs within the history of Christian transformation. The arrival of the church is equally central to local historical memory in Simbo, just south of Ranongga, where missionaries began working just one year after the Methodist Mission entered the Solomon Islands in 1902. In the early 1990s, Christine Dureau's elderly interlocutor described the men of Simbo awaiting the arrival of the mission ship "on the beach, carrying their axes, shields, spears"; the missionaries landed without violence, because they prayed to cool the anger of the local warriors (Dureau 2001: 147). In Simbo, Santa Isabel, and communities throughout the country and region, these dramas of arrival maximize the contrast between the violence of local ancestors and the peace of Christianity.

The dramas also enact a scene of "primal contact" between Europeans and local people (Young 1997: 96) that elides a century or more of sustained interactions. Their formulaic structures play on a crude contrast between benighted ancestors and their enlightened descendants. Not only are ancestors depicted as vicious cannibals and ruthless killers, they are also portrayed as stupid. A common, humorous trope in Solomon Islander stories caricaturing their forbearers involves an islander who finds Europeans to be delicious until he attempts to eat their boots! Such tropes are clearly beholden to racist missionary discourse that contrasted the benighted depravity of savage society with the enlightened virtue of Christian civilization (Thomas 1994). At the same time, as we have seen, they echo patterns evident in indigenous myths that depict the transformation from the ignorant amorality of proto-human beings to the knowledgeable morality of humanity (see Chapter 3). Those earlier myths focused on a movement out of primordial isolation into fully human engagement with strangers, an engagement that allowed ancestors to attain their fully human capacities such as birthing, cooking, speaking, and sharing food. In their Christian forms, these moral transformations entail a movement away from a world divided between strangers and kin into a utopia where there are no strangers, where humanity is completely united as members of the body of Christ and children of the same God. Like all effective ritual, these dramas combine formulaic structures with highly localized references, thus anchoring cosmic transformations in the here-and-now of local places and histories. In many cases, they are performed on the very same ground that the events occurred in the past by people descended from the modern-day culture heroes who brought Christianity to local shores.

People of the Western Solomons speak of Christianity as a thing that has traveled through space: they celebrate "the arrival of the faith" (*na lame na lotu*) or describe how ancestors "brought down the faith" (*na vagore na lotu*).[2] The arrival of Christianity is remembered, recounted, and re-enacted as a dramatic encounter on the beach, when the world was changed in a moment. In fact, conversion was a much longer and slower process. My interlocutors recalled the resistance of the old men who were unwilling to adopt these strange new ways, and who mocked and disrupted Christian worship. Their resistance seems to have focused less on the missionary's message than on its ritual form, and on the missionaries' bodily practices and modes of speaking. Stories about the early history of Christianity on the island thus offer a glimpse of a socio-spatial ordering of bodies now largely vanished. European missionaries worried about whether converts had really turned their hearts and souls toward God, but islander evangelists seemed to have focused more of their attention on localized powers that resisted the incursion of foreign persons, foreign speech, and foreign ways. Empowered by a spiritual force they experienced as more encompassing (but, perhaps, not so different than) the mantle of protection and empowerment offered by ancestors, these local pastors and teachers sought to neutralize the powers of dangerous spirits. They established Christian villages as spaces that were radically open, safe for locals and foreigners alike.[3]

Most of the processes I discuss here escaped the attention of the European missionaries posted at mission stations on neighboring islands.[4] Written missionary accounts occasionally mention local pastors or teachers, and the Seventh-day Adventist Mission records provide fairly extensive discussions of the work of early pastors in Ranongga. One of the best-known accounts of the conversion of an individual in the 1910s was written by Rev. R.C. Nicholson, an Australian posted at the Methodist station at Vonunu in Bilua just across the straight from Pienuna on the island of Vella Lavella. Nicholson's biography of Vella Lavella convert Daniel Bula articulated the tropes that Solomon Islanders have now made their own. Young Bula's father was the worst headhunter among the "vicious and blood-thirsty" people of Bilua, but, after being cured of an eye infection and taken on as a domestic servant, "Bula's heart opened to the Gospel Message as a flower opens to the sun"

(Nicholson 1923: 21). Yet many missionaries wrote of their frustration with a population that seemed slow, backwards, and unenthusiastic. According to historian David Hilliard, in the early days of the Methodist Mission in the Western Solomons, "the reaction of the Roviana people to the advent of the missionaries was one of indifference: both open opposition and enthusiastic support were noticeably lacking" (Hilliard 1966: 249). Many islanders, in turn, seem to have been frustrated that white missionaries, like other Europeans, rarely left their ships to come onto the beach to engage with local people on their own terms. Encounters between local people and Christian missionaries were probably marked by boredom, indifference, and misunderstanding, not the dramatic confrontations depicted in anniversary celebrations and contemporary welcome drama. Contemporary performances have mythologized this history of missionization, making the coming of Christianity the foundational moment of the contemporary social order.

In this chapter, I recount well-known narratives of dramatic encounters with missionaries and trace the subtler processes of spatio-social transformation that followed conversion to Christianity. Luqa was the site of the earliest mission efforts and the only region where the impetus came from mission headquarters, with Pacific Islander missionaries posted at Lale as early as 1903. In Kubokota, the Gospel arrived by accident, when young Paleo mistakenly boarded a mission ship and later returned as Pienuna's first missionary. In nascent Methodist communities of the 1910s, younger men championed the new practices of Christian worship against reticent elders. A decade later, the arrival of Seventh-day Adventism in Ganoqa was a top-down project, orchestrated by the last great war chief and carried out as the conclusion to his mortuary rituals. In the chapter's final section, I move forward two generations to consider a more recent phase in the embrace of new Christian work coming from beyond local shores: the arrival of women's fellowship. Throughout the Pacific, women's Christian groups have opened up new possibilities for women's collective action. Here I track parallels between accounts of the arrival of women's fellowship and the narratives of the arrival of the church, suggesting that women's fellowship can also understood as a force that originated beyond the island and was welcomed ashore to revitalize and transform local social life.

## Luqa: Desire and Disgust

Early Methodist evangelism focused on Ranongga's rugged western coast, densely populated at the turn of the twentieth century. Pacific Islander couples, first from Samoa and then from Tonga, were posted to Luqa and nearby Simbo in difficult conditions. Until two young men from Lale attended the mission school themselves, however, these foreign missionaries made little headway. Oral histories of the early encounters reveal ways of talking about bodies and persons that disappeared as converts adopted new bodily and discursive habits. Far from being a battle over souls, struggles around the Luqa mission in the early days focused on bodies: desire for the consumable bodies of missionaries, disgust at inappropriate practices of bodily excretion. Here as elsewhere, the problem is less the mission's message than its location.

According to oral history, the first missionary to alight on Ranonggan soil arrived at Kudu in 1903, just one year after the mission was established in Roviana. Dureau's Simbo informant recalls that after Chairman Rev. John F. Goldie and Rev. Stephen R. Rooney left Pacific Islander missionaries in Tapurai in 1903, they proceeded northward and stopped in Lale, Keara, and Kudu, where they left a married couple as teachers (Dureau 2001: 146; see also Hilliard 1966: 252). People of Luqa, however, do not recall that the teachers were allowed to come ashore. In 2000, Manase Resana told me of the encounter between his grandfather and the arriving missionaries:

> My grandfather, the chief Resana, Mata Resana, went down [to the beach.] Down he went. He saw and wanted the body of the ship man: "Ooh, if only that were mine, because it is so clean . . . it would be good eating because it's clean." So he went down. The dingy was coming ashore; he went down and waited with a battleaxe. He was quivering. He desired so strongly to quickly chop him down and eat him; to take him for his own. Because we are black, you see. So, when he saw that white man, he wanted him, he thought it was something that would be good to eat because it was clean.

According to Manase, Goldie and the other missionary hesitated, then turned around, went back to the ship, and headed back up to Munda. The tropes so common in narratives of the arrival of the Gospel, figuring ancestral figures as dirty, violent, and driven by desire, are evident in stark form in this story.

This was not Resana's first encounter with white men: two of his brothers and one brother-in-law had traveled to Queensland in previous decades. His son-in-law, Sado, had returned from Queensland not long after Goldie's first attempt to land a missionary at Kudu.[5] Manase told me that his grandfather Resana was so fierce that he would kill anyone who disagreed with him on the spot, but his worldly son-in-law dared to challenge his resistance to missionaries:

> Sado told Resana that Christianity was a good religion: There is no trouble, no drawing of blood; instead they just live peacefully, they are happy, and they eat together. Look at me. I'm a person from our

village and I went to Queensland. I was not killed, but I lived happily among them. So please don't chase away the missionary.

Sado convinced Resana that he had been wrong to threaten the missionaries. When Mr Goldie and a missionary Manase referred to as "Mr Adam" returned in 1904, Sado went with Resana to the shore and persuaded them to land (Goldie was hesitant because he recognized Resana as the axe-brandishing chief of the previous year). Mr Adam established a church on Ranongga and lived there with his wife and children from 1904 to 1908 under the protection of Resana.[6] In 1908, Mr Adam fell ill with malaria and departed on leave. Manase said that Mr Goldie agreed to send another Australian missionary to replace Mr Adam, but the white missionary (Rev. Tom Dent) was sent to Marovo instead.

Meanwhile, a few kilometers south near present day Lale, Samoan missionaries (whose names are not recorded in any mission histories I have consulted nor remembered by local people) did not enjoy the protection of a chief like Manase. According to people of Lale I interviewed in 2001, these teachers held *lotu* (services) and some people came to listen, but most were skeptical about this "new work."[7] The original mission lapsed in 1909 when one of the teachers died (Hilliard 1966: 295). Around the same time, two young men, Levani Ngopa and Matiu Koribule, went to school in Munda. When they returned to Lale, they held worship services, taught songs, and held reading and writing classes for anyone who would come.[8] Despite their own very partial knowledge of the Bible, or reading and writing, Ngopa and Koribule slowly paved the way for the re-establishment of the mission in 1914 with the arrival of Samu Aqarao, a Guadalcanal man who had worked as an indentured laborer in Fiji and was a member of the pioneering party of Methodists that arrived in Roviana in 1902. Facing resistance from the old chiefs, Ngopa led Aqarao to Ngaikeni, his own family's small hamlet, a fifteen-minute walk north along the coast from Lale.

Old men in Lale sought to undermine the work of the nascent mission, demeaning the missionaries and rejecting the new bodily practices that Christian ritual required. According to John Wesley of Lale, when Ngopa and Koribule instructed the congregation to close their eyes while praying, old men refused, saying they would fall asleep, or that someone could sneak up and kill them. They disrupted singing with comments like, "Why are you moving your mouth all around like that?"[9] While such a comment may seem inoffensive to non-islanders, it takes on a different meaning in a context in which any reference to the mouth, eyes, head, or face of an adult is deeply offensive. Indeed, to speak of the "mouth" of anyone in such a direct way would be either an insult or an example of the sort of "stupid" talk discussed in Chapter 3, and if old men made such comments, they surely did so in an effort to provoke an angry response. By recounting old men talking in such a way, contemporary interlocutors may again be drawing out a contrast between the crazy ways of the past and the sensible ways of the present, but it also conveys how profoundly Christian practice offended older bodily sensibilities.

Other stories seem to reverse racist caricatures of dirty ancestors and clean missionaries suggesting that, to traditionalists of Luqa, the missionaries were the ones who were filthy. The proper handling of bodily waste was and remains an issue of moral as well as hygienic concern throughout the Solomon Islands, a concern manifest most obviously in the menstrual taboos well known for Malaita (Akin 2004) but present in other forms throughout the country. Voerini Aqolo of Lale told me of a story she heard from the "time before," in which a small child was said to have defecated on a piece of large bamboo that was used for cooking. Because the panicked mother had no shell valuables to substitute for her child's life, she threw the child away into the river in order to avoid the retribution that would otherwise fall on her whole family. Voerini wondered at the "crazy" (*tuturu*) ways of people of the past: "A child is of great importance, but the fact that it squatted on the bamboo is unimportant." The chiefs of Lale, it seems, were worried that the missionaries who arrived in the 1910s brought sickness and epidemics (not an unreasonable anxiety, given the new diseases sweeping through the region). They were angry that the missionaries built their homes on the walking path along the shore, not inland. As John Wesley of Lale recalled the history, the old men kicked them out, saying: "They are going to defecate near the settlement (*pea tata*). These are people who have 'arrived from elsewhere' (*tio kamudi*), they will just shit all over the place."

From its base in Ngaikeni and under the leadership of Aqarao, the mission gradually grew. More and more people settled near the shore at Lale walked to Ngaikeni to join in the singing, feasting, and celebrations. At last, the chiefs offered to build a church and relocate the mission to the center of the settlements at Lale. There, it began to thrive under Devita Ofa (or "Opa"), a Tongan missionary posted to Lale whose name, unlike those of the earlier Samoan missionaries, is remembered by people of Luqa and recorded in the mission archives. A photo of Ofa from the early 1920s shows him at Lale with a large congregation of more than fifty people, both women and men, young and old (Bensley 1925). Ofa departed in 1925 following the death of his wife and infant twin babies, whose graves remain near the shore at Lale.

## Kubokota: A Lost Son

The arrival of Christianity in Kubokota is the narrative I know best. I first encountered it the evening of my arrival, when John Wesley Paleo told me of how his father, James Paleo, was send by Goldie to evangelize his relatives at Kubokota, and how the chiefly woman Takavoja welcomed him ashore against the resistance of old chiefs and priests.[10] I observed its dramatic re-enactment in two anniversary celebrations held in February, and, in modified form, on other occasions, such as the visit of Bishop David Havea in 1999 and at the time of the synod in 2005, and even when my parents visited Pienuna in 1999. The longer history of Christianization, which involved the neutralization of emplaced ancestral powers, emerged gradually as I asked my friends and interlocutors to tell me stories of the dozens of named and inhabited or formerly inhabited areas along the coast and inland on coastal paths around the village.

As with so many other stories, the arrival of the Gospel at Kubokota begins with the arrival of a ship. Sometime before 1910, two young men were processing copra with an old man, Noso, at Pejapeja, approximately half way between Pienuna and Obobulu. One young man's real name was Betijama, but he had been known by the nickname Paleo since he played with a fish of that name as a young child. The other young man was Nyatakera Tetebule. According to John Wesley Paleo:

> So there they were, drying copra, they were drying copra there, and they saw a ship heading toward Pienuna here. It had come from Gizo. So the old man said, "Hey, here's a ship!" when he saw it. "Hey, a ship for buying copra," they said. "Okay, you two kids, let's pack everything up so that we can load it and go up to the ship," said that old man Noso. So they packed up, loaded on the copra, got into the canoe, and took off. The ship there lowered its anchor at that island there, the island at Inuzauru.

Noso and the boys paddled up to the ship to sell their copra. When they came alongside it, young men from Roviana aboard the ship explained that it was not a trader's ship but a mission ship belonging to Reverend Goldie. Noso and the boys climbed aboard, and the Roviana crew told them of the school, where men were learning to read, write, and sing. Paleo and Tetebule listened with great interest to these stories. "Hey. What if the two of us followed, went off for school?" Paleo planted the idea and Tetebule agreed; overhearing their plans, the Roviana crew asked them if they really wanted to come, then sought permission from Mr Goldie, who agreed. Old Noso, however, began to argue with them. "I led the two of you here, and I didn't listen to your relatives, your mothers and your fathers. When I go back down, they will rebuke me." Tetebule was moved by Noso's objections and could not decide whether to stay on board the mission ship or go back ashore. He decided to go ashore, climbing back down into the dugout. Then as the ship pulled anchor and started its motor, he tried to climb back on.

But it was too late and he was left behind. Paleo continued on to Munda, where he was baptized "James," learned to read and write, and declared his intention to become a missionary.

John Wesley thought his father had probably been at Munda for nearly ten years when Mr Goldie announced that he would take him back to Pienuna to evangelize the people of Kubokota. With Paleo was a Roviana man named Nekulu, who was half-Ranonggan and wanted to take the trip with Paleo to visit his relatives. As in narratives recounting the return of war canoes, John Wesley narrated the return with close attention to the voyage itself, naming all of the many stops along the way, describing the ships they used, and the engine trouble they encountered on the way to Vella. In the end, the ship landed at Aena plantation (near present day Suava), and Goldie remained behind to oversee repairs, sending Paleo, Nekulu, and Pastor Makapivo of Vella Lavella in a small launch down to Pienuna.

At Pienuna, the old men who saw the ship coming raised the alarm, telling all the children to run and hide, lest this child-stealing mission ship strike again. As Paleo's launch was coasting ashore on the breakers south of the point, the old woman Takavoja, who lived at Pienuna with her husband and children, came down to see what was happening.

> So she recognized James Paleo. "Hey, he looks like my child. There," she said. "Oh, it is Betijama, Paleo!" So, she went down to Tiqi where they were landing, as they came up onto the landing place, Takavoja went down and hugged him, "Oh, my child, long ago you left, but now you have returned!" She was so happy, she wept. She was overjoyed, that old woman Takavoja, the *kalao bangara* (chiefly woman).
>
> So, Pastor Makapivo of Bilua spoke. "Here is your child, the missionary, the pastor. This is your missionary here. You look after your child. I've brought him down, so you look after him," said Pastor Makapivo.
>
> "Good," said the old woman, "very good." She took him up to her room, her family house, and settled him there.

The pastor from Bilua led a prayer service, then departed for Aena, where Goldie was waiting with the repaired ship.

This narrative mirrors the structure of stories of the return of war canoes in the days before pacification. Men ventured out to distant lands to take heads and captives; women played an important role in rituals of welcome, making foreigners safe in the local place. Throughout island Melanesia, they intervened after war raids, claiming captives as "children" and preventing them from being sacrificed (Macintyre 1983, 1995). White writes of an encounter in Santa Isabel that mirrors the events at Pienuna, in which a chief's wife protected an indigenous evangelist against warriors by hanging tapa (barkcloth) around his neck (White 1991: 39). In Biak, West Papua, too, Christianity arrived through efforts of a mother and her son, who was captured as a child in a raid and sold to a Molluccan trader who was a Christian convert; the boy became Biak's first evangelist and was brought home by his mother (Rutherford 2003: 33). Here as elsewhere in the broader Austronesian-speaking world (see Brenner 1998: 134–70), women are responsible for domesticating valuable but potentially dangerous foreign persons and practices.

No axe-and-spear-wielding warriors met James Paleo at the beach in the way that is depicted in welcome ceremonies and anniversary enactments of these events. John Wesley Paleo explained that Takavoja was chastised by the old men, including her brother Sagobabata and an ancestral priest Sagela:

> "What do you think you are doing, settling this youth here?" they said. "We don't want him to come and do any sort of work here in Pienuna. This is a sacred shore. Sacred. We propitiate ancestors in shrines on this shore." They argued, back and forth, but the old woman refused to back down. "So you, you want him to do this *lotu*, this thing he brought ashore here, you don't want to leave it? You carry it over to the rubbish place. You go over there and lay in it."

The "rubbish place" was the *sigu*, where women went to give birth, and also the women's toilet area. If the old men at Lale objected to the missionaries for fear that they would turn the shore into a toilet, in this account the old priests of Pienuna want to avoid such contamination by sending Paleo and Takavoja to carry out their newfangled foreign practices in the toilet.

But Takavoja prevailed and the *lotu* was not moved to the toilet. Later, the *sigu* area became, appropriately enough, the village medical clinic. Instead, the old men relocated ancestral shrines from the shore at Pienuna to Leva Point, which is thought to remain powerful and is forbidden to women. I learned of it just a few days after my arrival in Pienuna in October 1998. I was swimming in the direction of Leva Point when young Prudence Kevin, only seven years old at the time, yelled and waved me in to the beach, explaining that "we girls" cannot go there.

James Paleo began leading services in Takavoja's family house. As was the case in Lale, young men were especially attracted to Paleo, and he taught them songs, and then, after a few months, started a school. One of his tools was a roll of pictures of Jesus that he hung up as he explained that Jesus was the son of an invisible God. When Paleo held services, old men sat outside and heckled, yelling out when congregants were silent for prayer and laughing as worshippers sang hymns. They objected to the baptism of young men, saying that

**Figure 4.5.** James Paleo and Grace Nosequla with an unidentified soldier, in the hamlet of Zion in 1943 or 1944. Paleo and Nose are wearing traditional clothing for purposes of the photo. Interestingly, Nose wears a woven *bakia* necklace, which is part of male chiefly regalia. Photographer unknown, photograph courtesy of John Wesley Paleo.

this would incite ancestral anger. Not long after the church was established, an epidemic swept through the area (perhaps the devastating Spanish influenza of 1918), killing many of the most promising young men involved with the mission. The sickness was widely understood as ancestral punishment, and many residents fled back into the bush to propitiate the ancestors once more. By 1921, though, two of the men who had resisted Christian affiliation the longest, Sagela and Sagobabata, decided to leave their old "gods of darkness" and be baptized.[11] According to Sagobabata's grandson, Samuel Samata, when he was preparing to be baptized, the ancestors told him, "You will live nine days as a Christian, and then we will take you." Nine days past, then Sagobabata fell ill and died.

Around Ranongga, the Methodist Mission began to take root in the middle 1910s, not only in Luqa and Kubokota, but also around the Ganoqa settlements of Sabala and Qeuru. A pastor from Bilua (Vella Lavella), Pita Zitabule, was posted to Sabala in 1916, where he attracted the attention of a young orphan from Kudu, Devita Voeta, who became a missionary himself (Carter 1973). Zitabule was later posted in Kudu village, where he contracted pneumonia and died in 1924 (Bensley 1925).[12] In the mid 1920s, another Bilua pastor named Tevolo oversaw the construction of a large church at Sabala, opened by Rev. Goldie himself in a large ceremony that included the renowned Methodist bamboo band. Residents of Sabala told me that when Goldie blessed the church, he saw angels, and the original foundation post shone brightly. Not long after the church was opened, the mission instructed people of Sabala to move northward to Qeuru, which at the time had a small sheltered cove where the mission launch could land. Sabala was abandoned and gradually reverted to forest. Adventists from neighboring Modo removed most of the timber from the church except one post, which magically resisted all efforts to remove it, remaining in place until the early 1990s. After the 1952 earthquake, Qeuru was also abandoned when residents moved to the new village of Koriovuku. In the early 1960s, some disaffected Koriovuku residents returned not to Qeuru but to Sabala. At first, they "returned badly," suffering from illnesses that were blamed on "wild" spirits of abandoned ancestors who no longer recognized their descendants. Beikera of Keara, an ancestral priest turned Christian pastor, suggested that they protect themselves from these now unfamiliar and dangerous powers through prayer at the original post of the Sabala church blessed by Goldie in the 1920s. Although the church post had disappeared by the time I first visited Sabala in late 1998, the ritual was still being carried out for anyone staying overnight for the first time (*malabolo*); when I arrived, the pastor at the time took me to the site of the old church and prayed for my health and safety.

After a few years establishing the church at Pienuna in Kubokota, Paleo returned to Munda for further training, to be replaced by pastor-teachers from Bilua and Roviana. The best known was named Boazi Nunukujuku. Born in Vella Lavella, Boazi's mother was a woman of Kubongava, a *butubutu* that originated in Choiseul and had many descendants on Ranongga. Boazi arrived in Kubokota sometime in the late 1920s, married James Paleo's sister Emily, and lived in Pienuna until his death in the 1960s. Writing in the Methodist Mission periodical, Rev. A.A. Bensley reported that Kubokota (as Pienuna was known in missionary records of the time) was a "difficult village": family houses were in disrepair and people refused to work together for the community: "The people here seem most unresponsive and more difficult to deal with than out and out heathen" (Bensley 1931: 10). Later, he described Kubokota's pastor-teacher Boazi as "slow" in school and somewhat awkward in speaking, but loyal and dedicated; he won the trust of the uncooperative Kubokota people and completed a new church building on a hill above the shore at Pienuna (Bensley 1932). People of Pienuna remember Boazi not as slow and awkward, but as someone who possessed an almost crazy faith in God. Wherever there were dangerous devils, Matiu Matepitu of Pienuna told me in 2000, that was where old Boazi would make his garden or plant his copra. A stretch of coastline near Pienuna was known as Ole Tomete ("coast of the dead") until the early 1930s when Boazi renamed it Ole Tinoni ("coast of people") and established a coconut plantation there.

My interlocutors remembered one of Boazi's battles with non-Christian powers that occurred in the 1950s. In this instance, Boazi destroyed a powerful anthropomorphic wooden idol (*beku*) in a shrine a short distance south of the church at Pienuna. The story of this *beku* was told to me by John Pavukera of Pienuna. Long ago, four brothers of Nulu (the *butubutu* understood to be autochthonous to this part of Kubokota) saw frigate birds diving into the sea, and they launched their canoe to fish for bonito. Instead of fish, they found this *beku*, who looked just like a person and wore valuables around its neck. The youngest of the brothers brought the wooden figure onboard the canoe, which then demanded to be put down at Tobulu, a place on the northern coast of the island of New Georgia. The brothers explained that although they could not take it back to New Georgia, there was a place called Tobulu in Kubokota as well. The *beku* allowed them to install him there. When John Pavukera was young in the 1930s and 1940s, his elders still visited this *beku* in its shrine to ask for success in inaugural voyages of deep-water fishing canoes. Like most such shrine sites, it was dangerous to those who trespassed or sought to destroy it. A few years before Boazi destroyed it, Seventh-day Adventists from Modo reportedly cleared nearby land and disturbed the shrine area. When they returned to Modo, they fell ill, defecated blood, and died, a sure sign of having offended ancestral powers—at least from the perspective of people in the rival mission.

Precisely because it was so powerful, Boazi was determined to destroy this *beku*. He prayed to God, and then approached the *beku*, saying that if he did not fall sick in three days, he would come back. Three days passed and Boazi did not fall ill. He was unable to convince men of Kubokota to help him because they feared the power of the *beku*, so he recruited some men from Guadalcanal who were working on Panakera's plantations. At Tobulu, Boazi mocked the *beku* by presenting it with a packet of dirt instead a packet containing a root crop and nut pudding of the sort appropriate in ancestral propitiation. Then he set it alight. Matiu Matepitu told me that he was fishing on a canoe out at sea when he noticed a mix of light rain and sunlight, a sure sign that spirits were active, and so he paddled to the shore as fast as he could. Others remembered that thunder crashed terribly without a cloud in the sky. But Boazi prevailed. Laughing, Matepitu told me, "Boazi burned that *beku* to death; he killed it completely."

Other shrines around Pienuna were abandoned with less violence. Among them was a shrine at Tirovuku, a place near the present day village of Vonga. Like the *beku*, the powers installed in this shrine came from overseas. It belonged to Kubongava, the Choiseul *butubutu* that came to Kubokota via Vella Lavella. The Tirovuku shrine was home to the skulls of dead ancestors (*tomete*) and to a spirit being (*tamaza*), who was said to be a man of Choiseul, whose shark familiar dwelt in the outlet of the stream that flowed past the shrine. Paul Mumapitu witnessed the cooling of the shrine as a young child in the 1930s. He accompanied his uncles and two "*kastom* men" from Vella when they performed the final burnt offering at the shrine. It began with a kind of divination, known as *sabukai* (see Hocart 1922: 278). The *kastom* man of Vella swung his arm in a vertical circle while holding a shell ring, saying: "Today, your dwelling place will be cooled, so do not be angry, but accept our visit, so that we may leave you on good terms. These people whose shrine this is will then go back to Christian worship. So, when it is time for them to leave you, then, will you accept it?" The shell ring quivered at the apex of the circle, the sign for an affirmative answer. The party then began to prepare food, cooking bananas and cuscus in a stone oven. Though not prestigious foods, these constituted a proper traditional offering, not one intended to taunt the spirits like Boazi's dirt offering. When the food was cooked, they lit a fire on the shrine, putting first bits of banana and then cuscus into the flame while telling the *tomete* that this was their share. Then everyone present ate the rest of the food. Afterward, the Vella *kastom* man performed another divination:

> Now your authority and worship has ended. So they will leave you here to stay. We have already given you a share of the food, so don't be angry. You can't ask after them, you can't do any kinds of things or

ask about these men to whom this shrine belongs. The stream will be cool. All of you the *tomete* whose skulls lie here, you will stay still here and no one will bother you, in your dwelling place.

When this divination was finished, it began to rain, again with alternating showers and sunshine out of the blue sky. Then, the *kastom* man took a kind of ginger, chewed it, and then spit it all over the shrine. They went down again toward the coast to the stream that comes out at Vonga and he did the same into the water, and then jumped in. When he came out of the water, he declared the job done. The powers of the place were not completely neutralized until decades later when women began to bathe in the stream. The first woman to do so was Ezi, Mumapitu's wife and Boazi's daughter. After that, Mumapitu explained, the Kubongava shark familiar disappeared forever.

The idol at Tobulu and the shrine at Tirovuku suggest some of the ways that the pre-Christian spiritual landscape was animated by a range of foreign powers, some of which floated ashore (like the *beku*), some of which were sought out and captured in war raids (like the ancestors of Kubongava). Other stories suggest that the dead of migrant *butubutu* were sometimes enshrined in the shrines of their hosts or allies (this was the case for Vitu and Kubongava, for example), but sometimes then were able to establish their own distinct or linked shrines (like the Kubongava shrine at Tirovuku). As Keesing argued for Kwaio (Keesing 1970, 1982b), relations of kinship were determined less by birth than by death, and communities were defined by their shared propitiation of shared shrines. The destruction or abandonment of these shrines freed people to orient their lives around the new ritual center of social life: the church.

## Ganoqa: The Last Raid

When the first Seventh-day Adventist missionary arrived in Modo four years after Paleo returned to Pienuna, the old men neither mocked nor resisted the church. Here, Christian conversion resembles the "heroic history" that Marshall Sahlins describes for the conversion of Thakombau in Fiji, when the conversion of the entire polity followed from the actions of its leader (Sahlins 1985: 35–54). Adventists of Ganoqa would reject the ways of the past more vehemently than their Methodist kin on the island, but the narrative of the arrival of the mission follows historical precedent most clearly. The missionary was taken as a willing victim in one last great war raid commemorating the death of the chief Beibangara.

As a matter of policy, and in contrast to the Methodists, the Adventist Mission worked through strong chiefs and their regional alliances rather than relatively powerless young men like Paleo in Kubokota or Ngopa and Koribule in Luqa.

The church originally emerged in the context of millenarian expectations and disappointments in the United States in the 1840s and 1850s, officially founded in 1863 under the leadership of prophet Ellen G. White, who was still living when the mission spread from Australia to Solomon Islands. The opening was provided by Roviana-based England-born trader Norman Wheatley, who had become disillusioned with the Methodist Mission as it became clear that Goldie was making the church into a major competitor in the copra trade, and assisted Australian-born Pastor G.F. Jones to establish a base at Viru Harbour in 1914 (Hilliard 1966: 416–17, Steley 1983: 41–42). The Adventists expanded rapidly among Marovo communities that had refused to join the Methodist Mission. Hviding (1996: 119–20) suggests that many of the most powerful Marovo chiefs were unwilling to enter as junior partners in alliances the Methodist Mission had already established with rival polities. In an interview with me in 1999, Apusae Bei recalled that his father, Beibangara, was angry with Goldie for breaking a promise to establish the mission at Modo by landing the first missionaries at Luqa instead. When he heard of Wheatley's attempts to bring a different mission to the Solomons, Beibangara agreed to accept that new mission once he had completed the last great feast (*vavolo*) to install his successor.

Adventism came to Ranongga on the path of old routes of alliance between Ganoqa and Dovele district on northern Vella, a frequent launching point for raids across the New Georgia Sound to Choiseul. An Australian missionary, Pastor R.H. Tutty, and one of the first indigenous Marovo evangelists, Barnabas Pana, established a mission station at Dovele in 1918. In 1917/18, men of Ganoqa attended a great feast with their allies at Dovele.[13] According to Pastor Shem Niqu of Buri, whom I spoke to in 1999, Beibangara's brother Avoso attended and was impressed by the English language used for singing, saying that he wanted to get this language for his grandchildren (see Hviding 1996: 119–20; McDougall 2012). Soon after the Dovele mission was established, Pastor Jones also attempted to establish a mission on Ranongga. Hilliard reports that Pastor Jones traveled to Ranongga in 1918 with two indigenous missionaries, Riringi and Rono, but was unsuccessful in establishing them there because the powerful chief of Modo, Beibangara, was in Roviana at the time (Hilliard 1966: 431). According to Tonili and others of Modo who recounted the history of Adventism at Modo for me in 2000,[14] the missionaries arrived at a place called Kelekele.

> So, Pastor Jones said, "How would it be if I leave these missionaries here at Modo?" Tutijama and Kaptain replied, "Oh, no, this is the place of the *bangara* of Modo over there. It isn't us who are *bangara* here." "But, should I land these missionaries?" said Jones. "No, because the *bangara* went up to Roviana, so wait; he will be back soon and will welcome the missionary ashore," those two said.

The incident seems to show variability in the power of local chiefs of early-twentieth-century Ranongga—just a few kilometers to the south in Luqa, residents seemed willing to welcome Methodists ashore despite the objections of chiefs and priests. It also confirms the fact that welcoming missionaries ashore was seen as an assertion of sovereignty, not to be undertaken by those without proper authority.

Beibangara did not return. According to his son Apusae Bei, before he died in Roviana, he made his successor Niqusasa promise to bring the church to Modo. Up until then, the death of a chief like Beibangara would have required a long-distance raid to acquire skulls or captives. In this case, a raid was called at the conclusion of Beibangara's funeral rituals, but rather than returning with the skulls of slain enemies or war captives, the warriors returned with a missionary. Apusae Bei called the Seventh-day Adventist Church his father's *vavuluna*, the sacrificial victim whose capture or death ends the period of mourning and allows the enshrinement of the chief's skull.

In telling the story of the arrival of Adventism in Modo, Tonili of Modo and others I spoke to in 2000 drew out the parallels between this voyage and war expeditions of the past. Like John Wesley Paleo in describing his father's voyage from Roviana to Pienuna, they recounted the names of all the places where the canoes stopped. Two canoes departed to Baga, the island southwest of Vella Lavella, where one canoe remained while the other continued to Dovele. It went ashore at a place called Irivabika, and they found the missionaries bathing, a classic scenario in stories of surprise attacks in war raids.

> So, they sat down together and talked, "We want a missionary," the people of Modo said. "That is fine. So who do you want to go with you?" said their leader, Mr Tutty. "This one, this black man here, this is our missionary, the one we want," they said, and they took Pana.

With Pana loaded into the canoe, the Modo warriors left Dovele for Baga, where they stayed overnight, singing the song that the missionary had begun to teach them: "Come to Jesus." As the canoe crossed from Baga toward Vori, the canoe began to shake (*begobegolo*), and though the men paddled with all their might, the canoe would not move forward.[15] According to Pastor Shem Niqu, these were "devils" seeking to repel the missionary. Eventually, the voyagers said, "We do not belong to you; we have brought this man here and we are going to *lotu*." Thus abandoned, the devils no longer resisted, and the men paddled on to Vori, where they built a large fire to signal to those waiting at Modo that the expedition was successful and they had acquired a missionary. Departing from Vori and proceeding up the Ganoqa coast, they blew a conch to announce their triumph. The canoe landed at Sabala, but residents wanted to stay with the Methodist Mission, "where you get to eat nice things with your yam and taro . . . We like to chew betel nut and smoke, so we have no interest in [Adventism]." Proceeding to Modo, the canoe landed as the sun was going down. By the time that they arrived, the news had spread all up and down the coast. Pana waved a white flag to signal the start of the service and everyone came together at the shore. The first service was on 22 May 1920, with more than two hundred people.

The history of this Adventist community suggests a more instantaneous transformation and a more thorough rejection of past ways than occurred among the Methodists. Some aspects of the transformation were gradual. Would-be converts in Modo and elsewhere had to undertake extensive Bible study before they were baptized as full members of the church. The taboos that set Adventists apart from their neighbors (their avoidance of pork, shellfish, smoking, drinking, and betel nut) were also not immediately adopted. John Matepitu of Modo told me that Pana worried that this would be too difficult for new converts, so he observed them himself but did not force his followers to do so until they decided through Bible study that consumption of these foods and other things was forbidden. Before their baptism, residents of Modo killed all their pigs, had one last feast, and then abandoned pork forever. Ranonggan Adventists today emphasize the completeness of their grandparents' break with the past. According to Tonili:

> The old men from the time before also found the transformation of the people of Ganoqa to be a matter of great wonderment. The worship of the spirits of the dead that was practiced before, that was really, really strong among the people of Ganoqa before. But when the mission came, absolutely everyone abandoned those practices completely, so there was none, none—that is how the old men told it. [. . .] When they converted, not a single one of them maintained [the old practices], all of them left completely.

They burnt wooden carvings and threw shell valuables and stone figures into the sea. Shrines still remain in this area, but they are treated with disregard and they are denuded of the shell valuables that remain on many shrines within United Church areas. (See Fig 3.1.)

The contrast between Adventists and United Church adherents with regard to the lingering powers of places is striking. Like sacred spaces in Australia (Maddock 1974; Biernoff 1978; Munn 1996), the old emplaced ancestral powers are thought to reject foreigners. They sense foreign speech and respond particularly hostilely to questions like "what is this place?" or "who lived here before?" that are both ignorant and aggressive (knowing the stories of places is an important part of power over places). Whenever I ventured beyond garden areas in United Church communities, I was told not to ask such questions until we returned safely to the village. In such situations, my hosts were always careful to say something like, "Oh, all of you grandparents; this one is with us, she has white skin, but she's our daughter [or granddaughter, depending upon my relationship to the speaker]." United Church people do not approach ancestral shrines carelessly; I was told about several individuals rumored to have stolen shell valuables from shrines and to be suffering various life-long afflictions as a result. Some shrines are still forbidden to women, and all should be avoided by anyone not accompanied by someone with intimate knowledge of and connections to the places. Both times Jebede Toribule took me and other outsiders to the remarkable shrine complex of Kubokota, he watched the landscape for signs of ancestral approval or disapproval (once, for example, he feared that a snake across the path was blocking our way, but when it moved away upon our approach, he took it as a sign of assent). We visitors hung back until Jebede and other men cleared away the brush, spoke to the ancestral spirits, and opened the site for viewing. No such respect or caution is shown in Adventist areas. When John Matepitu led me to a skull shrine on the hillside above Modo, I was surprised when he told me to climb on top of the boulder housing the skulls to pull the moss from a carving on its side; it was a disconcerting disregard of the customary pattern whereby the sacred was associated with men and kept separate from and above women's bodies. John Matepitu told me not to worry: there is not a single place around Modo where a woman cannot go, no ancestral powers to be avoided. All people are now completely free to go where they wish.

Both missions required adherents to abandon the worship of old gods and destroy the things associated with that worship. Islander missionaries, whether Fijians, Samoans, Tongans, or native evangelists from within Solomon Islands like Pana and Boazi, appear to have taken up such projects of destruction with a great deal of zeal (see also Hilliard 1966; Steley 1989). Writing of the widespread destruction of images and temples throughout much of eastern Polynesia between 1815 and 1827, and the taboo-breaking communal feasts that followed, Jeffrey Sissons suggests that participants in this "Polynesian iconoclasm" believed they were taking part in "a large-scale sacrifice, the common objective of which was the acquisition of greater mana and the consequent revitalization of their societies" (Sissons 2011: 301; see also Sissons 2014). It seems plausible that something similar was occurring in Ranongga—pastors and teachers were simultaneously waging war against ancestral powers, and sacrificing them to God in order to reinvigorate the social order.

## Women's Fellowship: New Work

In Adventist and United Church communities alike, Christianity is celebrated because it is seen to bring freedom, a freedom that is understood as particularly transformative for women. This perspective is widely shared around the Solomons, even by those who are critical of Christian freedom and who blame diminished male potency and general moral decline on the loosening of constraints on women's movement, sexuality, and bodily practices.[16] Writing of Vanuatu, Annelin Eriksen (2008) has gone so far as to suggest that the church itself as a domain is gendered female, in contrast to a realm of *kastom* that is gendered male. Although such a characterization is perhaps overly reductionist (Jolly 2012), it captures something of the everyday sense that the church is a realm particularly open to, even dominated by, women.

Narratives celebrating the way Christianity liberated women are difficult to reconcile with evidence of the ways that mission Christianity exacerbated existing patriarchal tendencies in indigenous sociality. Where they are mentioned at all, women appear in colonial and mission archives as wives, and are often likened to servants and slaves (Douglas 1999). Missionaries systematically overlooked the brother–sister relationships that were so politically and cosmologically important in many societies of Polynesia and island Melanesia, and their policies diminished the significance of sibling relationships (Gailey 1987; Jolly and Macintyre 1989; Dureau 1993, 1998b). A woman like Takavoja, who appears to have had significant social and political authority on the eve of Christian conversion, would have been excluded from neo-traditional forms of customary authority developed through native administration that began in the 1930s (Monson 2012; McDougall 2014). Early Christianity appears to have been an exclusively male affair. Two of my oldest interlocutors, Pize (1910–1999), a woman who grew up in the area of Qeuru and Sabala, and Lokasasa (1906–2000), a man who grew up in Lale, recalled that when they were children, women were excluded from services because men feared that women would be made lazy by sitting around in church all day.

Solomon Islands Christianity thus presents a paradox familiar to scholars of the religion in many places of the world. As the sociologist of religion Linda Woodhead puts it, the task is to explain why "women appear to be more numerous and more active in the churches wherever and wherever we have hard evidence about such matters," despite the fact that "Christianity has traditionally excluded women from positions of power, and often places more emphasis on the connections between divinity and masculinity than divinity and femininity" (Woodhead 2004: 128). Woodhead suggests that although much of Christian teaching supports patriarchal institutions, the overall message is one that seeks to restrain male power; in Christian theology, this world may be ruled by violent domination, but traditionally female virtues like love, humility, and devotion will triumph in the world to come. For much of Christian history, the church has offered the only public space open to women, and devotion has been among the few activities women have been able to undertake without scrutiny by husbands and fathers. Paradoxically, perhaps, "Christianity is most successful as a 'woman's religion' when it finds itself in a 'man's world' – a world it helps to reinforce, whilst ameliorating its excesses" (ibid.: 145).

Anthropologists are wary of such sweeping generalizations about gendered patterns, and we cannot simply assume that "love" or "violence" mean the same things across cultures or history. Yet Woodhead's generalizations resonate with western Solomons situations, where love (*variroqu*) is strongly associated with Christianity, and where women are seen to have a particular capacity for kin-based love (see Dureau 1994, 2012). During a 1999 Easter Bible study, women of Pienuna were asked to explain why the resurrected Jesus first appeared to his female kin rather than his male disciples. They agreed that it was because it is always women who love and mourn more intensely: women in Solomon Islands, they reflected, weep over the body, brush away flies, and suffer the stench of decomposition, while men go out and chew betel nut (McDougall 2003; see also Cannell 1998).

The paradoxical relationship between gender and Christianity emerges clearly in analyses of women's fellowship groups in the Pacific (Dureau 1993, 1998b; Dickson-Waiko 2003; Douglas 2003; McDougall 2003, 2014; Paina 2000; Paini 2003; Pollard 2003; Van Heekeren 2003, 2004). Often apolitical and apparently anti-feminist, such groups have brought about significant transformations in gender relations and social life over the past two generations. As Dickson-Waiko has argued, churches "provided the opportunities and space for women to move out of their homes and into the public sphere"; women's church groups are thus "the missing rib" of indigenous feminism throughout the Pacific region (Dickson-Waiko 2003: 103). Two generations after Christianity's arrival, in 1962, a woman of Marovo "brought down" Methodist Women's Fellowship to Pienuna. When the Methodist Mission became the United Church in 1968, it became known as the United Church Women's Fellowship (UCWF). Like earlier stories of the arrival of the Gospel itself, narratives about the coming of women's fellowship suggest that enlightenment, power, and knowledge come from beyond local shores.

Born in 1914 and raised in Marovo as a Seventh-day Adventist, Joyce Dunateko was trained as a nurse and midwife. She was undertaking further training at the Adventist school at Kukudu on the island of Kolombangara when the terrifying power of global war exploded in the quiet backwaters of the Solomons. Behind Japanese lines in 1942/43, Kukudu became a base for the islander coast watchers, who radioed reports of Japanese movements to the Americans. Among them was Simion Panakera (1902–1996) of Pienuna village. As one of the first generation of young men educated through the Methodist Mission in Roviana, Panakera became a pastor-teacher and was posted throughout the Bilua circuit in the 1930s; after World War II, he would become a central figure in the native administration of Ranongga. Against the wishes of Dunateko's family, they eloped and returned to Pienuna village, where Dunateko became a Methodist. Dunateko's children and grandchildren—my hosts for much of my stay in Pienuna—remember her at the head of a bustling household, full of food and people, combining customary hospitality with modern sorts of order and cleanliness (which included, amazingly, ironing and starching Sunday clothing). Dunateko's approach to domestic life seems to have been shaped by her Adventist upbringing, with its emphasis on the nuclear family household and the sanctity of the home. Dunateko's example suggests that women also benefited from the Adventist emphasis on education—even as an unmarried woman, she was permitted to undertake professional training away from home.

As Ranongga's first female trained nurse, Dunateko transformed birthing practices on the island. Here and everywhere in Melanesia, birthing was considered a dangerous and contaminating business; in Ranongga, women gave birth in hastily constructed huts known as *sigu*, positioned some distance from family houses. Women who died in childbirth, like men who died in headhunting raids, were said to have "died badly" (*uke ikerena*). Instead of being mourned, enshrined, and remembered, these "bad dead" were summarily disposed of (often dumped at sea) and their names tabooed. Male nurses had worked on Ranongga before Dunateko arrived, but women were understandably loath to give birth in the presence of men. Dunateko worked in partnership with a traditional midwife named Suluana to help to birth hundreds of children in the relatively sanitary conditions of the clinic, helping to decrease both child and maternal mortality. Though none of my interlocutors made this connection, I am tempted to see Dunateko's work in the light of the widespread myths described in the previous chapter concerning the inability of proto-human ancestors to give birth properly until they engaged with outsiders bringing new knowledge.

Dunateko's work as a nurse meant that she was widely esteemed by the women of Ranongga when she was chosen to represent them at a regional workshop held in Munda in 1962. Marama Carter, the wife of the last expatriate head of the Methodist Mission in the Solomons, called for participants to join a five day training program led by an expatriate head of a Honiara women's club. Panakera paddled Dunateko across to the mission headquarters in Vella, where she joined three other women and traveled on the mission ship to Munda in Roviana. At the end of the training, Marama Carter and the Methodist women decided to form not a women's "club" but women's "fellowship," and Dunateko returned with instructions to start such a group on her own island. When she returned, she approached Mary Atunauru—Takavoja's daughter, who like her mother was known as the *kalao bangara*—to seek permission to undertake this "new work" in Pienuna. From Pienuna, Dunateko spread the gospel of women's fellowship throughout the island, often driven by Panakera in what was one of the first motorized canoes on the island. Dunateko founded the Methodist Women's Fellowship, but she also helped to influence Adventist women to start branches of the Adventist Dorcas society around the same time.

Like the arrival of the church, the arrival of women's fellowship is celebrated annually in Pienuna. In 2000, the anniversary was marked by the unveiling of a large stone monument with a marble plaque dedicated to the memory of Dunateko, who had died in 1977. Though marred by poor weather and the tragic death of a young man in a neighboring village, it was a large affair, attended by UCWF groups from all United Church villages, as well as pastors and leaders from Ranongga, Gizo, Munda, and Vella Lavella. One part of the two-day program featured skits that dramatically re-enacted the moments when Dunateko "brought down" the women's fellowship in villages around the island. These dramas elicited uproarious laughter, especially when a daughter accurately captured her (often long-deceased) mothers' mannerisms and ways of speaking. Like stories of the arrival of the church, these skits also dramatized (and parodied) local resistance to this new Christian work. The Pienuna group focused on the resistance of men. The woman playing Dunateko spoke eloquently of women's obligation to raise a Christian family and maintain a Christian household; she explained how this group would help them do it. Pienuna husbands, however, objected: "You've got children to care for, I don't know why you're bothering to go. I suppose there will be nothing to eat later." The drama presented by women of Koqu illustrated another barrier to women's participation: their own backwardness. Just as dramatizations of the arrival of the church tend to begin with stereotyped depictions of "custom" (warriors in loincloths brandishing spears), this skit portrayed women in dirty, markedly "customary" clothing, undertaking quintessentially traditional activities like looking for nuts, cooking *nyete* (rotten nuts that were a distinctive food of old Ranongga), and sweeping the ground with an old-style broom. Dunateko arrived dramatically in Panakera's motorized canoe, called the women from their work, and began explaining the work of Christian fellowship. Her hosts agreed that the work was a good idea, but balked when Dunateko asked them to take on leadership roles of president, vice-president, treasurer, and secretary. One by one, the women demurred, saying that they count not read, write, or count, and that they did not know the Bible well. Finally, Dunateko cajoled the younger women of the group to take up the leadership positions.

At a church service commemorating the founding of UCWF, the island coordinator Zinia Naorongo (one of Dunateko's many granddaughters) delivered a speech about Dunateko's life and work. She said:

> Women's fellowship has really changed the life of women in Ranongga. Before Duna started the Women's Fellowship, women

were afraid to stand and speak in front of a gathering of people. Only men were pastors, traveled, went to school, and preached the word of God. Women were expected to go to the gardens and attend to the children . . . Today, we women can and do preach, share the word of God and our own thoughts. Women have fellowship with women, not only in our own family but throughout Ranongga, Western Province, the Solomon Islands, and overseas.

Ranonggan women remember their efforts being dismissed by their husbands as a waste of time—it was called *qurupu pavu goboro*, "group that makes you tired for nothing."[17] Deborah Van Heekeren (2003) rightly points out that these groups did create new work for women, work that they often found burdensome. At points during my research, women have lamented the fact that other activities of the fellowship group are overtaken by an emphasis on fundraising, and that they are constantly busy "searching for money." Yet women's fellowship organizations are conduits for new ideas and training, especially on such topics of cosmopolitan concern as human rights. While these global agendas are sometimes transformed dramatically in translation, one of the reasons that women value the UCWF is the way that it connects them to a wider world beyond their homes, villages, and islands. In recent years, some UCWF leaders have come to take on authority in the previously male realm of neo-traditional leadership as "tribal chiefs." This chiefly authority is much attenuated from the authority of previous years, and arguably also simply adds to women's work (McDougall 2014), but it is hard to overlook the significance of women's fellowship groups in opening new kinds of space for women's collective action.

Dunateko's memorial stone stands in the center of Pienuna, but she is buried in Jericho, a hamlet established in the 1960s by Panakera. The land was given to Dunateko and her children by John Pavukera. He is the son of Atunauru, the chiefly woman who allowed Dunateko to establish the women's fellowship in 1962, and grandson of Takavoja, who allowed Paleo to establish the church itself a generation earlier. But John Pavukera's authority over the land of Jericho comes not from his mother's side but from his father's side, for it is land that his father had cleared and planted a generation ago. At a ritual that marked the cementing of the gravestone of Dunateko's eldest son Geoffrey Panakera, who headed the hamlet and the family until his untimely death in 2005, John Pavukera asserted that this was Dunateko's land, given to her because she was a *tio karovona* (a person who has crossed over) who had come under his care. In most narratives of encounter, men travel across the sea to capture foreign victims or foreign knowledge, while women remain at home and help to domesticate the foreign implants. In that sense, Dunateko broke this gendered pattern because she traveled beyond the island to bring back the "new work" of women's fellowship. In other ways, though, she is a

**Figure 4.6.** Monument to the memory of Joyce Dunateko Panakera, who founded the United Church Women's Fellowship in 1962. The monument is a decade old in the picture. The children are Virginia Dunateko (Dunateko's great-granddaughter), Anna Dunateko Edele, and Marita Jioni. 4 July 2010.

quintessential *tio karovona*: a foreigner who arrives on a local shore and transforms the local social order.

## The Foreign and the Local: Inversions, Paradoxes, Disappointments

The inhabitants of Ranongga have been Christian for generations; their society is suffused by Christian ritual and structured around Christian institutions. It is a far more Christian world than the post-Christian societies of Europe, Australia, or even the United States. Yet, every year, residents of villages remind themselves that Christianity arrived from beyond local shores. The arrival of any stranger provides an opportunity to re-enact and remember the epoch-changing arrival of Christianity from across the sea.

The arrival of Christianity coincided with, and was intricately connected with, the establishment of the colonial state, an equally exogenous form, albeit one adopted with considerably more ambivalence than Christianity. The imposition of colonial order is understood as the natural consequence of the embrace of Christian peace, and to the extent that people identify with their nation, it is as a Christian nation. Although church and state are formally separate in most Pacific Islands constitutions, Christianity is a taken-for-granted feature of the modern nation-state throughout the Pacific (Tomlinson and McDougall 2013). Given this strong association between the modern state and Christianity, social movements that challenge the authority of the state but still seek spiritual power in Christianity have often sought to uncouple the two by claiming local origins for Christianity. From anti-colonial movements in nineteenth-century Fiji (Kaplan 1990, 1995) to messianic movements in late-twentieth-century West Papua (Rutherford 2000, 2003, 2006a, 2006b), such movements invert dominant narratives of Christianity's arrival by claiming Jesus or Jehovah as indigenous ancestors. Claims about the autochthonous origins of Christianity are at the heart of widespread myths linking Pacific Islanders to the lost tribes of Israel (see e.g. Dundon 2011; Handman 2011; Newland 2013), myths that are particularly prevalent in contemporary Malaita (Burt 1982, 1983, 1994b; Stritecky 2001a; Timmer 2008, 2012; McDougall 2009a) and, in more subtle forms, in Makira (Scott 2005a, 2007b, 2013).

Both the dominant narratives where Christianity is figured as exogenous and the counter-hegemonic narratives in which it is figured as endogenous reveal a persistent concern about origins and precedence. As Greg Acciaioli (2009) argues, precedence in Austronesian societies does not presume a single encompassing value or a single contrast according to which societies may be ranked in the way that hierarchical societies often are. Instead, precedence is a set of recursively organized oppositions between elder and younger, male and female, or land and sea. The status differentiations thus generated are "structurally relative, temporally contingent, and often disputed" (Fox 1996: 134–35). Whether local or foreign takes priority, the boundary between them remains a focus of attention and cultural elaboration.

This persistent concern with the distinction between local and foreign is paradoxical because Christianity teaches that the distinction is irrelevant. Among the Bible verses most often cited in sermons and devotion services in Pienuna were those from the apostle Paul's letter to the Galatians, "There is neither Jew nor Gentile, neither slave nor free, nor is there male and female, for you are all one in Christ Jesus" (Gal. 3:28, New International Version). Throughout the Solomon Islands, such universalism required not simply a change of heart, but a change to the landscape. In the long process of Christianization that followed the arrival of the church, local pastors and new converts sought to marginalize or destroy ancestral powers who responded hostilely to foreigners; they created new Christian villages where strangers and locals alike could live safely. Yet Christian communities on Ranongga, like communities everywhere, are internally divided. Sometimes this division is mobilized in ways that resolve in a more encompassing sense of collectivity: every community fundraising activity, for example, creates competing sides, temporarily dividing people into "others" before coming back together as one. But in other ways, the divisions that emerged out of Christian conversion are seen as a failure of people to live up to their convictions.

Denominational difference has divided those who were "just one people" prior to conversion. After 1920, the once-entwined socio-spatial worlds of Methodists and Adventists diverged: they ate different foods, worshipped on different days, no longer came together for major feasts, and (with some notable exceptions) ceased to intermarry. The animosity was not marked by physical violence, but since the 1920s, land disputes have pitted Adventists against Methodists in ways that people today liken to warfare. In the generations that followed, cultural practices diverged. Others have remarked upon the distinctly modernist orientation of Seventh-day Adventists in the Pacific (e.g. Ross 1978; Miyazaki 2004; Jebens 2005). In Ranongga, Seventh-day Adventist villages have a higher proportion of timber and sheet-metal roofed "permanent" houses to bush-material houses than neighboring United Church villages, with a great deal of care taken in cultivating clover fields and flower gardens. Education is emphasized within Adventist teachings, and Adventist schools in Solomon Islands are of a higher quality than government schools; outside of school, English-language Bible studies seem to make Adventists more proficient and confident in the language of modernist advancement. Because of greater labor mobility and the wider reach of church networks, large Adventist villages have higher proportions of in-married residents from beyond Western Province than many United Church villages.

Macro-sociological differences in institutional structures and values are manifest in micro-sociological interactions, including language use and bodily habitus. While Kubokota and Luqa remain firmly the first language of children in United Church villages, Pijin appears to increasingly be the first language of many Adventist children, even in rural villages. As among Kwara'ae Anglicans (Watson-Gegeo and Gegeo 1991), Ranonggan adherents of the United Church retain markers of formality and hierarchy in everyday language; like Kwara'ae Evangelicals, Ranonggan Adventists have put aside such features of the language.[18] Similarly, the avoidance behavior between classificatory sisters and brothers that is mandatory in United Church villages is largely absent among Adventists, and while young women who wear trousers in United Church villages are accused of undermining the collective moral code, young Adventist women do so without attracting criticism.

Ranonggan Christians tend to see denominational differentiation as an unfortunate consequence of their inability to live according to God's plan (McDougall 2013). This denominationally driven schismogenesis can also be seen as testament to an ongoing valuation and amplification of diversity that is so evident in many societies of the western Pacific, where diversity is not the product of isolation but of "the over-elaboration of every way of boundary-marking between tiny communities" (Besnier 2004: 107). With the proliferation of new Christian and non-Christian groups in the country, religious differentiation is inescapably tied up with cultural diversification (Handman 2011, 2013, 2014; Scott 2013).

In the next chapter, I turn from transformations of spiritual worlds to the transformation of regimes of property. These two topics are intrinsically related. The Methodist Mission was heavily involved in encouraging the production of copra as a commodity for sale. Local men who studied at the Methodist school in Roviana learned to plant, tend, process, and market copra. Moreover, as we have glimpsed in the story of Boazi clearing the coast of dangerous spirits to plant his copra, the expansion of plantation capitalism is understood to have required not simply the clearing of coastal forest, but the clearing away of dangerous abandoned spirits. Above all, it is in regard to immovable property that Ranonggans feel the contradictions of their faith most acutely. When people reflect on their present lives, they are likely to lament the ways in which promises of Christian unity and amity are unfulfilled. Disputes about property make people fear that rather than being a Christian world where strangers are kin, the world today is one where kin have become strangers to one another.

## Notes

1. Writing of Simbo, Hocart recorded *kalao* as the wife of a chief and *bangara maqota* as a woman of rank (Hocart:1922: 78). My interlocutors did not make this distinction

consistently. John Pavukera and Samuel Samata defined *kalao* as the wife of the chief, but Takavoja was often referred to as the *kalao bangara*, and she was clearly a woman of the chiefly *butubutu* and the sister, not the wife, of the chief.
2. Throughout much of the central and western Pacific, Christianity and Christian worship is known as *lotu*, a term that appears to have originated in Tonga and was used in Samoa and Fiji, home of many of the pioneering Pacific Islander missionaries of various Protestant denominations. Ranonggan Methodists use the term *lotu*, but Adventists use the term "church" or Pijin *siosi*. On Malaita, missions were often referred to as *skul* (Keesing 1989; Burt 1994b).
3. The spatial dynamics of movement between ancestral religion and Christianity has been described in most depth for Malaita, where ancestralists and Christians continue to coexist (Keesing 1985, 1987b, 1989b; Akin 1996, 2003, 2004).
4. Neither the Methodist Mission (established at Kokeqolo, near Munda, in Roviana in 1902) nor the Seventh-day Adventist Mission (established at Viru Harbour in Marovo in 1914) had a headquarters or European missionary posted on Ranongga prior to World War II. In both churches, the nearest mission station was on Vella Lavella. Modo chiefs got their missionary from Dovele in Vella; after 1916, Ranongga fell within the Bilua (Vella Lavella) circuit of the Methodist Mission (Luxton 1955; Hilliard 1966). Ranongga figured more centrally in the literature of the Seventh-day Adventist Church after the entire population of Modo, about 200 people, embraced the faith in a single day.
5. Hugh Laracy (2000: 4) notes that three Ranonggans were taken aboard a schooner named *Albert* under trader Captain E. Ancell. They were so mistreated by the head pearl-shell diver (the notorious Niels Peter Sorenson) that they abandoned the ship somewhere in Santa Isabel and were said to have been killed. According to recruiting records, fifteen Ranonggans worked as indentured laborers in Queensland and five in Fiji in the 1870s and 1880s before the plantation economy got underway in New Georgia (Moore 2013).
6. Manase Resana's account is difficult to reconcile with the mission record because he clearly described Mr Adam as white (that is, a European); in other narratives, my interlocutors distinguished clearly between Europeans and the other Pacific Islander missionaries who arrived. Mission histories, which tend to leave Pacific Islanders nameless but invariably record the names of Europeans, give no indication of a European "Mr Adam" employed by the mission in the early years. The September 1903 trip to Simbo included Goldie, Rooney, a European builder, and unnamed Pacific Islander missionaries, including two Fijians who went ashore at Tapurai (Hilliard 1966: 252; Dureau 2001).
7. John Wesley, John and Voerini Aqolo, Jekop Ngopa, and Moses Tukebei were among those who told me about the coming of the church to Lale from 25 to 29 January 2001.
8. John Wesley said that they went to school and returned in 1903, and that Aqarao arrived in 1904. Manase and most others, however, said that Aqarao arrived in 1914, coming to Luqa via Simbo. Jekop Ngopa, Levani Ngopa's son, said that his father went to school at the time that a Tongan named Ngai was on Simbo. Hilliard notes fewer Samoan and Fijian teachers volunteered, as the first teachers became disgruntled with their very low pay, European missionaries' aloofness, and the shockingly high mortality rates (Polynesian teachers, like Europeans, had no resistance to malaria, but they were not given furloughs nearly as often as Europeans were; many died of malaria).

After 1910, Goldie turned mainly to Tonga for Polynesian teachers (Hilliard 1966: 286–90).

9. Dureau (2001) reports similar reactions in Simbo.
10. John Wesley Paleo related the story several times to me; I tape recorded a version on 5 June 2000. John Wesley's account is far more detailed than the briefer stories enacted during anniversary celebrations.
11. John Wesley stated that they were baptized by Nicholson, who left Bilua in 1921 (Hilliard 1966: 300).
12. I spell the name as my interlocutors seem to have pronounced it. Bensley (1925) wrote of Peter Jitubule, who died at Kudu in 1924; Carter (1973) refers to a Pita Zitambulu at Qeuru in 1916.
13. The season of calm seas between November and early February was the traditional time for both feasting and war raiding in the region, now replaced by Christmas celebrations.
14. When I expressed interest in the history of Modo, elders of Modo called a community meeting after Sabbath services on 22 July 2000. Among those who contributed were Tonili, Sonto, John Matepitu, Lamusasa, Bejamin, Benson, Mixina, and Resili.
15. According to Aimi Koito, the daughter of one of the last *iama* (priests) of Modo, a shrine located on the island of Goi had special powers that were able to cross a great distance. I spoke to her on 20 September 2000.
16. Within the Solomons, such critiques have been long voiced by ancestralist Kwaio of Malaita when reflecting upon their Christian neighbors; more recently, similar concerns have been documented among second- and third-generation Christian men, especially those raised within evangelical churches (Keesing 1987b, 1989; Burt 1994b; Akin 2003, 2004; McDougall 2009a). See Tuzin (1997) for a classic analysis of the "death of masculinity" in a New Guinea society due to the arrival of Christianity.
17. See Dureau (1993), who documents similar sentiments for Simbo.
18. An obvious example concerns references to eating and food (*ganigani*). In United Church communities, guests are invited to "look at" or "take" "this little bit" here; only children are instructed to "eat." In everyday speech in Adventist communities, "eat" (*ganigani*) is used in most contexts. Watson-Gegeo and Gegeo (1991) note that Kwara'ae people can often recognize denominational affiliation of an unknown person from afar based entirely on gesture and bodily habitus. Among Ranonggans, such visible recognition is amplified by subtly different ways of dressing, as well as the fact that devout Adventists do not chew the betel nut that often stains their United Church neighbors' teeth brown or red.

# 5

# No Love? Dilemmas of Possession

"There is no love anymore, because we are always marketing." Ziosi Luke and I were watching canoes leave Pienuna village laden with garden produce that women were taking to Gizo market. Ziosi was telling me how times had changed. In the past, she explained, if a man caught a lot of fish, he would divide it up so that every household would share in the catch. But today, when a canoe full of fish comes ashore, the fishermen call, "Market!" and you buy the fish. Even siblings (*tamatazi*) sell fish to one another—they are no longer like siblings. Such a lament is a familiar refrain not only in villages around Ranongga but throughout rural and urban communities in many Pacific Island societies, serving as a sad self-critical reflection on daily life.[1]

The narratives of conversion discussed in the previous chapter depict the pre-Christian past as a time of darkness, fear, and violence. Yet in other situations, Ranonggans valorize the premodern past as a time when people truly respected and loved one another. They sometimes marvel at the way that their ancestors lived in good, loving ways despite the fact that they were not yet Christian. Pastor Izikeli Moata addressed these themes in a Luqa-language essay written for a vernacular literacy project. He explained that there was love in the past too because people shared, did not buy things with money, worked together, and held their property in common. "So because of this, we might say that those people before were not really people of darkness but they were emerging as people of light" (Moata 2000: 24).[2] In such ways, dominant narratives about triumphant Christian faith are undercut by pervasive reflections on loss and decline, a point that Matt Tomlinson (2009) has explored in detail for Fijian Methodism. This loss is sometimes understood as a sort of physical diminution, a sense that people are smaller, weaker, less populous than in the past. It is also evident in nostalgia for a time when people were obedient and knew their places in a hierarchical social order.

Today, Ranonggan chiefs (*bangara*) are praised for being kind, self-effacing, and generous, but the violent, powerful chiefs of the past are remembered with a certain amount of awe and admiration. Above all, what many people throughout Oceania feel they have lost in the transition to modern life is unity, especially the capacity to work together "as one" for common purposes (Barker 1990, 1993, 2007; Brison 2007; Schram 2013). Most people blame the expansion of the market for the rise of selfish individualism that prevents people from working together, but Christian ideologies and institutions are also important in understanding this pervasive sense of loss and lack. The constantly reiterated call to live in Christian peace, harmony, and common purpose directs attention to discord, disagreement, and willful individuality.[3] Given the Christian exhortation to view all humanity as a single family under God the Father, it is hardly surprising that a discourse about the failure to achieve this unity is so widespread.

Laments about the decline of love and the rise of the market also reflect changes in local political economy that have been occurring for generations. Trading is nothing new: in precolonial times, people of New Georgia engaged in long-distance trade for goods like smoked nuts, valuables, and tools; early European traders noted that their local counterparts were capable of driving a hard bargain. Over the course of the twentieth century, however, land itself became commoditized in a novel way as local people contested colonial land alienation and participated in the transformation of coastal land into copra plantations. Populations have increased exponentially, creating pressure on land that would not have existed in previous centuries. More recently, the rise of market gardening has transformed food itself into a commodity in a way that is both novel and disturbing. As in other Melanesian contexts, such developments have led people to seek to articulate divisions between their own possessions and those of other relatives, giving rise to both incipient individualism and the moral critique of such individualism (see esp. Sykes 2007a, 2007b; Martin 2013).

At the same time, though, laments about the proliferation of self-interested commercial transactions seem counterfactual. In rural Ranonggan villages, and even in many of the urban neighborhoods of Gizo and Honiara where Ranonggans reside, markets in locally produced goods are generally kept firmly on the margins of community life. Although most Pienuna households earn their primary income by selling garden produce in the Gizo market, few sell vegetables to their neighbors, who include salaried teachers and nurses who are often keen to buy such produce. The only locally grown item regularly sold within the community is betel nut, betel leaf, and lime; otherwise, only goods produced with store-bought materials are sold for cash. Villagers run canteens selling commodities like rice, tinned tuna, noodles, sugar, tea and coffee, fishing line, kerosene, matches, and other goods. Some women occasionally sell fried ring-cakes made of store-bought flour. When fishermen come ashore to sell their catch in the way Ziosi described, they invariably explain apologetically that the only reason they are selling the fish is to cover the high cost of fuel used in deep-sea fishing. Only during community fundraising events are locally produced goods sold on a large scale, with profits donated to the village school, church, or various community organizations. "Bring and buys," small markets, large festivals with food and handicrafts for sale, and even concerts in which the audience pays to hear songs are a regular feature of social life.

Far from being seen as a sign of anomie, disunity, and selfish commercialism, however, such fundraising is celebrated as precisely the sort of collective activity essential to a thriving community.[4] Even the Gizo market hardly seemed like the epitome of heartless capitalism. Writing of Biak in West Papua, Danilyn Rutherford described markets as places for the "creation, maintenance, and mobilization of intimacies" where "Biak shoppers acted in a way that transformed strangers into kin" (Rutherford 2001: 308). As in Biak city, in Gizo market money changes hands quietly, no one haggles over prices, and vendors do not compete with one another. People catch up on news and visit relatives and friends from other places. Ranonggan women selling produce arrange themselves on the northwest to southeast axis of stalls of the Gizo market in such a way that the market mirrors the social geography of Ranongga Island.

Instead of "always marketing," most people go to considerable lengths to avoid engaging in market-like transactions within their communities. At the time that I had the conversation with Ziosi quoted above, I had already learned that it was quite difficult to pay for anything. When I arrived to begin fieldwork in Pienuna, I had offered to pay for the renovation of an unused teacher's house that was designated for my use, but the offer was refused, even when I suggested that the payment could take the form of a contribution to the school. If I was to be a guest in the village, then I should not pay cash for food, housing, or any of the other things that people say they get "for free" from the forest, sea, and gardens.[5] A few weeks after Ziosi and I watched that canoe head off to market, the driver of another over-laden canoe forced two women to disembark. It was the last canoe of the day, and the women were sorely disappointed because many of the greens that they had picked in the evening and carefully parceled late into the night would be wilted and worthless when the next canoe departed the following morning. I was eager to buy their vegetables, but even in this situation, they sold some to me with great reluctance and gave me far more than I bought.

It seems clear, then, that laments about the decline of kin-based morality in the face of market relations cannot be taken as a straightforward description of social life. These laments do, however, reveal the extent to which people feel that self-interested buying and selling is antithetical to community solidarity. Such sentiments are widespread, of course, and not only in so-called kin-based societies. As Marshall Sahlins (1965) observed decades ago, different kinds of exchanges are thought appropriate to different kinds of social relationship. Close kin share with one another without keeping track of things, while more distant relatives, friends, and in-laws engage in balanced reciprocity over the long term, with an emphasis on the relationship rather than on the goods exchanged. Only strangers try to get something for as little as possible, focusing on the value of the goods exchanged rather than on the relationship that is created and sustained through giving and taking. Commercial exchanges might be seen as balanced or neutral, but they are often understood as hostile because they deny bonds between the transactors. As David Graeber has argued, "relations of violence and economic self-interest . . . are really just variations of the same thing: both reflect the way one acts with people towards whose fate one is indifferent" (Graeber 2001: 154). The implicit violence of economically self-interested action is reflected in Ranonggan vernacular languages: the transitive verb *vai-* ("take") can means both hitting or killing a person and buying something, both actions in which agents assert their will without regard for the object of the action. To treat kinspeople with such disregard is more than a moral breach; it effectively severs the bonds of kinship.

When people of Ranongga speak about the risk of alienating kin by failing to share with them, they often focus on sibling relationships. Siblingship encapsulates many conflicting principles of Ranonggan sociability: equivalence and hierarchy, intimacy and distance, solidarity and respect. There is no distinction in Ranonggan kin terminology between siblings and cousins as there is in Euro-American kinship terminology; any cognatically related relative of one's own generation is addressed and referred to as a "sibling." However, kin terms do differentiate according either to age or gender, but not both: one set of terms indicates whether a sibling is elder (*tuqana*) or younger (*taina* in Kubokota; *tasina* in Luqa) regardless of relative gender, whereas another term (*luluna*) indicates that the sibling is of the opposite gender regardless of relative age. A pair or set of siblings is referred to as *tamaluluna* if the cross-sex sibling relationship is the focus, or as *tamatazi* if gender is not emphasized. *Tamaluluna* should show respect to one another by avoiding bodily contact, contact with clothing, reference to bodies or bodily processes, and a range of other behavior. The obligation is reciprocal, but the onus of such restrictions invariably falls more heavily on women than men. Unmarried young women are criticized not only for inappropriate sexual behavior, but also for giggling too loudly, wearing trousers rather than skirts, or engaging in the many other kinds of behavior that allegedly demonstrate a lack of respect (*pangaqa*) toward their brothers. The most flagrant disregard of the *tamaluluna* relationship is incest, an offense that is understood to split apart the kin group (McDougall 2004: 96–107; McDougall and Kere 2011: 151–53). If siblings as *tamaluluna* should respect one another and maintain their distance, siblings as *tamatazi* must care for one another and live together as just "one person" (*maka tinoni*). When siblings breach the *tamaluluna* relationship through incest or a lack of respect, or breach the *tamatazi* relationship by failing to care for one another, they are said to have forgotten one another or failed to recognize the relationship. While there are many parallels in laments about the collapse of *tamaluluna* and *tamatazi* relationships, the notion of *tamatazi* is most relevant in discussions of property that are my primary focus in this chapter.[6]

Anxieties about people's failure to recognize siblings are manifest in critiques of people buying and selling things like fish to one another, but they are most intense in discussions of landed property. When senior men mediated disputes over land and property, they invariably referred to and addressed disputants as *tamatazi*, and reminded them that they should not be arguing about land because they were "not different people" and should live as one. Even in ordinary conversations I had about land or property relations, my Ranonggan friends frequently reminisced about a time in the not-so-distant past when people lived together as siblings and owned all possessions in common. This sentiment was expressed poetically in vernacular languages: *qe vari-izongo, qe vari-tamatazi* (they owned things together, they were siblings together). Many evoked this sense of cooperation and oneness by describing the way that their grandparents and great-grandparents planted *Canarium* nut trees (*neni* and *ngari*) together in a grove (*aoro*) without worrying about which tree belonged to whom. Today, they explained, everyone is eager to assert their own individual claims over clearly delineated blocks of land. As much as they wished that they could share their possessions and live with relatives as "just one" in the way their ancestors had done, such a course was impossible in these selfish times. Sadly, the children and grandchildren of people who had lived according to these old ethics often found themselves without sufficient land for subsistence and commercial activities.

It is no surprise that worries about alienation and anomie are most pronounced in relationship to land. As in other Melanesian societies, kinspeople are not only those who are born from the same ancestors but those who live on, eat from, and are buried in or enshrined upon the same ground (e.g. Feld 1982; Fox 1997; Rumsey and Weiner 2001; Leach 2003; Scott 2007b; Sahlins 2013). Anxieties about alienation of kinspeople through transactions of land are focused less on outright buying and selling than on the assertion of discrete rights of ownership over land that could be claimed by a range kinspeople. Today, Ranonggans find it both necessary and deeply problematic to assert individualized rights to land against people of their own *butubutu*, their father's *butubutu*, and others who should be treated as siblings not "other people."

This moral dilemma presents a practical challenge to people who want to assert differential property rights without alienating their relatives. One

Dilemmas of Possession 129

**Figure 5.1.** Rosie Ekera gathering *Canarium* nuts (*ngari*) in a grove above Pienuna. August 2005.

way that they address this challenge is through ritual. Reflecting on Sahlins's discussion of the sociology of exchange, Joel Robbins and David Akin observe that "not only must people be in the right kind of relationship (or potentially in such a relationship), be transacting with the right kind of objects, they must also be doing so in the right way" (Robbins and Akin 1999: 9). In other words, the *mode* of exchange is crucial in moral judgments of transactions. Whether the context is mortuary prestations in Melanesia or Christmas gift exchange in the United States (Caplow 1984; Carrier 1993), ritual allows transactors to frame their giving and taking as a particular kind of action with a specific message about the nature of their relationship to one another. Ritual action is characterized by a certain formality of speech and action, and this formality offers clarity of interpretation. At the same time, though, ritual allows for a degree of paradox and contradiction difficult to sustain in non-ritualized transactions. Many of the rituals discussed here allow actors to "do" quite different things simultaneously.

The chapter begins to track dynamics of possession and alienation evident in many realms of Ranonggan life by focusing on a relatively simple transaction involving a canoe. What is particularly interesting here is the care that recipients of the canoe took to be sure that their gift was not interpreted as payment for services rendered, but as a token of their love for the canoe maker. To make this message clear, they presented the goods in the form of a nearly obsolete ritual that would "quiet the adze" of the canoe maker. Before turning to more complex transactions involve immobile property, I reflect on the different qualities of food, currency, and customary shell valuables called *bakia* as media of exchange, and tease out locally salient distinctions between "land" (*pezo*) and "property" (*izizongo*) that are sometimes mapped onto introduced legal concepts such as "primary" and "secondary" rights. The following three sections describe different forms of ritual through which people assert their possession of landed property. The most straightforward of these rituals is called *pajuku*, but while I heard a lot of talk about *pajuku*, these transactions were quite rare. More commonly, people asserted their property rights in funeral rituals and other events. Assertions of rights over property also occur in other kinds of ritual, and I conclude with a detailed analysis of a ceremony that sought to "heat the ground" of a recently resettled hamlet.

In analyzing these rituals, I focus not only on the material objects transacted but also the speeches that accompany these transactions. Scholars who have written about Melanesian relationality have suggested that ceremonial exchange serves to symbolically cut off relationships between cognatically related people (Wagner 1967; Strathern 1988; see also Chapter 1). The very act of exchange divides those who take part into two opposed sides as giver and taker, creating clearly bounded groups out of the webs of kinship that bind everyone to everyone else. In the Ranonggan examples I discuss here, gifts of food and, especially, money or shell valuables symbolically articulates such divisions, but the talk that accompanies such gifts serves the opposite purpose. As is common in Pacific societies (Myers and Brenneis 1984), Ranonggan ritual speech is often indirect, with a message that can be interpreted in multiple ways. Speakers often deflect responsibility for the outcome of the talk and give the audience a role constructing that outcome. Over and over, those presenting substantial quantities of food, money, and valuables dismissed these material objects as nothing more than the ongoing nurture that kin ought to expect from one another. Through the medium of material goods, actors assert rights over property in ways that exclude kinspeople; through their talk, they reassure their kinspeople that they will continue to share in the possession of the property.

## Transaction of a Canoe

In 1998, Grace Nose and her husband Joseph Sasapitu returned to Pienuna village after several years of residence in Choiseul. Energetic and concerned about earning money to pay school fees for their three young daughters, they planned to plant large gardens to produce vegetables for sale in Gizo and to run a trade store in Pienuna—endeavors that required a large wooden canoe that could carry a heavy load. They approached Grace's "grandfather" (her mother's maternal uncle) Simion Beto of Sabala village to ask for a canoe.

Beto's father Diavara was among the last men on the island who made plank-built canoes (*qeto*) used in long-distance trade, fishing, and warfare before the colonial government's pacification campaign of 1899/1900. As Hocart wrote in a paper on canoes and bonito, ritual was "just as much part of making a canoe as cutting of the boards" (Hocart 1935: 109). Plank-built canoes are not longer made in New Georgia, but Diavara passed his skills in carpentry onto his son Beto by sharing a bespelled betel nut. Beto was well known as a craftsman of large dugout canoes (*mola*), used with 15 or 25 horsepower outboard motors as the primary mode of transport from Ranongga to Gizo. Beto was an old man by 1998, and he had already passed this skill onto his descendants. It was manifest in different ways: one of his sons had exceptional skill in building modern-style houses with sheet-metal roofs and sawn timber frames, another son had skills in reading and writing and excelled at school, and a nephew had the ability to see designs in stone and pioneered modern stone carving on the island.

When Grace and her family asked for a canoe, old man Beto agreed to make it. Together, Beto's children and Grace's brothers and sisters worked several days together in the forest between Rava and Sabala to fell and hollow out a large tree that belonged to Beto. Forty or fifty people joined in pushing the canoe out of the bush down to the coast at Rava village, where a small feast was held to feed those who had helped. Beto lived in Rava while crafting the canoe with the help of his son. The work progressed slowly because Beto was frequently sick and, in the course of his efforts, he announced that this would be his last canoe because he was old and tired. The canoe was completed in August 1999, blessed by a minister of the United Church (Grace's sister's husband), and towed back to Pienuna.

Back in Pienuna, Grace, Sasapitu, and Grace's siblings and parents invited Beto's children and grandchildren to join them in what they called *moko temoko*, a nearly obsolete ritual aimed to "quiet the adze" of the canoe maker. Grace spoke first on behalf of her parents, brothers, and sisters. She thanked God, their grandfather, and all who had participated in making the canoe, blessing it, and preparing the feast. She then pointed out that although Beto had made two previous canoes for her brothers and sisters, this was the first time they had thanked him with a *moko temoko*. Finally, she said that the canoe was not for their family alone, but for everyone in the community. Although other canoe owners often charged fees to use their canoes, anyone in the community, the church, and the *butubutu* could use this canoe without paying. Then Nose's father, old man John Wesley Paleo, tearfully addressed his own children and grandchildren, entreating them to remember that Beto's children were their siblings. "Today it is not as it was before," he said. "Help one another. Recognize one another, and help one another." Today, he lamented, everyone

**Figure 5.2.** John Wesley Paleo and Simion Beto with the canoe made by Beto for Paleo's children. September 1999.

simply buys canoes. Turning to Beto, he apologized that they could not present him with a *bakia*. He hoped that the poor substitute of cash would adequately convey their feelings.

With this, Grace's brother Dixon brought out a large basket of cooked food, a 25 kilogram bag of rice, several tins of tuna, a few rolls of cloth, packets of soap, and other store-bought goods. Grace also handed Beto an envelope containing cash, saying, "Because you were hungry, you were tired, we want to give you a little, five hundred; it is not large." Receiving the cash and food, Beto said that this helped keep the families together. He said that he had made many canoes, but no one had prepared a *moko temoko* for him: "You have followed custom [. . .] We are all very happy." He began to sit down, but then stood up again, and told them all to keep asking his children for help, even though he was now too old to make any more canoes for them. He said that "other people" (*goto tinoni*) could not ask one another for help, but that they should not consider his children "other people." Finally, Grace's mother Sera spoke, tearfully, of the importance of continuing the connections in coming generations. She thanked her uncle for helping her children, and for his persistence through times of sickness and hunger. She said that this would have been difficult if they were "different people." She said she was glad that Nose organized the *moko temoko*: "My sons loved you with money," she said, "but my daughter has gone beyond that."

All of the speakers thus went to great efforts to frame the exchange in a particular way. If Nose and Sasapitu had simply handed Beto an envelope of cash without calling their relatives together and also preparing cooked food, it might have been seen as a simple purchase of the sort appropriate to a stranger. Downplaying the significance of the amount of cash ("it is not large"), stating that it was for the old man's hunger and fatigue, and presenting the cash in the context of the *moko temoko* made the transaction an example of kinspeople helping one another. The transaction was not tit-for-tat payment but a manifestation of values associated with customary times, when kinspeople worked for one another rather than for profit. The canoe, as well as the money and goods, were a sign of love, of *variroqu*. Sera, Wesley, and Beto—who were all elderly—were moved by this expression of love, and entreated their children to ensure that it would continue to bind them together after they were gone.

## Food, Money, *Bakia*: Mediums of Exchange

Like people throughout the world, Ranonggans express anxieties about a social world they sometimes feel is increasingly dominated by money (see Bloch and Parry 1989; Robbins and Akin 1999). Yet, the example of the *moko temoko* makes it clear that the problem is not the medium itself: money can serve as a vehicle of kin-based love (*variroqu*). Here and in many other contexts, cash is presented as a substitute for food, which it can be used to buy. Sharing food is the quintessential act of kinship the world over. Not only do kin share food with one another, but the sharing of food can temporarily transform non-kinspeople into a single united body, a process familiar to Christians everywhere through the sacrament of the Eucharist.

In Ranongga and elsewhere in Melanesia, food is shared among kinspeople who are "just one," but it is also mobilized with modern and traditional forms of money in formal exchanges that serve to highlight divisions between givers and receivers. The distinction between shared food and gifted food became clear to me at a feast marking the tenth day after a death of Evelyn Qago in Pienuna in 2000. I carelessly referred to the feast an *ivata*, a term that refers to the banana leaves that are spread out on the ground for food that is served to a large group that sits together and eats all the food. Muleduri of Obobulu quickly corrected me: "This isn't a birthday party! We're making baskets for distribution, not just spreading food out on banana leaves." In funerals and other occasions of formal exchange, root vegetables (taro, yams, sweet potatoes, or cassava), puddings (made of root vegetables pounded with *Canarium* nuts or coconut cream), fish, and sometimes pork are parceled into baskets, and organizers carefully plan who receives how much of each item. These locally produced foods are often augmented with store-bought food such as bags of white rice, sugar, tea, tinned fish, and noodles, or with money

**Figure 5.3.** An *ivata* (feast laid out on banana leaves) following a marriage exchange (*vaia reko*) between Manakera Samata and Laela. 30 December 2000.

that is described as a means of acquiring such consumable foods.[7] As a gift, food has a useful ambiguity because even in situations in which it is gifted in ways that mark social divisions, givers can describe it as little more than sharing between kin.

Such interpretive ambiguity is absent in exchanges of *bakia*, a traditional valuable made of large rings of giant-clam shell (*Tridacna* sp.) that has been fossilized under the soil of uplifted coastal terraces. Literally and symbolically heavy, *bakia* seem to have a special capacity for transforming social and territorial relationships. *Bakia* were made through a laborious process of water grinding that was sometimes undertaken by war captives who were treated as slaves (Walter and Sheppard 2000: 307–8). I was told that it took as long to make a *bakia* as it takes a coconut tree to mature, and that one of the reasons no one makes *bakia* any more is that they have lost the magic that allowed people to grind the impossibly hard shell. There are many different kinds of *bakia*, the most valuable of which are those with a reddish streak from the joint of the clamshell from which they are made. *Bakia* are the most important type of shell valuables that were in circulation throughout New Georgia prior to the twentieth century, which included shell rings called *poata*, which is one of the words used for modern cash today (the other is *seleni*, from "shilling"). *Poata* was used as bodily ornamentation and was exchanged for a wide range of goods and services in old New Georgia. In contrast, *bakia* was worn only by chiefs and remains one of the quintessential symbols of chiefly power. Chiefs could also transact *bakia* for rights in land and people, but I was told that each chief had to retain at least one *bakia* as the "base of the basket" (*puru mane*). If this *bakia* was given away, his chiefly authority would dissipate.

Like other forms of traditional currency (Robbins and Akin 1999), *bakia* play an important role in rituals of social reproduction, especially in United Church communities. Although marriage rituals in the past were said only to involve the gift of an ordinary shell ring (*poata*) to the bride's kin, today *bakia* are transacted in marriage exchange. The groom's side should give a *bakia* to the bride's side as a sign that she is now a married woman, along with cash to be distributed to her brothers (*luludi*) as compensation for being forced to hear of their sister's sexuality. A more formal and public exchange often follows a church ceremony. Ideally, the groom's side should present three separate *bakia*, although often cash is substituted for one or two: one for the bride's head, one for her middle, and one for her legs. In previous generations, I was told, the woman's side refused to take the "leg" payment, thereby asserting the bride's right to return to her own place. Today, the woman's side often accepts the whole payment but reciprocates with a sometimes-equivalent payment to the groom's side, a payment that is said to "open the way for her to come and go."

*Bakia* also play a critical role in rituals of compensation (*ira*) for a wide range of offenses, including adultery, incest, and swearing and, in the past, murder and other violent crimes. Strongly associated with the pre-Christian past, *bakia* tend not to be transacted by devout members of tradition-rejecting churches of the region, including members of the Seventh-day Adventist and smaller evangelical churches (cf. Akin 1999a; Robbins 1999). Evangelical Christians and Seventh-day Adventists prefer to solve problems by prayer alone; some say that Christ's death was the compensation for all of humanity's sins, and that people who pay compensation today deny the significance of this sacrifice. People of United Church communities also believe in the power of God's forgiveness, and all traditional compensation rituals are opened and closed by prayer (see McDougall and Kere 2011). They feel, however, that the exchange of money and especially of *bakia* creates a kind of closure that talk alone cannot; these payments are said to "cover" the offense and prevent others from "opening" it up again. Because offenses often involve wrongdoing on both sides, compensation payments often involve equal exchange, with each side presenting the same types of valuable or the same amount of cash. Senior men who oversee the "straightening" (*varivatuvizi*) of these problems almost always recall that, in the past, people were killed or banished for the kinds of offenses that are now solved through talk; only if a chief put down a *bakia* would the offender be saved from death or exile.

*Bakia* lend seriousness to rituals of social reproduction and reconciliation thought to be lacking when only cash is transacted. But they are scarce. For decades, members of the Pienuna Chiefs' Committee have worked to codify local forms of customary law and to establish some sort of equivalence between *bakia* and cash. As the late Apusae Bei reflected in a meeting on customary law convened by the conservation organization WWF in 1999, a *bakia* is worth a human life, for they ransomed those condemned to death: it is impossible to assign a monetary value to either *bakia* or human life. Unlike cash, *bakia* cannot be exchanged for food or other commodities. It ought to be passed from generation to generation, serving as a durable reminder of relationships made and breached. Ranonggan leaders reasoned that the cash equivalent of *bakia* ought to be high so that people are afraid to commit the offenses that require payment of *bakia*. But they also worried that if the cash equivalent were too high, ordinary villagers would not be able to settle their problems in a satisfactory way and that only people with modern wealth would be able to purchase *bakia* for cash.

Made of stuff originally from the sea taken from under the earth, *bakia* are understood as anchoring people and *butubutu* to territory. All around Ranongga, ancestral shrines (*tabuna*) are full of a variety of shell valuables (see Figure 3.2). Most are broken and appear to have been deposited with the dead who are enshrined at these sites. Some shrine complexes also contain intact valuables that were described to me as the "anchor" (*titi*) of the shrine; these *titi* were either *bakia* or *kalo* (a whale's tooth). Should this "anchor" be removed from the shrine, the people who own the shrine are said to be unmoored from the territory that encompasses it. Some such shrines are now associated with *butubutu* thought to be autochthonous to Ranongga, but others are associated with migrant *butubutu*. As we have seen, Ranonggan myth and oral history is full of accounts of people paying for land with *bakia* and other forms of shell valuables. Today, most people discuss these transactions as land sales, but stories of *bakia* anchoring *butubutu* to land suggest that these exchanges served less to alienate land than to attach strangers to the territory of their hosts.

Gifts of food, even when formally presented in baskets, can be framed as part of the normal give-and-take between kinspeople. Cash can have the same meaning when it is presented as a substitute for food in the way that it was in the *moko temoko* ceremony described above. *Bakia* is quite different, and so is cash when it is presented as a substitute for *bakia* rather than food. Kinspeople do not give and take *bakia* as part of ongoing nurturing relationships. Only "others" give and take these durable valuables. One gives *bakia* to affines in marriage, to enemies in peacemaking, and to people of other *butubutu* in land transactions. Thus, in situations where everyone is related to everyone else in one way or another, the transaction of *bakia* clearly articulates divisions between transactors, at least provisionally or temporarily. But the transaction of *bakia* also binds "different people" together; it rejoins kindreds that are split by incest, it establishes alliances and creates affinal relationships, attaches the dead to the living, and binds foreigners to local territory.

## Land and Property

Before turning to rituals through which people assert property rights, it is necessary to explore some of the distinctions that Ranonggans habitually make when talking about land and property. The most critical distinction is precisely between *pezo* (land) and *izizongo* (possessions or property): *pezo* is understood to be vested in matrilineal *butubutu*, whereas *izizongo* is held by those whose labor created it. Such vernacular distinctions are often understood in light of a distinction between "primary" and "secondary" that was introduced by colonial legal systems by the 1950s (Scales 2004: 109). Yet such a mapping obscures the very different nature of land and property in local thought, and leads to an underestimation of both the durability and significance of rights to property.

*Pezo* means soil, solid ground, even the earth itself. In vernacular renditions of the Christian Lord's Prayer, for example, one prays that God's will is done on *pezo* (earth) as it is in *nulu* (heaven). In discussion of land rights, *pezo* refers to named and bounded territories understood to be held by *butubutu* of the same name. People of the *butubutu* identified with *pezo* are often described as "tribal landowners," but the term "ownership" does not really capture the mutuality of the relationship between people and land. As Daniel de Coppet (1985) wrote of Are'are' of southern Malaita, "land owns people" at least as much as "people own land." People understand themselves to be inalienably connected to the territory of their *butubutu* through ontological relationships given at birth. To the extent that connections between *butubutu* and land were forged through human actions and interactions, they occurred in ancient times. As a result, there is a strong metaphysical dimension involved in relationships to territory. Emplaced powers, including non-human beings called *tamaza* and the ancestral spirits of the dead called *tomete*, may respond hostilely to strangers and also punish the transgressions of their own descendants. Christians today do not feel that they fully understand or can control these emplaced powers and seek protection through the mantle of Christian spiritual power. Yet the notion that land remains dangerous is evident in the widely articulated belief that people who lie or fight about land will die prematurely.

Property (*izizongo*) is clearly distinguished from land (*pezo*). The word *izizongo* is a reduplicated form of the transitive verb *izongo*, which could be glossed as "possess" or "own." When combined with the inalienable possessive suffix, the term means "name" (*izongona* is "his/her name"). In the contexts discussed here, *izizongo* consists of what people say are "things on the ground" (*zakazava pa pezo*). Prototypically, a person's or group's possessions comprise of three such "things": groves of *Canarium* nut trees (*aoro*), land previously cleared for gardens (*buzubuzu*), and land cleared for settlement (*ia*). For several generations, copra plantations have also constituted an important form of property, but people continue to refer to the symbolically resonant triad of *aoro*, *buzabuza*, and *ia* when speaking of the things they possess. In striking contrast to land as *pezo*, these possessions are the product of human labor of recent generations. *Izizongo* is a sign of the work of grandparents or perhaps great-grandparents, not the mythical movements of distant *butubutu* ancestors; people have a sentimental connection to *izizongo*, but there is little mystery of the sort that often marks relationships to *pezo*. Because of this emphasis on the transformative role of human labor, the term "property" captures something of the meaning of the Ranonggan term *izizongo* in a way that it does not capture the relationship between *butubutu* and land.[8]

I realized the critical importance of the distinction between land and property when I witnessed the abrupt end to a dispute settlement early in my research. The dispute arose when one man planted sago palms without asking permission from another man who felt he had rights to the area where the palms were planted. The second man uprooted the palms of the first man. The Pienuna Chiefs' Committee was called to hear the dispute. When the man who had planted the palms without permission said he wanted to straighten out the real story of the land (*pezo*) in the area by tracing out genealogies, *butubutu* histories, and naming all of the taboo sites, the committee chairman quickly stated that they were called to hear a discussion about the area (*ia*) not the land (*pezo*) itself, and he ended the discussion. In this case and in similar disputes, the failure to seek permission to create property (*izizongo*) was no mere oversight; it was an overt assertion of rights to land (*pezo*).

Despite such an insistence on the distinction between property and land, this case illustrates the intimate relationship between the two. People have the automatic right to clear land, build settlements, and plant tree crops on land of their own *butubutu*, but should seek permission to create property on any land that is not their own. Although many Ranonggans think that it is best to live, work, and hold property on the land of their own matrilineal *butubutu*, few actually do so. Extra-local marriage is common. Many people are of *butubutu* whose territory is in distant lands because they are descended from women who came from elsewhere, but they have lived for generations together with local people who originally invited their ancestors onto the land. Such people are said to remain "under" those who initially granted permission for their ancestor to use the land, and today they often feel insecure about their tenure.

Ranonggans are clear that *butubutu* identity is passed only through mothers, but they are strongly connected to their fathers' kin and *butubutu*. As is the case elsewhere in island Melanesia with matrilineal clan or lineage systems, paternal nurture is essential to the making of the person: a person *is* the clan of the mother, but is *made by* the clan of the father. In many societies, this principle is made visible through mortuary ritual. If the bones represent the enduring matrilineal essence of the person, the beauty, wealth, and even the flesh of the person is the product of paternal nurture. In mortuary rituals, as the flesh comes away from the bones, the clan of the deceased returns valuables to those who have contributed to the making of the person (Munn 1986: 163–80; Macintyre 1989 Weiner 1988: 125–38; Battaglia 1990; Foster 1995).

People of Ranongga say that they are the *butubutu* of their mothers, but that they are "born of" (*vinapodo*) the *butubutu* of their fathers. In marriage exchanges, paternal nurture is presented as the direct equivalent of maternal nurture. The groom's side may make a special gift for the bride's mother called *kura*, the sling that women use to carry young children, and another one for the bride's father called *bita*, the bark string bag that men tie around their ankles to grip the trunk of coconut trees when climbing for young coconuts. Speaking at a wedding in 2000, Pita Dimei of Varovo village explained, "When the mother's breast milk does not flow, the father has compassion for his family and climbs for young coconuts for the mother to drink so that her breast milk flows and the child may be fed." People may not marry into their father's *butubutu*; in weddings and some stages of funeral rituals, they stand as children of their father's *butubutu* without articulating any distinction. In the past, and today, there are no strict rules governing post-marital residence. Couples often move between the husband's and wife's home places before deciding to settle in one or the other; this means that children often grow up on (and are thus "fed by") their fathers' rather than their mothers' land.[9] In practice, children of men are just as likely as children of women to live in hamlets and use gardens established by their parents or grandparents. Yet today, at least, people say that the property rights of people descended from men are weaker than the rights held by people descended from women.

Descendents of migrants should not need to differentiate themselves from the descendents of the hosts who attached them to the ground. Similarly, those "born of" men should not need to differentiate themselves from their fathers' kin and *butubutu* in ways that suggests they are "other people" rather than children of the *butubutu*. Yet pressure on land due to increasing population and more intensive use of land for market gardening, as well as increasing emphasis on principles of "tribal" landownership (a point I return to in Chapter 6), makes both children of migrants and children of men of the landholding *butubutu* feel that such a differentiation is necessary.

Similar tensions between lineal and cognatic kin are evident throughout the Solomon Islands, including places like Malaita and Choiseul with kinship and land tenure systems oriented around the patrilineal transmission of rights (Tiffany 1983; Burt 1994a). Yet, the matrilineal orientation of Ranonggan *butubutu* gives rise to a distinctive form of struggle between nuclear families and the larger matrilineal *butubutu*. Although *butubutu* identities are passed through women, men tend to exercise political authority over *butubutu* land. Moreover, men, not women, are understood to be responsible for the work of clearing primary forest that is the necessary first step in creating settlement areas, garden land, nut groves, or coconut plantations (Hviding 1996: 155–60; Hviding and Bayliss-Smith 2000). In patrilineal systems, a man who passes this property onto his children keeps it within his own descent group, but in matrilineal systems father-to-children inheritance is understood to remove the property from his descent group.

Today, indigenous differentiations between land (*pezo*) and property (*izizongo*) are understood through the lens of an introduced distinction between "primary" and "secondary" rights. Primary rights are understood as land ownership vested in corporate descent groups. Secondary rights are understood as usufruct rights to property on the land held by individuals and families. This mapping obscures the different nature of land versus property relationships discussed above, and suggests that the really important ("primary") rights are those concerned with *butubutu* territory. In fact, as James Weiner has argued for Papua New Guinea (PNG), understandings of customary landownership that emphasize the collective or communal nature of ownership elide the fact that "everywhere" "custom supports individual proximate rights in land" (Weiner 2013: 12). Only in distinctly uncustomary situations, like projects involving the large-scale extraction of resources, do people feel the need to emphasize genealogically inherited rights to large territories. Moreover, contemporary discussions of primary and secondary rights incorrectly suggest that rights established by means other than genealogical inheritance through a descent group are insecure or transient. As Martha Macintyre and Simon Foale note for Lihir Island in PNG, "over decades, rights by virtue of birth are hard to tease out from those acquired by residence and gift" (Macintyre and Foale 2007: 50–51). Although secondary or use rights are understood as non-transferable, Carrier explains that in Ponam in Manus Province of PNG, "three or four granting groups could stand between those identified as the original, fundamental owners of a piece of land and those who were currently using it" (Carrier 1998: 94). Rights to use property held by individuals and families are at least as durable as the putatively permanent "primary" rights of land ownership held by *butubutu*.

Property rights cannot be understood without some consideration of the physical qualities of the things seen to constitute property—that is, in New Georgia, the prototypical nut groves, garden clearings, and settlement sites. Edvard Hviding and Tim Bayliss-Smith argue that theoretically temporary rights to property in Marovo take on a "long-term, rather permanent character" (Hviding and Bayliss-Smith 2000: 80–81) because after clearing areas for swiddens, people plant not only short-lived food crops but long-lived tree crops, including trees used for canoe building and nut trees. Even after fast-growing tropical forest covers garden swiddens, the tall white trunks of nut trees mark sites of former cultivation. Generations after people moved away from inland settlement sites at the turn of the twentieth century, their descendents continued to return to trees planted by their grandparents and great-grandparents to harvest nuts or wood for canoes. The rise of a copra economy meant that people turned their attention away from planting these traditionally valuable tree crops to coconut plantations. In some ways, this did not significantly change the nature of land tenure. Like nut groves, coconut plantations were a long-lasting form of property that meant that anyone given the right to plant coconuts acquired nearly permanent rights to land on which they were planted. Yet there were significant differences. Nut groves are focal points in the landscape amidst gardens and settlements, while coconut plantation are rectilinear blocks usually planted with a single crop. Coconut groves came to cover much of the most valuable coastal land of a group, thus freezing what might have otherwise have been quite flexible forms of tenure. This changed context means that even if some of the rituals people today use to assert property rights existed prior to the twentieth century, the contexts in which they are used have dramatically changed (see Martin 2013).

In part as a response to the sense that too much land has been alienated to "other" people outside of the clan, some people in the matrilineal societies of island Melanesia seem to have attempted to deliberately reshape their own "custom" to make it more purely matrilineal. They prescribe strict matrilocal and uxorilocal residence so that people create property on their own clan lands, and thus claims are "straight" (Nash 1984; Eves 2011). Others, in contrast, have sought to introduce patrilineal principles as a means of individualizing land tenure, an effort that dates back at least a century in areas of intensive commercial development (Martin 2013: 30–31; see also Scott 2007b: 253–60). Both strategies—reasserting matrilineal ownership or introducing patrilineal inheritance—would result in less entanglement among individuals and groups. This entanglement is precisely what my Ranonggans yearn for when they look back to the good old days when people lived together like siblings and shared their possessions.

## Transacting Property through *Pajuku*

In *pajuku*, guests give food, money, and (ideally) *bakia* to the people who originally invited them to live on and work the land. By doing so, they affirm their rights to the property (garden land, settlement areas, nut groves, or plantations) that they created on land not originally their own. Although *pajuku* rituals were usually focused on property (*izizongo*), not land itself (*pezo*), people of the landholding *butubutu* were described as the *kutana* (base, ground, or root) and could expect to be invited to share in the food and valuables presented. One interlocutor explained *pajuku* to me in the following terms: "If you *pajuku* something, then you are free. If you don't *pajuku*, when you die the *butubutu* can take it back. After *pajuku*, the other people do not have any power." As with similar transactions in other parts of island Melanesia, the status of *pajuku* is contested. Some people consider it to be customary, while others see it as a corruption of custom; sometimes it seems like a purchase, but at other times it would appear that *pajuku* does not unambiguously extinguish the claims of prior owners.[10]

Like land itself, property is supposed to be inherited matrilineally: if a man clears land, builds a settlement, or plants trees, those things should be passed to his sister's children, not his own children. However, many children grow up on their father's land and want to inherit the property he created or worked during his life. To affirm their rights to his property, they may present their father and his *butubutu* with food, money, and *bakia* in a procedure called "*pajuku*-ing the hand of their father." Some people told me that this sort of transaction was not *pajuku* at all, but should be referred to as *laena*, but most of the time it was called *pajuku*. Often, a man may not work on the land of his own *butubutu*. Many people I spoke to about *pajuku* complained that children today try to *pajuku* the hand of their father even when their father might not have *pajuku*-ed his property from those who originally gave him permission to work on the land.

I often heard rumors that someone was planning a *pajuku*, but in almost every case, those orchestrating the exchange denied that what they were doing was *pajuku*. In the end, I witnessed only one event unambiguously described as *pajuku*, and it turned out to be quite problematic. In 2007, Maka (not his real name) was attempting to *pajuku* a few hundred meters of shoreline that contained gravel used for house construction. Although gravel is normally not sold, some time earlier a woman of the village purchased gravel for her employer in Gizo, and a dispute arose over the distribution of the payment. The wider area had belonged to Maka's grandfather, but had already been split up after rancorous dispute in the generation of Maka's long-deceased father. This 2007 *pajuku* was overseen by two members of the Ranongga Island Chiefs' Committee, a body established in an attempt to reconstitute the native authorities of the late colonial era. It thus has a quasi-official status, and the president of the committee explained that this transaction would have legal status, and if anyone tried to challenge the rights that were established they would have to go to court.

The mood at this gathering was glum. Maka had not prepared any food to accompany the money and *bakia*, nor did the participants sit down to eat together after the proceedings. Stating baldly, "Today, I want to buy and take [place name] along with the gravel," Maka put down one *bakia* and cash amounting to more than SI$600 (about US$80), explaining that half of the amount was from his wife and children so that they would hold the area after him. There were also smaller contributions from his brothers' and sisters' children, as well as unrelated people who wanted to have the future right to take gravel without payment. This was to be given to Kori (not his real name), who spoke on behalf of the *butubutu* who held the larger territory on which Maka's grandfather's property was located. Kori was also Maka's cousin, also descended from the same grandfather who owned this area. Kori asked Maka about whether he would charge people of the community for gravel. Maka gave an equivocal answer, saying that he would not "charge" but he expected that people would show him "a bit of consideration" by offering a small payment. Despite this unsatisfactory response, Kori accepted his payment, saying that the *butubutu* of his and Maka's grandfather had stopped acting like a *butubutu* generations ago (he was referring both to disputes and to cases of incest). Individualizing ownership was the only way to stop this internal bickering. Later, this *pajuku* was criticized for excluding many people who had a claim on the area; just a few months later, the entire coastline would be transformed by the massive April 2007 earthquake.

Different *butubutu* have different approaches to *pajuku*: some allow it, whereas others forbid it. Nulu, one of the autochthonous *butubutu* of the island, has a history of bringing people onto their land and taking some sort of payment for the land. In the twentieth century, the previous chief of Nulu in Kubokota allowed many different people and groups to *pajuku* areas of land along the coast. Some people say that the chief was particularly keen to give land to non-*butubutu* guests after he won a land dispute in government courts that pitted him against people of another branch of Nulu who lived in the Adventist village of Modo. The migrant *butubutu* Vitu, in contrast to Nulu, is said to forbid *pajuku* outright and those who attempt to *pajuku* land are said to be punished by death or grave illness.

There is also considerable disagreement among individuals about the status and desirability of *pajuku*. Some people believe that *pajuku* represents progress: a move away from collective ownership toward individual ownership. During the *pajuku* of gravel discussed above, one of the members of the Chiefs' Committee opined:

> Today, there is no more trust in the *butubutu*. People today no longer think the *butubutu* owns anything. As I see it, people today think that each person should hold things alone. That way there will be no arguments, no disputes, none of all of these concerns that come to us. If the *butubutu* holds it, there is a whole lot of talk that will emerge in the future.

In another context, another man went even further, describing matrilineal inheritance as "rubbish custom" that makes people lazy. "If I work on my wife's land, it is for nothing because her brothers will come to claim it," he stated. He argued that Ranongga should embrace patrilineal inheritance because it is simple.

Others condemn the way that *pajuku* undermines the integrity of the *butubutu* and its land. One man told me that he did not attend a *pajuku* ceremony on the land of his father because were he to have taken the money and food, he would no longer have the authority to address any transgressions that might occur among people living on that land. As mentioned in Chapter 2, another man objected to the division of *butubutu* land into individually owned blocks because he though that this was a risky strategy on the unstable land of Ranongga's western coast. Someone who owns a small block will become landless if that block is washed into the sea by a landslide, but someone who shares in the large territory of the *butubutu* as a whole could simply move to another area. This man also doubted that *pajuku* was an authentic Ranonggan tradition. He said that his father had never heard of it when he was young, and it only became important after World War II. From his perspective, the proper "custom" of the island is not that children of men or other non-*butubutu* members buy land, but precisely the opposite: the landholding *butubutu* ought to buy the people. The *butubutu* should put down a *bakia* to anchor those outsiders more firmly on their ground. The desire to *pajuku* a block of land signals that guests have not been properly adopted by the local land or local people, and reflects poorly on both hosts and guests.

## "Cementing" Claims to Property in Funerals

Although I witnessed few events that were actually said to be *pajuku* ceremonies, a variety of rituals followed a logic similar to that described for *pajuku*. Many of these occurred in the context of mortuary rituals, especially the final ceremony in which the grave of the deceased is cemented, often with an elaborate headstone. With a few exceptions, the dead on Ranongga are buried in their family hamlets. People bury kin nearby because they want to be near to them and to keep them company; the practice also ensures that there is an unambiguous and durable sign of previous occupancy. Indeed, if old shrines with their heavy *bakia* "anchored" people in place, today Christian graves serve to "cement" claims of descendents on the property of the deceased.

The cementing (*sementi*) of the grave occurs a year or more after the death. Earlier parts of the funeral cycle are hosted by the *butubutu* of the deceased, often with the assistance of the dead person's children regardless of whether the deceased was a woman (and the children are of her *butubutu*) or a man (and they are *vinapodo*, "born of," the *butubutu*). On the tenth day after the death, for example, the entire community gathers to carry gravel to cover the grave, and then people of the deceased's *butubutu* present baskets of food to all the relatives who have helped. The division between the *butubutu* of the deceased and the children of the deceased is more marked, however, in the final rituals for important men. These cementing rituals are often hosted and organized by the deceased man's children; the most important recipients of gifts of food and money are often their father's *butubutu*, as well as his other kinspeople who might have claims on the property that their father created over the course of his life.

In 2000, I attended the cementing of the grave of Lokasasa, who was in his mid-nineties when he died the previous year. He had been particularly energetic in clearing forest, planting coconuts, and establishing hamlets on both Ranongga and on Vella Lavella, the land of his matrilineal ancestors. He was buried in Subolai village in Vella, and this was where the cementing ceremony was held. Lokasasa had been married three times; his second wife had been a woman of Malaita whom he met while working as a policeman during the period of Maasina Rule. She returned with him to Lale, but eventually returned home to Malaita, leaving behind their children with no connection to any matrilineal territory—though this would have probably also been the case even if she had stayed, since they lived far from her home, and people say the "side of the man" is strong in Malaita. Before he died, Lokasasa had announced that his sons from this marriage were members of his own *butubutu*, not their mother's. One of Lokasasa's nieces who attended the cementing gave food and *bakia* to his sons to firmly attach them to her as real brothers.

Lokasasa's grave was the most elaborate I have seen: the large gravestone had a *bakia* embedded in the cement, and the entire grave was enclosed in a small house constructed of sawn timber and metal roofing. Following an elaborate protocol outlined by a Vella chief, Lokasasa's children distributed large amounts of food, cash, and *bakia* to a range of people: to the man who built his grave monument, to Lokasasa's own *butubutu*, to the clan that originally held the land where Lokasasa had worked and where he was buried, and to other people who were connected to him or the places he worked. By making these prestations, Lokasasa's children sought to ensure that they would inherit the settlements, gardens, and plantations that their father had made.

During the event, the spokesperson for Lokasasa's *butubutu* accepted the food prepared by Lokasasa's sons. Unusually, this was a woman, among the few women who acted as *butubutu* chiefs at that time, though an increasing number of women would take on this role in the decade that followed (see McDougall 2014). Recalling Lokasasa's declaration that his children were not *vinapodo*, "born of," the *butubutu* but were true members of the *butubutu*, she said that she could accept the food they had prepared, but that she would not accept money: "If you give us money, we can't take it because then you will separate yourselves from us." Food is the medium of nurture flowing between kinspeople, but in this context, money is like *bakia*: it can only be exchanged between people who are reciprocally constituted as "others."

Other prestations in this event illustrated the generational recurrence of transfers from a *butubutu* to the children of men of the *butubutu*. The wife of one of Lokasasa's sons presented *bakia* and food to her husband, saying that she wanted to give her children "power" so that they would be sure that they could stay on the area that Lokasasa had cleared. Twenty-five years earlier, I was later told, her husband had made a similar prestation to Lokasasa himself. Later, some witnesses to the proceedings criticized her speech because she had failed to state that she was not giving the *bakia* in order to cut off her in-laws and that they were still welcome to share in the property. Without such an explicit mitigation of the implicit assertion she made by giving the *bakia*, her husband's relatives might have hard feelings that would jeopardize the relation of mutual regard (*variroqu*) and mutual help (*varitokai*) that ought to prevail between them and his children.

This breach in etiquette highlights the double movement of any such ritual exchange. Large amounts of cash and symbolically heavy *bakia* are given

**Figure 5.4.** The grave of Lokasasa, with a painted cross and a *bakia* embedded in the cement. The grave is within a "permanent material" house with a cement foundation and low walls, louvered windows, and galvanized iron roof. 20 December 2000.

**Figure 5.5.** Helena Enaduri speaking in front of baskets (*topa*) labelled for distribution at the cementing of the graves of Matiu and Lisa of Kolomali. 4 January 2007.

from one side to another in order to elicit recognition that the giver now has rights over the property: by accepting, the receivers have no power over the place. Yet, givers verbally downplay the significance of the objects presented. Vast quantities of food and large sums of money may be described as "a little something" or as a "sign" of love. When done well, such rituals allow people to simultaneously assert their differentiated rights to property and deny that they are separating themselves from their kin.

## "Heating the Ground" for a New Settlement

Funerals were not the only contexts in which people articulated differential rights to property. They did so in a wide range of gatherings that were rumored to be *pajuku* but then presented as something else. One such event was a ceremony to open a new settlement in an area of southeastern Luqa. The ceremony is of particular interest here not only for the way it illustrates the ways that people strive to assert and deny their rights to a place, but also because this area became the base for logging operations eight years after the events discussed here, a development I discuss in Chapter 6.

An old man of *butubutu* Degere, Panakolo, had invited his deceased brother's son Elison to come and live with him and build a hamlet at a place called Baniata, just south of the village of Paqe. Elison had begun to work in the area, cutting down the nut trees that were in a grove that belonged to Panakolo's mother Eda (Elison's paternal grandmother). At some point, Panakolo dreamed of an old man whom he did not clearly recognize, who said, "Hey, grandson, it would be good if you'd kill a pig, then come and live here." Panakolo suggested to Elison that they kill a pig, but Elison and his brothers and sisters decided to hold a much larger feast, with three pigs and two hundred attendees. When I first heard of plans for this event, it was rumored to be a *pajuku*. When I talked to Panakolo and to Elison's elder brother Edi Alaqeto, however, they explained that this was not *pajuku*, but just a feast to "heat the ground" (*va-mangini pezo*) so that Elison and his family could live there safely.

The complicated history of the land (*pezo*) encompassing the area at Baniata informed the ways that the event unfolded. As is the case in most areas of Ranongga, there are disagreements about the relative power of a *butubutu* thought to be autochthonous to the land and a *butubutu* that arrived later from somewhere else. Most people agree that the Degere ancestors emerged through the mating of a coconut crab and a pandanus tree on Degere territory, which encompasses the land at Baniata.[11] This union produced both humans and non-human beings (*tamaza*). The *tamaza* remained on the land and seas surrounding the island, and are still thought to have the power to afflict strangers and punish their descendents' transgressions. Some of the human sisters traveled to other areas of the New Georgia Group, but the ancestors of Degere people on Ranongga today remained on the island. At some point in the distant past, people of Vitu—a foreign *butubutu* originally from Baniata in southern Rendova Island in eastern New Georgia—arrived from the west coast of Luqa, where they had been living for generations.[12] Having outgrown the small area amenable for settlement above the steep sea cliffs, Vitu people were led by their local hosts across to Degere land. According to some people, the land was purchased by Vitu's local hosts because Vitu men had died for them in war. Other people said that Vitu people purchased the area themselves with baskets of money earned as payment for war service. A few also believed that the land was never transferred to Vitu, and that people of Vitu remained the guests of Degere.

During the "heating the ground" ceremony in 2000, no one spoke of the ultimate *butubutu* ownership of the land. Questions of ultimate ownership could not be entirely avoided, however, for any transaction involving property should recognize the landowning *butubutu*, who are described as the "base" or "root" (*kutana*). Failing to invite those who consider themselves the ultimate landowners is seen as an aggressive denial of the legitimacy of that ownership.[13] This was especially true here because Panakolo happened to be a man of Degere. If no representative of Vitu was invited, Panakolo might be understood to be asserting Degere's continuing ownership of its original territory against the claims of Vitu.

Instead of talking about the ancient history of Degere and Vitu, speakers focused on more recent histories of occupation. The forest inland from Baniata is full of ancestral shrines, house foundations, and nut groves that indicate intensive precolonial occupation, but on the eve of pacification in 1899/1900, these settlements appear to have been abandoned. Beginning in the 1920s and 1930s, men living in Saevuke and other west-coast villages returned to the land once occupied by their ancestors. They cleared the forest, planted nut trees and gardens, and built a church at a place called Ole Lavata just south of Baniata. During this period, people of many different *butubutu* are said to have lived together as siblings (*vari-tamatazi*) and shared their possessions (*vari-izongo*). Panakolo's maternal grandparents built their hamlet at Baniata, and his mother Eda lived there until everyone fled inland from the Japanese occupation in 1942. After the war, people returned to the coast to establish the village of Paqe, but did not reoccupy Ole Lavata or Baniata. Panakolo returned to Baniata on 20 June 1968, a date that he recalled precisely in 2000.

I traveled to Baniata with Panakolo's relatives living in Pienuna village on the evening prior to the feast. The plot had only recently been cleared; several temporary kitchens and a tarp-covered shelter for sleeping had been erected between the trunks of fallen nut trees that crossed the area. Pigs were tethered on the path that led from the canoe-landing place to the cleared settlement area. Canoes of people kept arriving laden with baskets of sweet potatoes, cassava, taro, and yams, and those who had arrived were fetching firewood. By the time darkness fell, more than one hundred people were milling around by the light of kerosene lanterns and the huge fires that were heating stones for the ovens. Then the women set to work in earnest, peeling mountains of sweet potatoes and grating heaps of cassava that would be mixed with coconut milk for puddings. Near midnight, visiting groups of young men and women began to sing and play panpipes to provide entertainment for the workers. By dawn, the work had slowed, but soon the relative calm of the gray early morning was broken by the angry scream of the first pig to be strangled. The work of the day proceeded doggedly despite a near-constant drizzle. The stone ovens with the cooked puddings were opened; ovens for sweet potatoes were prepared; the pigs were butchered, parceled, and baked; canoes arrived and unloaded bonito that had been baked during the night in neighboring villages; baskets of coconut fronds were woven. It was near evening by the time the food was prepared, the stone ovens were opened, and the baskets of food were ready for distribution.

Once the food was displayed, United Church Minister Abraham Toribule opened the proceedings. He framed it as "our custom": not just "some pork and sweet potatoes" but an acknowledgement of the area and the settlement. Next, Edi Alaqeto spoke briefly on behalf of his younger brother Elison:

> I am going to talk just a little bit, I won't speak long. There is a little bit of food for you to look at and take, for all of you of our father and our grandmother's group who own this area (*ia*) here. It is for you Panakolo, for you Egi [Panakolo's sister], for you Nesoni [the spokesman of the chief of Degere], for you Oqoro [a man of Degere], and some more of you who look at it. The thought behind all of this is that Elison will be living here; he will make a settlement here. If any of us siblings or any of our children want to come and live here, we will let Elison know first and then we will come. It is not as though Elison is buying all of the things here at Baniata, or all of the fruit trees and everything that belong to Panakolo. Instead, he is making it known that this is the area, these are the house foundations, so that he is going to stay here. So here is a little bit of potato, pig, a little rice, and a little money that has been put down. The thought behind it is that Elison and his children, and whoever else, will be living here at this place. That's it, my short speech on behalf of Elison and all of us siblings. Thank you.

Edi denies that this exchange is doing anything—a paradoxical, but widespread, feature of ritual. As Webb Keane has noted, "When most successful, ritual performance works by a circular logic in which it creatively *brings about* a context and set of identities that it portrays as *already* existing" (Keane 1997: 18). The clearest assertion of a transformed relationship to this place is Edi's announcement that if he wants to come "we will let Elison know first." This is not framed as an assertion of anything new—the speech just points to what already exists ("this is the area, these are the house foundations") by way of "making it known."

Old man Panakolo spoke next. He suggested more directly that a transfer of property was occurring, or that it would occur after his death. He began by explaining that he had repeatedly tried to invite his sisters and their children to stay with them. "None of them took notice," he said, wiping away tears, "up until this very day." Finally, he approached Elison:

> What about you, Elison, why don't you come down and stay with me, because my younger sisters, my sister's children, have not come. What will happen when I am gone? What will become of the things? [. . .] [I hoped Elison would] just come so he would stay with me. So however I might be, if I were to be sick or whatever might happen, Elison would take care of me.

Care for the elderly is called *barozo*. It is normally women, not men, who feed, clean, and care for those who are approaching their deaths. Panakolo had hoped to get a classificatory daughter to look after him, but none of them were willing.

Under normal circumstances, a daughter-in-law is expected to avoid bodily contact with her husband's parents and parents' siblings (whom he also calls parents). Caring for her in-laws in their old age requires her to break those avoidance taboos—a breach that is most striking in the act of cleaning the excrement of a person who is dying and unable to move from a sleeping mat. By providing such care, the daughter-in-law (who is, because of exogamy, the quintessential "other person") acts like a kinsperson rather than an affine. It is generally expected that when a daughter-in-law cares for a father-in-law or mother-in-law as though they were her own parents, she will inherit some of their property in a way that recognizes this daughter-like status. She is often granted a nut grove, parcel of garden land, or settlement area. The deceased may announce this gift before she or he dies, or the *butubutu* may show their gratitude for the care of their kinsperson after his or her death. The gift of property establishes the "other person" as a person of the place. Thus, as I understand it, by talking about who would care for him in old age, Panakolo pointed not only to the movement of the property to Elison but also to his wife and children.

After explaining that he just wanted Elison to come and live with him, Panakolo spoke of his worry when Elison prepared such a large feast:

> So, I wondered what this is about, but I thought about it, and I thought, that is all right, two people, Ruben and Jebede, are around. So it is okay, in that this is too much here, but those two will come . . . So it is very good that you have come, you Jebeti and Ruben, so that it is not me alone who will take the portion here.

Panakolo did not say anything here about the *butubutu* ownership of the land. However, by naming Ruben and Jebede—both from Pienuna, a village on Vitu territory under a Vitu chief, to whom both were closely connected—he implicitly acknowledged Vitu's stake in the land that encompasses the area at Baniata. In the next breath, though, Panakolo denied that it was really necessary to acknowledge these owners, for nothing was really going on in the ritual:

> But if you [meaning Ruben and Jebede] were not to come, or others who have not come, they may not see it, but that is all right. Because it is just food (*ganigani*), of no importance. Eat it and then it is finished.

*Ganigani* is a crude and direct way of referencing food and the process of consumption (the polite form, *tekutekuna*, could be literally translated as "something that is taken"), and Panakolo's use of it seems to underline the point that the food is just material stuff, to be shared with kinspeople and then forgotten.

The last part of Panakolo's talk was directed to Elison and his wife Ego, and articulated what he considered the ethics of landholding, an obligation to care for (*kopuni*) people and land:

> You Elison, you will stay here. You must care for people [inaudible] [. . .] Whatever they want, whatever they take, give it to them, you must not deny them. It is this way for you, Ego, as it is for you, Elison—the two of you must help one another during your lives here [. . .] You must be as I have been. I live here, and whatever people have wanted, I have told them, "Go take it." The things that I hold, I don't talk about them. The good and the bad, everything [. . .] It is all right with me. In such things, you two must be as I have been. You must do as I have done, until eventually we are all finished here. You will be gone, I will be gone, but this way of life must be followed.

The very essence of "holding" property for Ranonggans is the right to "talk about" it and the right to be asked for permission before anyone uses the property. Indeed, a year earlier, Panakolo had been involved in a dispute when someone planted sago on what he considered his area without asking his permission. In stating principles here, though, he emphasizes the idea that property ownership is the right to specifically include others, not the right to exclude them.

The most explicit "message" of this ceremony was not in the talk, but in the carefully planned distribution of food. The food was divided into baskets woven from coconut fronds, which were labeled with the names of the recipients, carefully listed by Edi Alaqeto in consultation with Panakolo the day before. Among the most important were Panakolo's sisters and their children, people whose fathers were Degere, and others whose ancestors had been given land in one way or another by Degere. Every family or individual who attended received a basket. A total of seventy-one baskets were distributed to named individuals on behalf of their households; the baskets were clustered into eighteen different villages or hamlets.

In front of these individual baskets was a large pile of food with the front half of one pig, four large bonito, many puddings and sweet potatoes, as well as a 10 kilogram bag of rice and a small amount of cash (just SI$60). Although the recipients of the seventy-one baskets were carefully named, the recipients of this larger prestation were not named. After the ceremony, I was told that it was divided between Panakolo, his sister Egi, and their other siblings, as well Jebeti Toribule, Ruben, and Nason Beikera, a man of Degere and the spokesman of the Degere chief. By avoiding any mention of land (*pezo*) or identification of "landowners," the organizers sidestepped any direct invocation of the contested histories of Degere and Vitu but acknowledged both.

The gifts thus served to articulate differences among the attendees even as the content of the speeches effectively denied that they existed. Moreover, the minister who acted as master of ceremonies spoke in a way that put all who were attending together as a united collectivity asking God for blessing upon the new settlement. The concluding prayer positioned everyone present as "witnesses" to the events (italicized words were spoken in English):

> Your servants have told what they know at this time, and we have come to *witness* this at this time [. . .] So Lord, plant these words in our ears so that we may recognize one another, we may lead one another, and we may help one another over the course of our lives. Now, as we come to the end, we want to *declare* in your name, the name of your Son and the Holy Spirit, the village is here. Your village. So Lord, you must live where the people live [. . .] It is declared, there is a village here [. . .] *Hip-hip hurray!*

Less explicit than the entreaty for God's blessing was the implicit propitiation of ancestral spirits that, as Panakolo's dream suggested to him, continue to inhabit the area. In such a case, the "warming" of the ground occurred not only in the ceremony but also in the preparations—the all-night singing, working, talking, and cooking that heated up the place and made it a site of collective activity once again.

## Intimacy, Alienation, Ambiguity

Anyone seeking a clear title to neatly delineated blocks of land is frustrated by the rituals described here. Are they purchases, or not?[14] To some extent, the answer depends upon the perspective of the transactors. Writing about transactions similar to *pajuku* between landowners and migrants working on oil-palm plantations in the Orokaiva region of PNG, George Curry and Gina Koczberski observe that block holders think that they are buying land as a commodity in a market: "Many outsiders acquiring land in this way believe that the cash payments give them 'ownership' of the land in the sense that their children can inherit the block or they can sell it on to a third party" (Curry and Koczberski 2009: 103). Landowners, on the other hand, do not believe that they are selling land: "land rights granted to outsiders are never permanent and exclusive . . . but are conditional for their ongoing validity on continued participation in indigenous (gift) exchange and fulfilling other obligations" (ibid.: 103).

Another answer is that *pajuku* and similar transactions are increasingly seen as purchases as people increasingly view land as a commodity. In the precolonial past, migrant groups seem to have used *bakia* to purchase land from original *butubutu*, yet those original *butubutu* rarely seem to have abandoned the land. Such transactions are perhaps best viewed not as alienating land but as "anchoring" strangers to unfamiliar places and attaching them to their hosts as allies rather than subordinates. Such payments appear to have given the newcomers power that they would not have enjoyed if they had come empty handed: the prerogative to establish their own ancestral shrines and the right to bring others ashore. Often, such powers seem to have superseded, but not really extinguished, the power of previous inhabitants. This is not to say that there was no alienation prior to colonialism. In an era before land shortages, however, alienation was less about selling off the land and more about cutting people off from the land through death or banishment. *Bakia* may have anchored people to land rather than alienating land to people, but this occurred in a broader context in which people had been cut of from relationships to their own territory and kinspeople.

The rituals I discuss here highlight a broader point that has been made about exchange in Melanesia and other contexts: the exchange of material goods, especially durable valuables like *bakia*, does not simply create relationships among people and groups. Such exchange also divides people from one another. In the decades since Sahlins (1965) outlined the relationships between social distance and types of reciprocal exchange, some scholars have suggested that labeling all forms giving and taking as "reciprocity" or "exchange" is misleading. Valerio Valeri pointed out that insofar as exchange or reciprocity implies that a gift will be returned, then relatives should not engage in reciprocal exchange because "there is no book-keeping among relatives and thus there can be no true reciprocity" (Valeri 1994: 6). Or, as Brenda Clay put it, "sharing expresses integration; exchanging communicates separation" (Clay 1975: 102; see also Woodburn 1998). We have seen this distinction between sharing and exchange materialized in Ranongga in the clear distinction between a feast laid out on banana leaves and a ritual prestation in which food is bundled in baskets for named persons or households.

Transactions of land and property do not involve neatly balanced exchanges between relatives who are not very close kin, but an emotionally charged oscillation between the poles of kinship and estrangement. There are strong parallels in land transactions and marriage transactions, for both involve life-giving powers of production and reproduction that can never truly be reciprocated with gifts of material objects.[15] In an interrogation of anthropological approaches to reciprocity, Valerio Valeri (1994) tracked the oscillation between alienation and solidarity in marriage exchanges among Huaulu people of Seram in eastern Indonesia. In this system of preferential cross-cousin marriage, affines are only ambiguously "other" to one another; although they are not part of the same patrilineally focused house, a woman's classificatory fathers and brothers consider themselves to be "one blood" with her husband. In the initial transactions following the announcement of the marriage, these soon-to-be affines de-emphasize their kinship ties and act in ways that highlights the distance between them. In theory, the woman is "bought" in a tit-for-tat exchange that has a crassly commercial tenor. The bride's relatives threaten violence and haggle over her price in antique porcelain plates, a form of durable valuable that (like New Georgia *bakia*) is only transacted between "others." Such hostility "evokes the moral perils of commodification" and maximizes a sense of otherness and social distance (ibid.: 13). But this purchase is not really a purchase, for it is never really possible to purchase the power to give life. Wife-takers remain indebted to the wife-givers. Over the decades of a successful marriage and through the life-cycle rituals of the children, these affinal sides increasingly engage with one another not as hostile "others" in the way they did in initial marriage exchanges but as loving "non others," re-emphasizing their own consanguineal relationships and their shared nurture of the children of the marriage. Their transactions do not involve durable valuables, but perishable foodstuffs, the universal medium of kin-based intimacy. Huaulu say that they "buy women" but do not "sell them"; and in Valeri's analysis, the statement captures what is a long-term and multi-faceted process involving both alienation and intimacy.

Similar dynamics of "buying but not selling" occur in Ranonggan rituals of property transfer through the different mediums of material exchange and speech. The articulation of otherness occurs via the exchange of material goods: the act of presenting food and money elicits recognition of differential rights to a place, positioning those who are siblings in other contexts on opposite sides of the transaction. But this articulation is undermined by the discourse during the distribution of these goods. Over and over, those giving the food asserted that their gifts were not really gifts at all, just a little bit of food that is shared among relatives.

The apparent ambiguity of *pajuku* and similar rituals allows Ranonggans to manage dilemmas arising from a complex set of assumptions, anxieties, and convictions. They believe that people are kin only if they share their possessions with one another, but they also believe that those who share in such a way are likely to impoverish their own children. An encompassing Christian moral framework arguably exacerbates this sense of failure because disunity is not just an inconvenient barrier to accomplishing large-scale work, but an affront to God's divine plan. According to the good old ways of the ancestors, now often seen as exemplifying Christian virtues, a person should not assert those rights but welcome others ashore and share their property. All is well as long as their rights are acknowledged, often in subtle and indirect ways that avoid inciting disputes over landownership. If this recognition is withheld, however, those who see themselves as rightful owners may have difficulty asserting their rights, for the very act of assertion undermines this authority.

Michael Scott (2000, 2007b) has discussed similar dynamics for Arosi people in Makira. In public, Arosi tended to agree that they had all come from elsewhere, stating that there are no longer any people who are truly autochthonous to the land that they were living on. In secret, however, representatives of matrilineages would tell Scott stories about their ancestral origins and the location of shrines, spirits, and stones in the landscape that they felt proved that they were, truly, autochthonous to the land. Knowing that others would contest the validity of these stories, few were willing to risk revealing these stories publicly, lest this be taken as an aggressive attempt to disentangle their shared lives on the land. Scott heard of only one instance where someone tried to "set the record straight, at least as he saw it, regarding who was who in the village" (Scott 2007b: 244). The man called a meeting and, when all were assembled, began to tell people where their grandmothers came from—thus "implicitly stating that the people of his matrilineage were the original people of the land, and that everyone else lived in the village through the goodness and hospitality of his lineage" (ibid.: 244). Villagers were indignant, and threatened to return to their home places. The elected village chief, the elder brother of the man who called the meeting, reasserted the public consensus that everyone in the village came from elsewhere and that there are no longer autochthonous owners. By denying any claims to precedence, this man was seen as bringing different people together to live in harmony in the way that a true chief, and a true Christian, ought to do (ibid.: 246).

Many Ranonggans believe that fighting over land, even trying to purchase land through *pajuku*, leads to illness or death. One elderly man told me that he had outlived all of the men of his generation who had repeatedly fought over land in the local courts that were active in the 1970s and 1980s because he had not been involved in land disputes. Fears about fighting over land became clear in a conversation with a knowledgeable old woman who told me that her *butubutu* arrived at the place where she is now living when it was empty of people (the more common narrative suggests that her *butubutu* was welcomed ashore by another *butubutu* that had arrived earlier). She said that she wanted people in America to hear the story, but I did not "need to bother" telling other people in Ranongga. A disagreement over the origin of this *butubutu* in previous years had given rise to serious conflict, and was thought to have been responsible for a recent death by sorcery. My interlocutor was seriously worried that if she told the true story, the others would become angry and cause her family harm. Besides, she told me, there was no need to straighten out who really came first, because in the past the two *butubutu* had lived as though they were "just one *butubutu*." Fighting about land could lead to death, but "as long as we have a little ground to plant sweet potatoes on, we'll live."

## Notes

1. Ziosi's sentiments are echoed, almost verbatim, by a woman of Rendova named Katie Soapi who speaks in a documentary film (Hawkins 2003) about the ill effects of logging in Rendova. In the past, she explained, when men went fishing, they would come home, bake the fish, and distribute parcels to each family up and down the village; today, people want to sell fish to one another. She also spoke of the way that people increasingly seek to cut off rather than include cognatic kinspeople. Today people fail to *luk save* (a Solomon Islands Pijin term meaning "recognize") their kinspeople.
2. See also Dureau (2001: 152) on Simbo, and Scott (2007b: 261) on Makira.
3. As Joel Robbins observed for newly Christian Urapmin in Highlands Papua New Guinea (PNG), "the Christian moral system virtually creates the conditions that ensure people's failure to live up to its demands [...] [T]he Christian concern to renounce the will has led people in Urapmin to attend assiduously to their wills and to talk ceaselessly about the problems they cause. Enjoined always to be looking for the sinful will, they are bound to find it" (Robbins 2004: 249).
4. Akin (1999a) describes a similar dynamic among Kwaio people of eastern Malaita, who are quite happy to sell shell valuables to one another only in situations where the shell money is being collected for a mortuary feast.
5. Many ethnographers working in village settings experience something similar. A classic discussion of reciprocity is Counts (1990).
6. Christine Dureau (1993, 1998b) has analyzed the changing meaning and significance of sister–brother (*tamaluluna*) relationships on nearby Simbo. There are interesting parallels between the dynamics of sibling relationships and the relationship between chiefs and people in the western Solomons. As Geoff White discusses for Santa Isabel, chiefs were thought to embody two contrasting ethno-psychological principles, which he labels "solidarity" and "dominance" (White 1991: 65–72). Like chiefs and people, in New Georgian societies brothers and sisters are simultaneously in a relationship of solidarity (as *tamatazi*) and dominance (as *tamaluluna*). All of the respectful behaviors that sisters are supposed to demonstrate toward brothers are precisely those that ordinary people were supposed to show toward chiefs of the past. Discourses about the lack of respect between brothers and sisters mirrors discourses about the lack of respect given to chiefs today.
7. On the symbolism of store-bought versus garden food among Orokaiva of PNG, see Bashkow (2006: 145–208).
8. There is a large literature on problems in applying Western notions of property rights to non-Western and especially indigenous contexts; starting points can be found in Povinelli (1993), Hann (1998), and Wagner and Talakai (2007).
9. See Scott (2007b: 59–67) for the case of Arosi.
10. *Pajuku* is a transitive verb: one *pajuku*-s something (*za pajuk-i-a*). Ceremonies in which people *pajuku* property are called *pajupajuku*. These kinds of transactions are common in the region; ethnographically well-documented examples include *huihui*

in Ngella (Foale and Macintryre 2000), *tsupu* or *chupu* in Guadalcanal (Allen 2012; Monson 2012: 229–33), *pondo* in Oro Province, PNG (Curry and Koczberski 2009), and *kulia* among Tolai of New Britain, PNG (Martin 2013: 61–74).

11. Like all *butubutu* narratives, this one is contested. Disagreements focus on the relationship between Degere and another *butubutu* that is sometimes said to have preceded Degere, and sometimes said to have been the same as Degere until one or the other committed an offense and was banished from Degere land.

12. At the time of Vitu's arrival, the land was already occupied by people of Patukaqo or Tiro. There is some disagreement about the relationship between these two *butubutu*; some people say they were originally different, but became "just one" by co-residence; others say that one or the other originated on the land and the other arrived; some say that Tiro originated when a woman of Patukaqo was looking for *ngali* nuts (an activity know as *tiro ngari*) when she unexpectedly gave birth. To complicate things further, some people told me that the two *butubutu* had exchanged names several times to be sure that no one could disentangle one from the other. The migrants did not arrive with the name "Vitu"; this was the name given to them by their local hosts because they arrived in seven (*vitu*) canoes; according to some accounts, their original name was taken by their Ranonggan hosts as their own.

13. Some weeks prior to the "heating the ground" ceremony, a powerful Vitu chief was enraged when graves of the long-deceased founders of Paqe village were cemented without the presence of a Vitu representative. Because this man is thought to have supernatural power (I was told that he could cause thunder and lightning), it was a matter of serious concern for those involved.

14. This puzzle is the focus of Kier Martin's (2013: 61–74) discussion of the Tolai practice of *kulia*, which is very similar to *pajuku*.

15. There are some compelling parallels between contemporary discussions of bridewealth exchanges, described in Solomon Islands Pijin as *peim gele* (buying the girl), and more important in societies of the eastern Solomons, especially Malaita, than in the western Solomons. In the case of bridewealth exchanges, local people and anthropologists have suggested that market logic is changing the meaning of a transaction that traditionally bound families to one another. For discussions of the changing meanings of bride price or bridewealth in Malaita, see Keesing (1987b, 1989b), Kwa'ioloa and Burt (1997), Akin (1999a, 1999b), and Pollard (2000a: 57–66).

# 6
## Estranging Kin
### *The Tribalization of Land Ownership*

A decade after the "heating the ground" ceremony described in the previous chapter, Baniata was denuded of vegetation except a small cluster of pandanus on the edge of the shoreline. Between 2008 and 2010, it was the camp and operating base for logging of Degere land undertaken by the multinational Glengrow Limited—the place where round logs were deposited and then floated out to waiting ships for transport. Ole Lavata, lying on a small rise just south of Baniata, had been cleared for housing for the company's laborers, primarily Iban men from Sarawak in Malaysia. When I visited in June 2010, old Panakolo was there, living alone in a dilapidated house of sago leaf, and so was his sister Egi. Elison was no longer living in Baniata, but his brother Alfred had taken advantage of the activity by setting up "Al's 24 hour shop," which now stood without customers in the middle of the abandoned camp.

No one had received logging royalties. Nor had any of the other hoped-for boons of "development" materialized: there was no school, no clinic, no wharf, no toilets, no aluminum or fiberglass canoes, no outboard engines, and no water supply. Many people were enthusiastic about the logging road the company built, thinking that it would make it easier to traverse the difficult terrain between Paqe and Lale to the south and Saevuke to the west. Just a few weeks after operations ceased, however, the road had begun to erode and one bridge had collapsed. As anyone with knowledge of logging in Solomon Islands could have predicted, the operations caused land disputes. A court case was initiated soon after operations began in 2008, and was concluded after the company had left in 2010, pitting neighbors and relatives against one another. Youth had come to blows and threatened one another with machetes when they met in the bush. In mid 2010, a reconciliation ceremony was being planned but had not yet occurred.

Logging physically obliterates the kind of property created by the work of previous generations: nut groves, garden areas, and settlement sites. Often, it also destroys the ancestral shrines that mark ancient settlements and are the focus of narratives about the origins and movements of clans. The law dictates that such important heritage sites be identified and preserved prior to

Figure 6.1. Baniata after the completion of logging opeartions. 22 June 2010.

logging, but the required archeological surveys are often not carried out and, when they are, companies tend to destroy the sites and then later pay compensation if landowners have the leverage to demand it. Multinational mining companies tend to be more careful about preserving ancestrally significant sites than logging companies. As Bainton, Ballard, and Gillespie (2012) have noted for Lihir, however, even where an ancestral site is preserved, the paths linking people to the site are destroyed or transfigured, thus changing both the meaning and context of those sites. Disarticulated from the other marks of habitation and occupation, and in the absence of groves, gardens, and old settlements, such shrines do not index the entangled histories that were the focus of the "heating the ground" ceremony discussed in the previous chapter.

A similar process of disarticulation occurs on the level of social relations through the "tribalization." Long problematized by anthropologists, the term "tribe" is used by Solomon Islanders and outsiders alike to refer to kin-based groupings larger than the extended family, especially those that can be traced to some founding ancestor—the sorts of social formations that I refer to as clans and other anthropologists may call lineages. When speaking English or Pijin, Ranonggans translate the term "*butubutu*" as "tribe," although as discussed in Chapter 2, such a translation captures only one aspect of the polysemous term *butubutu*. In legal and development discourse, customary land tenure is also often described as tribal landownership. It is often assumed that rights to build dwellings, plant gardens, or harvest the fruit of tree crops are determined by membership in a particular tribe. As we have seen in Chapter 5, things are much more complicated than that. *Butubutu* identities continue to link people to the home territories of their matrilineal ancestors, but rights on the ground are established through ties to many different relatives. Many of these rights are not given by birth, but established through exchange or practical labor undertaken over the course of a lifetime or many generations.

This chapter focuses on projects of large-scale economic development and environmental conservation undertaken in the late 1990s through the 2000s on Ranongga. I argue that complicated histories of occupation and engagement with land are downplayed or disregarded in such situations, and Ranonggans are pushed to portray themselves as landowners by virtue of descent alone. Similar dynamics have been documented by anthropologists working elsewhere in Solomon Islands and the wider region. As Pei-yi Guo argues for Langalanga people in Malaita, legal discourse has encouraged people to "lean toward the principle of precedence and downplay the importance of incorporation" (Guo 2011: 237; see also Tiffany 1983). Gerhard Schneider noted that when people of Roviana dispute genealogy, "claimants try to turn closely related people into people of separate social origins," a process that "entails the negation of former common social identities" (Schneider 1998: 193). Land disputes in Roviana and elsewhere around the Solomons predated the rise of logging, but because logging and other forms of resource extraction promise royalties to landowning groups that are legally bounded, it has raised the stakes of those disputes. All of the processes that create landowning corporations require people to retell their local histories in ways that exclude, rather than include, others: "relationships with outsiders, previously a source of wealth, status and corporate identity, are reconsidered and deliberately limited, truncated or severed entirely" (Allen 2013b: 155; see also Filer 1997; Weiner and Glaskin 2007; Bainton 2009). Linking low-level conflicts over the spoils of resource extraction to the large-scale violence that has erupted in Papua New Guinea (PNG) and Solomon Islands since the 1990s, Matthew Allen calls resource capitalism the "crucible" that "turbo-charged" the ideologies of ethno-nationalism and indigeneity that became central to these conflicts (Allen 2013b: 153).

Recent work in Melanesian anthropology, and anthropology more generally, has questioned the foundational assumptions of descent theory. Rather than assuming that corporate groups exist as the building blocks of any society, scholars focus on the ways that corporate groups emerge out of practices like gift exchange. Such approaches are consonant with a disciplinary embrace of practice theory, which sought to escape the "realism of the structure" that "hypostatizes systems of objective relations by converting them into totalities already constituted outside of individual history and group history" (Bourdieu 1977: 72; see also Ortner 1984). In some way, however, social reality seems to move in the opposite direction to social theory (Golub 2007). As anthropologists have eschewed the search for corporate groups, processes of resource extraction have led to the hypostatization—or, "entification" as Thomas M. Ernst (1999) has called it—of what once might have been fluid structures of organization and leadership. Corporate groups may not have existed in Melanesia, but they have been created through legal processes of incorporation—processes that, as Nick Bainton (2009) points out, keeps networks of entangled relationships "out of view." In legal discourse about customary landownership, such emergent quasi-legal semi-corporate groups are often called "tribes."

Anxieties about processes of corporatization that are my focus in this chapter parallel anxieties about processes of individualization that I discussed in the previous chapter. Wherever it occurs, corporatization is a form of individualization: it transforms a messy entanglement of rights and responsibilities into a neatly delimited "corporate sole" that functions legally as a single person. When my Ranonggan friends spoke nostalgically about an earlier era when people lived together as siblings and shared property, they condemned both individuals who cut off their relatives and matrilineal clans that defined themselves in ways that excluded the children of men. As Kier Martin (2013) points out, both individualization and corporatization involve the denial of histories of reciprocal engagement. Tolai-speaking residents of the Gazelle Peninsula in New Britain, PNG, and anthropologists alike tend to view patrilineal forms of inheritance as the modernist individualization of traditional corporate matrilineal clan ownership. Martin, in contrast, sees both patrilineal inheritance patterns and matrilineal clan ownership as responses to pressures arising from population growth and agricultural intensification. Indeed, the assertion of corporate clan landownership creates the condition under which such individualization is necessary. As matrilineal clans assert exclusive landownership in ways that exclude non-members, it becomes even more important that non-members assert individualized property rights.

Outsiders and Solomon Islanders alike often assume that clarifying land boundaries and genealogical membership in corporate landowning groups is a precondition of development (McDougall 2005). Yet, empirical research shows that non-registered customary land is often mobilized more intensively for commercial purposes than land that has been formally registered to individuals or groups (see e.g. Fingleton 2005; Allen 2008a, 2012). In systems where ownership is not formalized, people who do not use their land are likely to lose it regardless of their genealogical connections to it. Registration of land can create a class of absentee landowners who need not use their land to hold onto it. More importantly for my purposes in this chapter, attempts to clarify ownership can undermine the potential for collective action that is often necessary for the kinds of development that rural Melanesians want. Clarification of corporate landownership always gives rise to unanswerable questions about the origins and movements of mythic ancestors. As we have seen, in ordinary negotiations of land use away from the crucible of resource capitalism, these impossible questions were avoided by claims like "we aren't different anyway" and "it does not matter as long as we live like siblings and share our possessions." In situations of outsider-driven resource capitalism, people are required to articulate divisions they often prefer to avoid. Ironically, a similar process is evident in conservation projects that seek to counter destructive forms of resource capitalism.

In this chapter, I consider the tribalization of landownership in two projects that seem to encapsulate alternative visions of outsider-driven "development" for rural Solomon Islanders: the logging operation on Degere land that began in Luqa in 2008, and a conservation and development project led by a non-governmental organization that was undertaken a decade earlier on Nulu land in Kubokota. Despite their different goals and modes of operating, both projects required local people to constitute themselves as "tribal" landowners. To do this effectively, people had to represent themselves as members of bounded corporate groups defined by unilineal descent that owned a delineated territory. Yet in both contexts, actors worked together in ways that subverted this tribal framing; they sought to work together not as tribal landowners, but as members of church-based communities.

## Colonial Contradictions and Resource Capitalism on Customary Land

By the late twentieth century, customary land tenure was firmly defined in terms of corporate landowning groups, a definition that has shaped both development projects and the capacity of local people to engage with and contest these projects. But as is the case for "custom" generally, customary land tenure makes little sense outside of the expansion of both capitalism and the formal state over the past century. As David Akin (2013) has argued in his study of the emergence of Malaitan *kastom*, colonial approaches to indigenous social life, including land tenure, were riven by contradictions. Colonial agents misrecognized local social forms as being fixed and tradition-bound at the same time that they dismissed evidence of flexibility and change as a modern corruption of authentic tradition. With "custom" defined as static and communal, colonial administrators believed that their challenge was to foster more flexible and individualized forms of tenure that would allow Solomon Islanders to use their land for commercial purposes. As it turned out, however, the major form of commercial development in the postcolonial era has not required this individualization of tenure. In order to invite multinational logging companies to strip their customary land of trees in exchange for royalties, islanders must assert corporate rights of tribal ownership.

Early land policy in the British Solomon Islands Protectorate was focused on alienation to expatriates with minimal attention to local principles of land tenure. Early-twentieth-century land alienation took place in an era when colonial administrators, missionaries, and other Europeans believed that the indigenous population of Melanesia was dying out (Rivers 1922; Bayliss-Smith 2014; Bennett 2014; Lawrence 2014: 301–7). Government administration could only ease the death pangs of the dying race; it could not assume that local people would play a role in any future economic development. Under pressure to foster the commercial activity necessary to generate the tax revenue that could make the Protectorate economically self-sufficient, Resident Commissioner Charles Woodford declared large swathes of forest not visibly occupied to be "waste land," often without even coming ashore to investigate (Bennett 1987: 131). In the 1900s, resident European traders also purchased land directly from islanders. Some of them sold the land a few years later at fantastic profits to large companies like London-based Lever Brothers (later Levers Pacific Plantations Ltd.) and the Sydney-based trading firm Burns Philp and Company that were interested in the potential of the Solomon Islands for copra production (ibid.: 142–43). Outright land sales ended in 1914 with legislation that stipulated that native owners could sell land only to the government, which would then provide long-term leases (mostly of ninety-nine years) to would-be investors in the colony. The policy was not primarily an attempt to protect native owners; it was a strategy to increase state control over land, minimize market forces, and divert profits from land speculation from private traders to the government (ibid.: 146–48; Monson 2012: 126–27). Although land alienated in the early years of the Protectorate amounted to only about 10 percent of the total landmass, much of it was prime coastal land. Throughout the Solomons, land alienation created lasting resentment of the government, and fear that land would be stolen if not occupied (Bennett 1987, 2000; Scales 2004; Scott 2007a, 2007b: 100–4; Akin 2013: 34–35, 187–88).

Some early land "sales" seem to have been voluntary, possibly occurring in ways similar to the *pajuku* transactions discussed in Chapter 5. By most accounts, New Georgia chiefs were eager to attract European traders by granting them land. People of Kolombangara, where large areas of land were declared to be "wasteland" by the government, began objecting to land alienation only when they realized that Europeans violated local norms of landownership by forbidding people from accessing their property on the land, cutting down valuable trees without compensating the owners, transferring land to third parties without seeking permission, and importing foreign laborers (Scales 2004: 119). Prior to government pacification, such a breach of local norms would have been met with violence, but in the early twentieth century, local residents no longer had this option. As Ian Scales (ibid.: 117–26) points out, the only way that islanders could challenge colonial land alienation was by working through the colonial apparatus itself.

Widespread dissatisfaction with the ways the land was alienated prompted the First Land Commission of 1919 to 1923 (known as the Phillips Commission), a watershed in establishing the forms of political authority and conceptions of land tenure that would be taken for granted later in the century (Bennett 1987: 195; Scales 2004: 117–126; Monson 2012: 131–36). The documents from the Phillips Commission reveal a widespread awareness among local people that Europeans viewed land as a commodity. Commissioner Phillips observed that local ideas of landownership were in a state of rapid transformation, and that people were representing themselves as landowners in new ways, but he did not reflect upon the ways that the commission itself might be encouraging such reformulations. Like all later European inquiries into customary tenure, the Phillips Commission expected customary land to be held by corporate descent groups, not individuals or families. When islanders spoke of owning land or property, it was understood that they were speaking on behalf of their corporate descent groups.

After World War II and the exit of many expatriate planters, the colonial administration finally began to envision an economic future for the Protectorate with Solomon Islanders as small producers. In 1953, a Special Land Commission was established to assist the government in formulating land policy in this new era. Colonial official Colin Allan's report on the Commission's findings encapsulates many of the contradictions of colonial land policy that have continued to shape the ways that Solomon Islanders themselves understand their proprietary relationships to land. The Commission sought to develop policy that would simultaneously recognize customary tenure, for which there was a "present continuing need," and transform customary tenure "along progressive lines toward the emergence of a modern tenure system, based on adjudication and registration of individual title" (ibid.: 277). Anticipating that "progressive" islanders would voluntarily register individual property rights, Allan predicted "the ultimate extinction of native custom" (1957: 217, 278). In the meantime, though, he sought to identify authentic forms of customary tenure—by which he meant ownership of land by clearly delineated, genealogically defined, corporate groups.[1] He also proposed that the government take possession of land that had been unused for twenty-five years, thus reviving the hated "wastelands" policy of the previous generation and emphasizing the importance of continuing occupation.

Allan sought to formulate policy that would encourage individualized tenure, but like Phillips, he assumed that authentic customary land tenure was communal ownership by bounded descent groups. As discussed in Chapter

5, the most important rights to property in Ranongga and elsewhere in the Solomons are established by individuals on the basis of their labor and dwelling on the land, not inherited genealogically. Even though these sorts of individualized rights were what Allan thought government policy should encourage, when he observed them in existing indigenous practices he dismissed them as a non-customary distortion of authentic customary principles of clan or "line" ownership. Anthropologists critiqued Allan for disregarding then-current research on non-unilineal descent systems in favor of Rivers's speculative theories concerning evolution from matrilineal to patrilineal kinship systems (see e.g. Hogbin 1958; Scheffler 1971). As Hviding (2003c: 77–79) has observed, Allan was particularly vexed by the bilateral nature of New Georgian kinship systems, seeing it as a cynical manipulation of rules that multiplied interests in land. Having thus dismissed any sort of flexibility in inheritance or individualized rights to landed property as "non-customary," Allan argued that the system would have to be modernized by introducing principles of individual inheritance in order to foster commercial development.

Land tenure was transformed in the decades following the Special Land Commission, but not in the ways envisioned by Allan or anticipated by legislation. In 1959, the Protectorate government passed a Land and Titles Ordinance with two aims: first, expanding government-held public land by taking control of undeveloped alienated land and supposedly vacant customary land; and second, encouraging islanders to formally register either individual or group title to land (Heath 1979; Bennett 2000: 164). The legislation was not effective in either goal. Islanders adamantly resisted any government incursion onto land they considered to be their own, and few took up opportunities to formalize their own land claims through government schemes. As Tony Hughes wrote of these schemes, "in the 1960s we underestimated the degree of group resentment which could be created by separating off the holdings of such farmers from the rest of the group" (Hughes 1979: 236; see also Maenu'u 1979; Totorea 1979a, 1979b). Without capital for investment, transportation infrastructure, agricultural expertise, venues for marketing, and other factors, the registration of title did little to foster commercial agriculture. In the decades since the 1960s, land rights have been formalized not through an orderly process of land registration but through messy and disruptive land disputes that challenged and eventually overwhelmed the court system.

Large-scale logging has transformed the political and economic context for discussions of land tenure. Aside from an operation in Vanikoro in Santa Cruz that had begun in 1920, commercial logging in Solomon Islands began in the 1960s on government-controlled land. A significant operation was undertaken by Levers Pacific Timbers (a subsidiary of Levers Pacific Plantations Ltd.) on alienated land on Kolombangara and New Georgia. On the eve of national independence in 1978, Levers sought to expand operations from government land onto the vast swathes of heavily forested customary land in sparsely populated North New Georgia. A special act of parliament in 1979 set up the North New Georgia Timber Corporation to alienate timber rights and distribute profit from logging on customary land. Some Methodist leaders and most Seventh-day Adventists were in favor of logging on customary land, but leaders of the indigenous Christian Fellowship Church (CFC) offered fierce resistance that involved direct action against the company in 1981 and 1982 when Levers' machinery and staff housing at Enoghae were burned. The resistance was effective: in 1986, Levers cut its losses and left the province (Tausinga 1992; Bennett 2000: 213–24; Hviding 2011). A few years later, however, CFC leaders used the North New Georgia legislation to form a partnership with Golden Springs, a multinational based in Indonesia (Bennett 2000: 247; Hviding 2011: 68). This apparent turnaround reveals that CFC objections were less about logging per se than about the way that Levers and the government sought to bypass landowners (Bennett 2000: 225; Hviding 2003b).

Under an independent Solomon Islands government, logging on customary land swiftly expanded. By 1985, 95 percent of logging was on customary land. Logging brought large windfall profits to people unaccustomed to high incomes, but with a few significant exceptions little of that money was invested in projects of lasting value that could lead to improvements in quality of life. In theory, federal and provincial governments along with local councils were charged with enforcing legal regulations governing the negotiation of timber rights, the payment of royalties, and limiting environmental damage. In practice, however, the logging sector has been effectively unregulated (Frazer 1997; Dauvergne 1998: 524; Bennett 2000; Kabutaulaka 2006). The central regulatory legislation had been formulated in the late 1970s and applied only to government land, leaving the Timber Control Unit without jurisdiction over customary land where most logging was occurring (Bennett 2000: 237). From the 1980s onward, the Forestry Division was systematically underfunded.

Logging is widely understood to have fundamentally corrupted the fledgling political system of the independent Solomon Islands in ways that helped to lay the ground for the ethnic conflict that began in 1998. At independence in 1978, Solomon Islands inherited a Westminster-style political system without a system of political parties, so every government has been comprised of an unstable coalition held together by pragmatic concerns rather than ideology or consistent policy (Larmour 1983; Steeves 1996). Since the 1980s, much of the money that has greased the wheels of this high-level patronage politics has come from the logging industry. One prime minister, Solomon Mamaloni, who ruled for three terms (1981 to 1984, 1989 to 1993, 1994 to 1997), was known as the logger's friend; a champion of allowing local landowners to do with their resources as they wished, he undermined the legal restrictions and processes that should have ensured a sustainable rate of extraction and a better return on this valuable resource. On all levels, government officials granted tax exemptions, overlooked transfer pricing, pushed through logging licenses without due process, and engaged in numerous other dubious practices in exchange for direct and indirect support from loggers. A 1993/4 reform-oriented coalition government led by Ranongga-Simbo MP Francis Billy Hilly (son of George Hilly, the post-World War II era leader discussed in Chapter 2) was brought down by a no-confidence motion by Mamaloni widely understood to have been funded by Malaysian loggers (Kabutaulaka 1996). Mamaloni's governments continued to devolve regulatory responsibility to provinces and local councils, well aware that they lacked infrastructure to set and implement policy or enforce regulations (Bennett 2000: 253, 356–60; 2002; Fraenkel 2004: 39–41; Moore 2004). In 1997, widespread popular discontent about logging-fueled corruption resulted in a record number of incumbents losing their seats and brought another reform-oriented coalition government headed by Bartholomew Ulufa'alu to power. This was the government that would be destabilized by the ethnic conflict that began in 1998, and eventually pushed out of office by the 2000 coup.

In somewhat more subtle ways, logging has also transformed systems of informal political authority throughout the rural Solomons. These systems of "customary" or "traditional" authority were not timeless holdovers from precolonial times. By the eve of the boom of logging on customary land, they had already been transformed by two or three generations of engagement with plantation capitalism. Writing of New Ireland province in PNG, Robert Foster suggests that colonial pacification helped to amplify the authority of local big men, who expanded their influence into the emerging copra industry. After World War II, however, these modern big men lost control of copra production, which was increasingly controlled by households and cooperatives (Foster 1995: 67–92). This pattern is also evident in Ranongga, with the rise and demise of men like Simion Panakera and George Hilly (Chapter 2). Writing of Marovo, Hviding and Bayliss-Smith argue that copra production "in a sense 'democratised' access to wealth and status earlier this century because there was no aspect of the copra industry that could be brought under the sole control of local leaders"; the timber industry, however, has had the "opposite effect" (Hviding and Bayliss-Smith 2000: 232). Processes of determining ownership and distributing royalties have concentrated power in the hands of a few men, appointed as trustees for tribal landowning groups.

## Logging and the Constitution of Tribal Landowners

For most of the 1990s and 2000s, the Solomons-wide logging boom bypassed Ranongga. After decades of extraction of natural forest logs at rates far above sustainable levels, however, commercially exploitable stocks in other parts of the Solomons were swiftly running out. Even small, steep, densely populated, landslide-prone Ranongga became attractive to a company seeking to eke out a few more logs before departing from the country.

Logging came to Ranongga by way of the Christian Fellowship Church, an indigenous church of the Western Solomons with origins in the Methodist Mission. The founder of the CFC was Silas Eto, an indigenous Methodist pastor-teacher known for his innovative spiritualist style of worship and the new form of collective village life he introduced among his congregations in remote North New Georgia (see Harwood 1971; Tuza 1975, 1977). Considered backwards by many of his contemporaries, Eto became known among his followers as Holy Mama (*mama* is an affectionate term for "father" in the Roviana language.) The movement gained momentum in the late 1950s, when a large-scale revival broke out across the Roviana lagoon; in 1960, the CFC seceded from the Methodist Mission. The movement's numbers peaked in the late 1960s when nearly one-third of villages in traditionally Methodist areas had joined the CFC; over the following years, many villages away from New Georgia Island reverted to Methodism. Eto died in 1983, and after a period of uncertainty, leadership of the church passed to his younger son Ikan Rove, who took the title of the Spiritual Authority and led the church until his death in July 2014. Knighted in 2005 in recognition of his "services to religion and community," Rove was also known as "the living god" (*tamaza toana*) and Papa Hope (*hope* is "holy" in Roviana), and many of his followers understood him to be the living incarnation of God on Earth, capable of blessing those who obey and cursing those who do not. Rove's elder brother Job Dudley Tausinga led the CFC community in the realm of secular politics as premier of Western Province from 1983 to 1987; he was also the nation's longest serving member of parliament, holding the North New Georgia seat from 1984 until his surprise defeat in the 2014 national election. Hviding (2011: 66–77) describes this division of authority between the two brothers as consistent with the division of authority between chiefs and priests in old New Georgia.[2]

Like the Methodist Mission on which it was modeled, the CFC embraced a theology that focused very much on collective work for commercial production. In the 1950s and 1960s, Silas Eto established enormous copra plantations in the Kusage area of New Georgia, and the church was known for building the largest traditional material "leaf house" anywhere in Solomon Islands. His successors would involve the church community in logging on an equally large scale. Reverend Rove described his father's leadership as the "time of the church" and his own leadership as the "time of development." According to Hviding (ibid.), royalty money from logging operations undertaken since the 1980s on CFC land has been consolidated rather than distributed. He argues that it forms the basis for the remarkable projects of rural development undertaken by the CFC, projects that include large-scale reforestation of logged areas in teak and oil palm, and supported rural development in the face of civil crisis and state collapse.

As a church, kinship network, and corporate business entity, the CFC is unlike any other landowning group in Solomon Islands. The spiritual and secular leaders of the CFC derive some of their authority from genealogical relationships to landowning *butubutu*, but the CFC membership is most powerfully bound together as a religious community, subject to the power not only of the Christian God but also the spiritual authority first of Silas Eto and then his son Ikan Rove. The singular effectiveness of the CFC as a corporate landowning group must also be understood in the context of the unique legal situation of the North New Georgia Timber Corporation (NNGTC). Tausinga was highly critical of the way the NNGTC bypassed landowners, but after the CFC leadership wrested control away from the national government and foreign interests they were able to use the NNGTC as the business wing of the CFC. Under local control, the NNGTC retained special status granted by the colonial government, a status that meant the CFC could obtain timber despite a 1983 ban on round-log exports and without the usual messy processes of determining land rights (Bennett 2000: 246). Through a legal entity established by the colonial government to bypass landowners, the CFC was thus able to undertake logging on its own terms with minimal interference from either the national government or individual landowners.

The CFC is a powerful force throughout Western Province, but there are few members on Ranongga. One of them is Nason Beikera, and it is no coincidence that he was among the people most active in promoting logging on Degere land. In 2006, Nason escorted me to North New Georgia to meet the Spiritual Authority and see CFC development at Duvaha.[3] While traveling to North New Georgia, and waiting for my audience with the leader, Nason talked to me at length about the CFC theology of development as he had come to understand it (he explained that he only understood a "shadow" of the core theology expounded by the Spiritual Authority). Jesus told us to move mountains, he explained, but we can't do that with our hands; we need the assistance of a company and its earthmoving equipment. Nason knew that there wouldn't be much royalty money from Ranongga, but royalties weren't the point. Royalty money is "dead money," but the roads and opportunity to create plantations in cleared areas produces "living money." He foresaw the major problem he would face: getting his non-CFC neighbors and relatives to unite behind his plan for developing Ranongga.

That dissent was already obvious as news about plans for logging on Degere land began to circulate in mid 2005. I learned about these plans in the context of a large synod of the United Church of Solomon Islands at Pienuna village. In the 1980s, the United Church had sought to foster ecologically and socially sustainable alternatives to large-scale logging by establishing the Solomon Western Islands Fair Trade (SWIFT) Trust, which encouraged small-scale milling of timber for export to European markets. Unfortunately, the under-resourced United Church administration could not manage complex fair-trade regulations, its overseas partners did not effectively market SWIFT timber, and the small scale of production made it unattractive to producers (Bennett 2000: 284–86; Hviding and Bayliss-Smith 2000: 276–90; Bird 2007, 2008). Yet the effort is notable because it was among the few attempts to foster sustainable timber extraction in the region. Despite this initiative, however, the authority of the church over land matters was limited. While some people gathered for the United Church synod in Pienuna in 2005 privately discussed their fears that logging would destroy already fragile land and cause divisive disputes, most were resigned to the fact that it was on "the side of the landowners, the side of the chiefs" rather than the church. Others planned to contest the logging operations, but did not want to do so until the company actually arrived because they hoped to claim a share of royalties or compensation for damages (see also Macintyre and Foale 2004).

In order to obtain a logging license, a foreign corporation must gain permission from landowners to log their land. Earlier in 2005, Kalena Timber Company, which had been active previously in Choiseul (Bennett 2000: 213), submitted its application for a license to the Commissioner of Forests, with a letter stating that the company had consulted "Degere Tribe" and proposed to log 2,000 hectares of land for 40,000 cubic meters of timber annually. The application was accompanied by a letter undersigned by the "Chief" and "Spokesperson" of Degere tribe, stating that "after having consulted our tribe," they invited Kalena to "enter and harvest our timber resources on our customary land known to our tribe as Degere land for purposes of round logs export." Until the mid 1990s, such an application would have been approved by the Commissioner of Forests, and a timber rights hearing would have been held by the Local Area Council. Area Councils were dismantled around 1996, however, and since that time, the Western Province Executive approves applications, even though its members know nothing of the detailed history of the lands in question. In theory, timber rights hearings should gather all "stakeholders" in an area to consult about the history and ownership of the land in question. In practice, the hearings are often poorly publicized in ways that ensure that opponents to the application will be excluded. If the determination is in favor of the applicant, a Second Notice is posted, inviting objectors to submit arguments in writing to be heard by the Customary Land Appeals Court. Even when hearings are publicized and objectors attend, the debate focuses not on the potential benefits or drawbacks of logging for communities involved. These hearings focus only on contests over landownership.

For several years, nothing happened on the Degere logging project. The license should have expired. However, in 2008, a different company, named Glengrow, suddenly began logging operations around Baniata without any further applications or hearings. Opponents requested an injunction for the company to halt operations and launched a High Court case challenging the legality of the license granted to Degere and Glengrow. The first defendant in the case was the Commissioner of Forests and the Western Provincial Government (represented by the Solomon Islands attorney general); the second defendants were Ezekiel Daveta and other named members of "Degere Tribe"; the third was Nason Beikera, who was doing business under the name Degere Development Company; the fourth was Glengrow (SI) Company Limited.

The series of court cases that followed were understood by many villagers as a contest over landownership between two *butubutu*: Vitu and Degere. Importantly, however, the claimants did not initially present themselves as landowners, but as representatives of "all persons" of the villages within the logging concession and on the other side of the logged ridge (*Zobule v. Attorney General* 2008). The first named claimant, Alpheaus Zobule, a highly respected Bible translator with a PhD in theology (see McDougall 2012), explained to me in 2010 that he took up the cause when he was presented with a petition signed by residents of southern Ranongga villages who were concerned that logging would further damage their earthquake-ravaged land. His co-claimant was a man of Vitu, but they were not challenging Degere's ownership of the land. Instead, they sought to challenge the legality of the license-granting procedure. The challenge had several grounds: the license had been reissued four years after it was initially approved, even though the law allowed only three months; there was no public notice of a timber rights hearing held in December 2007; the hearing was held in the provincial capital of Gizo, not in the area of the concession as the law specified.[4]

The claimants did not seek to speak as tribal landowners, but as the case unfolded they were required to do so. In a successful petition to quash the injunction, the defendants' lawyer did not defend his clients from the charges of illegality but instead argued that only landowners can put a halt to logging operations. In the ruling, Justice Faukona wrote: "There is no evidence that people from those villages claim ownership of any customary land within the concessionary area, or within Degere land" (*Zobule v. Attorney General* 2008). Faukona argued that these ownership claims were implicit in the request for an injunction: "If the Claimants claim trespass then they have to allege ownership." And while agreeing that the late revalidation of the logging license, and the hearing's location in Gizo rather than Ranongga, breached the Forest Resources and Timber Utilisation Act 1996, he drew on earlier judgments to claim that the question of the "logging license cannot be entirely separated from the issues of ownership of customary land" (ibid.).

This initial ruling pushed the claimants to establish themselves as customary landowners and to challenge Degere's tribal ownership of the land within the logging concession. As discussed in Chapter 5, Vitu arrived on Degere land many generations ago. According to some, Vitu purchased land from Degere, but according to others they remained guests on Vitu land. What is clear is that people of the two groups had long lived together on the contested land, and that extensive intermarriage and interaction had made people say, in contexts outside of logging hearings, that the two were no longer "different people." In 2009, a meeting in Lale village on Ranongga was arranged to determine which *butubutu* was the real landowner. The Kubokota Chiefs' Committee heard the arguments and determined that Vitu clan owned the contested land. According to the people I spoke to, Degere leaders were summonsed but did not attend the meeting, though I suspect they would say that they were not informed of the meeting. The defense lawyer proceeded to seek a "quashing order" from the High Court against the findings of the Chiefs' Committee (*Daveta v. Kotomae* 2010) on the basis that the Kubokota Chiefs' Committee had no jurisdiction to hear claims regarding land in Luqa; that the committee was biased toward people of Vitu; and that his clients were not properly summonsed. The judge in this case (Justice Chetwynd) rejected these claims and found that the Kubokota Chiefs' Committee did have jurisdiction and that no bias had been proved. He ordered the claimants, Beikera and Daveta, to pay the court costs and take their disagreements to either the Local Court or the Customary Land Appeal Court, which, unlike the High Court, have jurisdiction over the substance of customary land claims.

With this decision in their favor, the High Court returned to the original case, again led by Zobule. In a ruling in August 2010, Justice Chetwynd found that the defendants had failed to pay court fees and, because of the incompetence of their lawyer, had failed to file objections by the deadline. He did not strike out the defense, but he did reinstate the original injunction against the logging operation. By that time, however, the injunction was pointless because the fourth defendant, Glengrow, had "left the scene." Owing tens of thousands of Solomon Islands dollars in court fees, local defendants were not present for the hearing, having reportedly returned to Ranongga. Chetwynd instructed their lawyer to contact them by public service announcement to "tell them what a serious situation they are in," and warned that they would face punitive charges if court fees were not paid (*Zobule v. Attorney General* 2010).

Only two parties emerged from the legal proceedings unscathed: the company and the state. Glengrow absconded before the injunction on operations was reinstated, leaving its Ranonggan partners with court fees owing. The Ranonggan defendants were forbidden from engaging another company, but there was no mention in the rulings that Glengrow would be banned from undertaking further activities in the country. The Commissioner of Forests and the Western Provincial Government, the first defendants in the case, will presumably continue to process licenses without adequate attention to legal requirements. Aside from noting that "there will still be serious issues to be dealt with," Chetwynd did not indicate how the government would be held accountable. Instead, he reiterated the previous ruling, which claimed, "The issue of the propriety of the logging license cannot be separated from issues of ownership of customary land" (ibid.). In his ruling, he chastised claimants and defendants alike for not "dealing with the fundamental issue in the case" (ibid.). By foregrounding the need to sort out ownership issues, questions about state complicity were sidelined.

In a final High Court case (*Zobule v. Attorney General* 2011), the claimants sought payment for damages. There were no records of the volume of timber extracted, but Justice Chetwynd cited evidence that timber valued at US$1,348,172.26 was exported. Although Chetwynd stated that he considered the claimants' map of Vitu land to be inadequate (it accurately recorded boundaries on the coast, but was vague about inland borders), he nevertheless estimated that 40% of the logs that were taken from the land came from the claimant's land and ruled that they should be paid a total of US$146,613.73 (15% of the proportion of their timber export as royalty, and 25% as profit from the operations). It is not clear whether the claimants—or the defendants, for that matter—ever received these royalties.

As a result of the logging, southern Ranongga is now left more vulnerable to landslides, with people struggling harder to make a living. The real tragedy of the story is that this damage occurred with minimal benefit to anyone: even if the few hundred thousand dollars of royalty money and profits had been distributed, it was not invested in a way that improved quality of life for most of the population. What was remarkable about the High Court challenge in the case of Degere land was that it was initially motivated by a church leader's concern for the interest of all village communities on the southern half of the island. But the rulings made it clear that a coalition of concerned citizens could not stop a logging operation, even one that had so clearly breached legal procedures. Only customary landowners could mount such a challenge. The legal process essentially thwarted the emergence of a broader concerned public.

## Conservation and the Misrecognition of Community

In the 1990s, global conservationists were moving away from the idea that the environment could only be preserved in nature reserves taken out of the hands of local people. The decade saw an expansion of funding for projects aimed at "integrated conservation and development" that sought to involve communities as "stakeholders." The shift away from ideas of permanent reserves was partially philosophical and partially pragmatic: in much of the decolonized world, large nature reserves were not politically feasible. As a wide range of studies of community conservation projects have now documented, the conservationist embrace of "community" was not accompanied by much critical examination of what the term might mean (see Agrawal 2005; Brosius, Tsing, and Zerner 2005; West 2006). I now turn to the examination of such a project in Ranongga, wherein "community" was initially defined as "tribe," an approach that provided the ideal conditions for igniting a long-smoldering dispute about chiefly succession.

The frenzy of logging in the Solomons in the 1980s and 1990s attracted the attention of global environmentalism. A large number of non-governmental and governmental initiatives sought to offer an alternative to the destructive logging that would wreck land and livelihoods. The Worldwide Fund for Nature (WWF) began community-based conservation work in Marovo Lagoon in 1991 with funding from Australia and the European Commission. In 1995, it began a five-year community resource conservation and development project (CRCD), coordinated by the WWF South Pacific Program and based in Gizo, with funding from the UK Overseas Development Administration's Joint Funding Scheme with WWF (WWFSPP 2003). The project attempted to convince landowners of the value of their forests and reefs, and offered assistance to help them undertake forms of development that were more sustainable than the destructive round-log operations run by multinational corporations. Writing of the WWF project, Simon Foale notes that environmentalists tend to value rainforest and coral reefs for the sake of "biodiversity," something that has become a transcendentally valuable moral good in ways that are no longer rooted in biological science. While few rural Solomon Islanders share this sense of the transcendent value of species diversity, they are concerned with the continued viability of ecosystems upon which they depend for their livelihoods. While this could be a common ground for cooperation with global environmentalists, Foale argues that environmentalists romanticize rural life, overestimate the solidarity of the "community," and underestimate villagers' aspirations for economic advancement (Foale 2002; see also Foale and Manele 2004; Macintyre and Foale 2004; Foale and Macintyre 2005).[5]

WWF began its project on Ranongga in April 1997. Like many similar projects, this one commenced without any real inquiry into local social or territorial organization. The location of the project seems to have been chosen because of a unique form of karst topography in the mountains of Ranongga, as well as the interest of the Ranonggan field officer, who lived in the project area. The project was initially known as the "Nulu land project" and the "community" was defined as the "Nulu tribe." Nulu is the name of a territory and a *butubutu*: the first Nulu ancestors are said to have descended from heaven (*nulu*) by sliding down a mango tree onto Mount Kela, Ranongga's highest mountain. Over the course of events discussed below, the WWF project was renamed the "Kekoro community," a neologism derived from the names of the uninhabited peaks on the central ridge (Kela, Korotina, and Rioroqe). The project involved people of two United Church villages of more than 300 people each (Pienuna and Obobulu), one Seventh-day Adventist village of approximately 120 people (Vonga), and numerous smaller hamlets scattered along the coast whose inhabitants attended church in one of the larger villages. All of the people living in the area had various crosscutting kinship ties; many inhabitants of the Adventist village were related to people of one or the other of the United Church villages, though mostly at two or more generations remove. Nulu territory is bounded by a point south of Obobulu, a small stream north of Pienuna, and the highest point of the ridge of the island is known as Nulu land. Within this territory, however, the village of Pienuna is held by the clan named Vitu, and numerous other family groups control smaller areas of land.

The project quickly became embroiled in a heated dispute over chiefly succession within Nulu. This particular dispute had been brewing for several years and was linked to conflicts of the previous generation. At the core of the dispute were the relative rights of two branches (*kaesusu*) of Nulu, one of which was resident on Nulu land and the other which was resident on the other side of the island. According to a well-known story, a Nulu woman married a chief of Galagala, another *butubutu* whose territory encompassed Modo village. As this woman and her children were crossing from the Kubokota to the Ganoqa side of the island, they were ambushed by warriors from Vella Lavella. The son was slain and the mother hanged herself in mourning. Only the daughter survived, and she joined her father in Ganoqa. Her father decided that his own Galagala people were unable to look after themselves and passed the chieftainship to his daughter and her Nulu descendants, who were chiefs of this area in historical times (thus Beibangara, the last non-Christian chief of Modo, was a Nulu man). The transfer of power from Galagala to Nulu was at the core of a land dispute fought in the early 1980s (see *Mamipitu v. Ragoso* 1980; *Mamipitu vs. Ragoso (Appeal)* 1981). That case, which many residents of both Modo and Buri continue to reference when discussing land tenure, hinged on the question of whether the Galagala father transferred only the chieftainship to his daughter, or whether he also transferred actual ownership of the land to her. In the context of the WWF project, a different issue came to the fore: the extent to which the branch of Nulu who had taken over the chieftainship of Modo in Ganoqa also retained power over Nulu land in Kubokota.

Prior to the twentieth century, there had been considerable movement back and forth across the mountains, often taking the form of a woman being "called back" onto the land of her clan following generations of exogamous marriage and patrilocal and virilocal residence (McDougall 2004: 173–79).

Soon, though, mission rivalry overlaid the geographic differentiation of the two branches. According to oral accounts of a dispute heard by a British district officer in the 1930s, Adventist men of Modo cut a tree for a canoe on Nulu land without asking Amos Nake, the Methodist chief of the Kubokota branch of Nulu.[6] Nake reportedly won the court case that followed, though the result continues to be contested by some Adventists, who attribute his victory to colonial government favoritism toward Methodists. Some of my interlocutors suggested that when it was clear that Amos Nake had no direct matrilineal relatives (sisters' sons) who could replace him, he called a Nulu woman from Modo to settle and marry at Obobulu, but he decided not to appoint her son as his successor because of a dispute. In the end, Nake appointed his own son, Timote Nake, to "look after" Nulu land and people with the help of Samuel Samata, a man of Nulu. None of these appointments were public in the way that chiefly installations in the past were. Many people today complain that there are no more chiefs on the island because none have been seated on top of *bakia* in front of representatives of all the island's *butubutu* in the way that customary procedures once required. In the late 1990s, Timote was living quietly in his family hamlet at Qiloe, some distance from Obobulu village. Along with Pienuna village chief John Pavukera (his cousin) and a few other relatives, Timote belonged to the World Wide Church of God, an American church founded by American radio evangelist Herbert Armstrong. Like many contemporary chiefs, Timote had a "spokesman," his nephew Derek Alekera Jiru, whose father Alekera had been a justice in the government local courts and had established the World Wide Church on Ranongga. Shortly before the WWF project commenced, Timote decided that first his younger brother, then his own son, should succeed him as chief of Nulu.

When WWF began its work on Ranongga, the first step was aimed at increasing awareness of the environment and mapping out relationships between people and the land. Most of the public mapping of relationships focused on lateral ties between *butubutu*, villages, and church and community organizations. A few individuals closely related to the Ganoqa branch of Nulu, however, began to compile an exhaustive genealogy from the first Nulu woman to the current generation of Nulu people. Given the underlying history of disputes over the territory, it is little wonder that this was interpreted as an attempt to regain control of the territory.

In late 1998, the chief's spokesman wrote to WWF to declare the project closed. The letter forbid "any further enforcement or monitoring the land" [*sic*] by a foreign organization, arguing that the land should be held by "traditional custom" and that no more details about the land should be revealed. In responding to the letter, the expatriate country manager explained that the information collected was to help them against foreigners who might take advantage of them, and that it would only be made available to the "community" who would control it. In a second letter, the spokesman reiterated the demand that the project be ended, and stated more explicitly that the Nulu chief had enemies in his own "tribe."[7] WWF leadership sought to work out these conflicts between the WWF and "the community," and also to establish a clear line of chiefly succession. In September 1998, the Pienuna Chiefs' Committee was involved in a WWF meeting focused on the question of Nulu chiefly succession. Bruce Ragoso, the recognized chief of the Ganoqa branch of Nulu, asserted his authority, stating that the chieftainship should remain with the *butubutu*; only if all members of the "tribe" around the region are consulted can chieftainship pass onto someone of another *butubutu*. Distance did not erase connections to or knowledge of land: "We live far away, but we know the house foundations, the genealogy, the land." Having asserted his authority, Bruce said that Samuel Samata of Pienuna would be a local "custodian." Timote did not object, saying only he agreed with the others. From the point of view of the WWF, conservation and development work could then proceed because leadership structures were clear.

In the months after the September 1998 meeting, work on the project proceeded in ways that made little reference to those leadership structures. Bruce Ragoso was minimally involved in the project. Samata attended most WWF meetings but did not take a leading role; my sense was that he intentionally downplayed his own authority in favor of leaders chosen from within the community. Project meetings were announced following Sunday church services, when other kinds of community work for the school and church were discussed. During the first part of 1999, committees and subcommittees were laboriously put together over several days of meetings. The field officer drew on WWF guidelines for structuring and organizing the management program, but villagers were already well acquainted with the formation of committees, having been involved in both churches and local government for generations. These committees aimed to be inclusive, with membership balanced across different hamlets (thus different extended families) and including women and men, youths and elders. The chairman who was eventually chosen to lead the committee was not a landowner, but a prototypical outsider, a man from Choiseul married to a Pienuna woman.

Controversies over the role of chiefs as landowners periodically came to the surface. In a February 1999 meeting, a project executive was labeled "chiefs' committee," and was thus seen to exclude anyone who was not a chief of the landholding *butubutu*, a point that angered many in-married people who were involved in the project. The name was changed to "Kekoro" committee so that it was clear that anyone, not just chiefs, could be on the committee. When one participant suggested that the community give more thought to who should be members of the Kekoro committee, a man originally from Vella Lavella became angry because he thought that this implied that outsiders should not serve on the committee. He threatened to take his family back to his own land rather than stay and work in a community that did not appreciate him. The original speaker sought to placate him by explaining that he only meant that they should choose people who had the time, interest, and education to be part of the conservation work rather than arbitrarily choosing a certain number of women, men, elders, youths, and people from all hamlets. He had not meant to suggest that in-married residents from other islands should not participate and had no authority in managing resources.

Six months after the chief's hearing that had appeared to resolve the debate over chiefly succession, WWF called another meeting intended to, once again, "get things out in the open." The expatriate WWF management at the time continued to assume that problems were centered on the relationship between "the community" and WWF, rather than internal tensions within the community. People of Pienuna and Obobulu who had taken part in the project were bewildered about why the issue was being revisited. As Samata said: "They say tell it all out, then it will be clear. But there isn't anything else that is hidden." The Nulu chief's spokesman took the opportunity to tell WWF to stay out of internal discussions of landownership: "WWF can continue to help people, but WWF should not be involved in any conflict about things involving our land system . . . Totally leave those things . . . That is our issue and it isn't tied up with WWF." During this meeting, committees were reconstituted to include a wider range of hamlets and families. After this meeting, however, WWF's local field officer and Gizo-based management stopped trying to bring controversies over land and chiefly succession within the scope of the project.

In September 1999, a resource management order was prepared and officially launched at a large gathering in Obobulu. Prior to the launch, the order had been discussed on Sunday evening following a church service in Pienuna. A well-educated man, who had returned to live in his parents' hamlet after several years spent working in town, angrily opposed the order, saying that "blocks" that belonged to individual families would fall under restrictions imposed by WWF, the committee, or even the village chiefs. After some harsh words were exchanged, the pastor exhorted everyone to calm down and speak in order. In opposition to the first man's aggressive outburst, another man said that he was happy to "follow the thoughts of the chiefs" regarding the organization of blocks of land because "we are all adopted and you [chiefs] know what is best." Another man who had taken part in meetings explained that people were free to saw timber as they saw fit within their own "blocks." What seemed to placate the objector, however, was the comment of a Kekoro committee member, who pointed out that the committee meetings were open to all and he had chosen not to participate. In this fashion, questions about tribal landownership were subsumed through reference to a bureaucratically constituted community committee.

The management plan order stipulated that trees not be felled for gardening more than 200 meters above sea level, and that reefs along the coast be closed for one year from spear fishing and harvesting mollusks, sea snails, and bêche-de-mer. Few people paid attention to the limitation on gardening, in part because no one really knew where 200 meters elevation was located on the landscape. The reef taboo, however, was effectively enforced around Pienuna. Again, however, Nulu "tribal" leadership had very little to do with it. Instead, village chief John Pavukera (a man of Vitu, not Nulu) and the families that controlled the reef areas associated with the "blocks" they held closed the reefs to harvesting. A year later, the field officer reported non-compliance with the reef closing on Nulu land around Obobulu, but no one attempted to enforce the closure.

From the perspective of most people in Pienuna, the reef closure was a terrific success. By Christmas 2000, the reefs were full of mollusks, crayfish, and fish. The Kekoro committee and the village chiefs lifted the taboo on the reef in time for the 2001 New Year's feast. Following annual tradition, the village was organized into teams (that year, we were named for Pacific Islands countries). Along with the usual soccer and netball games, choir competitions, races, and traditional skill competitions (scraping coconuts, weaving baskets, and so on), the teams competed to see which could gather the most food for the New Year's feast. The reefs that had built up stock for more than a year were cleared out within a few days, an endeavor that lead to a huge feast at the end of the week. From the point of view of anyone interested in long-term conservation, the ban was less effective. Here and elsewhere in Western Province, WWF supported traditional forms of short-term closures that were unlikely to have any long-term effect on fish stocks (Foale 2002; Foale and Manele 2004). Foale et al. (2011) argue that in the situations of low population density that have characterized most of island Melanesia until recently, such resource taboos have followed human social cycles, not the reproductive cycles of marine species.

One of the ironies of the early years of the project was that, although people were genuinely interested in managing their resources for future generations, they gained little relevant information and few skills in resource management through their involvement with the project. Early WWF workshops in 1997/8 focused on "awareness," as if all that was necessary to lessen people's desires for the kind of development promised by logging companies was some reflection on their own environmental knowledge and values. As the resource management order was being drafted in 1999, a large part of the budget for capacity building funded work led by Lawrence Stubbs, who had recorded custom stories in Ranongga in the late 1980s and early 1990s (Stubbs 1989, 1991). Stubbs was tasked with consulting with Ranonggan chiefs to produce a "book of custom law" and to set up an island-wide chiefs' committee. Unfortunately, the book of custom law had little to do with environmental resources, and, to my knowledge, the island-wide chiefs' committee met only once after it was established.

Following the launch of the resource management plan and the closure of reefs, in early 2000 the project turned to "community resource development ventures," that is, something that would offer income that many villagers hoped would be a trade-off for closing their reefs and sitting for hours in meetings and workshops. Under the leadership of the Ranonggan field officer's energetic wife, the Kekoro Women's Association was formed in 2000 and visited a project in Rarumana that used simple equipment to produce high-quality coconut oil for local sale and export. Such a project would have effectively made use of the otherwise worthless coconut plantations. The movement into the "venture" stage of the project, however, initiated a new round of clarification efforts, when the Gizo-based resource-planning officer (a man of the western Solomons) told the Kekoro committee in Pienuna that WWF could not sponsor any development project until the boundaries between Vitu and Nulu land were clarified.

Like so many other places on the island, the history of Pienuna involves an engagement between an autochthonous clan and a migrant clan. People of Nulu and Vitu agree that many generations ago, two sisters of the clan Vitu living in Luqa quarreled after one broke a shell tool used for scraping taro. One sister fled northward onto Nulu land, and encountered two old men of Nulu. She gave them a basket of shell valuables for the land that would become Pienuna. The precise boundary of the land she purchased hinges upon a contested detail in the narratives about the Vitu woman's path from Luqa to Nulu land. If she traveled along the shore (*poana*), it is assumed that her purchase was limited to the coastal areas. If she followed an inland route (*are*), however, then it is assumed that it included more inland territory. In everyday practice, the precise location of the boundary does not matter. Since Vitu's arrival, Nulu and Vitu people have been allies and affines, and people today say they are "not different people."[8] Disagreements about the limits of Vitu and Nulu land arise occasionally, but they are usually kept under wraps by reference to these histories of entanglement.

In the case of the proposed WWF venture there was absolutely no need to clarify the boundaries of Vitu and Nulu land. It was not a logging or mining operation that would generate royalties to be distributed to one or the other clan. People would simply harvest coconuts that they already had access to and would earn money from the products they made. Had the project been highly successful, disputes about the possession of coconut plantations might have arisen. Such disputes would not have had anything to do with the disagreement about the boundaries of Nulu and Vitu land because coconuts are a kind of property (*izizongo*) that has little to do with the large named territories (*pezo*) held by clans (see Chapter 5). Some WWF staff believed that people of Nulu or Vitu or others would object to the placement of the equipment on their land or seek to claim profits from operations. But the grounds for demanding that Nulu and Vitu clarify their land boundaries were weak. It seemed to be little more than simply a reflexive expression of the common wisdom that no development can succeed unless tribal disputes are sorted out—common wisdom that is based on a misunderstanding of the nature of land tenure, land disputes, and social organization in rural Solomon Islands societies.

As it turned out, the WWF coconut-oil project was not funded, though not because of the concocted land dispute at Pienuna. The project did not get off the ground because of the worsening civil crisis that made everything very difficult, as well as a rather tepid commitment on the part of WWF to the "development" side of "conservation and development" projects. However, rumors of a land dispute nearly ruined Pienuna's possibility of being the site of a junior secondary school, something most residents were enthusiastic about. The new school was to be located on a plateau a few hundred meters inland, in an area where people disagree over whether the land belongs to Vitu or Nulu. Again, the clan ownership of this densely used area is almost irrelevant. Many different people of many different clans have used the area in the past, clearing land for settlements, gardens, and coconut plantations. People of different clan groups had given land to the school and church.

In the end, the school was built without any dispute and without any clarification of the boundaries between *butubutu* territories. When the chairman of Pienuna's school board learned that the Education Department was seeking to locate the junior secondary school elsewhere to avoid a land dispute in Pienuna, I helped to draft a letter from the village school committee, village chief John Pavukera (of Vitu), Samuel Samata (of Nulu), and leaders of other *butubutu* that explained that everyone was united in their support for the new school. Their parents and grandparents had donated the land for the original primary school, and so-called tribal ownership was irrelevant.

Over the ensuing years, WWF changed its strategy, moving away from a model that promised local communities income-generating "development" projects in exchange for their cooperation in projects aimed at environmental conservation. As Simon Foale has explained, the project began to put "greater emphasis on providing a range of clearly defined 'technical' services aimed at assisting landowners with basic sustainable resource management strategies" (Foale 2002: 65). The Kekoro project continued into the post-conflict years, with WWF staff working with families who actually controlled access to areas of reef (and not just people of the autochthonous *butubutu*) to assess the reef and provide advice on management. Following the 2007 earthquake, WWF was involved in damage assessment, but its largely marine-focused management activities ceased after the project area's fringing reef was exposed and destroyed. Neither WWF-constituted institutions including the Kekoro committee and the island-wide chiefs' committee, nor individuals involved in WWF's consciousness-raising work offered significant opposition to the logging that began a few kilometers south of the project area in 2008.

Although both are considered to be a form of "development," it is hardly fair to suggest any direct comparison between logging operations undertaken by a rapacious logging company and conservation workshops led by a well-intentioned environmental NGO. By putting these diametrically opposed projects in the same analytical frame, however, I have tried to show that they elicit a very similar form of social organization: tribal landownership. In the context of logging, the legal apparatus of the state requires that local people who seek to establish or contest timber rights must organize themselves as tribal corporations, rather than as churches, kindreds, or a group of concerned citizens. In the context of conservation, the NGO leadership simply assumed that communities were by definition tribal communities, and ignored other aspects of social organization. Yet because this project operated outside of the formal legal apparatus of the state, there was scope for local people to bypass such divisive tribalism. Rather than continuing to engage with the NGO as members or non-members of Nulu "tribe," people of Pienuna, Vonga, and Obobulu engaged with it through civic institutions of the church and community.

## Tribes, Villages, and Emergent Collectivities

Solomon Islanders and outsiders alike blame tribalism and land disputes for thwarting the projects that might allow communities and the nation as a whole to "develop." In this chapter, I have tried to put this argument on its head by showing how diverse forms of development actually incite tribalism and create disputes. Tribalism is not a natural feature of indigenous sociality; it is a social formation that has been elicited through engagements with the apparatus of the colonial state and engagement with projects of capitalist development. The British colonial administration consistently defined social organization and land tenure in terms of tribes, even when the purported goal was more individualized forms of ownership. Today, whether seeking to exploit or conserve resources, Ranonggans find themselves constituted by outsiders and by the state as tribal subjects.

My analysis in this chapter resonates with Mahmood Mamdani's discussion of late colonialism in Africa (Mamdani 1996). Africans were tribal by definition; those aspects of sociality and territoriality that did not fit the tribal mode were systematically downplayed or ignored. These assumptions led colonial agents to fundamentally misunderstand indigenous systems of land tenure. First, they assumed that land was owned either by an individual or a bounded community, and that property rights were exclusive, with no overlapping ownership of land. Second, colonial authorities mistook ritual authority for ownership, and assumed that chiefs were also landowners. And finally, land policy drew a clear line between tribal members and strangers; it "identified the community with the tribe and thus defined all migrants not belonging to the tribe—all strangers—as without a traditional right of access to the land" (ibid.: 140). All of this is as true for Solomon Islands as it is for much of Africa. However, whereas Mamdani emphasizes the hegemonic nature of this tribal frame, I have also tried to tease out the ways that local people subvert such a framing, often without explicitly critiquing that framing.

Both the logging project and the conservation project began with the assumption that corporate descent groups (*butubutu* in the vernacular language, tribes in legal discourse) were the core unit of local socio-territorial organization. Over the course of both projects, however, people acted collectively as entities that were not tribes, clans, or any other kind of corporate descent group. In the context of logging, Degere had to constitute itself as a tribal landowning corporation to seek timber rights, but translocal church connections played an important role in bringing the company to Ranongga. Opponents of Glengrow did not initially speak as a genealogically defined tribe but as a coalition of village communities led by a charismatic religious leader. In the context of the conservation project, participants were pushed to clarify issues of tribal succession, but the designated tribal custodian allowed his authority to be subsumed within the broader structures of the village community.

Such dynamics reveal the ongoing importance of place-focused social organization analyzed in Chapter 2. In A.M. Hocart's analysis of Simbo at the turn of the twentieth century, the district (*gusu*), not a genealogically defined corporate group such as *butubutu*, was mobilized for collective action under chiefs (Hocart 1922). In Ranongga today, despite widespread ideologies about tribal landownership, *guguzu*—now church-centered villages—are still the groups that are most effectively mobilized for collective action. Villages are not united; far from it. The centripetal pull of the church is matched by the centrifugal forces of everyday conflicts, which often dissolve into denominational schism (McDougall 2008, 2013). Yet despite the reality of social fragmentation, when people do come together and work for a common cause, it is almost always in the form of church-based communities.

Social scientists have now effectively debunked myths about the solidarity of supposedly traditional communities. Yet in critiquing naive assumptions that communities exist and are automatically cohesive, many seem to suggest that we ought to discard the concept entirely. Thus, Agrawal and Gibson (1999) argue for more attention to multiple actors, multiple interests, the interactions of these actors and interests, and the institutional arrangements of these interests and actors. In such a framework there is no need to think about something like "community." Yet, in my experience, it would be a mistake to ignore the possibilities of community, particularly because "community" is something that Ranonggans themselves are passionately concerned with. "Community" cannot be understood as a thing that is out there, but as something that people are constantly seeking to achieve; community is the goal, not the ground, of social life.

## Notes

1. Many of the contradictions in Allan's report on customary land tenure are also evident in his evaluations and reflections on the Maasina Rule movement (Allan 1989; see also Akin 2013). As a district officer in Malaita in 1949, and then its district commissioner between 1950 and 1952, Allan had taken part in the arrest for coordinated civil disobedience of thousands of Malaita's Maasina Rule followers, and he left the island with acute antipathy for the movement, for its ideology of *kastom*, and for Malaitans in general (Akin 2013: 440 n.53). This antipathy was manifest in his report on customary land tenure in the way he blamed many problems of contemporary tenure on islanders' growing self-consciousness about their own customary practices.
2. Beginning around 2010, rifts developed between followers of Rev. Rove and Tausinga (though not, it seems, between the brothers themselves). Conflicts, which were sometimes violent, centered on the distribution of the considerable assets of the CFC (Lyons et al. 2012). Tausinga's 2014 election loss to John Dean Kuku, associated with the other faction of the CFC, resulted from this schism.
3. Uninvited visitors to CFC villages are not welcome. My host Nason Beikera worked hard to gain permission for my visit; I also had an introductory letter from Edvard Hviding, who has a long and cordial relationship with CFC leaders. Yet when we arrived at Duvaha late in the evening after a long day's ride across open seas, we were almost turned away by a group of young "sentries" who had come from Baraulu in Roviana Lagoon on their regular service rotation. They had known of my arrival, and were under the impression that I should not be allowed ashore. Panicked, Nason hurried to find out what had happened. He returned greatly relieved after the Spiritual Authority himself gave us permission to land. Once our invitation was clear, we were warmly welcomed. The incident highlighted the power of the Spiritual Authority, as well as the complexity of relationships amongst different villages within overall CFC control.
4. According to the "background facts" reported in the first judgment issued, the first Form I application was lodged on 28 August 2003 but was not activated. It was then renewed on 9 September 2007. The claimants argued that there was no publicly displayed notice for the timber rights hearing, which was held not on Ranongga Island but in the provincial capital, Gizo, in December 2007. The High Court documents make no mention of the application procedures that were underway during my visit to Ranongga in July and August 2005. The file on Ranongga that I obtained from the Western Province secretary in 2005 had no record of any earlier application in 2003. In July 2010, I attempted to track down documents relating to Degere land and the entire file had been misplaced so there was no paper trail, at least in Gizo. In 2005, the

applicant was Kalena Timber Company, but the company that actually undertook the logging operations in 2008 was Glengrow Ltd.
5. Even when attempting to oppose a major oil-palm plantation that would involve the clear felling of thousands of hectares of forest on Vagnunu—a project, Foale (2002) suggested, that would result in "few if any beneficial changes" to the lives of landowners and negligible returns for the government—WWF failed to present any reasonable sort of "alternative" to this counterproductive development.
6. I was not able to locate the records for this court case, which may have been destroyed in World War II as many other records were. It seems to have followed the well-documented pattern whereby denominational competition between Adventists and Methodists was carried over into disputes over land (Monson 2012).
7. I viewed these letters in the Gizo office of WWF in 1998 and have copies in my files.
8. The point is clear in the genealogies of the key leaders of both *butubutu* in Pienuna over my period of research: all were the grandsons of the last great precolonial chief of Kubokota, a man named Sagobabata, and his sister Takavoja, and they all worked closely together and with church leaders to solve disputes and maintain social harmony in Pienuna and surrounding hamlets.

# 7

# Losing Passports
## *Mobility, Urbanization, Ethnicity*

When outsiders have lived for many years on Ranongga, people may joke that they have "lost their passports" and become "citizens." Such joking calls attention to the difference between connections to ancestral territory and connections to a nation-state mediated by bureaucracy. At the same time, these jokes reflect real worries that prolonged absence can sever connections to ancestral land. Such anxieties have become acute in the context of the transformations of kinship and land tenure discussed in the previous two chapters. As landowners increasingly define themselves in terms of genealogically bounded groups that exclude outsiders rather than as place-based collectivities that include them, the position of outsiders becomes less and less secure.

It is not easy to "lose a passport" to an ancestral home. Even in this era of bitter land disputes, long-lost descendants may reconnect to ancestral homelands even after generations of absence. A remarkable example concerns the descendants of Awana, who was captured with her child from the Sabana area of Santa Isabel in the late nineteenth century (Chapter 3). In 2009, a Ranonggan great-granddaughter of Awana was in a crowded health clinic in Honiara seeking treatment for her sick child when she began chatting with some Santa Isabel women. When the women named the cave where their kinswoman had tried to hide from the Ranonggan warriors who eventually took her, the Ranonggan woman knew that they were speaking of Awana. The following year, a delegation of Santa Isabel men from Sabana traveled to Ranongga, visited the grave of Awana, and "worked custom" on the shrine that housed the skull of Awana's murdered child, whom the Santa Isabel relatives revealed to be her younger brother, not her son. When they returned to Santa Isabel, a young woman raised in Pienuna accompanied them and lived there for a year, coming to know the land, people, and language of her great-great-grandmother.[1]

Maintaining a "passport" to a rural home remains important to many modern migrants living in town. As long-term resident of Honiara Michael Kwa'ioloa, a man of eastern Kwara'ae in Malaita, put it: "A man who is not connected to his home is a nobody. He is no longer a person" (Kwa'ioloa and Burt 2012: 147–48). In two autobiographical books co-written with anthropologist Ben Burt, Kwa'ioloa argues for the ongoing relevance of tradition in contemporary Solomon Islands life by describing his own intensive engagement with his lineage and land in Kwara'ae and his relatives visiting or living in Honiara (Kwa'ioloa and Burt 1997, 2012). According to Kwa'ioloa, townspeople who neglected their ties to "grassroots" people suffered the consequences during the civil conflict, when some twenty thousand Malaitans living in Honiara and northern Guadalcanal were forced to return home to an island that many of them had never even visited: "When they reached home they went straight to the place which they thought was their land, but people there didn't want them to stay because, they said, 'You left a long time ago'" (Kwa'ioloa and Burt 2012: 148). One of his acquaintances returned to disputed land in To'ambaita in Malaita's north. Rather than being welcomed back as a kinsperson, he was killed – "cut up like fried chicken" (ibid.: 148).

Place-based identities remain important for urbanites, but they take on new meanings because urbanites are often unable to connect to their adopted land in the same way that in-married spouses or other long-term residents in rural areas do. As we have seen, even though dominant ideologies emphasize the way that genealogically defined groups own territory in rural areas, the more important rights are property rights, not land rights, and these are forged through the activities of life. Men clear the land, build settlements; women bear children, care for the elderly and infirm; both men and women plant trees and gardens that provide their livelihood and nurture their children. In rural areas, migrants die and are often buried on the land of their adopted homes, and their graves become a focus of memory and belonging for their descendants. These processes do not occur in the same way in urban locales and amongst people who earn their livelihood through wage labor or salaried employment rather than subsistence agriculture. To be sure, urban and rural worlds are not radically separate. Ben Burt observes that urban Kwara'ae "seem to treat their experience of town and rural life, of Western and local culture, as contrasting aspects of a single world, inextricably linked" (Kwa'ioloa and Burt 1997: 8). Despite many continuities, however, the risk of "losing a passport" to one's own ancestral lands without becoming a "citizen" on someone else's ancestral land is greater for people living in urban areas, especially for those on the margins of the formal economy.

In town, a sense of belonging to a particular place is often overlaid with a quite different kind of place-based identity: ethnicity. Ethnicity does not necessarily involve a lived connection with people and places. It is always oppositional: one is a particular kind of person only in contrast to another kind of person. The most powerful oppositions at the national level in Solomon Islands today tend to involve provincial-level identities, like "Malaitan," or

"Guadalcanal," or "Western," which themselves encompass diverse and complexly inter-related peoples. A sense of ethnic or regional self derives not only from precolonial networks of interaction or broadly shared cultural similarities, but also the accidents of colonial boundary drawing and oppositional contrasts to an ethnic "other." "Western" identity is shared by people of the New Georgia Group and, depending on context, people of the Shortland Islands (which is part of Western Province), Choiseul (which was part of Western Province until it became a separate province in 1991), and Bougainville (part of Papua New Guinea but with close connections with the northwestern Solomon Islands) (Dureau 1998a; Scales 2007; Hviding 2011, 2014). For people of the western Solomons, Guadalcanal, Makira (Scott 2012), and elsewhere in the country, the oppositional "other" against which ethnic identity is articulated is Malaita, the Solomon Islands' most densely populated island. For more than a century, Malaitans have migrated in significant numbers to all centers of commercial development, including Western Province and northern Guadalcanal. Ethnonationalist identities are not the result of formerly isolated societies being thrown together by a colonial state without adequate efforts to bring these culturally disparate groups together, as is suggested in influential analyses of the causes of the civil conflict between 1998 and 2003. Contemporary ethnic tensions are not the result of a lack of engagement between Malaitans and "Westerners," or Malaitans and Guale people, but from a form of engagement that does not encourage amicable intercultural relationships: laborers arrive on local land at the behest of outsiders, not local landowners.

In this chapter, I describe the ways that my neighbors and friends in Pienuna approached the diversity that was part of their everyday lives, and sketch some of the patterns of inter-village and inter-island mobility that gives rise to such diversity. A medium-sized village reasonably accessible from a provincial capital, Pienuna is similar to many other rural places, especially in provinces and regions that are now, or were once, a focus of commercial development. In many contexts, and especially in community events like fundraising carnivals, church gatherings, or holidays, diversity in Pienuna was a focus of pleasure and enjoyment. Yet here as elsewhere, relations between local people and Malaitans are sometimes tense—a tension that cannot be understood outside of the context of a long history of engagement under conditions established by a colonial administration that was, for much of its existence, maximally concerned with a fostering a plantation economy and minimally concerned with the well-being of indigenous inhabitants of the Solomons. Without denying that cultural differences between people of Malaita and Western Province can strain relationships, I argue that the conflicts that arise between Ranonggans and Malaitans are not dramatically different to conflicts amongst Ranonggans themselves. Drawing on an interview with a Malaitan who settled with his family in Ranongga in the 1960s, I show that even when migrants arrive at the behest of an outsider and live on alienated land, they may go out of their way to put themselves "under" the real people of the place to act as good guests.

Migrants or sojourners in urban places, especially Honiara, face special challenges in remaining connected to their own home places or feeling that the place where they reside is really home. Urbanization in Solomon Islands has not necessarily diminished the importance of a connection to home places. But, as Rupert Stasch has observed, "villages are geographic figures of nostalgia for a past that is felt to have been lost in the biographical and historical present of urban life, even as urbanites' actual ties with village settings are morally ambivalent and socially fraught" (Stasch 2010: 56; see also Stasch 2013). The ambivalence is particularly pronounced among younger people who may still think of themselves as people of a particular place, but who have never lived on the land or learned to speak the local language of that place. Ethnicity emerges most intensely precisely in these situations, where a connection to home is tenuous and ambivalent.

## Mobile Lives at Home and in Town

In June 1999, residents of Pienuna and surrounding villages held a four-day carnival for the village primary school to raise funds for materials for new housing for teachers. Among the activities was a skit performed by teachers, nurses, and members of the school committee that played upon the linguistic and cultural diversity of the community. All the performers sang the chorus (the tune was something like "For He's a Jolly Good Fellow") in the national lingua franca, Solomon Islands Pijin, with the vernacular Ranonggan word *qokolo* (which I translate as 'guy') interjected for effect:

| | |
|---|---|
| *Hao nao toktok blong qokolo ia?* | What is this guy's language? |
| (repeated three times) | |
| *Iu tok mekim mi harem!* | Speak, let me hear it! |
| (repeated twice) | |
| *Hao nao toktok blong qokolo ia?* | What is this guy's language? |
| *Iu tok mekim mi harem!* | Speak, let me hear it! |

Following the chorus, one performer after another stood forward to speak in a foreign language. Among the speakers was the head nurse of Pienuna, Lynnette Roga, a Seventh-day Adventist from Malaita married to a teacher, Kent Roga, from Vonga village south of Pienuna. She spoke in the Kwaio language of Malaita to announce that she was off to look after her pigs. This elicited uproarious laughter, since Lynette is both Malaitan (Malaitans in general, and traditionalist Kwaio in particular, are depicted as being obsessed by pigs) and a Seventh-day Adventist (who do not raise or eat pigs). Then school principal Jeffrey Sem spoke in the Bugotu language of Santa Isabel, the home of his wife Marion. Others stepped forward to speak Bilua (the non-Austronesian language of nearby Vella Lavella), Roviana (from the lagoon areas to the east, the former church lingua franca), and Babata (from Choiseul, where Ranonggans have long-standing ties). One man spoke Pijin with a distinctly old-fashioned Malaitan accent. Performers used phrases that are ubiquitous in discourse throughout the Solomons, like "Where are you going?" They referred to distinctive foods or iconic practices of the places they were representing. These speeches included distinctive vernacular words for "person" (like Ranonggan *qokolo*), terms that are often known by non-native speakers and often index the language as a whole.[2]

This playful accentuation of difference fits into a broader cultural logic that becomes visible in such community work. Rather than simply working together for a particular goal, people tend to divide themselves into competing divisions that then, at the conclusion of the work, join together as one in a community feast. At the 1999 school carnival, the community was divided into sections, each competing with one another to raise more funds through bazaar sales, raffles, games, and other activities. I was part of the winning section, and our success was attributed in large part to the leading role taken by two Choiseul *roroto* (in-married spouses from other places), who have the reputation on Ranongga for being good at business. A similar structure of competitive giving was routine within women's fellowship. Rather than simply paying annual dues to the organization, women were organized into pairs (*baere*, "friends" or "trading partners") who competed with one another to present a larger and more beautiful gift (one year it was a basket of food, another year gifts of woven mats or store-bought goods), each far more valuable than the dues paid to the organization (McDougall 2003). At Christmas and New Year's, villages are divided into sections often named after foreign nations that compete for points in debates, sports, games, and other activities. A similar logic informed the New Year's festivities in 2007, when Pienuna was divided into "Germany" and "America" to celebrate my own marriage (described in the Introduction). Cultural differences and social divisions are accentuated or invented in ways that make the unity that is the result of collective activity all the more surprising and delightful.

When I conducted a census in late 1998 and early 1999, Pienuna's approximately 300 residents included people from Luqa, Simbo, Vella Lavella, Roviana, Marovo, Choiseul, Santa Isabel, Guadalcanal, Malaita, and Gilbertese (ni-Kiribati) communities in Gizo. People born and raised in Pienuna are similarly living all around the region and nation, with a few overseas. As the site of a rural health center, a primary school, and a junior secondary school (which opened in 2005), people from around the island visit or stay with relatives in Pienuna. Professional staff from the clinic and school tend to have some connection to Ranongga, but all have undertaken training far from the island, mostly in Honiara, and several come from other parts of the country or have spouses from elsewhere. Several staff posted in Pienuna over the years were adherents of the Seventh-day Adventist Church rather than the United Church. Within easy reach of the provincial capital of Gizo, Pienuna's residents are able to earn cash from market gardening, which makes it a relatively attractive place for people with kin ties to many places to reside. It is not dissimilar from many other rural places around the Solomon Islands where people enjoy reasonable access to commercial centers. Villages further from commercial opportunities attract fewer people from other places.[3]

Intra-village diversity is the result of inter-island mobility. As is the case for much of island Melanesia, in New Georgia, mobility was once the domain of powerful men who traveled along paths of alliance or controlled access to such paths. The most famous example of this may be the societies of the Massim region of Papua New Guinea and the famous system of *kula* exchange, analyzed by Nancy Munn (1990) in terms of the way that subjects were able to extend their influence across space and time. Of the ranked societies of northern Vanuatu, Joel Bonnemaison has written:

> A man of high grade has often been defined by the political authority acquired through the use of economic power; he can just as well be distinguished by his geographical mobility and the control exerted upon the movements of others and the traffic of goods . . . By definition, the high chief ("big man") is one whose fame reaches far beyond the limits of his territory. (Bonnemaison 1985: 137)

Yet this mobility is not shared by everyone: "For common people, fixity and stability are the norm: mobility is both a privilege of power and a means of acquiring it" (ibid.: 137–38). This principle held even in societies without traditions of long-distance sea travel, including pre-contact northwestern Guadalcanal; as Murray Bathgate observed, "how often and how far people moved was thus an index of their social status" (Bathgate 1985: 86). Ordinary people moved frequently but within closely delineated home territories, whereas the powerful men of the society, sorcerers and *tavoa* (chiefs), moved across the borders of their home territories and engaged with allies in potentially hostile territory.

Colonial pacification had contradictory effects on mobility. On the one hand, in New Georgia the destruction of large seagoing canoes dramatically curtailed the mobility of powerful chiefs and warriors. On the other hand, pacification eliminated barriers to ordinary people's travel, allowing common people and women to travel the paths once reserved for powerful men. War canoes were replaced by mission cutters and, later, motorized dugout canoes.

While control of such vehicles remains both a sign and avenue of power (and is largely restricted to men; I knew only one woman who occasionally drove her own canoe in Kubokota), everyone may travel on them.

Both in the past and today, marriage between people of different islands is responsible for much of the cultural diversity present in rural villages. Patterns of inter-island marriage reflect patterns of mobility—people find spouses when they travel to visit kin, attend church rallies, work or study in other areas—but also drive much of the travel that people undertake. Clan exogamy is a feature of most Solomon Islands societies, but Ranonggans seem to take these principles of exogamy to an extreme: in theory, at least, people are forbidden from marrying a person of their own *butubutu*, their father's *butubutu*, their paternal grandfather's *butubutu*, or anyone with whom any blood or adoptive kin relationship can be traced. My Ranonggan friends were bemused by the fact that some people in Santa Isabel and Guadalcanal frequently married their cross-cousins (that is, the child of their mother's brother or father's sister). In Ranongga, cross-cousins are not of the same named *butubutu*, but they are nevertheless considered to be "just one people"; marriage between cross-cousins is therefore considered to be incestuous. These extensive rules of exogamy are frequently breached, but they still encourage people to look beyond the village and island for spouses.

Husbands and wives who come from different places often follow a dual residence pattern, moving between their home places over the course of their marriage.[4] An example of this mobility comes from the family of Grace Nose of Pienuna and her husband Joseph Sasapitu, from Sepa village in southern Choiseul. The couple met at a church youth rally but their families were already acquainted: Sasapitu's father had worked as a policeman during the construction of the new village of Koriovuku under George Hilly in the 1950s (Chapter 2). After their marriage, Grace and Sasapitu lived for a decade with Sasapitu's family in Choiseul, then moved to Ranongga in 1998. Sasapitu has returned to his village occasionally, and one of their daughters has stayed for more extended periods, thus continuing to anchor the family in Choiseul. Another example of multi-local family life is the family of Jebede Toribule and his wife Marion, a woman of Santa Isabel who frequently joked in the late 1990s and early 2000s about "losing her passport" because she hadn't been home for decades. Shortly after the birth of their first grandchild in 2007, Jebede and Marion relocated their whole family to her home in Santa Isabel in order to re-establish their children's connection to their mother's land and kin. At the time of writing, they had not yet (to my knowledge) returned to Pienuna.

According to the latest census held in 2009, 80 percent of the country's population of just over 500,000 lives in rural areas, but rates of urban growth are 4.7 percent per annum, which is double the average rate of population growth (SISO 2012). The largest and most rapidly growing urban center is Honiara, with a population of nearly 65,000; next in population comes Malaita's provincial capital, Auki, with over 5,000 residents. Western Province is also relatively urbanized, with nearly 10,000 urban residents across several towns: Gizo, the provincial capital (population approximately 3,500); Noro, the former site of a tuna cannery and headquarters of a fleet of long-line tuna-fishing vessels owned by the joint venture company Solomon Taiyo (3,300); and Munda and Nusa Roviana, centers of the United Church administration in Roviana lagoon (1,315 and 1,528 respectively) (ibid.). Although only 20 percent of the country's population is counted as urban, a far larger percentage has lived for a significant period of time in provincial towns or the national capital during some period of their lives. Many of my neighbors in Pienuna had lived for months or years in Honiara for work, to visit relatives, to seek treatment at the National Referral Hospital, or to approach politicians for funds for household projects, businesses, or school fees. Conversely, almost anyone with formal employment in towns or as teachers or nurses in rural areas invest in building a "permanent" (metal-roofed) home in their own or spouses' home village. People move between rural and urban areas, and some town residents remain influential in the affairs of their local kinspeople.

Although worlds of town and home are connected and people move frequently between them, they are often depicted by Solomon Islanders themselves as radically different life worlds. A favorite topic for debate during community celebrations in Pienuna is whether life in town or life at home is better. In those I have witnessed, the "town" teams argue that life is easy in town because you do not have to toil in the hot sun; you travel by truck rather than foot; you purchase food rather than growing it yourself; you can enjoy many different kinds of activities and entertainment. Those arguing in favor of "home" point out that although you must work hard, in villages you do not have to worry about money; you can eat the food that you grow on your own land and build houses with the materials you gather in the forest; you do not have to worry about feeding visitors who come to live with you.

Despite the relatively fluidity with which people move between urban and rural worlds, long-term town dwellers face special difficulties in maintaining their ties to rural homes and villages. Those who earn wages must respond to innumerable requests for money to pay for school fees, weddings, funerals, transport costs, church building and many other village projects. They also must host rural kin who visit town with no other means of support. Such obligations are often a great burden on people earning modest wages and struggling to pay for Honiara's shockingly expensive food and housing. Worse still, visits home entail expenses far beyond the fare on a ship. A friend who was steadily employed in a non-governmental organization in Honiara complained to me that, in the past, when town dwellers went home for the holidays they could live for free, but now village relatives expect you to return with enough rice and other food to share with everyone for the duration of the visit. Returning home (and thus keeping one's "passport" active) thus presents wage-earning town dwellers with problems that villagers visiting other rural locales do not face.

## Oppositional Identities: Malaita and the "West"

The language skit described above figured difference as a source of pleasure and mobilized ethnic stereotypes for fun. In other contexts, ethnic stereotypes are mobilized in derogatory ways. Other people of Western Province refer to Ranonggans as "*nyete* eaters," a reference to the smelly flesh of rotted *Canarium* nuts that was the quintessential food of old Ranongga. Ranonggans, in turn, dismiss Roviana people as haughty and lazy (*tinoni tabuna paji*, "those who are forbidden to get themselves dirty"). Ranonggans call people of Rendova "axe-blade people" because of their supposed proclivity for violence in the precolonial era. "Gilbertese" people are called "raw-fish eaters" and "shark eaters."[5] The most politically fraught stereotypes concern people of the island of Malaita. Ranonggans sometimes referred to Malaitans, like people of Rendova, as "axe-blade people" (a reference to a reputation for violence), "red people" (a reference to their lighter complexions), or simply "people from up there," a reference to Malaita being southeast ("up" in local terms) of Western Province. When people complain about "those from other islands," it is usually Malaitans that they are referring to.

The "West" is often contrasted to Malaita in essentialist terms. Christine Dureau (1998a) has outlined some of the many cultural differences that "Westerners" highlight to contrast themselves with Malaitans. Malaitans may be stereotyped as pagan rather than Christian, with several thousand Kwaio people who still practice their ancestral religion standing for the whole of otherwise overwhelmingly Christian Malaita. "Westerners" say that while women are respected in the predominantly matrilineal Western Solomons, they are treated badly in patrilineal Malaita. Finally, Westerners characterize Malaitans as innately more prone to violence and retaliation. Such characterizations elide variation within Malaita Province, which is comprised of two islands, some eleven distinct language groups, and a range of different polities. They also downplay many of the fundamental similarities between "Westerners" and Malaitans, which include cognatic patterns of land tenure, whereby children of women (in Malaita) and men (in the "West") often inherit rights to property and sometimes become important landowners in their own right; an approach to conflict resolution that involves the exchange of money and valuables; similar patterns of subsistence agriculture; and, for the many Seventh-day Adventists in both regions, shared religious affiliation. Some cultural differences do prove problematic in interactions between Malaitans and "Westerners," but the animosity between Malaita and the "West" cannot be understood outside of the expansion of plantation capitalism over the course of the twentieth century.

Malaitan history and identity has been profoundly shaped by the experience of overseas and inter-island labor migration that is not shared with many people of Western Province. Beginning in the early 1870s and continuing until the early twentieth century, tens of thousands of Solomon Islanders (almost all men) signed on as indentured labors for work in Queensland (on sugarcane plantations, as well as pastoral and maritime work), Fiji (on sugarcane and copra plantations), and other Pacific Island territories. In the early years of the labor trade, a few hundred islanders from the western Solomons went overseas.[6] By the time recruiting intensified in the 1880s, European traders were already active in the New Georgia Group, so local leaders could obtain European goods, including steel tools and weapons, through trade rather than by sending young men to work on plantations (Bennett 1987; Hviding 1996). In the eastern Solomons, labor recruits and the local leaders who encouraged or coerced them to sign on had few other ways to obtain the trade goods that were quickly becoming essential to local life. Many labor recruits came from other areas like Guadalcanal, Makira, and parts of Central Province, but from the start of the labor trade, a large majority of recruits came from Malaita, which "has been the premier reservoir of Solomon Islands plantation labor ever since" (Akin 2013: 14). Although most indenture contracts were undertaken voluntarily, and recruits were aware of what conditions they could expect, they deeply resented their mistreatment at the hands of plantation owners. The memory of humiliation at the hands of Europeans remains an important force in contemporary political identities (Bennett 1987: 188, 2003; Moore 2007; Akin 2013: 14; Allen 2009).

In the nineteenth century, most recruited laborers traveled overseas to work, but after the first decade of the twentieth century, labor migration occurred within the boundaries of the British Solomon Islands Protectorate. Australia's White Australia policy, specifically the Pacific Island Labourer's Act 1901, led to the deportation of some 5,000 Solomon Islanders, including 2,500 Malaitans, some of whom had lived for many years in Queensland (Corris 1973: 130). The end of overseas labor was a boon to the Protectorate administration, which was under increasing pressure to foster commercial activity that would make the colony self-sufficient. The scale of this inter-island labor migration was significant. At the time of the Protectorate's first census in 1931, some 10 percent of the total population of Malaita (and a much greater percentage of adult males) was away during any single year, even after the Great Depression and the collapse of copra prices had led to a fall in the number of labor recruits (Bennett 1987: 165; Akin 2013: 94).[7] As an early site of plantation development by smaller European and Chinese traders and large companies like Levers Pacific Plantation Ltd. and Burns Philp and Company, Western Province was an important destination for labor migration until the 1960s, when Honiara and northern Guadalcanal began to offer more possibilities for potential laborers than Western Province.

Part of the reason laborers on Western Province plantations were recruited from other areas was the fact that local people had better options: they planted and sold their own copra to resident traders and missions. Extra-local recruitment was also an intentional strategy on the part of planters, and was encouraged by Protectorate labor policies. Writing of plantations in northwestern Guadalcanal, Murray Bathgate observed that even though local men were engaged in plantation labor (many traveled to New Georgia and Santa Isabel), the plantation managers recruited outsiders mainly from To'ambaita and Kwaio on Malaita in order to "guarantee a captive work force for the period of contract" (Bathgate 1985: 92). When planters justified their need for non-local workers to the colonial administration (which often suggested that they ought to deal with chronic labor shortages by recruiting local laborers), they often invoked colonial stereotypes of different groups, depicting Malaitans as industrious and local people (whether they were from Guadalcanal or New Georgia) as lazy.

An example comes from C.P. Beck, a European who ran Aena plantation in southern Ranongga.[8] Beck enjoyed cordial relations with his Luqa neighbors: he married a local woman and is remembered without any animosity by people of Suava and Keara, who claim the land on which Aena was located. In correspondence with the resident commissioner in 1920, Beck complained bitterly about the plight of small planters like himself, who paid much higher rent for land than large companies like Burns Philp that had purchased freehold land for a pittance in the past. He also resented the power of the Methodist Mission over local residents. In explaining to the resident commissioner why he could not draw workers from Ranongga, Beck stated:

> The young generation prefer to walk about and hang round the so-called Mission schools. They think (and say) that if they go to school that they should do no work. Their villages are filthy and the men's principal occupation is chewing betel-nut and walking about visiting. The women do all the work. The men make a few canoes or ramshackle houses occasionally or cook a bit of copra with the help of the women, when they run out of tobacco. They are not doing much of this now and there are tons of nuts rotting on the ground... After living amongst these people for 11 years I think I know them better than most people and believe that they are dying out for want of work. (BSIP 18/I/41)[9]

He continued by complaining that when he did hire local men, they stayed only for three weeks. In one instance, all the laborers left when influenza broke out (perhaps the deadly Spanish influenza pandemic of 1918 to 1920); in another instance, a local laborer died following an illness contracted on the plantation, and the rest "packed up and went home" because "they did not like work and that was a good excuse to clear out" (ibid.). These ethnic stereotypes would become internalized by Solomon Islanders themselves.

Plantation conditions frequently brought Malaitans and "Westerners" into proximity without opening many opportunities for real engagement. According to Bennett (1987: 174), even though plantations in the Protectorate were often near local villages, laborers on large plantations owned by big companies had minimal contact with locals: Malaitans formed an enclave. Smaller planters like Beck were often more dependent on casual labor from neighboring villages, and in such contexts interactions between local and non-local laborers probably occurred frequently and were not always friendly (Bennett 1987: 173; Dureau 1998a: 210; Scales 2007: 193). Yet, against the odds, Malaitan laborers and local people of Western Province sometimes established amicable relationships across the boundaries of the plantation enclave. A striking example comes from David Akin, whose Kwaio friend Ma'aanamae (probably born around 1900) fondly recalled his encounter with a kind woman from Western Province when he was working on a plantation owned by a Chinese trader. For some reason, wages and rations for the laborers were delayed, so Ma'aanamae and other Kwaio men started off down the road to try to buy rice on credit from a local store. As Akin recounts it:

> A woman from Western [Province] living there on her land with her husband hailed them on the road and asked where they were going. They told her and she said to come in first. They did and she fed them all. Then she said when her husband got home [that] they would go to the garden. They went there and the couple filled two big bags of *kumara* [sweet potatoes] for them to take home. They told them that they were going to be going to some sort of meeting for a month (they were Adventists) and that they should consider the garden theirs to take *kumara*, bananas, sugarcane, or whatever they wanted, while they were gone. Ma'aanamae and the other Kwaio were so impressed with the hospitality that when they were away they brushed all of their property with their bush knives, and doubled the size of their garden and planted it in *kumara* for them. The couple was very happy when they returned.[10]

Encounters between such exceptionally hospitable hosts and exceptionally gracious guests may have been unusual. Yet, given that an encounter like Ma'aanamae recounts is unlikely to have found its way into any colonial officer's report in the way that a major brawl would have, cordial relations between locals and laborers may not be as rare as archival records suggest.

Early hostility between Malaitans and people of the western Solomons must be understood in the context of extraordinarily violent times. In the 1880s and 1890s, New Georgian warriors killed about a dozen Malaitans working for European traders, not necessarily because they were Malaitans but because they happened to be there at a time when a war party was seeking victims (Bennett 1987: 390–96). Malaitans were involved as both victims and perpetrators of what became known as the Binskin affair (Bennett 1987: 108; Dureau 1998a: 211). This debacle began when Western District's resident magistrate, Thomas Edge-Partington, had attempted to arrest the Vella Lavella warrior Sito Latavaki, who was wanted for an 1897 attack on a trader. The attempt was botched and the government party shot and killed Sito's wife and children. In retaliation, Sito sent men to kill the Malaitan wife and children of the European trader Binskin, based on Baga Island in Vella Lavella's southwest. The response was a punitive expedition undertaken in 1909 by government officers, traders, and a Malaitan militia, who have been described as sweeping "over Vella Lavella in a random wave of killing and destruction" (Bennett 1987: 108). The violence was ended through the mediation of the Methodist missionary R.C. Nicholson, who convinced the government to allow Vella Lavella people to capture Sito themselves. Dureau argues that Malaitan involvement in the raid "forms part of the litany of Malaitan violence so constantly cited in New Georgia" (Dureau 1998a: 211).

Conversely, "Westerners" earned the ire of Malaitans for their involvement in police action on Malaita. When Edge-Partington was posted as resident magistrate to Malaita later in 1909, he brought around twenty men from Western District as policemen to assist in what were largely futile efforts to bring the island under government control (Akin 2013: 38). The police force of his successor, William Bell, was comprised primarily of Malaitans from the island's north. After Bell and some of his police were assassinated by a Kwaio warrior at Sinalagu in 1927, it was primarily north Malaitan troops and militias (not "Westerners") who committed most of the violence and atrocities against innocent civilians (Keesing and Corris 1980; Akin 2013: 39–49; cf. Dureau 1998a: 211), a reminder that not all colonial violence was committed across what would later become the dominant ethnic cleavages. Later, however, during the government campaign against Maasina Rule, large numbers of "Western" police were deployed to arrest the movement's leaders and guard prisoners in a heavy-handed campaign called Operation Delouse. According to Akin, "Many Malaitans for decades after resented people of the west, especially Choiseul, for their role in suppression" (Akin 2013: 418 n.1).

Yet, even in a situation where Solomon Islanders found themselves in inherently antagonistic relationships, hostility was not inevitable. Among the western Solomons policemen working to suppress Maasina Rule on Malaita was a Ranonggan man, Lokasasa, who befriended many of the Malaitan men he was charged with guarding. In 1999, he remembered them as "good, generous men," and sympathized with the work they were trying to do. Lokasasa was already a widower at the time, and, because he treated his Malaitan charges so kindly, they decided to give him a local woman as a wife. David Akin suggests that such sentiments may not have been unusual, and that his Kwaio interlocutors recount that many non-Malaitan Solomon Islands police, including men from the western Solomons, secretly sympathized with Maasina Rule.

Like all large islands or island groups of the Solomons, Malaita has many distinct language groups; since the advent of Christian missions on the island, it has been more religiously divided than any other region, with tension not only between Christians and a significant population of non-Christians, but also within the four historical missions working on the island. Scholars have argued that the experience of working first overseas and then in other areas of the Solomons helped to foster a sense of shared identity among the otherwise diverse people of Malaita. The post-World War II Maasina Rule movement played an enormous role in crystallizing a sense of island-wide identity and a shared ideology of *kastom*. As David Akin (2013: 171–73) has argued, one of the most remarkable aspects of Maasina Rule was the way that it brought together this deeply divided island in a truly popular collective movement. Maasina Rule simultaneously resisted and sought to appropriate the apparatus of the British colonial administration after the upheavals of World War II; adherents protested against unjust labor and taxation policies, sought more control over the administration of justice and the formation of laws, and attempted to establish the institutions that would allow Malaita to develop economically. Akin argues that an ideology of *kastom* became central to the movement because this was the one realm in which colonial administrators gave islanders some scope in ruling themselves: far from being static, "*Kastom* became a voracious category, encompassing all things over which Malaitans now claimed authority" (ibid.: 7). As Matthew Allen (2009, 2013a) has pointed out, Malaitan combatants who took part in the civil conflict known as the Ethnic Tension echoed the anti-colonial stance of their fathers and grandfathers, and built upon the sense of Malaitan-ness established during Maasina Rule.

In contrast to Malaitan identity, "Western" identity was not anti-colonial. It built upon pre-existing cultural affinities and connections that arose during the twentieth century, but emerged most clearly in opposition to the perceived threat of Malaitans who migrated to the region. New Georgia, and to some extent Choiseul and Santa Isabel, were connected by routes of trading and raiding prior to colonialism. The Methodist Mission, which limited its scope to the Western Solomons, and the powerful figure of Rev. John Goldie, created new networks focused on Roviana. These forms of pan-"Western" identity were crosscut by bitter divisions between Methodists and Adventists dating from 1914 and, in the 1960s, a division between Methodists and the indigenous breakaway Christian Fellowship Church. In modern politics, "Western" identity has been articulated most palpably in opposition to Malaitans, fueling ongoing desires for regional autonomy within the nation (Herlihy 1982: 580–81; Premdas, Steeves, and Larmour 1983; Dureau 1998a; Scales 2007; Hviding 2011). At independence and during the time of the Ethnic Tension, separatist arguments have focused on fears that revenues from resource-rich Western Province would be diverted away from the western Solomons to subsidize the development of Malaita and Honiara, which is often viewed from the western Solomons as a Malaitan-dominated enclave. People of the western Solomons also desire greater political autonomy because of the dominance of demographically more numerous Malaitans within the political system of the Solomon Islands. As is the case in Guadalcanal, resentment is also focused on a sense that Malaitans have come into the province without the permission of the province or the invitation of local landowners, sometime joining Malaitan relatives already living in the region.

Anti-Malaitan sentiments were palpable in 1999 in the midst of the exodus of Malaitans from Honiara, and in an atmosphere where anti-migrant sentiments had already been heightened by decades of logging-related land disputes in many parts of Western Province. Some people of the western Solomons feared that Malaitans fleeing Honiara would come to join relatives in Western Province and Choiseul rather than going home to Malaita. A vocal minority suggested that "Westerners" ought to evict Malaitans in a similar manner to that employed by Guadalcanal people. In mid 1999, around the Munda and Noro area, some local men burned Malaitan property and attempted to evict Malaitan residents who were living mostly on the alienated land of abandoned plantations (Scales 2007: 195). The Western Provincial government produced a Munda Accord that resolved to restrict the movement of unemployed people from outside of Western Province, take action against people of Western Province who allow outsiders to settle on their land, and prevent the allocation of land to outsiders. At the time of the coup in Honiara in June 2000, Bougainville militants arrived in Gizo town to provide "security" against a feared incursion by Malaitan Eagle Forces from Honiara. People of Western Province were reportedly targeted in Honiara as reprisals for the anti-Malaita actions of "Westerners" and Western Province. In what Ian Scales called "the coup nobody noticed" (Scales 2007), Western Province declared itself an independent state on Independence Day, 7 July 2000 (see also Hviding 2011). Analyzing the Western State movement in the context of landowner frustrations about economic development and ongoing political discussions of provincial government reform, Scales concluded that, "The 1998–2000 conflict in the West began with ethnic violence, but was quickly channeled away from a specific conflict with Malaitans and propelled into a direct contestation with the national government over its failure to serve landowner interests" (Scales 2007: 189). As we will see in the next chapter, Allen (2013a) makes a similar argument for the ethnic conflict in Guadalcanal: the targets of violence were the ethnic "other," but each side blamed the national government for its failure to manage migration and economic development.

Ethnic identities like "Malaitan" and "Western" are not the extension of local connections to kin and land; they emerged in the context of the expansion of the colonial state and plantation capitalism. Given these historical circumstances, it is hardly surprising that relations between Malaitans and people of Western Province are sometimes fraught. More remarkable is the way that, against structures that made antagonism so likely, "Westerners" and Malaitans have often worked hard to establish cooperative, productive relations with one another.

## Peace Talks: Mediating Intercultural Disputes

Conflicts between Ranonggans and people from Malaita living on Ranongga tended to focus on the same thing as conflicts among Ranonggans or among people from other parts of the western Solomons: illicit sexual affairs. Yet conflicts between Malaitans and Ranongga take on additional complexities because of real cultural differences that are manifest strongly in gender and sexual relationships.

Both Malaitans and Ranonggans struggle to reconcile their different approaches to marriage transactions. In Malaita, the man's side is expected to provide a large bridewealth payment (comprised of traditional valuables, cash, and other goods) to the woman's side, a payment that is seen to both establish the man's right over the woman and their children's membership of his descent group. Women and their kin seem to see such a payment as a measure of their worth, and may demand very high bridewealth payments. In most of Western Province, by contrast, payments at marriages are relatively small and are ideally equal in order to "open the road to come and go." Western Solomon Islanders are often unwilling to pay the high payments sometimes demanded by Malaitan women's kinspeople. And although many "Westerners" assume that Malaitans are eager to obtain women "for free," many Malaitans do not want to marry a woman without giving a large amount of bridewealth. Two Kwaio men told David Akin about breaking off relationships with western Solomons women because they felt it would be humiliating to marry a woman without giving a respectable bridewealth payment, and they feared that other men wouldn't respect their sexual rights over their wives. The women's fathers refused a large amount of bridewealth because this would mean the children of the union would be members of their father's group whose land was back in distant Malaita, and would therefore have no rights on their mother's land in this matrilineally-oriented region where the couple planned to reside.[11]

In both regions, prior to government pacification, certain kinds of sexual offenses were punishable by death or banishment. In Ranongga and other areas of the western Solomons, incest was considered a capital offense but premarital sexual relationships among young people were not uncommon. Indeed, women who were *tugele* (prostitutes) working for chiefs were said to have been treated with considerable respect. On Malaita, however, premarital sexual relationships were considered a capital crime (Keesing 1982b: 19). From the early colonial period, administrators responding to Malaitan demands that adultery be treated as a criminal offense struggled with the fact that Malaitans wanted to impose far harsher punishments on sexual offenders than did Solomon Islanders from many other societies (Laracy and Laracy 1980; Akin 2013: 90–91).

Yet the Malaitan reputation for rage at sexual offenses should not overshadow the fact that sexual affairs also cause serious conflict among people of the western Solomons. The difference is that intra-'West' conflict focuses less on the fact that a woman has had a sexual affair and more on the ways in which her brothers learn about the relationship. In Ranongga, if a woman is to be married, her parents will circulate "compensation" (*ira*) to her brothers before the news comes out. In the past, this was a payment given to the eldest of various groups of brothers, but today it often takes the form of a small payment (sometimes just SI$1 or a rolled cigarette) given to each of the woman's brothers. In cases when such a payment has not occurred and young men hear of their sisters' affairs, their rage is visceral and often violent. I was shocked when I first witnessed such an outburst early in my fieldwork. A soft-spoken, kind, and gentle young man bellowed and wept as he berated his "sisters" (the daughters of his father's sisters) who had been lingering in the dark giggling with some young men of the village during late-night Christmas celebrations. Ranonggan men often lash out at their own sisters; their anger is quelled by small amounts of compensation paid by their own parents (or senior relatives) that mirror the payment of compensation preceding the announcement of a legitimate marriage. Malaitans, in contrast, tend to threaten and demand compensation not from their own "sisters," but from their sisters' boyfriends or boyfriends' families, either as a kind of "down payment" on the bridewealth that will follow if the affair leads to marriage, or as compensation for "spoiling" the woman and lowering the amount of bridewealth she might draw in a subsequent marriage arrangement.[12]

Aside from such cultural differences, historically inculcated forms of ethnic animosity sometimes play into conflict concerning marriage and sexuality.

Some Ranonggans do not want their children to marry Malaitans, an attitude that reflects the negative stereotypes discussed above as well as a sense that the children of such unions will have weaker rights to land in Ranongga and no effective rights in densely populated and distant Malaita. Scales (2007: 194) notes that marriage between Kolombangara women and men of Langalanga in the 1960s and 1970s were controversial, but that controversy faded as the families became well established. Anti-intermarriage sentiments resurfaced again in the late 1990s, when young women were called together by their elders and harangued about the dangers of affairs with Malaitan men.

Several conflicts focused on sexual affairs and marriage arrangements between Malaitans and Ranonggans erupted during the various periods of my fieldwork. The most serious occurred in early 1999. News emerged that a young man of Pienuna village was having an affair with the niece of a Kwaio woman living in Pienuna, and the young woman was pregnant. This young woman had cousins living in Taquaba, a hamlet founded near the old plantation of Aena by a Kwaio man who had settled on Ranongga in the 1950s and married a local woman; she also had relatives in Suava village and Gizo. These relatives demanded SI$4,000 (more than four times per capita GDP at the time and more than ten times what might have been considered appropriate by local standards) from their sister's lover's family, and threatened to come and burn down the entire village of Pienuna if compensation was not given. Pienuna's village chief and the young man's father sought contributions from all residents (myself included) to help meet the demand. Those contributions, along with a sizable donation from the young woman's aunt (held responsible by her kin for not properly guarding her niece), and from the member of parliament for Ranongga and Simbo, were eventually handed over to the young woman's Malaitan relatives and Malaitan chiefs in Gizo. The couple later married and resided with the young man's parents in Pienuna.

Another incident that seemed to foreground the cultural differences between Malaita and Ranongga ended more amicably. A young Ranonggan man, whom I will call Joseph, had begun to live with a young woman whose mother was Ranonggan and father was Malaitan, long resident in his wife's village on Ranongga. Her parents consented to the marriage, and did not demand large compensation or bridewealth payments because they were members of the Seventh-day Adventist Church, which forbids such practices. Joseph's senior relatives informed the young woman's classificatory brothers about the marriage by distributing amounts of compensation, following accepted practice in Ranongga. Trouble arose when some of the girl's male cousins arrived from Malaita after the marriage was made public. When Joseph attended a big soccer competition at his fiancée's village, he was confronted by a number of his fiancée's recently-arrived cousins, who threatened him with a machete, accused him of "stealing" their sister instead of "buying" her properly, and demanded several thousand dollars of compensation. Joseph was forced to leave but was angry that these Malaitan men did not accept Ranonggan custom and that they were starting a fight when they ought to act like guests on someone else's island. He and his friends began to prepare to attack the Malaitan youth. Two of Joseph's uncles stopped the boys and went to speak to the girl's senior Malaitan relatives. As one uncle later told me, these Malaitan elders explained that Ranonggans often demand less than they expect to get, but Malaitans demand far more than they expect. As a result of the discussion, Joseph's uncles gave the girl's Malaitan uncles SI$70, a fraction of the amount originally demanded, so that they could inform the girl's recently arrived cousins that she would be married. Then Joseph's uncles requested compensation from the Malaitan men because their youth had threatened Joseph with a machete. Joseph's uncles reminded them that Malaitans were not the only violent people in the Solomons; Ranonggans, too, had once been warriors but, they said, now we are all Christian and none of us may threaten violence. The Malaitan men presented Joseph's uncles with SI$70, exactly the same amount as they had received.

A third example of a conflict involving Malaitans on Ranongga illustrates how rumors and stereotypes themselves can complicate what are otherwise quite ordinary conflicts. The dispute occurred in October 2000 and involved tit-for-tat sexual affairs, a sort of hostile sister exchange. There were two sets of siblings: let us say that Michael is the brother of Mary, Geoff is the brother of Gina. All of them were born and raised on Ranongga, but Michael and Mary had a Malaitan mother; Geoff and Gina had a Guadalcanal father. The affair began when Michael and Gina fell in love, and Michael ran away with Gina. In angry retaliation, Gina's brother Geoff ran away with Michael's sister Mary. Now, Michael and Mary had a cousin, related to them on their mother's side, who was visiting from Malaita. This Malaitan cousin was angry that Geoff had "stolen" Mary. He said that if he found Geoff, he would beat him up or kill him. The story was complicated by the fact that, not long before, another Malaitan kinsman living with Mary and Michael's family learned that a relative was killed in Honiara by Guadalcanal militants as part of the raging Ethnic Tension. This visiting Malaitan kinsman said—in jest—that he would get revenge by killing Gina and Geoff's father because he was a man of Guadalcanal. As rumors circulated, the joke about revenge for Tension-related violence on Guadalcanal was conflated with the more earnest threat of violence in retaliation for a sexual offense. People started to worry that the conflict on Guadalcanal really was making its way to Ranongga.

Samuel Samata of Pienuna, a senior relative of one of the parties involved and well known to all, was called to straighten out the dispute. I met him when he returned. Earlier that day, Solomon Islands Broadcasting Corporation radio had been reporting on the negotiations that would lead to the signing of the Townsville Peace Agreement between the Guadalcanal and Malaitan militants. In light of current events, Samata wryly explained to me that he had "held some peace talks between Guale and Malaita." After he explained the tangled net of events and rumors to me, he reflected on the fact that everyone blames any kind of trouble on Malaitans. "Sometimes people from Malaita do cause trouble," he said, "but they are blamed even when they don't cause any trouble."

Such examples show that, sometimes, cultural differences do raise problems for relationships among people from different parts of the country. But these conflicts are often no more disruptive to social life than similar conflicts arise amongst people of the western Solomons. Moreover, despite differences in expectations about issues like the appropriate amount of compensation for a sexual offense, Ranonggans and Malaitans alike share a basic sense that the exchange of money or valuables, along with Christian prayer, is the most effective way to solve conflicts. People of both islands are accustomed to compromising across different church denominations with different rules about compensation and marriage. Finally, in the cases where Ranonggans were most angry about Malaitan aggression, the aggressors were often not long-resident Malaitans but kin who had arrived more recently or were visiting temporarily, and who were perceived by both Ranonggans and long-resident Malaitans to be acting in ways inappropriate to being guests on other people's land.

## Living Amicably on Alienated Land

The era of plantation labor drew to a close in the decades after World War II. In the late 1950s and 1960s, many Malaitans continued to work for larger companies like Levers Pacific Plantations Ltd. under shorter contracts and with a greater range of opportunities until many moved to other forms of employment in the mid and late 1960s (Frazer 1985a). Smaller plantation owners, already weakened by the Great Depression of the 1930s, failed to win reparations for wartime damage to their property, and most abandoned their plantations. Traces of this old plantation era are visible on maps of Western Province, which are dotted with villages called "New Mala" or named after places in Malaita, even when no Malaitans have remained on the land. Some Malaitan men working in Western Province married women and were integrated into local families; others remained on the theoretically alienated land of abandoned plantations. Many of the Malaitans who have settled in the western Solomons, and the people of the western Solomons who have welcomed them, have worked to establish amicable and cooperative relationships as morally legitimate hosts and guests.

The settlement of New Mala on the northeastern coast of Ranongga was established by James Suafo in 1966 after he had worked on the land since 1959. He arrived toward the end of the period when Malaitans came to Western Province to work on copra plantations. I interviewed James and his wife in 1999 about their life on Ranongga, and their story illustrates the ways that people who migrate in the context of wage labor may seek to engage with local landowners and transform a relationship mediated by capitalist economic relationships into one mediated by shared understandings of customary forms of land ownership.

James was born in north Malaita sometime in the 1910s. He said he was already "big" when his father joined in the punitive expedition that followed the murder of District Officer W.R. Bell by Kwaio warriors in 1927 (Keesing and Corris 1980; Akin 1999b), which suggests he was born around 1920. In the late 1940s and early 1950s, James recalled, he worked as a clerk for the postwar Maasina Rule movement. After Maasina Rule ended, he worked as a tax collector for the government, but the wages were poor. Kitchener Wheatley, the son of English trader Norman Wheatley, whom Judith Bennett described as having "virtually established a dynasty in the Western Solomons" (Bennett 1987: 75), was looking for men to work on a copra plantation on northeastern Ranongga, and James eagerly signed on.

Beginning in 1959, James led a team of twelve Malaitan men to the area that would become known as New Mala. The area was then still sparsely populated: George Hilly's project at Koriovuku was just beginning, and a few families were living at Kolomali. James and his crew worked for six months at a time and, during this period, James left his wife and family home in Malaita. In 1966, he learned that his eldest daughter, then ten years old, was the fifth of their children to die on Malaita. At that point, he decided to bring his wife and surviving children, along with a niece, Ela, and her husband, Mesia, to settle at the site he named New Mala. The move was to be temporary. "We wanted to go back," he explained to me, but Kitchener Wheatley and his children "held us here." Later, he said that life on Ranongga is good: "Many of my brothers in Malaita are already dead, but here some people are old men before they die. That's why we stay here. And because the people here love us too."

James is unusual in the fact that he was already married and had a family when he began working on Ranongga. James and his family were also careful to point out that they had never invited other relatives from Malaita to join them in New Mala, a point that Ranonggans living in surrounding villages mentioned approvingly when they told me of their high regard for old James. Indeed, when we were talking about events on Guadalcanal, one of James's nephews said that Malaitans settled in Guadalcanal or Western Province had no right to bring their relatives from Malaita with them. "Guale people," he said, "have a right to be angry." When I asked them whether they missed their home in Malaita, James and his in-law Mesia talked about how Malaita was in their bodies; custom is something that you take no matter where you go (see also Gegeo 2001). At the same time, though, they lived "underneath" Ranonggan custom: "the custom of *this place* holds us." Mesia's wife, Ela, told me how good Ranonggan women were to her, repeatedly mentioning that they had helped her in childbirth and with her children. One woman of Pienuna, Evelyn Qago, had brought her food in the clinic after she gave birth to her daughter and, as a result, she named one daughter after Evelyn's daughter Otelyn. Ela had been back to Malaita three times since 1966 to visit her mother, but she had no further plans to return. Six of her seven children were born here and had never set foot on Malaita. They didn't know Malaitan custom.

Even as he emphasized the fact that he was living under the chiefs of "this place," James also subtly affirmed his own rights to live at New Mala by recalling his work in clearing the land for the plantation. When he arrived in 1959, he said, the place was just big bush, completely overgrown. He had spilled his sweat and that was why both Kitchener Wheatley and the people of Ranongga wanted him to stay. Throughout the Solomon Islands, clearing primary forest is a powerful assertion of ownership. Such claims are particularly powerful in Kwara'ae and other areas of northern Malaita, where origin myths posit an original ancestor who arrived from across the sea rather than ancestors who emerged on the island itself (see Burt 1982, 1994a; Keesing 1982b). James was not claiming any kind of primary right, however, because after describing his work in clearing the land, he explained that he was careful to "ask" for any land that he used for gardening or settlement. The people of this place were good and generous and never said no, he said. Samuel Samata of Pienuna had given them permission to build a small hamlet at Nikue, near New Mala, where coconuts planted by one of Samata's uncles stood.

When I asked about the status of the land that New Mala was part of, James explained how Kitchener Wheatley came to lease the land: Wheatley had owned an island near Gizo where the British Protectorate had resettled a community of Gilbertese people. In exchange for this island, the Western District government gave him the alienated land south of Koriovuku. Then James added that it was not really Wheatley who owned the land: "The land belongs to the people here. It was only the government who gave it to Wheatley." James and his neighbors treat this alienated land as though it is still customary land.

One of Ela and Mesia's sons explained that they had no connection to Malaita and were "just like citizens" of Ranongga. Yet, it was clear they were uncertain of the future, especially in light of the mass eviction of Malaitans from Guadalcanal that had begun the previous year. Not long after our interview, anti-Malaitan violence around Noro and Munda was directed largely at Malaitans who had, like James and his family, settled on the officially alienated land abandoned by expatriate plantation owners (Scales 2007: 194). Other

Ranonggan-based Malaitans I knew spoke during this period of returning home to Malaita to develop their own island; one man cited a rumor of great mineral wealth on the island that would help them lift Malaitan standards of living. James, however, had no desire to return to Malaita. He would die on Ranongga, but he was not sure about his children. Would the next Ranonggan generation be as generous as their parents and grandparents? Was land getting scarce? According to rumors, some people in neighboring villages were attempting to reclaim the alienated land and start their own development projects.

The story of New Mala in rural Ranongga is not strikingly different to stories of a range of rural and urban settlements founded by Malaitans on Guadalcanal during this same period. By the time that James traveled to Ranongga to work the land transferred to Kitchener Wheatley, many of his compatriots were pursuing the swiftly expanding opportunities offered by the expansion of Honiara. Among them was Michael Kwa'ioloa's brother John Maesatana, who had previously worked for Levers in Western Province but in the 1960s decided his chances were better in Honiara (Kwa'ioloa and Burt 1997: 42). Then and now, housing in Honiara was inadequate for the numbers of workers residing there, and Kwa'ioloa's brother approached local Guadalcanal landowners around Mount Austin for permission to found a settlement that would become Kobito 2. Kwa'ioloa carefully names the Guadalcanal leaders who granted this permission, and lists the Malaitan men who first established Honiara's settlements. The Guale landowners "had to offer sacrifices to their ancestral ghost to declare everything before anyone settled or cleared an area of land. Otherwise the ghosts would not know these persons and would cause sickness or even death to those settling the land" (Kwa'ioloa and Burt 2012: 201). Writing of Kobito 2, Kwa'ioloa describes the relationship between his family and the landowners as one of "children" and "fathers." He and his family worked on behalf of the Guale landowners, inviting them to feasts, helping them with land disputes, contributing to community projects; the Guale landowners granted them permission to use land for gardening, harvest housing materials, and collect firewood that allowed Kwa'ioloa's family to live better than many other families in town (ibid.: 197, 68).

In addition to asserting their legitimate status as guests of Guale people, Kwa'ioloa justified the legitimacy of Malaitan occupation of Guadalcanal land in terms of what he describes as Kwara'ae tradition. First, and perhaps most controversially, Kwa'ioloa suggests that Guadalcanal people are actually descended from Kwara'ae people, figuring Malaitans as genealogically senior to Guadalcanal people.[13] Second, he argues that Malaitans were responsible for clearing all of the forest on Guadalcanal, and that clearing forest has always conveyed primary rights over land. This justification resonates with James's comments about clearing the bush around New Mala. Finally, Kwa'ioloa argues that Malaitan sacrifices during World War II should have been acknowledge with a large gift of pigs and valuables, or a gift of land: "This is why we have done no wrong in settling Guadalcanal land, because our fathers and grandfathers were shot dead on the island of Guadalcanal, so that the Guadalcanal people could all remain on their island" (ibid.: 194).

While Guadalcanal people would probably contest many of Kwa'ioloa's justifications for Malaitan settlement of Guadalcanal, his basic account of the friendly relationship between settlers and local landowners is affirmed by other sources.[14] As early as the 1950s, Guadalcanal people expressed fear of being overwhelmed by Malaitans who had migrated to work on expatriate-owned plantations (Fraenkel 2004: 24–26, 32). Yet pressure to evict all Malaitans from Guadalcanal in the 1990s came not from those landowners who were most intensely engaged with Malaitan settlers, but from Weather Coast people who claimed ownership of the land and did not accept the arrangements made by Guale people living near Honiara (see Chapter 8).

What is striking in both the Ranonggan and the Honiara case is that neither settlers, nor landowners, accepted the legitimacy of the government's designation of the land as alienated. In articulating their rights to settle the land, both James and Kwa'ioloa focused on their connections to local landowners, not the legal status of the land. In explaining the causes of the conflict, Kwa'ioloa points to the fact that many Malaitans who arrived later in Honiara did not establish a connection to landowners in the way that he and his brothers did. Instead, they went to Honiara Town Council or the Lands Department, which automatically issued "temporary occupation licenses" within the extended boundaries of the town without any consultation with the landowners (Kwa'ioloa and Burt 2012: 198). Like James's son on Ranongga, Kwa'ioloa admits that Guadalcanal people had a right to be angry. And like many of the men of both Malaita and Guadalcanal who took up arms during the civil crisis (Allen 2013a), Kwa'ioloa ultimately blames the state for failing to respond to the legitimate grievances of Guadalcanal people and for failing to protect the lives and property of Malaitans with a legitimate right to live on Guadalcanal.

## Ambivalent Urbanism and Emergent Ethno-nationalism

Since the 1960s and 1970s, research on the nascent urbanism of Solomon Islands has emphasized the fact that migration to Honiara is not unidirectional. Working in town was not necessarily different than other forms of short-term migrant labor that men of Malaita, Guadalcanal, and other southeastern Solomons societies had been undertaking for generations (Chapman 1969, 1985, 1992; Bathgate 1985; Frazer 1985a, 1985b; Friesen 1993). As Honiara grew into a major urban center and the focus of significant inputs of British development aid in the late 1950s (Bellam 1970), people of the western Solomons also began to pursue opportunities in Honiara. Wage laborers tended to see a stay in town as a temporary strategy to earn money before returning home; professionals and skilled migrants might see work as ongoing, but often they intended to retire to their rural home. Yet even by the 1970s it was clear that purportedly temporary sojourns were increasingly permanent, and that a stated intention to return home might not result in an actual return home. As Marilyn Strathern (1985) wrote of Hagen migrants in Port Moresby in Papua New Guinea, the tie home was becoming "disconcerting" both to migrants and to those researching them.

The late colonial era of the late 1960s and early 1970s was a time of growing opportunity for indigenous Solomon Islanders, and also a time of growing class distinctions. Ian Frazer (1985a) observed that after generations of being stuck in low-wage and relatively low-status jobs with little possibilities for advancement, To'ambaita people of north Malaita with some education could expect significant upward mobility, though the prospects of those with minimal education remained limited. Most To'ambaita living in Honiara expressed a strong intention to return home, but by the mid 1970s some had established an urban lifestyle that was an alternative to rural lives. Upwardly mobile urbanites with ongoing rather than temporary employment were not necessarily loosening their connections to their rural homes; many were taking leading roles both in the ethnic community in town and in rural development projects at home. Frazer observed that patterns of mobility were changing the nature, if not the intensity, of relations to rural homes.

By the 1990s, a generation of young people had been raised in town with minimal connections to the rural villages they thought of as "home," and new forms of urban, class, and national identities were emerging (Gooberman-Hill 1999; Berg 2000; Stritecky 2001b). Christine Jourdan, who has conducted research among Honiara residents since the 1980s, only began to notice expressions of nationalist consciousness in the early 1990s. Suggesting that national identity was being fostered through schooling, Solomon Islands Pijin, and popular culture, Jourdan argued that it was not a coincidence that it was emerging most powerfully in Honiara: "Towns as cultural marketplaces allow for new negotiations of meaning to take place while at the same time allowing for wider circulation of new symbols and modes of identification. Nationalism is one of them, negotiated publicly and privately, by urbanites who have to shape a future for themselves away from culture and tradition (*kastom*)" (Jourdan 1995: 144).

The period of civil conflict revealed the fragility of the sense of shared national identity that Jourdan had identified as emerging over the previous few years. Rather than distancing themselves from what they saw as *kastom*, many of the educated and urbanized men who joined in the militant struggle transformed it into a key symbol in the struggle (Allen 2013a). It is important to remember, however, that nationalism is not simply a positive identification with a nation. In much of postcolonial Melanesia, nationalism takes the form not of pride but of shame, anger, or frustration at the weakness, backwardness, or corruption of the nation-state (Robbins 1998; see also Bashkow 2006; Scott 2012). This sense of negative nationalism was very strong in the Solomons by the turn of the twenty-first century and was shared across the ethnically defined militias.

Localized and ethnic identities did not necessarily become less important in the context of rapid urbanization, but the meaning of those identities changed. These changes are evident in quotidian practices, including language use. By the late 1980s and 1990s, Solomons Pijin had become the first language of many second- and third-generation settlers in Honiara (Jourdan 1989, 1990). Parents were often concerned with their children's fluency in English and Pijin as languages of social advancement and schooling, but assumed that they would simply pick up the language of their home places because they were people of the place. Yet according to Jourdan, even as vernaculars have "become marginal in the lives of many city people," they "keep their status as 'true' language even in the eyes of those who do not know them" (Jourdan 2007: 35). In vernacular languages and in Solomon Islands Pijin, *langgus* refers only to vernaculars (see Jourdan 2002: 118), and the term *ples* only refers to rural villages. If residence in town leads to the attenuation of ties home, and fluency in Pijin and English replaces vernacular fluency, people may come to feel they have no place, they have no language. Even upwardly mobile youth who function almost entirely in English and Pijin may scatter a few words or phrases from their home languages as a way of marking island identity. No longer the primary medium of communication, vernacular language becomes a marker of ethnic identity.

A sense of belonging to the nation, rather than a particular home area, has developed in tandem with the emergence of an urban elite and middle class. In research conducted in Honiara on the eve of the conflict, Rachel Gooberman-Hill (1999) described the strategies through which her middle-class interlocutors sought to distance themselves from their rural kin. They sought a sense of feeling "free" from the burdens of kinship. They downplayed their ethnic identities in favor of a class identity that depended upon the suppression of ethnic loyalties and the minimization of obligations to grassroots kin (see also Gewertz and Errington 1999). Against theories that ethnicity is malleable, Gooberman-Hill argued that for middle-class urbanites ethnicity is fixed. Thus, she noted, a woman who married a man from a different island might be praised by his kin as a "real person" of that island because she carefully respected distinctive forms of avoidance behavior, spoke his language, or cooked foods distinct to her husband's home. Yet such comments are just a manner of speaking: ethnic identity remains the same. These comments mirror the joke with which I began this chapter, in which in-married spouses are said to have become "citizens" of Ranongga, but with a significant difference: I have argued that long-term residents of land in Ranongga really do become local because of the way in which physical labor (clearing land and planting gardens) or emotional labor (caring for local people) anchors them to the place. In the absence of a generative relationship with the ground that defines people's identity, ethnicity can become fixed, something to be overcome in search of a more encompassing class or national identity.

If some urbanites distance themselves from the demands of rural kin, other town dwellers continue to embrace an ideology framing urban living as a temporary sojourn. Like many urban residents, Michael Kwa'ioloa has some secondary schooling and has moved back and forth between Kwara'ae in Malaita and Honiara, working in a variety of occupations: as a clerk, within a family contracting business, and as a special constable within the police force. He described himself being in the middle of the emerging class system of Solomon Islands: not part of the governing elite (despite several unsuccessful attempts at running for office) who are rich and keep getting richer, nor the "grassroots" who struggle to get any money at all, but someone who continues to struggle to make businesses work, sometimes succeeding and sometimes failing (Kwa'ioloa and Burt 2012: 270). Despite the fact that his family has clearly worked hard to give some legitimacy to their ongoing residence in Honiara, Kwa'ioloa claims, "We stay in Honiara just to work, to pay school fees for the education of our children" (ibid.: 135); he describes towns as places to make money temporarily in preparation for an eventual return home. Like the To'ambaita residents of Honiara that Frazer interviewed in the 1970s, Kwa'ioloa works hard to maintain connections with rural kin, using his moderate affluence in the context of traditional exchanges, especially bridewealth and compensation payments, to remain significant in the lives of his kinspeople in Honiara and in Kwara'ae. He states explicitly that he does this to make sure that no one back home forgets about him or his sons, and that they will be welcomed when they return.

For some twenty thousand Malaitans resident in Honiara in the late 1990s, returning home was not a choice in the way that it was for Frazer's upwardly mobile interlocutors in the 1970s. After years, decades, and in some cases generations of absence, they were compelled to return home—a home that many had never even visited. David Gegeo and Karen Ann Watson-Gegeo (2012) describe the pressure that massive return migration put on rural west Kwara'ae communities. They overwhelmed the capacity of institutions like schools, which were already struggling because of state collapse. More strikingly, many of these return migrants were unable to speak Kwara'ae language fluently, did not follow Kwara'ae traditions as villagers practiced them, and were blamed for a wide range of social problems. Many return migrants were not welcomed onto customary land. The combination of being violently evicted from Guadalcanal and rejected in the places they considered home fueled anger toward the government and, in some cases, a search for a sense of community and belonging through new religious affiliations (McDougall 2009a; Timmer 2012).

By the late 1990s, few Solomon Islanders felt that their prospects for upward social mobility were great. The public service, which had offered so many possibilities to the previous generation, was undergoing dramatic cuts in the context of a broader program of structural adjustment. The forced eviction of thousands of urban Malaitans during the period of Ethnic Tension led to a situation not unlike that documented by James Ferguson (1999) for Zambia in the midst of an economic downturn in the 1980s, when many urbanites found themselves forced to return to the land. In the years of economic prosperity, some urbanites developed distinctly modernist styles and sought to disentangle themselves from the obligations and constraints of their rural connections. Others were traditionalists who had continued to invest in land and livestock and had maintained close ties with their country cousins. In a context of economic collapse, traditionalists fared better than modernists. In the Solomons, town residents who extricate themselves from the often burdensome obligations of kin networks may "lose their passports" home without becoming "citizens" of another place.

## Diversity, Division, and Cooperation

We cannot understand the ethnic or island-based identities of town dwellers, nor the ethno-nationalist identities at play in the civil conflict of 1998 to 2003, as the extension of the place-based identities of people living in rural villages. Ethnicity has its own complex dynamics that grow out of particular kinds of interactions, not ancient animosities or isolation. Ethnic tensions between Malaitans and people of the western Solomons or Guadalcanal are the product of colonial state building and the expansion of markets in land, labor, and commodities, not the extension of timeless social formations isolated from capitalist economies and a weak state. Moreover, as Simmel (1964) observed a century ago, the metropolitan experience of being immersed in a world of strangers does not necessarily lead to a more intense engagement with strangers, but often a greater sense of distance and even antagonism.

Indigenous Solomon Islands polities are politically fragmented and culturally diverse. In this chapter, I have shown that such fragmentation and diversity has not prevented people from various areas of the Solomons—including people on opposite sides of the most polarized ethnic divides like Malaitan and "Western" or Guadalcanal—from interacting in amicable and cooperative ways. I have focused primarily on small-scale negotiations involving marriage and land rights, but the same argument holds with regard to broader macro-political movements in the colonial and postcolonial history of the country. To the surprise, and often dismay, of many colonial administrators, from the 1930s onward, Solomon Islanders from around the Protectorate proved able to unite for common causes, like better conditions for laborers and more political autonomy. Maasina Rule drew together people from Malaita, Guadalcanal, Makira, Gela, and even Santa Isabel.[15] One of the predecessors of Maasina Rule, the Fallows Movement, drew people together across an even wider geographic expanse and across even greater socio-cultural and linguistic differences, from Makira in the southeast to the Shortland Islands in the northwest. Akin (2013) suggests that British colonial administrators systematically misunderstood the nature of indigenous political fragmentation and consistently underestimated the capacity of Solomon Islanders to work together. In a similar vein, many contemporary analysts continue to blame the failure of the modern state in the Solomon Islands on the long-standing fragmentation of indigenous polities, thus downplaying the most obvious drivers of the crisis: a profound frustration with a postcolonial state that, like its colonial predecessor, has better served the needs of outsiders than the people of the Solomons themselves.

In the Introduction I posed the question of why the ethnically inflected conflict between migrants and indigenes on Guadalcanal was not worse than it was. This chapter suggests that part of the reason is that ordinary Solomon Islanders have been dealing with these kinds of tensions for generations. Over the course of mobile and multi-sited lives, most ordinary Solomon Islanders have been in the position of both migrant and landowner; each can see the position of the other. Even in situations where the state suggested the land did not belong to any local group, migrants often sought to act like good guests and landowners to act like good hosts.

## Notes

1. For other examples of long distance and multigenerational reconnections, see Kwa'ioloa's accounts of meeting with people of north Malaita and Santa Isabel to track the connections between his Kwara'ae ancestors and theirs (Kwa'ioloa and Burt 2012: 150–58).
2. *Qokolo* is not normally used by native speakers of Kubokota or Luqa as a term of reference: if the chorus above were sung in the vernacular, the word *qokolo* would have been replaced by *tinoni*, a term with cognates in the other Austronesian languages of New Georgia (e.g. *tio* in Roviana). In vernacular language discourse, *qokolo* has a dual discursive function: it is a vocative or address term, and an interjective or discourse marker (the exclamation "*Qokolo!*" functions much like 'Oh, man!' in English). Unlike the word *tinoni*, *qokolo* does not have cognates in regional languages; it can better stand for Ranongga. Some non-Ranonggans living in the provincial capital Gizo called

out "*Qokolo!*" when they saw me and asked me to speak in Ranonggan languages "so that they could hear it"—precisely as the song suggests.
3. Murray Bathgate's (1985) description of changing patterns of mobility in northwestern Guadalcanal some forty years ago resonates strongly with my description of Pienuna. He describes an increasingly diverse community as people increasingly meet, and marry, women and men from around the country drawn to nearby Honiara; many in-married people sought to reside in villages in northwestern Guadalcanal because of the proximity to Honiara and the opportunities it afforded. The centralization of development in Honiara after 1960 intensified population pressures in northwestern Guadalcanal in the 1990s and 2000s (Monson 2012: 211–65) in a way that they did not occur in Pienuna or other areas of Ranongga.
4. Writing of northwestern Guadalcanal, Bathgate (1985: 83–85) discusses the way that marriage drove movement between hamlets along a similar dynamic of "dual residence" as couples move between the home of the husband and wife.
5. The people referred to as "Gilbertese" in Solomon Islands are descendents of people who were resettled between 1957 and 1963 on Gizo Island and other locales in Western Province and Choiseul in Solomon Islands from what was then the British Gilbert and Ellice Islands Protectorate, and is now the republic of Kiribati (Knudson 1977).
6. Moore (2013) provides tables of numbers of recruits from different regions in Solomon Islands: between 1870 and 1887, 85 laborers were recruited from Choiseul and 165 from Western Province, including 15 Ranonggans. After 1888, the number of laborers recruited from both Western Province and Choiseul is zero.
7. The proportion was slightly lower for Guadalcanal at 7 percent, but it would have been even higher in remote areas like the Weather Coast. Surveys of adult men on both Guadalcanal and Malaita undertaken by Bennett in the 1970s indicate that virtually everyone had worked on a plantation or a ship, with the few exceptions being men who had assisted on missions, and that the average time away was ten years (Bennett 1987: 189; see also Chapman 1969; Chapman and Pirie 1974; Bathgate 1985).
8. With his brother H. Beck, C.P. Beck had obtained a lease for a plantation at Kudu (which never seems to have been put into operation) and for Aena plantation on Povana land (just south of the present day village of Suava) in 1914, and operated it through the Great Depression of the 1930s, but he did not return after World War II (BSIP 21/II).
9. On the general tendency of Europeans to attribute depopulation to local culture or society, rather than the devastating effects of introduced diseases, see Akin (2013: 114–28), Bayliss-Smith (2014), and Bennett (2014).
10. David Akin, personal communication by email, 29 May 2014, from unpublished fieldnotes from early 1996.
11. David Akin, personal communication, 6 June 2014.
12. Kwa'ioloa describes such negotiations undertaken in Honiara in detail (Kwa'ioloa and Burt 1997: 73–87, 103–12; 2012: 85–116); see also Akin (1999b) on Malaitan compensation claims more generally.
13. Ben Burt (Kwa'ioloa and Burt 2012: 15) acknowledges that such a claim would be contested by many Guadalcanal people. Kwa'ioloa also describes a gathering in which he told people of eastern Guadalcanal where their place names came from, something that most other Solomon Islanders would find highly objectionable.

14. I heard similar stories from founders of Adaliua, a neighborhood beyond the town boundary where I lived for a month in 2006, also established in the 1960s: he described Guale people who held the land as good, generous people who had always welcomed their presence.
15. Most discussions of Maasina Rule have focused primarily on Malaita, but as Michael Scott notes, it was a formative moment in the development of a distinct Makiran identity, which in recent years has taken on an oppositional relationship to Malaita (Scott 1991, 2007b, 2008, 2012). It was equally important in Guadalcanal, influencing the development of the Moro Movement (Davenport and Coker 1967; Allen 2013a: 81–84).

# 8
# Amity and Enmity in an Unreliable State

Welcoming strangers ashore is a powerful assertion of sovereignty over land. In Ranonggan myth and history, this act also transforms territorial relations. In some narratives, strangers are adopted to replace a group facing extinction. In others, they succeed chiefs who have been unable to look after local territory and people. In times of violence, migrants gained rights to territory through sacrifice in ritual or in war. More often, though, migrants became anchored to their new homes through the productive labor of clearing land, building settlements, and planting trees, and through the reproductive labor of bearing children, nurturing children, and nursing the aged and infirm. Even as migrants become attached to their new home, *butubutu* identities continue to point back to the places of matrilineal origin, reminding people of ancestral ties to distant lands.

In mundane reality, strangers arrive in all kinds of ways. But in ceremonies that memorialize such arrivals, there is a clear pattern. Strangers arrive from beyond local shores. The land seems empty, but as the canoe comes ashore, warriors rush down to defend their territory. Threatened, the strangers are immobilized until a chief of the land steps forward, holding shell valuables to welcome the strangers ashore as guests. I discussed such ceremonies in Chapter 4 in the context of Ranonggan conversion narratives, but the basic scenario is re-enacted far beyond Ranongga. In the biggest media event of recent Solomon Islands history, for example, the Duke and Duchess of Cambridge were greeted with such an attack when they stepped onto the tarmac at Henderson Airport near Honiara.[1] When chiefs welcome strangers ashore in such ceremonies, they do so within the frame of *kastom*. They carry the traditional valuables—*bakia* for the western Solomons, strings of shell money for the eastern Solomons—that are the medium of peacemaking, used to ransom lives and attach strangers to a place. By enacting this message of peace, these *kastom* authorities also usher in the new era of Christianity, understood as a time when all strangers should be welcomed because all humanity is united as children of the same God. They simultaneously assert ancestral sovereignty and re-enact the moment when ancestral power was subjugated to the Christian God.

Warrior welcomes are touristic performances of native culture, in which the threat of violence is feigned. Yet they also remind visitors and locals alike that people themselves have the right to decide who may, and who may not, arrive on their ancestral land. The civil war of 1998–2003 can be partially understood as an attempt by Guale people to reassert this right against a national state that had ignored it for generations. The Guale uprising of 1998 violently persecuted migrants, yet it was not simply xenophobic. The problem was not only that many outsiders had settled on northern Guadalcanal since the 1950s, but also that these outsiders came without an invitation by the rightful people of the land. Indigenous residents of Guadalcanal felt forgotten and disregarded by people from other islands and, most significantly, by their own government.

Perhaps the most surprising thing about the so-called Ethnic Tension is the fact that the victims of Guale violence largely accepted the legitimacy of Guale grievances. Many settlers from the island of Malaita who suffered from Tension-related violence, and even some who later took up arms against the Guale militants, accepted that their hosts had the moral right to evict them. Malaitans objected to the brutal treatment they received at the hands of Guale militants, and were angry that their efforts in good faith to establish themselves as legitimate guests on the land were ignored, but, like the Malaitans living on Ranongga whose perspectives were discussed in Chapter 7, they agreed that Guale people had a right to be angry.

Many commentators have blamed the Ethnic Tension between 1998 and 2003 on underlying cultural diversity and political fragmentation. Far from demonstrating deep-seated tribal differences, however, the conflict played out in ways that reveal broadly shared cultural ground. Like the people of Ranongga who have been my focus in this book, migrant Malaitans and indigenous people of Guadalcanal alike agree that the land ultimately belongs to local people. They also agree that migrants who are given permission to work on the land should not be evicted without cause. These understandings apply to customary land, and to alienated land where settlers have arrived at the behest of outsiders rather than the invitation of local people. Furthermore, Guales, Malaitans, "Westerners," and citizens from all across the country share traditions of peacemaking involving the exchange of material valuables that stand for the lives of people and rights to land. Despite denominational differences, they draw on a common corpus of Christian texts, and they participate in similar Christian rituals of prayer and forgiveness. Finally, they share a profound disappointment in governments that they believe have systematically failed to protect their interests and improve their lives.

Insofar as many Solomon Islanders blame the government for the conflict, local interpretations of the conflict resonate in some ways with the "weak state" paradigm that has helped to shape—and has been re-enforced by—the approach of the Regional Assistance Mission to Solomon Islands (RAMSI). As discussed in the Introduction, the policy report that made the case for Australia to intervene militarily in the affairs of this "failing neighbour" depicted the institutions of the modern state as a superficial overlay whose legitimacy was undermined by resilient indigenous political structures (Wainwright 2003: 28). Colonialism contributed to the conflict because it did not sufficiently penetrate local social, economic, and political life: the "perfunctory" British Protectorate administration made minimal effort to "develop the country economically or socially" and "has left little imprint on the country today" (ibid.: 19). From this perspective, the most pressing challenge is improving the capacity of the state to encompass and subordinate these localized political structures.

Many scholars have suggested that this narrow focus on the institutions of the state obscures the underlying political-economic drivers of conflict. Terence Wesley-Smith observes that although commercial activity is necessary for the functioning of a modern state, "some types of modern economic activity have been so disruptive, particularly of local communities, as to weaken rather than enhance state capacity" (Wesley-Smith 2008: 44). Matthew Allen (2013b) suggests that the failure of Melanesian states to regulate the exploitation of resources and distribute the benefits to citizens has undermined their legitimacy, but the weakness of the state is a secondary cause of violent unrest in the region; the core drivers are the divisive and corrupting effects of resource capitalism. Since the very beginning of the colonial administration, the state has been justified largely in terms of its ability to foster the capitalist development that will generate the revenues necessary to support the state. Writing of the early history of the British Solomon Islands Protectorate, Judith Bennett has observed that, "The capitalists had received far more than 'a little help from the authorities' and the Islanders far less in this new colonial world" (Bennett 1987: 149). To the profound disappointment of many of its citizens, the same can be said of most governments comprised of the democratically elected representatives of Solomon Island people themselves.

Ranonggans, and Solomon Islanders all around the country, lament the fact that their government appears unable to protect their interests or improve their quality of life. They complain about unreliable government services, the failure of the government to foster rural development, a lack of government control over internal migration, and, above all, a political system in which big money seems more influential than the will of ordinary people. Their experience during the years of civil conflict underlined the extent to which many things they believe make their lives better—things like schooling, health care, and transportation—depend upon a functioning nation-state. Without denying that Solomon Islanders deserve a more reliable state, it is worth remembering that for much of the history of the modern Solomon

Islands, state expansion has served the interests of outsiders or political elites. Arguably, the expansion of state power in the service of resource capitalism has done much to undermine the cosmopolitan dynamics of everyday life I have documented throughout this book. Citizens may have much to gain from a better government, but they also have much to lose from the strengthening of a state that they have good historical reasons to mistrust.

## Enemy Friends: Tension Times (1998 to 2003)

The outbreak of ethnic violence in Solomon Islands in the late 1990s is not particularly surprising. Strong correlations between civil war and the degree to which a country's economy is dominated by resource wealth made Solomon Islands an ideal candidate for a resource conflict (Allen 2013b). But what is surprising is that the conflict was not worse. Writing in mid 2000, Julian Treadaway, the director of the University of South Pacific Solomon Islands, wondered, "Where else can you find 20,000 people expelled from their homes and an attempted government coup with so little violence or loss of life?" (quoted in Fraenkel 2004: 91). Many acts of everyday intimidation, as well as terrible acts of sexual violence, occurred during the Tension and do not figure in official estimates of the casualties of war. Nevertheless, as the authors of a book-length evaluation of the regional military intervention that ended the conflict observe, "At every stage, it might have spiraled into something much worse without the restraining influences of church leaders and women leaders, and the efforts of many ordinary Solomon Islands villagers in general" (Braithwaite et al. 2010: 32). Attention to macro-political structures and transnational economic forces is necessary to understand the drivers of the conflict, but attention to local cultural patterns and social processes of the sort that I have documented for Ranongga is important in understanding why violence was limited.

The roots of the ethnic conflict are to be found in colonial history, but not merely in the weakness of the colonial state. For most of its existence, the colonial government was primarily focused on fostering the capitalist development that would generate revenues that would allow it to fund itself. These priorities were evident in policies of land alienation and labor regulation—policies that allowed foreign investors to avoid paying a fair price for land and labor, and restricted the ability of laborers to negotiate for better pay or leave oppressive conditions. The Protectorate was never really profitable but, as Bennett has pointed out, the "failure of an exploitative policy no more excuses it than does success" (Bennett 1987: 166). This state-supported exploitation of land and labor in the interest of foreign capital—not simple "weakness"—constitutes the poisonous legacy of colonialism.

Far from leaving "little imprint," the state-driven expansion of capitalism in the twentieth century fostered both inequality and ethno-nationalist forms of identity that emerged in virulent form in the late 1990s (Kabutaulaka 2001; Bennett 2002; Akin 2013; Allen 2013a). This expansion created lasting divisions between the "haves" who were close enough to European commercial infrastructure to sell their products and the "have nots" who had nothing to sell but their labor. It created divisions between landowners whose territory was appropriated by foreign interests and laborers who left their homes to work for those foreign interests. Contemporary identities did not arise only as a reflex of incorporation into global capitalist structures, but also through a wide range of social movements that sought to contest the oppressive labor conditions and autocratic nature of colonial rule. Various social movements — whether Gizo tax revolts or the Fallows Movement of the 1930s, Maasina Rule in the 1940s and 1950s, the Guadalcanal-based Moro Movement of the 1960s, or even the Christian Fellowship Church that has continued until today—have sought to create alternative political structures that would allow a more efficacious participation in the transnational economy. Partly in response to the global postwar consensus regarding decolonization that emanated from the British Colonial Office in London after World War II, and partly in response to the persistent demands of Solomon Islanders, especially as articulated through Maasina Rule (Akin 2013), in the 1950s and 1960s, the Protectorate administration sought to develop the country's infrastructure in ways that would benefit Solomon Islanders more directly, and began to open avenues for local people to participate in government (Bennett 1987: 31). Today, many Solomon Islanders look back on this late colonial period with a degree of nostalgia that sometimes overlooks earlier struggles against the worst excesses of colonialism.

To the dismay of Solomon Islanders, their independently elected representatives do not seem to have served them much better than the late colonial administration. In the 1980s and 1990s, political corruption associated with logging undermined the ability of elected representatives in the independent Solomon Islands to serve the interests of their constituents. In 1997, Prime Minister Bartholomew Ulufa'alu came to power at the head of the Solomon Islands Alliance for Change with an intention to reform the logging industry. At the same time, the Asian economic crisis led to a dramatic drop in revenue within the Solomons, and international donors including the World Bank, the Asian Development Bank, and the International Monetary Fund pushed programs of "structural adjustment" that aimed to reduce debt by cutting government expenditure. Scholars have argued that Ulufa'alu's 1997/8 reforms helped to trigger the conflict in two ways: by creating a faction of political elites with a vested interest in undermining the reformist government, and by increasing unemployment through cuts to the public service (Fraenkel 2004: 41–42, 64; Moore 2004: 61–63; Hameiri 2007; Allen 2011).

While political elites had an interest in destabilizing a reform government, the ordinary rank-and-file men who took up arms during the conflict were motivated by a deep sense of frustration with a state that had served them poorly. In his analysis of former-militant perspectives on the conflict, Matthew Allen argues that despite their differences, fighters from both Guadalcanal and Malaita were motivated by the perception of "social and economic deprivation relative to other Solomon Islanders and relative to people in other parts of the world" (Allen 2013a: 188). Both also focused on the way that their opponents had offended *kastom*, the pan-Melanesian term that points to ancestrally sanctioned, locally distinctive, ever-changing ways of living that has come to stand for many forms of local self-determination. Finally, both sides ultimately blamed the government for failing to regulate internal migration, allowing land alienation, refusing to compensate Guale people for offenses committed against them, and ignoring persistent demands for rural development.

According to Allen, Guale militants were motivated to "defend the motherland" from what they saw as exploitation and invasion by outsiders (Allen 2013a: 103). In addition to being the site of the postwar capital city, northern Guadalcanal was the location of other large-scale enterprises that drew large numbers of migrants. Gold Ridge Mine, located about 30 kilometers east and inland from Honiara, opened in 1998 after years of negotiations that had divided the owners of the lease area from the non-landowners living there. The mine became an important symbol of the hidden wealth of the island, and the violent extraction of that wealth by foreigners (Kabutaulaka 2001; Moore 2004: 107). Solomon Islands Plantations Limited (SIPL) was a massive oil-palm plantation that covered 6,000 hectares, had 1,800 employees, and housed some 15,000 people, more than half of them Malaitans.[2] Most Guale landowners established supportive and hospitable relations with the Malaitans who came to live and work at SIPL and in other locations around northern Guadalcanal. Many settlers had acquired rights to use land through transactions called *tsupu* or *chupu* that are similar to Ranonggan *pajuku* transactions discussed in Chapter 5 (Stritecky 2001b: 83; Kwa'ioloa and Burt 2012; Monson 2012: 229–37; Allen 2013a: 92). It is no coincidence that the Guale insurgency arose and found strongest support among people of Guadalcanal's Weather Coast, people who were not party to these transactions but who claimed ownership rights on land of northern Guadalcanal.[3] By the late 1990s, land transactions were increasingly "resented by a younger generation of Guadalcanal people who view the act of sale as a sale of their 'birth right'" (Kabutaulaka 2001: 15). Kabutaulaka points out that anger was focused as much on the Guale sellers of land as the Malaitan buyers (ibid.).

Anger at Malaitan settlers was sparked by a series of murders and rapes committed by Malaitans against Guale people. These offenses featured in petitions presented to the government in 1988 and again in 1998 that demanded compensation for crimes against indigenous inhabitants of the island, restrictions on internal migration, and the relocation of the national capital. The failure of the national government to address these claims was seen as evidence that people of Guale were not taken seriously and were "second class citizens" on their own land (Fraenkel 2004: 50).[4]

When the Guadalcanal Revolutionary Army (GRA) began a violent campaign of eviction against Malaitan settlers on the island's northern plains in late 1998, tens of thousands of Malaitans flooded into Honiara from outlying areas and then, along with many Malaitans living in town, traveled back to their "homes" on Malaita. After a 1999 visit to the peri-urban neighborhood of Gilbert Camp, where she had lived the previous year, anthropologist Jolene Stritecky reflected:

> Nothing had been burned or destroyed. Its residents had left pre-emptively and proactively, before they were driven out. Their choice to leave represented a subtle triumph of volition over violence. Their exodus was an act of conflict avoidance, carried out en masse yet un-orchestrated at a time when tension was so pervasive as to make violence seem inevitable. (Stritecky 2001b: 105)

At the time, and retrospectively, many people were surprised at the apparent acquiescence of Malaitans over this eviction campaign (Moore 2004: 125; Kwa'ioloa and Burt 2012; Allen 2013a: 142–46). According to David Gegeo and Karen Ann Watson-Gegeo, many people of Kwara'ae (the largest language group in Malaita), "acknowledge that the Guales had a right to defend their land, and some were embarrassed by the known violations of Guale *kastom* (custom, tradition) by Malaitans. 'Wouldn't we do the same if it happened to us?' was a theme in Malaitan discourse" (Gegeo and Watson-Gegeo 2012: 237). In addition to sympathizing with Guale grievances, many Malaitans seemed to hope that by returning home they could finally develop their own island rather than investing their labor in other areas of the country. Yet, the scale of return migration—approximately 10 percent of the entire population of Malaita, and up to 25 percent in some areas of northern Malaita—put enormous strain on what were already limited resources (Fraenkel 2004: 61–62). Many long-time Honiara residents found that they no longer fit into, or were welcome, in the places that they had long considered "home," an experience that appears to have radicalized them.

If many Malaitans accepted that people of Guadalcanal had the right to demand they leave, no one accepted the brutality of the GRA campaign. According to Allen (2009, 2013a: 140–43), former Malaitan militants said that they were motivated to take up arms because of offenses against civilians including murder, rape, and other acts they described as being against Malaitan *kastom*, and that can also be described as grave violations of human rights. The militia that came to be known as the Malaita Eagle Force (MEF) originated in vigilante groups established to protect outlying settlements of Honiara in the first year of the conflict, but took concerted action only after it became clear that the Malaitan-dominated police force was immobilized by political interference (Fraenkel 2004: 78; Allen 2013a: 142–46). The rank and file militants who took part in these operations came to see themselves as defenders of a city and nation they characterized as having been built by Malaitan labor—taking up an ethno-nationalist and class identity that had been established during Maasina Rule a generation earlier.

After the MEF-led coup on 5 June 2000, the GRA (by then known as the Isatabu Freedom Movement, or IFM) and MEF engaged in battles around Honiara's outskirts. Yet even this all-out warfare was tempered by cross-cutting friendships between militants, and by the efforts of civilians acting in the name of church organizations and civil society. George Gray, a GRA/IFM commander, recalled:

> I remember once during the height of the crisis one of my best Malaitan friends manning the enemy banker [*sic*] on the other side passed his greetings, good luck and best wishes across to me. The Melanesian Brotherhood (*Tasiu*) who brought me the message told me that my 'enemy friend' really wanted to see me and cautioned me to take extra care during the firing. The next I heard about him was that he had died during one of the shootouts. (Gray 2002: 30)

The Melanesian Brotherhood that Gray mentions are a religious order within the Anglican Church of Melanesia comprised of indigenous men who take mostly temporary vows. Understood to wield supernatural power, they moved between the militant groups throughout this period of conflict (Carter 2006). Other men and women acting under what many described as the spiritual protection of churches and church organizations took up similar mediating roles. A United Church minister from Western Province told me of how he helped to bring medicine from Honiara to communities of rural Guadalcanal, facing hostile armed men as he crossed roadblocks or rough seas when traveling by canoe at night. Women for Peace, drawn from Christian and secular women's organizations, held prayer meetings with militants on battle fields, as well as promoting a peace agenda through the media (Liloqula and Pollard 2000; Pollard 2000b; McDougall 2003).

These grassroots peacemaking efforts did not end the conflict. Ceasefires were negotiated, but both militant sides lacked the strict command structures necessary for enforcing them. Eventually, following negotiations on New

Zealand-owned warships anchored outside Honiara, representatives of both militias, as well as representatives from Guadalcanal and Malaita provinces, the premiers of other provinces, and the national government were flown to Queensland to negotiate peace in October 2000, negotiations that excluded the churches and civil-society groups that had been so active in lobbying for peace. The Townsville Peace Agreement was signed on 15 October 2000 and promised sweeping reforms of the state, a federal constitution, and compensation for victims of the violence. A National Peace Council was established to oversee disarmament, and an unarmed international Peace Monitoring Committee was established. After the treaty was signed, former enemies walked arm in arm in a parade in front of the jubilant residents of Honiara.

Rather than ending the violence, the signing of the Townville Peace Agreement marked a new phase of conflict, characterized by schisms among the militant leadership and a general collapse of many state functions. Guale militant leader Harold Keke refused to join the peace talks and established the Guadalcanal Liberation Front (GLF). Following several unsuccessful attacks on the GLF by the police, the former MEF, and their former Guale comrades of the GRA/IFM who had signed the Townsville Peace Agreement, Keke became increasingly unstable. His reign of terror led to some of the worst atrocities of the Tension committed against the long-suffering people of Guadalcanal's Weather Coast and the murder of Anglican clergymen sent to negotiate with Keke. In Honiara, leadership of the MEF also fragmented. Prime Minister Manasseh Sogavare, who came to power after Ulufa'alu was forced to resign, followed a policy of "money before peace," paying large amounts of compensation to the supposed victims of the Guale uprising. Former Malaitan militants, many of whom were designated "special constables" under the terms of the Townsville agreement, threatened and attacked ordinary citizens, and extorted large sums of money from the national government. They burned the law offices of Andrew Nori, the spokesman for the MEF in the wake of the June 2000 coup, because he had appropriated much of the compensation. Most traditional aid donors cut funding to the compromised government, seeking instead to channel funds through non-governmental channels. Ironically, perhaps, the collapse of the state led to the efflorescence of civil society movements in Honiara and Gizo, movements in which citizens worked together in attempts to demand peace and better government. But they seemed unable to counter the powerful and violent men who seemed to be running the country.

The conflict took an ethnic shape not because it emerged out of primordial loyalties or ancient divisions, but because Solomon Islanders have come to locate their grievances within what Allen calls "micronationalist narratives" (Allen 2013a: 13) that emerged over the course of the twentieth century. Not only did civilians act in ways that minimized violence, but militants themselves seemed to see their enemies not as absolute "others" but as "enemy friends." Many militants on opposite sides of the battle lines had gone to school together, had been part of the same churches, or were related by marriage. Both sides accepted the moral right of landowners to determine who comes to settle on their land; both were angry about forms of uneven development that caused some people to get rich and others to remain poor; both blamed the government for failing to defend their interests. Far from incommensurable differences, there was a great deal of common ground between the two rival groups. The war was an argument in shared terms.

On the surface, the openness to other people that I have analyzed for Ranongga seemed to be absent in an ethnic conflict that pitted indigenous Guales against migrant Malaitans. Yet people of Guadalcanal have themselves been migrant laborers, and Malaitans are also landowners—a situation that meant that each side could see the point of view of the other. Accounts of the conflict from the perspective of local people suggest that even at the height of conflict, people and communities on opposed ethnic sides were able to empathize with their enemies. If political economic forces made the conflict likely, this broadly shared cultural ground arguably made the conflict less deadly and made peace more feasible.

## Hope and Frustration: The RAMSI Decade (2003 to 2013)

In mid 2003, new strangers arrived on the shores of Solomon Islands. Following an abrupt policy shift, the Australian government responded to a request for military assistance from beleaguered prime minister of Solomon Islands, Allen Kemakeza. With the support of New Zealand and the regional Pacific Islands Forum, Australia initiated the Regional Assistance Mission to Solomon Islands (RAMSI). Following the passage of enabling legislation by the Solomon Islands parliament, more than 2,000 military, police, and civilian personnel from Australia, New Zealand, and other Pacific Islands countries were deployed to the Solomons beginning on 24 July 2003. Civil-society activist John Roughan described the scene in Honiara: "The Australians arrived, commando style and heavily armed, and secured the airstrip as though it were Afghanistan. They were met by children, a choir and gifts" (quoted in Anderson 2008: 4). A month after the initial deployment, Australia's prime minister, John Howard, arrived in Honiara. As he stepped onto the tarmac of Henderson International Airport to meet waiting Solomon Islander dignitaries, men dressed as traditional warriors rushed forward, thrusting spears in Howard's direction until local chiefs intervened, presented him with shell money, and welcomed him to the country. Howard traveled along the main road into Honiara, passing throngs of schoolchildren waving Australian flags. One memorable placard read "Thank you, Uncle Howard."[5]

**Figure 8.1.** "Freestyle" dancing in Adaliwa, a peri-urban neighborhood of Honiara. 17 November 2006.

RAMSI was the most obvious example of a broader reorientation of Australian foreign policy toward increasingly direct "cooperative" intervention.[6] During the period leading up to and following the 2000 Townsville Peace Agreement, international actors were involved in peace negotiations and monitoring. Despite direct requests from previous Solomon Islands prime ministers for military intervention, however, the government of Australia, Solomon Islands' largest donor and the largest regional military power, refused.[7] As late as January 2003, Australia's foreign minister, Alexander Downer, described intervention as "folly in the extreme" because "foreigners do not have answers for the deep seated problems affecting the Solomon Islands" (quoted in Kabutaulaka 2005: 287). Just a few months later, Howard and Downer portrayed intervention as unavoidable. Howard described the new interventionism as "a very important exercise in Australia being a good neighbour," and emphasized Australia's self-interest in making sure "things in our part of the world, on our patch, aren't allowed to deteriorate."[8] The Australian Strategic Policy Institute report justifying intervention warned that the "failed state" of Solomon Islands could become "a Petri dish for transnational threats," including drug smuggling, gun running, fraud and "perhaps" terrorism (Wainwright 2003: 13). The internal strife of the Solomons was thus framed as part of the global war on terror; Australian intervention was part of a broader "securitization" of development aid in the early 2000s (Dinnen 2004; Nguyen 2005; Greener-Barcham and Barcham 2006; Fry and Kabutaulaka 2008; Hameiri 2008).[9] More than a military or peacekeeping operation, RAMSI took a "whole of government" approach, with expatriate advisors working alongside Solomon Islands civil servants in key ministries like finance and justice. Australia's prime minister and foreign minister are reported to have said that they would have to "re-engineer" and "completely redesign the place" (Braithwaite et al. 2010: 51). Yet as RAMSI progressed, it became clear that the primary goal was stabilizing the government, and that such grand aspirations were overambitious.

Many ordinary Solomon Islanders also hoped that RAMSI would facilitate a radical remaking of their broken political system. In this deeply Christian nation, many citizens understand possibilities for social and political change through the model of a Christian movement from law to spirit, from sin to forgiveness, from fear to grace; they also understand these possibilities through their own village histories, which center on the epoch-changing arrival of the church. As we saw in Chapter 4, however messy and undramatic Christian conversion really was, the arrival of the church is now remembered as a dramatic shift from a time of violence to a time of peace. Narratives of the arrival of Christianity from abroad are as foundational to the national psyche in Solomon Islands as, say, the Anzac legend is in Australia or an American sense that their nation has a quasi-divine relationship to liberty. Although I have never heard any Solomon Islanders directly compare RAMSI to Christian missionaries, I suspect that RAMSI's arrival is implicitly understood through this mytho-historical frame—it was a powerful force that arrived on local shores and opened the space for local people to transform their own sociopolitical worlds. Such a perspective helps us understand both the remarkable openness to transformation demonstrated by civilians and former militants alike, and the deep frustration felt by many when the transformations they prayed for did not come to pass.

When RAMSI arrived, apparently hardened warlords quickly surrendered themselves and most of their weapons. Among them was Harold Keke, who had thwarted the implementation of the Townsville Peace Agreement and terrorized his own people on the Weather Coast of Guadalcanal. In an Australian television program recorded a few days before RAMSI arrived, Keke asked Prime Minister Howard to investigate who was right and who was wrong in the struggle on Guadalcanal.[10] In a sermon filmed during the visit, Keke preached about the ancient Israelites claiming the Holy Land in the name of the almighty Father. Keke seems to have believed that both God and the Australian prime minister would find that he was in the right.

Many perpetrators of violence sought to personally reconcile themselves with their former enemies and victims. Some of the most astonishing instances of reconciliation come from Honiara's overcrowded Rove prison. In the first three years of RAMSI's operations, more than 6,000 people (1 percent of the entire population) were arrested (Braithwaite et al. 2010: 49–50; Allen 2013a: 19). Crowded prisons filled with frustrated inmates could have very well become a hotbed of violence and radicalism. Instead, Rove prison became the most important site for "meaningful reconciliation" between former combatants, leaving prison staff amazed after observing "ex-combatants living together in a small prison for years and never observing unpleasant interactions, let alone violence" (Braithwaite et al. 2010: 83–86). One RAMSI prisons advisor observed, "In Port Philip prison [Victoria, Australia], inmates blame me for putting them away. Here in Solomon Islands they thank me for looking after them" (quoted in Fraenkel, Madraiwiwi, and Okole 2014: 23).

Unguarded in prison, former enemies seem to have been less likely to get into fights than to form prayer groups. Braithwaite et al. report:

> In one famous occasion, a Guadalcanal Liberation Front (GLF) prisoner was mistakenly put on the MEF side of Rove prison. When the police rushed to the prison to correct the mistake, he was found with his arm around Jimmy Rasta [i.e. Jimmy "Rasta" Lusibaea, former supreme commander of the Malaita Eagle Force], with whom he had reconciled. (Braithwaite et al. 2010: 83)

Although initially criticized for arresting rank-and-file militants but not the "big fish" responsible for fomenting the Ethnic Tension, RAMSI oversaw the arrest of prominent politicians. Among them was former prime minister and premier of Guadalcanal Province Ezekiel Alebua, who told interviewers that "he liked being in prison very much," comparing it to a monastery where he could spend time in contemplation "developing his spiritual side" (ibid.: 85). With the exception of Harold Keke and his former associate Ronnie Cawa, all of the militants in prison were reconciled with one another by 2009, when a joint work team of former members of the IFM and MEF was observed working harmoniously to rebuild the prison chapel (ibid.: 82).

Within and beyond prison, these processes of reconciliation were often undertaken under the auspices of Christian churches and organizations, and were saturated by the narratives, rituals, and doctrines of Christianity. Rove was the site of an evangelical prison fellowship program linked to the US-based group Prison Fellowship International and undertaken by a local evangelical church; it was funded largely by former militants themselves, including Jimmy Rasta Lusibaea, who was "born again" in prison and went on to win a seat in the 2010 parliamentary elections.[11]

Some militants explained their willingness to be arrested in terms of Christian notions of sin and redemption. One Guale militant explained to Joy Kere that he initially avoided arrest but, after he began attending church again, realized that he had to surrender to pay for his sins; a Malaitan militant confessed that he was happy to have gone through a trial and a prison sentence because it "helped straighten me out." Kere said that many men in prison were initially bitter and angry that they were imprisoned while many of the political elites responsible for the conflict were free. "Then the churches went in, complementing the work of the prison and helping the prisoners forgive those who had used them" (McDougall and Kere 2011: 155). Outside of prison, reconciliation ceremonies involved both the transaction of customary forms of compensation and prayer for forgiveness. Recounting ceremonies in rural Guadalcanal and Malaita that were supported by the Ministry of Peace and Reconciliation, Kere observed that "the speeches by women and men, youth, church leaders, and chiefs emphasize over and over that if it wasn't for our Christian principles—our belief in God, love, forgiveness, and all of these things—it would be very difficult for them to forgive one another" (ibid.: 149).

Of course, the role of Christianity in the conflict and post-conflict reconciliation is more complex than such accounts might suggest. While there is almost unanimous agreement that religious actors intervened to minimize violence and assist civilians during the Ethnic Tension, religious ideologies do seem to have played some part in lending a cosmic dimension to what might have been a socio-political conflict (Juergensmeyer 2004).[12] Within the Guale militancy, some leaders embraced the ideals of the Gaena'alu Movement (formerly known as the Moro Movement), while others including Keke rejected association with *kastom* in favor of evangelical Christianity (Allen 2013a: 125). A vast majority of Solomon Islanders are Christian, but not all of them. A Solomon Islander of the Bahai'a Faith I spoke to in 2006 described the conflict itself as a failure of the Christian leadership and its moral teaching. Newly converted Sunni Muslims from northern Malaita in Honiara condemned Christianity in more direct terms, bitterly recalling the hypocrisy of their supposedly Christian communities in Malaita who ostracized them during the Tension (McDougall 2009a, 2013). Yet even those who reject Christianity tend to view the problems of the nation "through a moral lens" (Stritecky 2001b) and believe that the transformation of the nation will occur through the spiritual transformation of its citizens.

As the decade wore on, many Solomon Islanders became increasingly frustrated at the apparent failure of both RAMSI and Solomon Islander political leaders to bring about meaningful change. Government revenue during the RAMSI decade improved dramatically from the nadir of the period of the Tension. Aid revenue increased markedly and, by most accounts, RAMSI significantly improved the capacity of the Solomon Islands government to collect revenue and manage its economy. RAMSI played a role in negotiating the reopening the two major pre-conflict enterprises that were a spark for violent conflict in 1998: Solomon Islands Plantations Limited and Gold Ridge Mine.[13] Yet much of the post-2003 growth came from logging, which in 2010/11 accounted for 70 percent of export income. Such resource dependence leads to economic volatility and vulnerability, especially given the imminent exhaustion of this non-renewable resource within the next few years (Hameiri 2007, 2012; Allen 2010, 2011: 8; Braithwaite et al. 2010: 118–19).

More generally, RAMSI's very presence helped to exacerbate the sense of relative depravation that Allen and others identified as a core driver of conflict. As is often the case with international interventions, the presence of thousands of well-paid expatriates threw local poverty into sharp relief. Australians who occupied in-line positions in the administration were accused of having an attitude of superiority and a lack of respect for local knowledge (McDougall 2006; Roughan 2006; Roughan, Greener-Barcham, Barcham 2006; Anderson 2008; Brown 2010, 2013; Marai et al. 2010). An urban-based middle class, many of whom have a Chinese background, arguably benefited from the expansion of public services and the retail sector in Honiara (Fraenkel, Madraiwiwi, and Okole 2014: 590), and property owners, including many political elites who had privatized government-owned real estate over the previous decades (Williams 2011), were able to make a small fortune in a skyrocketing real-estate market. For the working poor in Honiara, however, the rising cost of living in Honiara made life more difficult.[14]

Possibilities for completely re-engineering the Solomon Islands government were limited by the fact that the terms of the enabling agreement meant that RAMSI was a guest of the government and was bound in partnership with it. During the first three years, the partnership was one-sided because Prime Minister Kemakeza was dependent upon RAMSI for his survival. Yet this partnership with a government deeply implicated in wrongdoings during the Tension period arguably undermined RAMSI's legitimacy in the eyes of ordinary people. Issues around sovereignty came to the fore in 2006 when Manasseh Sogavare took power after post-election riots that saw the destruction of much of Honiara's Chinatown (Morgan and McLeod 2006; Alasia 2007; Dinnen 2007, 2008a, 2008b; Allen 2008b; Dinnen and Firth 2008; Kabutaulaka 2008; Moore 2008; O'Callaghan 2008). Tension between the Sogavare government and Canberra centered on a Commission of Inquiry set up to look into causes of the riots, as well as Sogavare's appointment of Australian lawyer Julian Moti as the country's attorney general.[15]

The tension between Australian-dominated RAMSI and the Solomon Islands government eased after 2007, when Sogavare lost a no-confidence vote and an election put a Labour government in power in Canberra, but the conflict led RAMSI's leaders to scale back rhetoric of "state building" and to emphasize the limitations of RAMSI's mandate. Against accusations that it was deaf to local feedback, RAMSI instituted consultative forums and an annual performance review that included independently conducted "People's Surveys" to document ordinary citizens' perceptions of RAMSI, the Solomon Islands government, and improvements to their lives. These consistently revealed a double-edged message about the effectiveness of the mission: on the one hand, respondents overwhelmingly approved of RAMSI's ongoing presence, but on the other hand, the survey revealed an ongoing lack of confidence in the police, lack of optimism about economic opportunities, and significant anxieties about the possibility of renewed unrest (ANU Enterprise 2010, 2011; Dinnen 2012: 68; ANUedge 2013).

In 2003, donors and Solomon Islanders alike hoped RAMSI would dramatically change a flawed political system. In 2013, as the functions of RAMSI were moved into regular channels of development aid in a period of "transition," few of these hopes had been fulfilled. Many Australians and Solomon Islanders wondered whether the modest results justified the enormous expense of this multi-billion dollar decade-long operation (Hayward-Jones 2014; Wood 2014). All agree that RAMSI helped to break a cycle of violence. In remarks made in late July 2012, Special Coordinator Nicholas Coppel called the absence of weapons in the Solomons "one of the most remarkable successes" of the intervention; although post-conflict societies are typically "awash" in weapons, the Solomons has had only nine reports over as many years of any firearm being discharged. "There would probably be no other post-conflict society," Coppel reflected with genuine surprise, "that has as few weapons."[16] There is also broad agreement that RAMSI helped to improve the justice system, increase revenue collection, strengthen systems of financial management, and improve parliamentary support systems. Policing has improved, but the presence of well-equipped regional forces in some ways has highlighted the shortcomings of the local police force (Dinnen and Allen 2012). Scholars differ in the extent to which they believe RAMSI should have—or could have—undertaken more fundamental changes. Fraenkel, Madraiwiwi, and Okole (2014) describe causes of the conflict as too amorphous to be addressed directly, and they argue that without broad support among the political elite, RAMSI had little possibility of implementing significant reform. In contrast, Braithwaite et al. (2010) fault RAMSI for ignoring the specific drivers of the conflict, for failing to build on the work of the National Peace Council and local churches in fostering peace and reconciliation, for discouraging debates about constitutional change, and for failing to prosecute international commercial interests that shirked taxes, destroyed the regulations that might have ensured the sustainability of logging and fishing, and funded political corruption.

Though often described in the bloodless language of "capacity building" or "institutional strengthening," state building is rarely peaceful or orderly. Even Francis Fukuyama, a proponent of the sort of neoliberal state building that RAMSI represented, admitted that state building is inherently violent:

> It is sobering to realize that ... there are virtually no instances in which customary land was converted into modern property voluntarily, that is, without some degree of coercion or fraud. People in the developed West conveniently forget the degree to which their own institutions were shaped and made possible by violence and conflict in earlier historical periods. (Fukuyama 2008: 22; cf. Brigg 2009)

The failure of the state in Solomon Islands might be understood as a failure of what Karl Polanyi described some seventy years ago as a "double movement" of the state and market (Polanyi 1944). The state was essential in creating markets in land, labor, and money—which Polanyi dubbed "fictional commodities" because they were not produced for the market (ibid.: 71–81). The market in these fictional commodities was "the outcome of a conscious and often violent intervention on the part of the government which imposed the market organization on society for noneconomic ends" (ibid.: 58). In nineteenth-century England, the democratizing state stepped in to protect society from the devastating consequences of markets by introducing labor laws, tariffs, banking control, and other protective mechanisms for its own citizens. Yet these protective measures at home were accompanied by a further expansion of empire, and exploitative practices were moved "offshore." In the Solomon Islands and other colonies, the colonial state sought, with various degrees of success, to impose market organization on society, but did little to protect the population from the worst effects of the market. This failure to protect citizens is understandable in the context of colonialism, where almost by definition the government is answerable to foreign powers rather than the people subject to its rule. Unfortunately, post-independent governments in Solomon Islands and many other postcolonial nations continue to be more powerfully beholden to outside interests, and have also done little to protect their populations from the ravages of markets.

Solomon Islanders want—and deserve—a better government. Yet the expansion of the power of a state that is beholden to outside powers and not responsive to the citizenry may serve to undermine the local socio-political formations that sustain ordinary people without replacing them with reliable forms of social welfare that many of us living in rich postindustrial nation states like Australia have the privilege to take for granted. Further commoditization of land and labor—always a core aim of state building in Solomon Islands—may leave people far poorer than they are today.

## Cosmopolitan Spaces in the Margins of the State

This ethnography has analyzed a social world in which radical openness to others is compatible with a deep connection to ancestral ground. Ranonggan social life has been profoundly transformed through engagements with strangers in the precolonial past, the colonial era, and the present. This engagement with strangers from distant shores has been more intense in Ranongga and elsewhere in New Georgia than in other regions in the Solomons. Precolonial New Georgia was a maritime world with traditions of long-distance seafaring lacking in other areas of the country. In the colonial and postcolonial era, extensive commercial development has made the western Solomons a destination for migrants rather than a source of migrant labor. Despite this variation, however, I have argued that understandings about the proper relationship between people of the place and migrants are broadly shared by most Solomon Islanders and other people of island Melanesia. This shared understanding was evident even in the midst of a civil war, and arguably helped to mitigate its violence.

Far from being insular, atomistic, or tribal, these social worlds and the people who inhabit them are cosmopolitan: open to the world beyond local shores, constantly engaging with people from other places and speaking other languages. Moreover, because Solomon Islanders have embraced Christian notions of universalism, contemporary Ranonggan ethics of hospitality share roots with the Western philosophical cosmopolitanism that has been so influential in the development of the institutions of international law. Yet, the differences between the cosmopolitan hospitality evident in many Solomon Islands societies and Western philosophical cosmopolitanism are also striking. Most Western traditions of cosmopolitanism presume the existence of a nation-state to enforce the cosmopolitan rights of citizens; the challenge for cosmopolitan thinkers is formulating overarching institutions that can enforce these rights beyond the limited boundaries of the nation-state. The cosmopolitan modes of life I discuss here, in contrast, exist largely outside the institutions of the formal state.

In the 2000s, a historical era in which counter-cosmopolitan sentiments seemed to be on the rise, the ancient philosophical tradition of cosmopolitanism was revived within the social sciences, including anthropology.[17] Pnina Werbner (2008b: 4–5) suggests that cosmopolitanism emerged as the counterpart of globalization theory: theories of globalization focus attention on the movement of people and capital, whereas theories of cosmopolitanism focus attention on the positive ethic of orientation to otherness that may emerge through such translocal movement. The combination of cosmopolitanism and anthropology is somewhat counter-intuitive since cosmopolitanism has tended to focus on similarity and the possibility for universal community, whereas anthropology has focused on diversity and the autonomy of small-scale communities. In engaging with cosmopolitanism, anthropologists have turned attention from elites to the "cosmopolitan everyday" (Hannerz 2010: 449), jettisoning the pejorative "rootless" by exploring vernacular, rooted, discrepant, patriotic, ethnic, demotic, and many other pluralized and localized cosmopolitanisms (summarized in Werbner 2008b). Although some forms anthropological cosmopolitanism appear to advocate a methodological individualism that contradicts many core principles of the discipline,[18] much recent anthropological work on cosmopolitanism reiterates arguments anthropologists have been making for a long time: no local worlds are truly isolated, no cultures are really bounded.

At the same time, much of what is sometimes called the "new cosmopolitanism" in philosophy and the social sciences is grounded in progressive narratives that anthropologists have long sought to combat—that is, the notion that civilization is evolving from simple to complex, closed to open, relatively insular to increasingly cosmopolitan. Although it is not always explicitly articulated, the vanguard of complex open societies in this framework is the advanced liberal democracies of the West. For many liberal cosmopolitan thinkers, the modern state form and global capitalism are essential in the expansion of cosmopolitan consciousness. Cosmopolitanism may be useful in understanding how people come "to think and feel beyond the nation" (Cheah and Robbins 1998) and account for transnational forms of engagement increasingly important in the everyday lives of many of the world's people. Yet this focus on getting "beyond" the nation has arguably directed attention away from the ways that people engage with strangers on a level "below" or outside of the structures of the modern state. As Bruce Kapferer (2007) suggests, the turn to cosmopolitanism within anthropology is a sign of the ongoing "metropolitanisation" of anthropology—a turn away from rural or marginalized places of the sort that anthropologists have long studied.

Most work on cosmopolitanism assumes the existence of a nation-state, and much of it assumes that the expansion of state-like structures beyond the boundaries of nations are necessary to foster cosmopolitan forms of social life. In an idiosyncratic contribution to a volume on cosmopolitanism and anthropology, David Graeber (2008) argues that far from fostering the expansion of democratic ideals, states squelch the possibility of sorts of democratic practices by imposing an overarching power to which all are subject. The truly cosmopolitan spaces of the modern age were not to be found in metropolitan centers of Europe or America, but in the nooks and crannies of the Atlantic world, spaces like frontier communities of settlers and Native Americans, and the intercultural communities of pirate ships. Graeber suggests that states and elites only began to espouse democratic ideals when forced to do so by populist pressure emerging from these cosmopolitan zones on the edges or interstices of state power. Democratic practices, Graeber writes, usually emerge in "zones of improvisation" outside of the control of state, "in which diverse sorts of people with different traditions and experiences are obligated to figure out some way to get on with one another" (ibid.: 291).

The rural worlds of Ranongga are such cosmopolitan spaces on the margins of state power. Against "weak state" theories that suggest that state structures have had limited impact on local worlds, I have argued that the state is an important (and not always benign) force in local social life. Yet it is also true that rural citizens are not entirely reliant on the nation-state in the ways that citizens of metropolitan states are. When the state effectively collapsed in the early 2000s, people continued to earn their livelihoods and maintain social order. The colonial state effectively asserted its monopoly on legitimate violence through its pacification campaign, thus establishing an internal peace that lasted, with the exception of World War II, until 1998 with the Guale uprising. The state has possession of national territory including (to the consternation of customary land owners) rights to the minerals that lie under the ground, but it is a sovereignty that has been difficult to assert in the face of a tenacious commitment to the idea that all land is held by the people whose ancestors lived and worked there, not in the abstract institutions of the state.

The ethics of hospitality I have discussed throughout this book rely on local territorial sovereignty in a way that is counter to the influential vision of cosmopolitan hospitality articulated by Immanuel Kant in a text that has been foundational in the formulation of international law and influential in recent work on the "new cosmopolitanism." Writing in the late eighteenth century, at a time when Western Europe had only recently begun to move from being a cultural and economic backwater to being a global power, Kant decried the "inhospitable conduct of the civilized states of our continent" that display "appallingly great" injustice on those unfortunate foreigners they visit (Kant 1991: 106). In this emerging global world, Kant saw states as necessary in enforcing the "cosmopolitan right" to hospitality as one of the conditions necessary for "perpetual peace":

> *hospitality* means the right of a stranger not to be treated with hostility when he arrives on someone else's territory. He can indeed be turned away, if this can be done without causing his death, but he must not be treated with hostility, so long as he behaves in a peaceable manner in the place he happens to be in. The stranger cannot claim the *right of a guest* to be entertained, for this would require a special friendly agreement whereby he might become a member of the native household for a certain time. He may only claim a *right of resort*, for all men are entitled to present themselves in the society of others by

virtue of their right to communal possession of the earth's surface. (ibid.: 105–6, original emphasis)

Communal possession meant "no-one originally has any greater right than anyone else to occupy any particular portion of the earth" (ibid.: 106). A right to be received without hostility is thus derived from a universalism that sees all humans as bearing the same fundamental rights and sees the earth as neutral ground.

Insofar as they embrace a vision of the world embedded in Christian theology, this sort of universalism is part of the thought-worlds of people of Ranongga and other Christian societies of Oceania. Yet Kant's vision of an un-owned earth is anathema to indigenous people everywhere who claim special rights to territory grounded in ontological connections among land, ancestors, and living people. The relationship of ownership is grounded in people's very being, not in laws externally imposed by national or supra-national states. A stranger may be welcomed as a guest or repelled as an enemy, but there is no culturally elaborated middle ground of hospitality without friendship. To live on land requires a relationship with the people who are bound to the land. This principle emerges not through abstract philosophical precepts, but through everyday experience. How could a stranger be given refuge but not welcome? What would she eat? Where would he live? And how can people with no prior right to "a particular portion of the earth" be good hosts? How could they grow the food necessary to feed their guests?

Arguably, Ranonggan engagements with strangers go much farther than a right to universal hospitality. In their most exalted moments as Christians, they strive to treat everyone with the love that ought to be shown to fellow brothers and sisters in Christ. The universalist ethics of Christianity both resonate with and contradict those ethical orientations of longer standing concerning the proper treatment of those who come from across the sea. As we have seen, strangers were not always treated with loving regard, and the ongoing memory of past violence gives special poignancy to the kindness that is shown to them today. Kinspeople are *owed* regard, but strangers may be *given* regard that they are not owed. Hospitality is not neutral tolerance of the stranger in one's midst on ground that already belongs to everyone. It is the movement across the gap between strangers that begins the process of transforming them into kin.

## Notes

1. A video of the event is online "Kate and William Ride Open-Top 'Canoe' Float in Solomon Islands," *Daily Telegraph*, 16 September 2012 (retrieved 6 February 2015 from: http://www.telegraph.co.uk/news/uknews/prince-william/9546342/Kate-and-William-ride-open-top-canoe-float-in-Solomon-Islands.html).

2. SIPL was a focus of landowner discontent because of migrant labor and lack of Guadalcanal ownership. This resentment was exacerbated in 1997 when Ulufa'alu reduced the government's share in the enterprise from 30 percent to 10 percent as part of a structural adjustment privatization scheme, but refused requests that some shares be transferred to Guadalcanal Province or to a landowners association (Moore 2004: 74; Fraenkel, Allen, and Brock 2010).
3. Like Ranongga's eastern coast, Guadalcanal's northern coast was depopulated in the immediate precolonial era when many residents fled to the more easily defensible southern coast. Postcolonial peace allowed people to relocate to the north, but many contemporary residents of the Weather Coast claim that the land of the northern coast really belongs to their clans.
4. The 1988 petition was directed to Prime Minister Ezekiel Alebua who was from Guadalcanal's Weather Coast. As prime minister, Alebua did not act on this petition, but ten years later, as premier of Guadalcanal Province, Alebua presented essentially the same demands to Prime Minister Ulufa'alu (Frankel 2004: 48–51; Moore 2004: 105). The precedent for compensation payments in the wake of ethnic slurs was set by the payment by the central government to Western Province after the publication of an incendiary pro-Malaitan poem on the eve of national independence. Throughout the 1980s and 1990s, the national government had paid compensation to Malaita and other provinces following crimes against individuals or ethnic slurs (see Akin 1999b; Moore 2004: 107–19). Shortly before Alebua presented the petition in 1998, two Malaitan girls at a Guadalcanal secondary school claimed to have been raped. Without a trial or arrest, the national government met demands for compensation for the crime, deducting the money from the grant to Guadalcanal province. This was taken as a sign that only Malaitans were respected by the government (Moore 2004: 105).
5. "Island Children Greet 'Uncle Howard,'" *Melbourne Age*, 25 August 2003 (retrieved 1 September 2003 from: http://www.theage.com.au/articles/2003/08/25/1061663718397.html); "Solomons Welcome Howard Visit," *BBC*, 25 August 2003 (retrieved 18 June 2013 from: http://news.bbc.co.uk/2/hi/asia-pacific/3178661.stm).
6. The reorientation was also evident in Australia's muscular intervention in the affairs of other Pacific Islands states. Australia sought to implement a new "enhanced partnership program" in Papua New Guinea involving in-line policing (an effort stymied by local opposition to immunity provisions for Australian personnel), rebuilt Nauru as a sovereign state following fiscal collapse, redeployed troops in East Timor in 2006, and sought the leadership of the regional Pacific Islands Forum (Fry and Kabutaulaka 2008). This new interventionism was not necessarily as radical a departure from previous policy as might initially appear. The state-building project of the 2000s built on the neoliberal reforms of the 1980s and 1990s, which were implemented in Australia by the Labour governments of Hawke and Keating. Fry argues that, in the 1990s, the Pacific Islands featured prominently in a "forthright salvationist message that warns of an approaching 'doomsday' or 'nightmare' unless Pacific Islanders remake themselves—just as Australians have had to do" (Fry 1997: 305). This earlier attempt at neoliberal reform was carried out through diplomacy as well as foreign development aid, the latter increasingly conditional upon the recipient government implementing policies seen as favorable to economic growth and good governance (Fry and Kabutaulaka 2008: 14, 16).

7. Before the de facto coup in 2000 that removed him from power, former Prime Minister Bartholomew Ulufa'alu appealed to his Australian counterpart for assistance in containing a conflict that he felt was aimed at destabilizing his reform-oriented government. His successor, Manasseh Sogavare, also appealed to the Australians for assistance in 2001. Moore (2004: 205–6) suggests that Kemakeza's March 2003 request to the Indonesian government for military assistance spurred Australia into action.
8. "Transcript of the Prime Minister the Hon. John Howard MP." Press conference, Canberra, 22 June 2003 (retrieved 4 September 2006 from: http://www.pm.gov.au/news/interviews/Interview382.html).
9. Greg Fry concluded: "Humanitarian concern has not been given as the ultimate rationale for Australia's new hands-on approach in the Pacific. In all ministerial statements the dominant rationale is put in terms of Australia's national interest" (Fry 2008: 75). Fry and others (Moore 2004: 209; Dobell 2008) argue that Prime Minister John Howard used the intervention as an excuse for not committing more Australian troops to a war in Iraq that was unpopular with the Australian electorate.
10. "Harold Keke—Rebel or Raskol," *SBS Dateline*, 30 July 2003 (Program transcript retrieved 12 August 2015 from: http://www.sbs.com.au/news/article/2003/07/30/harold-keke-rebel-or-raskol).
11. When Lusibaea was given yet another jail sentence in 2010 and forced to resign, his wife Vika Lusibaea won a by-election to become the second woman in Solomons history to enter parliament.
12. See also Timmer (2008, 2012) and Hermkens (2013) for Melanesian cases.
13. SIPL was a major focus of the conflict, and efforts to re-establish the enterprise have sought to give Guadalcanal landowners a greater sense of control and ownership in the project (Fraenkel, Allen, Brock 2010; Allen 2012). Gold Ridge Mine remained controversial and subject to some forms of resistance by those who felt excluded from its benefits, but by 2014 it was producing some 20 percent of Solomon Islands' GDP. In the wake of devastating floods in Honiara and Guadalcanal in April 2014, the Australian-based company running the mine pulled out its staff and halted operations, leaving questions about ongoing responsibility for the tailings dam. Prime Minister Darcy Lilo accused the company of abandoning the mine in the context of a plummeting share price, though the company cited concerns over staff safety in light of the flooding and security incidents over previous months ("St Barbara Insists It Hasn't 'Abandoned' Gold Ridge Mine in Solomon Islands," *ABC Radio Australia*, 12 April 2014; retrieved 29 November 2014 from: http://www.abc.net.au/news/2014-04-11/an-st-barbara-insists-it-hasnt-pulled-out-of-gold-ridge-mine/5385660; "Police Deployed to Gold Ridge Mine Site," *Solomon Star News*, 15 August 2014; retrieved 29 November 2014 from: http://www.solomonstarnews.com/news/national/3485-police-deployed-to-gold-ridge-mine-site). Recent talks focus on turning over the mine to the Solomon Islands government ("Talks over Gold Ridge Held," *Solomon Star News*, 14 November 2014; retrieved 29 November 2014 from: http://www.solomonstarnews.com/news/business/4951-talks-over-gold-ridge-held).
14. I saw the effects of this housing bubble directly in the lives of Ranonggan friends in Honiara. One friend employed in a local non-governmental organization was able to rent a small house with a reliable water supply within the town boundary in the years prior to 2003. By the time I stayed with him and his family in late 2006, they had moved beyond the town boundary, renting a house with no water or indoor toilet (see

Amnesty International 2011). He rented this second house from Malaitans who had purchased the area from Guadalcanal landowners a generation earlier, precisely the sort of transaction whose legitimacy was challenged by Guadalcanal militants who effectively evacuated this neighborhood in 1999. To help make ends meet, his wife also worked at one of the many cafés that have sprung up since 2003 to cater for foreigners, but after she deducted the cost of transport, she earned just a few SI dollars a day, about the price of one cup of coffee in the café where she was employed.

15. Sogavare convened a Commission of Inquiry into the causes of the riots, and accused the Australian-appointed police commissioner of negligence in preventing them. RAMSI had purged the Royal Solomon Islands Police of many senior officers involved in the Tension; by 2006, the force was dominated by the Participating Police Force that lacked (or disregarded the importance of) local knowledge. Respected journalist Mary-Louise O'Callaghan argued that in failing to predict the crowd's reaction, the RAMSI-controlled police demonstrated either a "failure of intelligence" or "an alarming lack of institutional memory" (O'Callaghan 2008: 192; see also Braithwaite et al. 2010: 63). For their part, Australian leaders saw the Commission of Inquiry as an attempt by Sogavare to stall a police investigation into the role played by two of his cabinet ministers in fomenting the violence. The diplomatic row came to a head over Sogavare's controversial appointment of Fiji-born Australian lawyer Julian Moti as the country's attorney general; Moti was allegedly wanted in Australia for child sex offenses committed in Vanuatu. In actions that the High Court of Australia later ruled to be unjustifiable political interference in the pursuit of justice, the Australian Federal Police sought to extradite Moti from Solomon Islands (Fraenkel, Madraiwiwi, Okole 2014: 17–19).

16. "Transition of the Regional Assistance Mission of Solomon Islands," video podcast, ANU Channel, 24 July 2012 (retrieved 11 August 2015 from: https://youtu.be/SZIEOdAu-7w).

17. In the mid 2000s, several special issues of journals of social theory were dedicated to the theme of cosmopolitanism (for example, Beck and Sznaider 2006; Fine and Boon 2007). Cosmopolitanism also emerged as an orienting concept in anthropology. "Cosmopolitanism and anthropology" was the theme of the annual meetings of the UK Association of Social Anthropologists in April 2006, and has given rise to several edited volumes (Campbell 2008; Nowika and Rovisco 2009; Wardel 2010; Werbner 2008a; Josephides and Hall 2014). "Indigeneities and Cosmopolitanisms" was the theme of the May 2007 meetings of the Canadian Association of Social and Cultural Anthropology and the American Ethnological Society; "Cosmopolitan Anthropologies" was the theme of the November 2014 conference of the Association of Social Anthropologists of Aotearoa/New Zealand and the Australian Anthropological Society.

18. Nigel Rapport, for example, argues that "the constituent units of humanity are individual actors—energetic, self-conscious, intentioning—not collectivities, their discourses and symbolic classifications"; he also argues that attention to cultural ideologies "should not obscure individuality as a human universal" (Rapport 2006: 24). Granting the obvious fact individual persons are biologically bounded organisms, such an approach takes a particular late-modern ideology of personhood as a human universal. A sense of personhood embedded in social relationships is not mere "cultural ideology" in the way that Rapport might suggest. As we have seen with reference to

Ranongga, this embeddedness is manifest in the nitty-gritty material details of life. Land is not acquired by purchase but by virtue of inherited or acquired social relations. Life depends upon the nurturing care of others who feed children and clean the feces of elderly people who can no longer get up from their mats. A wealth of literature on emerging individualism in Melanesia explores the contradictions and tensions inherent in situations where people strive to disentangle themselves from social relations in order to experience themselves as individuals in the way that Christian theology and Western modern capitalism suggests they ought to be. I have discussed this in relationship to Joel Robbins's work on Christian individualism (McDougall 2009b; cf. Robbins 2004). See also Sykes (2007a, 2007b) and Martin (2013) for ethnographically grounded discussions of individualism in Melanesia. Accepting the notion that individual actors are the constituent units of humanity as empirical statements or a methodological starting point turns our attention away from those on-the-ground struggles that occur when ordinary people seek to adopt, reject, or otherwise engage with individualism as the dominant ideology of our age. It also directs our attention away from the ways in which the institutions of modern states and capitalism allow people to experience themselves as autonomous individuals.

# Glossary

This glossary lists Kubokota terms that appear frequently in this text. Other terms in Kubokota, Luqa, and Pijin are glossed in the text.

| | |
|---|---|
| *aoro* | grove of nut-bearing trees called *neni* (*Canarium salomonense*) or *ngari* (*Canarium indicum*) |
| *bakia* | large rings made of fossilized giant clam shell, the most important traditional valuable of the New Georgia Group |
| *bangara* | chief, leader; "Lord" in Christian discourse |
| *butubutu* | named clans linked to territory of their origin; also, any sort of grouping based on similarity |
| *buzabuza* | secondary forest that was cleared for gardening but has been allowed to regrow |
| *goto tinoni/nake goto tinoni* | "other people" (non-relatives, strangers, foreigners)/ "not other people" (relatives, friends, neighbors) |
| *ia* | to share, or a portion (of food, for example); in relation to land, a place or area cleared for settlement |
| *iama* | ancestral priest who oversaw mortuary rites and the propitiation of ancestors |
| *iliganigani* | ogre or giant, an important figure in folk tales |
| *ivata* | feast laid out on banana leaves |
| *izizongo* | property, especially that created by clearing land, planting trees, and cultivating gardens |
| *kalao bangara* | chiefly woman or female chief |
| *kale* | side, half; term frequently used in ritual and in reference to kin relations |
| *kastom* (SI Pijin) | custom or tradition; ways of doing things that adhere to indigenous rather than exogenous values |
| *lotu* | Christian faith, Christian services, Christian worship |
| *maka tinoni* | "one person" or "one people"; kinspeople or relatives |
| *mola* | dugout canoe |

| | |
|---|---|
| *pajuku* | transaction transferring rights to property from host to guest or from father to children |
| *pezo* | territory, land, or earth; named territories identified with named *butubutu* |
| *pinauzu* | captives who were taken in long-distance warfare |
| *poata* | shell armbands used as currency in old New Georgia, now a general term for money |
| *qeto* | large plank-built canoes formerly used in deep sea fishing and long-distance trading and raiding expeditions |
| *tabuna* | ancestral shrine |
| *tamaluluna* | cross-sex siblings |
| *tamatazi* | siblings |
| *tamaza; Tamaza* | pre-Christian spirits; the Christian God |
| *tinoni or tio* | person or people |
| *tinoni kamudi* | "people who have come"; migrants or guests |
| *tinoni karovona* | "people who have crossed over"; migrants from other islands |
| *tinoni vaka* | "ship people"; Europeans |
| *tite* | grandparent |
| *tomete* | the dead, especially ancestral dead |
| *tuturu* | mad, stupid, or morally senseless; also, forest spirits with these characteristics |
| *vaia* | to buy, to strike or hit, to kill |
| *variroqu* (Luqa: *vairoqu*) | love, compassion, mercy, or mutual regard |
| *vavuluna* | sacrificial victim |
| *vinapodo* | "born of"; relationship of children to their father's *butubutu* |
| *zona* | path, road, route |

# References

## Archival Sources

Solomon Islands National Archives, Honiara, Western Pacific Archive, Western Pacific High Commission, British Solomon Islands Protectorate (BSIP).
BSIP 7/I/DCW/124–127. Vella Lavella Native Council. Office of the District Commissioner, Western District. General Correspondence 1943–1970.
BSIP 7/I/DCW/130. Emu Harbor Scheme. Office of the District Commissioner, Western District. General Correspondence 1943–1970.
BSIP 7/III/34/5. General Administration, Vella Lavella. Office of the District Commissioner, Western District. General Correspondence 1943–1970.
BSIP 13/I. Papers related to land matters, 1959–1968.
BSIP 18/I/41. Reports, notes, proceedings, and other papers relating to land claims. Land Commissioner's Office, Lands Commission 1920–1924.
BSIP 21/II. Gizo District: Dispatches from the Resident Commissioner and general correspondence, 1908–1928.

## Court Cases

*Daveta v. Kotomae.* 2010. High Court of Solomon Islands 13. HCSI-CC 288 of 2009, 15 April 2010. Retrieved 10 July 2010 from: http://www.paclii.org/sb/cases/SBHC/2010/13.html.
*Mamipitu v. Ragoso.* 1980. Gizo/Kolombangara Local Court, 1/80. Copy in author's possession.
*Mamipitu v. Ragoso (Appeal).* 1981. Gizo/Kolombangara Local Court. Copy in author's possession.
*Zobule v. Attorney General.* 2008. High Court of Solomon Islands 87. HSCI-CC 297 of 2008, 22 October 2008. Retrieved 10 July 2010 from: http://www.paclii.org/sb/cases/SBHC/2008/87.html.
*Zobule v. Attorney General.* 2010. High Court of Solomon Islands 39. HCSI-CC 297 of 2008, 5 August 2010. Retrieved 22 October 2010 from: http://www.paclii.org/sb/cases/SBHC/2010/39.html.
*Zobule v. Attorney General.* 2011. High Court of Solomon Islands102. HCSI-CC 297 of 2008, 30 September 2011. Retrieved 11 August 2010 from: http://www.paclii.org/sb/cases/SBHC/2011/102.html.

## Other Sources

Acciaioli, Greg. 2009. "Distinguishing Hierarchy and Precedence: Comparing Status Distinctions in South Asia and the Austronesia World, with Special Reference to

South Sulawesi." In *Precedence: Social Differentiation in the Austronesian World*, ed. Michael P. Vischer. Canberra: ANU E-Press, pp.51–90.

Agrawal, Arun. 2005. *Environmentality: Technologies of Government and the Making of Subjects*. Durham, NC: Duke University Press.

Agrawal, Arun, and Clark C. Gibson. 1999. "Enchancement and Disenchantment: The Role of Community in Natural Resource Conservation." *World Development* 27 (4): 629–49.

Akin, David W. 1996. "Local and Foreign Spirits in Kwaio, Solomon Islands." In *Spirits in Culture, History, and Mind*, ed. Jeanette Mageo and Alan Howard. New York: Routledge, pp.147–72.

———. 1999a. "Cash and Shell Money in Kwaio, Solomon Islands." In *Money and Modernity: State and Local Currencies in Melanesia*, ed. David Akin and Joel Robbins. Pittsburgh: University of Pittsburgh Press, pp.103–30.

———. 1999b. "Compensation and the Melanesian State: Why the Kwaio Keep Claiming." *Contemporary Pacific* 11 (1): 35–67.

———. 2003. "Concealment, Confession, and Innovation in Kwaio Women's Taboos." *American Ethnologist* 30 (3): 381–400.

———. 2004. "Ancestral Vigilance and the Corrective Conscience: Kastom as Culture in a Melanesian Society." *Anthropological Theory* 4 (3): 299–324.

———. 2013. *Colonialism, Maasina Rule, and the Origins of Malaitan Kastom*. Honolulu: University of Hawaii Press.

Alasia, Sam. 2007. "Rainbows across the Mountains: The First Post-RAMSI General Elections in Solomon Islands, April 2006, and the Policies of the Second Sogavare Government." *Journal of Pacific History* 42 (2): 165–86.

Allan, Collin H. 1957. *Customary Land Tenure in the British Solomon Islands Protectorate. Report of the BSIP Special Land Commission*. Honiara: Western Pacific High Commission.

———. 1989. "The Post-War Scene in the Western Solomons and Marching Rule: A Memoir." *Journal of Pacific History* 24 (1): 89–99.

Allen, Matthew G. 2008a. "Land Reform in Melanesia." State Society and Governance in Melanesia Briefing Note. Retrieved 18 Jan 2011 from: http://ips.cap.anu.edu.au/sites/default/files/BriefingNote_LandReformInMelanesia.pdf.

———. 2008b. "Politics of Disorder: The Social Unrest in Honiara." In *Politics and State Building in Solomon Islands*, ed. Sinclair Dinnen and Stewart Firth. Canberra: ANU E-Press and Asia Pacific Press, pp.39–63.

———. 2009. "Resisting RAMSI: Intervention, Identity and Symbolism in Solomon Islands." *Oceania* 79 (1): 1–17.

———. 2010. "The Political Economy of Logging in Solomon Islands." In *The Political Economy of Economic Reform in the Pacific*, ed. Ronald C. Duncan. Manila: Asian Development Bank, pp.277–301.

———. 2011. "Long-Term Engagement: The Future of the Regional Assistance Mission to Solomon Islands." Australian Strategic Policy Institute Strategic Insights 51. Retrieved 10 Oct 2011 from: http://www.aspi.org.au/publications/publication_details.aspx?ContentID=284.

———. 2012. "Informal Formalisation in a Hybrid Property Space: The Case of Smallholder Oil Palm Production in Solomon Islands." *Asia Pacific Viewpoint* 53 (3): 300–13.

———. 2013a. *Greed and Grievance: Ex-Militants' Perspectives on the Conflict in Solomon Islands, 1998-2003*. Honolulu: University of Hawaii Press.

———. 2013b. "Melanesia's Violent Environments: Towards a Political Ecology of Conflict in the Western Pacific." *Geoforum* 44: 152–61.
Allen, Matthew and Sinclair Dinnen, Daniel Evans, and Rebecca Monson. 2013. "Justice Delivered Locally: Systems, Challenges, and Innovations in Solomon Islands." Washington, DC: The World Bank.
Amnesty International. 2011. "'Where Is the Dignity in That?' Women in Solomon Islands Slums Denied Sanitation and Safety." London: Amnesty International. Retrieved 3 March 2012 from: http://amnesty.org/en/library/info/ASA43/001/2011/en.
Anderson, Benedict. 1991. *Imagined Communities: Reflections on the Origin and Spread of Nationalism*, 2nd. edn. London: Verso.
Anderson, Tim. 2008. "The Limits of RAMSI." Sydney: AID/WATCH. Retrieved 12 February 2015 from: http://www.aidwatch.org.au/publications/reports/.
ANUedge (with the University of the South Pacific). 2013. "Solomon Islands Government RAMSI People's Survey Report." Canberra: Australian National University. Retrieved 27 June 2013 from: http://www.ramsi.org/solomon-islands/peoples-survey.html.
ANU Enterprise. 2010. "People's Survey 2009." Canberra: Australian National University. Retrieved 15 March 2010 from: http://www.ramsi.org/solomon-islands/peoples-survey.html.
———. 2011. "Solomon Island Government—RAMSI People's Survey 2010." Canberra: Australian National University. Retrieved 28 July 2013 from: http://www.ramsi.org/solomon-islands/peoples-survey.html.
Appadurai, Arjun. 1995. "The Production of Locality." In *Counterworks: Managing the Diversity of Knowledge*, ed. Richard Fardon. New York: Routledge, pp.204–25.
Appiah, Kwame Anthony. 1997. "Cosmopolitan Patriots." *Critical Inquiry* 23 (3): 617–39.
———. 2006. *Cosmopolitanism: Ethics in a World of Strangers*. London: Allen Lane.
Aqar, Andrew. 1989. "Story of a Giant." In *Manoga Maka Vavakato Pa Ganoqa: Eleven Stories from Ranongga*, ed. and trans. Laurence Stubbs. Gizo, Solomon Islands: Western Province Government, pp.66–69.
Argyle, John. 2008. "'Receiving Insiders' and 'Stranger Clients'." *Indonesia and the Malay World* 36 (105): 219–33.
Aswani, Shankar. 2000. "Changing Identities: The Ethnohistory of Roviana Predatory Headhunting." *Journal of the Polynesian Society* 109 (1): 39–70.
Aswani, Shankar, and Peter Sheppard. 2003. "The Archaeology and Ethnohistory of Exchange in Precolonial and Colonial Roviana: Gifts, Commodities, and Inalienable Possessions." *Current Anthropology* 44 (S5): S51–S69.
Bainton, Nicholas A. 2009. "Keeping the Network out of View: Mining, Distinctions and Exclusion in Melanesia." *Oceania* 79 (1): 18–33.
Bainton, Nicholas A., Chris Ballard, and Kirsty Gillespie. 2012. "The End of the Beginning? Mining, Sacred Geographies, Memory and Performance in Lihir." *Australian Journal of Anthropology* 23 (1): 22–49.
Ballard, Chris. 1997. "It's the Land, Stupid! The Moral Economy of Resource Ownership in Papua New Guinea." In *The Governance of Common Property in the Pacific Region*, ed. Peter Larmour. Canberra: National Centre for Development Studies and Resource Management in Asia-Pacific Project, pp.47–65.
Barker, John. 1990. "Mission Station and Village: Religious Practice and Representations in Maisin Society." In *Christianity in Oceania: Ethnographic Perspectives*, ed. John Barker. Lanham, MD: University Press of America, pp.173–96.

———. 1993. "'We Are *Ekelesia*': Conversion in Uiaku, Papua New Guinea." In *Conversion to Christianity: Historical and Anthropological Perspectives on a Great Transformation*, ed. Robert W. Hefner. Berkeley: University of California Press, pp.199–230.

———. 2007. "All Sides Now: The Postcolonial Triangle in Uiaku." *The Anthropology of Morality in Melanesia and Beyond*, ed. John Barker. Aldershot, UK: Ashgate, pp.75–92.

Barnes, John A. 1962. "African Models in the New Guinea Highlands." *Man* 62: 5–9.

Bashkow, Ira. 2004. "A Neo-Boasian Conception of Cultural Boundaries." *American Anthropologist* 106 (3): 443–58.

———. 2006. *The Meaning of Whitemen: Race and Modernity in the Orokaiva Cultural World*. Chicago: University of Chicago Press.

Bathgate, Murray. 1985. "Movement Processes from Precontact to Contemporary Times: The Ndi-Nggai, West Guadalcanal, Solomon Islands." In *Circulation in Population Movement: Substance and Concepts from the Melanesian Case*, ed. Murray Chapman and R. Mansell Prothero. London: Kegan Paul, pp.83–118.

Battaglia, Debbora. 1990. *On the Bones of the Serpent: Person, Memory, and Mortality in Sabral Island Society*. Chicago: University of Chicago Press.

Bauman, Zygmunt. 1995. "Making and Unmaking of Strangers." *Thesis Eleven* 43 (1): 1–16.

Bayliss-Smith, Tim. 2003. "Commentary on Aswani and Sheppard." *Current Anthropology* 44 (S5): S70–S71.

———. 2014. "Colonialism as Shell-Shock: W.H.R. Rivers's Explanations for Depopulation in Melanesia." In *The Ethnographic Experiment: A.M. Hocart and W.H.R. Rivers in Island Melanesia, 1908*, ed. Edvard Hviding and Cato Berg. New York: Berghahn Books, pp.179–213.

Beck, Ulrich. 2002. "The Cosmopolitan Society and Its Enemies." *Theory Culture and Society* 19(1/2): 17–44.

Beck, Ulrich, and Natan Sznaider. 2006. "Unpacking Cosmopolitanism for the Social Sciences: A Research Agenda." *British Journal of Sociology* 57 (1): 1–23.

Bellam, M.E.P. 1970. "The Colonial City: Honiara, a Pacific Islands Case Study." *Pacific Viewpoint* 72: 66–96.

Bennett, Judith A. 1987. *Wealth of the Solomons: A History of a Pacific Archipelago 1800–1978*. Honolulu: University of Hawaii Press.

———. 1995. "Forestry, Public Land, and the Colonial Legacy in the Solomon Islands." *Contemporary Pacific* 7 (2): 243–75.

———. 2000. *Pacific Forest: A History of Resource Control and Contest in Solomon Islands, c. 1800–1997*. Cambridge: White Horse Press.

———. 2002. "Roots of Conflict in Solomon Islands. Though Much Is Taken, Much Abides: Legacies of Tradition and Colonialism." State Society and Governance in Melanesia Discussion Papers, No. 2002/5. Retrieved 28 July 2013 from: http://hdl.handle.net/1885/41835.

———. 2009. *Natives and Exotics: World War II and Environment in the Southern Pacific*. Honolulu: University of Hawaii Press.

———. 2014. "A Vanishing People or a Vanishing Discourse? W.H.R. Rivers's 'Psychological Factor' and Depopulation in the Solomon Islands and the New Hebrides." In *The Ethnographic Experiment: A.M. Hocart and W.H.R. Rivers in Island Melanesia, 1908*, ed. Edvard Hviding and Cato Berg. New York: Berghahn Books, pp.214–51.

Bensley, A.A. 1925. "Devita Ofa." *Open Door* 3 (4): 11.
———. 1931. "A Difficult Village." *Open Door* 10 (3): 10.
———. 1932. "Church Opening at Kubokota, Ronongo, Bilua Circuit, Solomon Islands." *Open Door* 11 (2): 10.
Besnier, Niko. 2004. "Diversity, Hierarchy, and Modernity in Pacific Island Communities." In *A Companion to Linguistic Anthropology*, ed. Alessandro Duranti. Malden, MA: Blackwell, pp.95–120.
Berg, Cato. 2000. "Managing Difference: Kinship, Exchange and Urban Boundaries in Honiara, Solomon Islands," MA dissertation. Bergen: Department of Social Anthropology, University of Bergen.
———. 2008. "'A Chief Is a Chief Wherever He Goes': Land and Lines of Power in Vella Lavella, Solomon Islands," PhD dissertation. Bergen: Department of Social Anthropology, University of Bergen.
———. 2014. "The Genealogical Method: Vella Lavella Reconsidered." In *The Ethnographic Experiment: A.M. Hocart and W.H.R. Rivers in Island Melanesia, 1908*, ed. Edvard Hviding and Cato Berg. New York: Berghahn Books, pp.108–32.
Berglund, Eeva. 2006. "Generating Nontrivial Knowledge in Awkward Situations: Anthropology in the United Kingdom." In *World Anthropologies: Disciplinary Transformations within Systems of Power*, ed. Gustavo Lins Ribeiro and Arturo Escobar. Oxford: Berg, pp.181–200.
Biernoff, David. 1978. "Safe and Dangerous Places." In *Australian Aboriginal Concepts*, ed. L.R. Hiatt. Canberra: Australian Institute of Aboriginal Studies, pp.93–106.
Bird, Cliff. 2007. "Blowing the Conch Shell: A Baseline Survey of Churches Engagement in Service Provision and Governance in the Solomon Islands." Honiara: AusAID and Solomon Islands Christian Association. Retrieved 16 June 2009 from: http://www.ausaid.gov.au/Publications/Documents/solomons_church_survey.pdf.
———. 2008. "*Pepesa*—the Household of Life: A Theological Exploration of Land in the Context of Change in Solomon Islands," PhD dissertation. Canberra: School of Theology, Charles Sturt University.
Bloch, Maurice, and Jonathan Parry. 1989. "Introduction." In *Money and the Morality of Exchange*, ed. Jonathan Parry and Maurice Bloch. Cambridge: Cambridge University Press, pp.1–32.
Bonnemaison, Joel. 1985. "Territorial Control and Mobility within ni-Vanuatu Societies." In *Circulation in Population Movement: Substance and Concepts from the Melanesian Case*, ed. Murray Chapman and R. Mansell Prothero. London: Kegan Paul, pp.57–79.
———. 1994. *The Tree and the Canoe: History and Ethnogeography of Tanna*. Honolulu: University of Hawaii Press.
Bourdieu, Pierre. 1977. *Outline of a Theory of Practice*, trans. Richard Nice. Cambridge: Cambridge University Press.
Braithwaite, John, et al. 2010. *Pillars and Shadows: Statebuilding as Peacebuilding in Solomon Islands*. Acton, ACT: ANU E-Press.
Brenner, Suzanne A. 1998. *The Domestication of Desire: Women, Wealth, and Modernity in Java*. Princeton: Princeton University Press.
Brigg, Morgan. 2009. "Wantokism and State Building in Solomon Islands: A Response to Fukuyama." *Pacific Economic Bulletin* 24 (3): 148–61.
Brison, Karen J. 2007. *Our Wealth Is Loving Each Other: Self and Society in Fiji*. Lanham, MD: Lexington Books.

Brosius, J. Peter, Anna Lowenhaupt Tsing, and Charles Zerner, eds. 2005. *Communities and Conservation: Histories and Politics of Community-Based Natural Resource Management*. Walnut Creek, CA: AltaMira Press.

Brown, Terry M. 2010. "A Flawed Design: RAMSI and Capacity Building in Solomon Islands." Paper presented at the meeting of the European Society for Oceanists, St Andrew's, Scotland, 7 July.

———. 2013. "RAMSI: A Few Reflections on Its Tenth Anniversary." *DevPolicy Blog*. Retrieved 12 February 2015 from: http://devpolicy.org/ramsi-a-few-reflections-on-its-tenth-anniversary-20130627/.

Burt, Ben. 1982. "Kastom, Christianity, and the First Ancestor of the Kwara'ae of Malaita." *Mankind* 13 (4): 374–99.

———. 1983. "The Remnant Church: A Christian Sect of the Solomon Islands." *Oceania* 53 (4): 334–46.

———. 1994a. "Land in Kwara'ae and Development in the Solomon Islands." *Oceania* 64 (4): 317–35.

———. 1994b. *Tradition and Christianity: The Colonial Transformation of a Solomon Islands Society*. Philadelphia: Harwood Academic.

Caldwell, Ian, and David Henley, eds. 2008. "Stranger-Kings in Indonesia and Beyond." *Indonesia and the Malay World*, special issue, 36 (105).

Campbell, Ben. 2008. "Environmental Cosmopolitans." *Nature and Culture*, 3 (1): 9–24.

Cannell, Fenella. 1999. *Power and intimacy in the Christian Philippines*. Cambridge: Cambridge University Press.

Caplow, Theodore. 1984. "Rule Enforcement without Visible Means: Christmas Gift Giving in Middletown." *American Journal of Sociology* 89 (6): 1306–23.

Carrier, James. 1993. "The Rituals of Christmas Giving." In *Unwrapping Christmas*, ed. Daniel Miller. Oxford: Claredon Press, pp.55–74.

———. 1998. "Property and Social Relations in Melanesian Anthropology." In *Property Relations: Renewing the Anthropological Tradition*, ed. Chris M. Hann. Cambridge: Cambridge University Press, pp.85–103.

Carsten, Janet, and Stephen Hugh-Jones, eds. 1995. *About the House: Lévi-Strauss and Beyond*. New York: Cambridge University Press.

Carter, George G. 1973. *David Voeta: The Story of a Pioneer Missionary*. Auckland: Proceedings of the Wesley Historical Society.

Carter, Richard. 2006. *In Search of the Lost: The Death and Life of the Seven Peacemakers of the Melanesian Brotherhood*. Norwich: Canterbury Press.

Chambers, Mary Ruth. 2009. "Which Way Is Up? Motion Verbs and Paths of Motion in Kubokota, an Austronesian Language of the Solomon Islands," PhD dissertation. London: School of Oriental and African Studies.

Chapman, Murray. 1969. "A Population Study in South Guadalcanal: Some Results and Implications." *Oceania* 11 (2): 119–47.

———. 1985. "Me Go 'Walkabout', You Too?" In *Circulation in Population Movement: Substance and Concepts from the Melanesian Case*, ed. Murray Chapman and R. Mansell Prothero. London: Kegan Paul, pp.429–43.

———. 1992. "Population Movement: Free or Constrained?" In *Independence, Dependence, Interdependence: The First 10 Years of Solomon Islands Independence*, ed. Ron Crocombe and Esau Tuza. Suva: University of the South Pacific, pp.75–97.

Chapman, Murray, and Peter Pirie. 1974. *Tasi Mauri: A Report on Population and Resources of the Guadalcanal Weather Coast*. Honolulu: East–West Population Center, University of Hawaii.

Cheah, Pheng, and Bruce Robbins. 1998. *Cosmopolitics: Thinking and Feeling Beyond the Nation*. Minneapolis: University of Minnesota Press.

Ching, Barbara, and Gerald W. Creed, eds. 1997. *Knowing Your Place: Rural Identity and Cultural Hierarchy*. New York: Routledge.

Clay, Brenda Johnson. 1977. *Pinikindu: Maternal Nurture, Paternal Substance*. Chicago: University of Chicago Press.

Coppet, Daniel De. 1985. "... Land Owns People." In *Contexts and Levels: Anthropological Essays on Hierarchy*, ed. R.H. Barnes, Daniel de Coppet, and R.J. Parkin. Oxford: JASA Occasional Papers, pp.78–88.

Corris, Peter. 1973. *Passage, Port and Plantation: A History of Solomon Islands Labour Migration 1870–1914*. Melbourne: Melbourne University Press.

Counts, David. 1990. "Too Many Bananas, Not Enough Pineapples, and No Watermelon at All: Three Object Lessons in Living with Reciprocity." In *The Humbled Anthropologist: Tales from the Pacific*, ed. Philip DeVita. Belmont, CA: Wadsworth, pp.18–24.

Curry, George N., and Gina Koczberski. 2009. "Finding Common Ground: Relational Concepts of Land Tenure and Economy in the Oil Palm Frontier of Papua New Guinea." *Geographical Journal* 175 (2): 98–111.

Damon, Frederick H. 2000. "From Regional Relations to Ethnic Groups? On the Transformation of Value Relations to Property Claims in the Kula Ring of Papua New Guinea." *Asia Pacific Journal of Anthropology* 1 (2): 49–72.

Dauvergne, Peter. 1998. "Corporate Power in the Forests of the Solomon Islands." *Pacific Affairs* 71 (4): 524–46.

Davenport, William, and Gulbun Coker. 1967. "The Moro Movement of Guadalcanal, British Solomon Islands Protectorate." *Journal of the Polynesian Society* 76 (2): 123–75.

Davis, Karen, ed. 1991. *Vivinei Ruruhu Pa Hoava/Custom Stories from Hoava*. Gizo, Solomon Islands: Western Province Government.

Delanty, Gerard. 2006. "The Cosmopolitan Imagination: Critical Cosmopolitanism and Social Theory." *British Journal of Sociology* 57 (1): 25–47.

Dening, Greg. 1980. *Islands and Beaches. Discourse on a Silent Land: Marquesas, 1774–1880*. Honolulu: University Press of Hawaii.

Derrida, Jacques, and Anne Dufourmantelle. 2000. *Of Hospitality: Anne Dufourmantelle Invites Jacques Derrida to Respond*, trans. Rachel Bowlby. Stanford: Stanford University Press.

Dickson-Waiko, A. 2003. "The Missing Rib: Mobilizing Church Women for Change in Papua New Guinea." *Oceania* 74 (1/2): 98–119.

Dinnen, Sinclair. 2002. "Winners and Losers: Politics and Disorder in the Solomon Islands 2000–2002." *Journal of Pacific History* 37 (3): 285–298.

———. 2004. "Lending a Fist? Australia's New Interventionism in the Southwest Pacific." State Society and Governance in Melanesia Discussion Papers, No. 2004/5. Retrieved 27 July 2013 from: http://hdl.handle.net/1885/42136.

———. 2007. "A Comment on State-Building in Solomon Islands." *Journal of Pacific History* 42 (2): 255–263.

———. 2008a. "Beyond State-centrism: External Solutions and the Governance of Security in Melanesia." In *Intervention and State-Building in the Pacific: The Legitimacy of "Cooperative Intervention"*, ed. Greg Fry and Tarcisius Tara Kabutaulaka. Manchester: Manchester University Press, pp.102–18.

———. 2008b. "Dilemmas of Intervention and the Building of State and Nation." In *Politics and State Building in Solomon Islands*, ed. Sinclair Dinnen and Stewart Firth. Canberra: ANU E-Press and Asia Pacific Press, pp.1–38.

———. 2012. "The Solomon Islands: RAMSI, Transition and Future Prospects." *Security Challenges* 8 (4): 61–71.

Dinnen, Sinclair, and Matthew Allen. 2012. "Paradoxes of Postcolonial Police-Building: Solomon Islands." *Policing and Society* 23 (2): 222–42.

Dinnen, Sinclair, and Stewart Firth, eds. 2008. *Politics and State Building in Solomon Islands*. Canberra: ANU E-Press and Asia Pacific Press.

Dobell, Graeme. 2008. "Australia's Intervention Policy: A Melanesian Learning Curve?" In *Intervention and State-Building in the Pacific: The Legitimacy of "Cooperative Intervention"*, ed. Greg Fry and Tarcisius Tara Kabutaulaka. Manchester: Manchester University Press, pp.54–71.

Douglas, Bronwen. 1999. "Provocative Readings in Intransigent Archives: Finding Aneityumese Women." *Oceania* 70 (2): 111–29.

———. 2003. "Christianity, Tradition, and Everyday Modernity: Towards an Anatomy of Women's Groupings in Melanesia." *Oceania* 74 (1/2): 6–23.

Dundon, Alison. 2011. "DNA, Israel and the Ancestors: Substantiating Connections through Christianity in Papua New Guinea." *Asia Pacific Journal of Anthropology* 12 (1): 29–43.

Dureau, Christine. 1993. "Nobody Asked the Mother: Women and Maternity on Simbo, Western Solomon Islands." *Oceania* 6 (1): 18–35.

———. 1994. "Mixed Blessings: Christianity and History in Women's Lives on Simbo, Western Solomon Islands," PhD dissertation. Sydney: Department of Anthropology, Macquarie University.

———. 1998a. "Decreed Affinities: Nationhood and the Western Solomon Islands." *Journal of Pacific History* 33 (2): 197–220.

———. 1998b. "From Sisters to Wives: Changing Contexts of Maternity on Simbo, Western Solomon Islands." In *Maternities and Modernities: Colonial and Postcolonial Experiences in Asia and the Pacific*, ed. Kalpana Ram and Margaret Jolly. Cambridge: Cambridge University Press, pp.239–74.

———. 2000. "Skulls, *Mana*, and Causality." *Journal of the Polynesian Society* 109 (1): 71–97.

———. 2001. "Recounting and Remembering 'First Contact' on Simbo." In *Cultural Memory: Reconfiguring History and Identity in the Postcolonial Pacific*, ed. Jeannette Marie Mageo. Honolulu: University of Hawaii Press, pp.130–62.

———. 2012. "Translating Love." *Ethos* 40 (2): 142–63.

———. 2014. "Acknowledging the Ancestors: Vexations of Representation." In *The Ethnographic Experiment: A.M. Hocart and W.H.R. Rivers in Island Melanesia, 1908*, ed. Edvard Hviding and Cato Berg. New York: Berghahn Books, pp.44–70.

Eriksen, Annelin. 2008. *Gender, Christianity and Change in Vanuatu: An Analysis of Social Movements in North Ambrym*. Aldershot, UK: Ashgate.

Ernst, Thomas M. 1999. "Land, Stories, and Resources: Discourse and Entification in Onabasulu Modernity." *American Anthropologist* 101 (1): 88–97.
Errington, Frederick, and Deborah Gewertz. 1994. "From Darkness to Light in the George Brown Jubilee: The Invention of Nontradition and the Inscription of a National History in East New Britain." *American Ethnologist* 21 (1): 104–22.
Evans-Pritchard, Edward Evan. 1948. *The Divine Kingship of the Shilluk of the Nilotic Sudan.* Cambridge: Cambridge University Press.
Eves, Richard. 2011. "Puzzling over Matrilineal Land Tenure and Development in New Ireland, Papua New Guinea." *Pacific Studies* 34 (2/3): 350–73.
Feld, Steven. 1982. *Sound and Sentiment: Birds, Weeping, Poetics, and Song in Kaluli Expression.* Philadelphia: University of Pennsylvania Press.
Ferguson, James. 1999. *Expectations of Modernity: Myths and Meanings of Urban Life on the Zambian Copperbelt.* Berkeley: University of California Press.
Filer, Colin. 1997. "Compensation, Rent and Power in Papua New Guinea." In *Compensation for Resource Development in Papua New Guinea*, ed. S. Toft. Canberra: National Centre for Development Studies, Australian National University, pp.156–89.
———. 2014. "The Double Movement of Immovable Property Rights in Papua New Guinea." *Journal of Pacific History* 49 (1): 76–94.
Fine, Robert, and Vivienne Boon. 2007. "Introduction: Cosmopolitanism: Between Past and Future." *European Journal of Social Theory*, 10 (1): 5–16.
Fingleton, Jim. 2005. "Privatising Land in the Pacific: A Defense of Customary Tenure." Canberra: Australia Institute.
Foale, Simon J. 2002. "'Where's Our Development?' Landowner Aspirations and Environmentalist Agendas in Western Solomon Islands." *Asia Pacific Journal of Anthropology* 2 (3): 44–67.
Foale, Simon J., and Martha Macintyre. 2000. "Dynamic and Flexible Aspects of Land and Marine Tenure at West Nggela: Implications for Marine Resource Management." *Oceania* 71 (1): 33–45.
———. 2005. "Green Fantasies: Photographic Representations of Biodiversity and Ecotourism." *Journal of Political Ecology* 12: 1–22.
Foale, Simon J., and Bruno Manele. 2004. "Social and Political Barriers to the Use of Marine Protected Areas for Conservation and Fishery Management in Melanesia." *Asia Pacific Viewpoint* 45 (3): 373–86.
Foale, Simon J., et al. 2011. "Tenure and Taboos: Origins and Implications for Fisheries in the Pacific." *Fish and Fisheries* 12 (4): 357–69.
Foster, Robert J. 1995. *Social Reproduction and History in Melanesia.* Cambridge: Cambridge University Press.
Fox, James J. 1994. "Reflections on 'Hierarchy' and 'Precedence'." *History and Anthropology* 7 (1–4): 87–108.
———. 1996. "The Transformation of Progenitor Lines of Origin: Patterns of Precedence in Eastern Indonesia." In *Origins, Ancestry and Alliance: Explorations in Austronesian Ethnography*, ed. James J. Fox and Clifford Sather. Canberra: Research School of Asia and the Pacific, Australian National University, pp.133–56.
———. 1997. "Place and Landscape in Comparative Austronesian Perspective." In *The Poetic Power of Place: Comparative Perspectives on Austronesian Ideas of Locality*, ed. James J. Fox. Canberra: Research School of Asia and the Pacific, Australian National University, pp.1–21.

———. 2008. "Installing the 'Outsider' Inside: The Exploration of an Epistemic Austronesian Cultural Theme and Its Social Significance." *Indonesia and the Malay World* 36 (105): 201–18.

Fraenkel, Jon. 2004. *The Manipulation of Custom: From Uprising to Intervention in the Solomon Islands*. Wellington: Victoria University Press.

Fraenkel, Jon, Matthew G. Allen, and Harry Brock. 2010. "The Resumption of Palm-Oil Production on Guadalcanal's Northern Plains." *Pacific Economic Bulletin* 25 (1): 65–75.

Fraenkel, Jon, Joni Madraiwiwi, and Henry Okole. 2014. "The RAMSI Decade: A Review of the Regional Assistance Mission to Solomon Islands, 2003–2013." Honiara: Independent Review Commissioned by Office of the Prime Minister and Cabinet, Solomon Islands Government. Retrieved 12 Feb 2015 from: http://devpolicy.org/pdf/Independent-RAMSI-Review-Report-Final.pdf.

Frazer, Ian L. 1985a. "Circulation and the Growth of Urban Employment Amongst the To'ambaita, Solomon Islands." In *Circulation in Population Movement: Substance and Concepts from the Melanesian Case*, ed. Murray Chapman and R. Mansell Prothero. London: Kegan Paul, pp.225–48.

———. 1985b. "Walkabout and Urban Movement: A Melanesian Case Study." *Pacific Viewpoint* 26 (1): 185–205.

———. 1997. "The Struggle for Control of Solomon Islands Forests." *Contemporary Pacific* 9 (1): 39–72.

Friesen, Ward. 1993. "Melanesian Economy on the Periphery: Migration and Village Economy in Choiseul." *Pacific Viewpoint* 34 (2): 193–214.

Fritz, Hermann M., and Nikos Kalligeris. 2008. "Ancestral Heritage Saves Tribes During 1 April 2007 Solomon Islands Tsunami." *Geophysical Research Letters* 35 (1): L01607, doi:10.1029/2007GL031654.

Fry, Greg. 1997. "Framing the Islands: Knowledge and Power in Changing Australian Images of 'the South Pacific'." *Contemporary Pacific* 9 (2): 305–44.

———. 2008. "'Our Patch': The War on Terror and the New Interventionism." In *Intervention and State-Building in the Pacific: The Legitimacy of "Cooperative Intervention"*, ed. Greg Fry and Tarcisius Tara Kabutaulaka. Manchester: Manchester University Press, pp.72–86.

Fry, Greg, and Tarcisius Tara Kabutaulaka. 2008. "Political Legitimacy and State-Building Intervention in the Pacific." In *Intervention and State-Building in the Pacific: The Legitimacy of "Cooperative Intervention"*, ed. Greg Fry and Tarcisius Tara Kabutaulaka. Manchester: Manchester University Press, pp.1–36.

Fukuyama, Francis. 2008. "State Building in Solomon Islands." *Pacific Economic Bulletin* 23 (3): 18–34.

Gailey, Christine Ward. 1987. *Kinship to Kingship: Gender Hierarchy and State Formation in the Tongan Islands*. Austin: University of Texas Press.

Gegeo, David Welchman. 2001. "Cultural Rupture and Indigeneity: The Challenge of (Re)Visioning 'Place' in the Pacific." *Contemporary Pacific* 13 (2): 491–507.

Gegeo, David Welchman, and Karen Ann Watson-Gegeo. 2012. "The Critical Villager Revisited: Continuing Transformations of Language and Education in Solomon Islands." In *Language Policies in Education: Critical Issues*, ed. James W Trollefson. New York: Routledge, pp.233–52.

George, Kenneth M. 1996. *Showing Signs of Violence: The Cultural Politics of a Twentieth-Century Headhunting Ritual*. Berkeley: University of California Press.

Gewertz, Deborah, and Frederick Errington. 1993. "First Contact with God: Individualism, Agency, and Revivalism in the Duke of York Islands." *Cultural Anthropology* 8 (3): 279–305.

———. 1999. *Emerging Class in Papua New Guinea: The Telling of Difference*. Cambridge: Cambridge University Press.

Goldie, John F. 1909. "The People of New Georgia: Their Manners and Customs and Religious Beliefs." *Proceedings of the Royal Society of Queensland* 22 (1): 23–30.

Golub, Alex. 2007. "Ironies of Organization: Landowners, Land Registration, and Papua New Guinea's Mining and Petroleum Industry." *Human Organization* 66 (1): 38–48.

Gooberman-Hill, Rachael. 1999. "The Constraints of 'Feeling Free': Becoming Middle Class in Honiara (Solomon Islands)," PhD dissertation. Edinburgh: Department of Social Anthropology, University of Edinburgh.

Graeber, David. 2001. *Toward an Anthropological Theory of Value: The False Coin of Our Own Dreams*. New York: Palgrave.

———. 2008. "On Cosmopolitanism and (Vernacular) Democratic Creativity: Or, There Never Was a West." In *Anthropology and the New Cosmopolitanism: Rooted, Feminist and Vernacular Perspectives*, ed. Pnina Werbner. New York: Berg, pp.281–308.

———. 2011. "The Divine Kingship of the Shilluk: On Violence, Utopia, and the Human Condition, or, Elements for an Archaeology of Sovereignty." *Hau: Journal of Ethnographic Theory* 1 (1): 1–62.

Gray, George. 2002. "Habuna Momoruqu (The Blood of My Island): Violence and the Guadalcanal Uprising in Solomon Islands." State Society and Governance in Melanesia Working Papers, No. 2002/4. Retrieved 4 January 2008 from: http://ips.cap.anu.edu.au/ssgm/publications/working_papers/wplist.php?searchterm=2002.

Greener-Barcham, Beth K., and Manuhuia Barcham. 2006. "Terrorism in the South Pacific? Thinking Critically About Approaches to Security in the Region." *Australian Journal of International Affairs* 60 (1): 67–82.

Guo, Pei-Yi. 2011. "Law as Discourse: Land Disputes and the Changing Imagination of Relations among the Langalanga, Solomon Islands." *Pacific Studies* 34 (2/3): 223–49.

Gupta, Akhil, and James Ferguson. 1997. "Beyond 'Culture': Space, Identity, and the Politics of Difference." In *Culture, Power, Place: Explorations in Critical Anthropology*, ed. Akhil Gupta and James Ferguson. Durham, NC: Duke University Press, pp.33–51.

Hameiri, Shahar. 2007. "The Trouble with RAMSI: Reexamining the Roots of Conflict in Solomon Islands." *Contemporary Pacific* 19 (2): 409–41.

———. 2008. "Risk Management, Neo-Liberalism and the Securitisation of the Australian Aid Program." *Australian Journal of International Affairs* 62 (3): 357–71.

———. 2012. "Mitigating the Risk to Primitive Accumulation: State-Building and the Logging Boom in Solomon Islands." *Journal of Contemporary Asia* 42 (3): 405–26.

Handler, Richard, and Jocelyn Linnekin. 1984. "Tradition, Genuine or Spurious." *Journal of American Folklore* 97 (385): 273–90.

Handman, C. 2011. "Israelite Genealogies and Christian Commitment: The Limits of Language Ideologies in Guhu-Samane Christianity." *Anthropological Quarterly* 84 (3): 655–77.

———. 2013. "Mediating Denominational Disputes: Land Claims and the Sound of Christian Critique in the Waria Valley, Papua New Guinea." In *Christian Politics in*

Oceania, ed. Matt Tomlinson and Debra McDougall. New York: Berghahn Books, pp.22–48.

———. 2014. *Critical Christianity: Translation and Denominational Conflict in Papua New Guinea*. Berkeley: University of California Press.

Hann, Chris M. 1998. "Introduction: The Embeddedness of Property." In *Property Relations: Renewing the Anthropological Tradition*, ed. Chris M. Hann. Cambridge: Cambridge University Press, pp.1–47.

Hannerz, Ulf. 2010. "Afterthoughts: World Watching." *Social Anthropology* 18 (4): 448–53.

Hanson, Allan. 1989. "The Making of the Maori: Cultural Invention and Its Logic." *American Anthropologist* 91 (4): 890–902.

Harrison, Simon. 1993. *The Mask of War: Violence, Ritual, and the Self in Melanesia*. Manchester: Manchester University Press.

———. 2003. "Cultural Difference as Denied Resemblance: Reconsidering Nationalism and Ethnicity." *Comparative Studies in Society and History* 45 (2): 343–61.

———. 2006. *Fracturing Resemblances: Identity and Mimetic Conflict in Melanesia and the West*. New York: Berghahn Books.

Harwood, F.H. 1971. "The Christian Fellowship Church: A Revitalization Movement in Melanesia," PhD dissertation. Chicago: Department of Anthropology, University of Chicago.

Hayward-Jones, Jenny. 2014. "Australia's Costly Investment in Solomon Islands: The Lessons of RAMSI." *Analysis*. Canberra: Lowy Institute for International Policy.

Hau'ofa, Epeli. 1993. "Our Sea of Islands." In *A New Oceania: Rediscovering Our Sea of Islands*. Suva: School of Social and Economic Development, University of the South Pacific, pp.2–19.

Hawkins, Russell, dir. 2003. *Since the Company Came*, 52 mins. East Molesey, UK: New South Wales Film and Television Office/SBS Independent/Journeyman Pictures.

Heath, Ian, ed. 1979. *Land Research in the Solomon Islands*. Honiara: Land Research Project, Lands Division, Ministry of Agriculture and Lands.

Henley, David. 2004. "Conflict, Justice, and the Stranger-King: Indigenous Roots of Colonial Rule in Indonesia and Elsewhere." *Modern Asian Studies* 38 (1): 85–144.

Henley, David, and Ian Caldwell. 2008. "Kings and Covenants." *Indonesia and the Malay World* 36 (105): 269–91.

Herlihy, J.M. 1982. "Decolonization Politics in Solomon Islands: The Model that Never Was." In *Melanesia: Beyond Diversity*, ed. R.J. May and Hank Nelson. Canberra: Research School of Pacific Studies, Australian National University, pp.571–600.

Hermkens, Anna-Karina. 2013. "Like Moses Who Led His People to the Promised Land: Nation- and State-Building in Bougainville." *Oceania* 83 (3): 192–207.

Hilliard, David. 1966. "Protestant Missions in the Solomon Islands 1849–1942," PhD dissertation. Canberra: Department of History, Australia National University.

Hocart, A.M. 1914. "Mana." *Man* 46: 97–101.

———. 1922. "The Cult of the Dead in Eddystone of the Solomons (Parts 1 & 2)." *Journal of the Royal Anthropological Institute* 52: 71–112, 259–305.

———. 1931. "Warfare in Eddystone of the Solomon Islands." *Journal of the Royal Anthropological Institute* 61: 301–24.

———. 1935. "The Canoe and the Bonito in Eddystone Island." *Journal of the Royal Anthropological Institute* 65: 97–111.

———. 1969 [1927]. *Kingship*. Oxford: Oxford University Press.

———. 1970 [1936]. *Kings and Councillors: An Essay on the Comparative Anatomy of Human Society*, ed. Rodney Needham. Chicago: University of Chicago Press.

Hogbin, Ian. 1958. "Review of *Customary Land Tenure in the British Solomon Islands Protectorate* by Colin H. Allan." *Oceania* 28 (4): 336.

Horton, Robin. 1975. "Rationality of Conversion." *Africa* 45 (3): 219–35, (4): 373–99.

Hughes, Tony. 1979. "Evaluating Land Settlement." In *Land in the Solomon Islands*, ed. Peter Larmour. Suva: Institute of Pacific Studies, University of the South Pacific and the Ministry of Agriculture and Lands, pp.232–83.

Hviding, Edvard. 1993. "Indigenous Essentialism? 'Simplifying' Customary Land Ownership in New Georgia, Solomon Islands." *Bijdragen to de Taal-, Land- en Volkenkunde* 149: 802–24.

———. 1996. *Guardians of Marovo Lagoon: Practice, Place, and Politics in Maritime Melanesia*. Honolulu: University of Hawaii Press.

———. 2003a. "Commentary on Aswani and Sheppard." *Current Anthropology* 44 (S5): S72–S73.

———. 2003b. "Contested Rainforests, NGOs, and Projects of Desire in Solomon Islands." *International Social Science Journal* 55 (4): 539–54.

———. 2003c. "Disentangling the Butubutu of New Georgia: Cognatic Kinship in Thought and Action." In *Oceanic Socialities and Cultural Forms: Ethnographies of Experience*, ed. Ingjerd Hoem and Sidsel Roalkvam. Oxford: Berghahn Books, pp.71–113.

———. 2011. "Re-Placing the State in the Western Solomons: The Political Rise of the Christian Fellowship Church." In *Made in Oceania: Social Movements, Cultural Heritage and the State in the Pacific*, ed. Edvard Hviding and Knut Mikjel Rio. Wantage, UK: Sean Kingston Publishing, pp.51–90.

———. 2014. "Across the New Georgia Group: A.M. Hocart's Fieldwork as Inter-Island Practice." In *The Ethnographic Experiment: A.M. Hocart and W.H.R. Rivers in Island Melanesia, 1908*, ed. Edvard Hviding and Cato Berg. New York: Berghahn Books, pp.71–107.

Hviding, Edvard, and Tim Bayliss-Smith. 2000. *Islands of Rainforest: Agroforestry, Logging and Eco-Tourism in Solomon Islands*. Aldershot, UK: Ashgate.

Hviding, Edvard, and Cato Berg. 2014a. "Introduction: The Ethnographic Experiment in Island Melanesia." In *The Ethnographic Experiment: A.M. Hocart and W.H.R. Rivers in Island Melanesia, 1908*, ed. Edvard Hviding and Cato Berg. New York: Berghahn Books, pp.1–43.

Hviding, Edvard, and Cato Berg, eds. 2014b. *The Ethnographic Experiment: A.M. Hocart and W.H.R. Rivers in Island Melanesia, 1908*. New York: Berghahn Books.

Jackson, K.B. 1975. "Headhunting and the Christianization of Bugotu, 1861–1900." *Journal of Pacific History* 10: 65–78.

Jebens, Holger. 2005. *Pathways to Heaven: Contesting Mainline and Fundamentalist Christianity in Papua New Guinea*. Oxford: Berghahn Books.

Jolly, Margaret. 1982. "Birds and Kastom Banyans of South Pentecost: Kastom in Anticolonial Struggle." *Mankind* 13 (4): 338–56.

———. 1992. "Specters of Inauthenticity." *Contemporary Pacific* 4 (1): 49–72.

———. 1994. *Women of the Place: Kastom, Colonialism, and Gender in Vanuatu*. Philadelphia: Harwood Academic.

———. 2012. "Material and Immaterial Relations: Gender, Rank and Christianity in Vanuatu." In *The Scope of Anthropology: Maurice Godelier's Work in Context*, ed. Laurent Dousset and Serge Tcherkezoff. New York: Berghahn Books, pp.110–54.

Jolly, Margaret, and Martha Macintyre, eds. 1989. *Family and Gender in the Pacific: Domestic Contradictions and the Colonial Impact*. Cambridge: Cambridge University Press.

Jolly, Margaret, and Mark S. Mosko, eds. 1994. "Transformations of Hierarchy: Structure, History and Horizon in the Austronesian World." *History and Anthropology*, special issue, 7 (1–4).

Josephides, Lisette, and Alexandra Hall, eds. 2014. *We the Cosmopolitans: Moral and Existential Conditions of Being Human*. New York: Berghahn Books.

Jourdan, Christine. 1989. "Nativization and Anglicization in Solomon Islands Pijin." *World Englishes* 8 (1): 25–35.

———. 1990. "Solomons Pijin: An Unrecognized National Language." In *Language Planning and Education in Australasia and the South Pacific*, ed. Richard B. Baldauf and Allan Luke. Clevedon, UK: Multilingual Matters, pp.166–81.

———. 1995. "Stepping-Stones to National Consciousness: The Solomon Islands Case." In *Nation Making: Emergent Identities in Postcolonial Melanesia*, ed. Robert J. Foster. Ann Arbor: Michigan University Press, pp.127–50.

———. 2002. *Solomon Islands Pijin: A Trilingual Cultural Dictionary*. Canberra: Pacific Linguistics.

———. 2007. "Linguistic Paths to Urban Self in Postcolonial Solomon Islands." In *Consequences of Contact: Language Ideologies and Sociocultural Transformations in Pacific Societies*, ed. Miki Makihara and Bambi B. Schieffelin. Oxford: Oxford University Press, pp.30–48.

Joyce, Rosemary A., and Susan D. Gillespie. 2000. *Beyond Kinship: Social and Material Reproduction in House Societies*. Philadelphia: University of Pennsylvania Press.

Juergensmeyer, Mark. 2004. "Is Religion the Problem?" *Hedgehog Review* 6 (1): 21–33.

Kabutaulaka, Tarcisius Tara. 1996. "Melanesia in Review: Solomon Islands." *Contemporary Pacific* 9 (2): 487–97.

———. 2001. "Beyond Ethnicity: The Political Economy of the Guadalcanal Crisis in Solomon Islands." State, Society and Governance in Melanesia Working Papers, No. 2001/1. Retrieved 15 November 2005 from: http://eprints.anu.edu.au/archive/00001992/.

———. 2005. "Australian Foreign Policy and the RAMSI Intervention in Solomon Islands." *Contemporary Pacific* 17 (2): 283–308.

———. 2006. "Global Capital and Local Ownership in Solomon Island's Forestry Industry." In *Globalisation and Governance in the Pacific Islands*, ed. Stewart Firth. Canberra: ANU E-Press, pp.239–57.

———. 2008. "Westminster Meets Solomons in the Honiara Riots." In *Politics and State Building in Solomon Islands*, ed. Sinclair Dinnen and Stewart Firth. Canberra: ANU E-Press and Asia Pacific Press, pp.96–118.

Kant, Immanuel. 1991 [1795]. "Perpetual Peace, a Philosophical Sketch." In *Kant: Political Writings*, ed. and trans. Hans Reiss. Cambridge: Cambridge University Press, pp.93–130.

Kapferer, Bruce. 2007. "'Anthropologists Are Talking' About Anthropology after Globalisation." *Ethnos* 72 (1): 102–26.

Kaplan, Martha. 1990. "Christianity, People of the Land, and Chiefs in Fiji." In *Christianity in Oceania: Ethnographic Perspectives*, ed. John Barker. Lanham, MD: University Press of America, pp.189–207.

———. 1995. *Neither Cargo Nor Cult: Ritual Politics and the Colonial Imagination in Fiji*. Durham, NC: Duke University Press.
Keane, Webb. 1997. *Signs of Recognition: Powers and Hazards of Representation in an Indonesian Society*. Berkeley: University of California Press.
Keesing, Roger M. 1970. "Shrines, Ancestors, and Cognatic Descent: The Kwaio and Tallensi." *American Anthropologist* 72 (4): 755–75.
———. 1982a. "Kastom and Anticolonialism on Malaita: 'Culture' as Political Symbol." *Mankind* 13 (4): 297–301.
———. 1982b. *Kwaio Religion: The Living and Dead in a Solomon Island Society*. New York: Columbia University Press.
———. 1984. "Rethinking Mana." *Journal of Anthropological Research* 40 (1): 137–56.
———. 1985. "Kwaio Women Speak." *American Anthropologist* 87 (1): 27–39.
———. 1987a. "African Models in the Malaita Highlands." *Man* 22 (3): 431–52.
———. 1987b. "*Ta'a Geni*: Women's Perspectives on Kwaio Society." In *Dealing with Inequality: Analysing Gender Relations in Melanesia and Beyond*, ed. Marilyn Strathern. Cambridge: Cambridge University Press, pp.33–62.
———. 1989a. "Creating the Past: Custom and Identity in the Contemporary Pacific." *Contemporary Pacific* 1 (1/2): 19–42.
———. 1989b. "Sins of a Mission: Christian Life as Kwaio Traditionalist Ideology." In *Family and Gender in the Pacific: Domestic Contradictions and the Colonial Impact*, ed. Margaret Jolly and Martha MacIntyre. Cambridge: Cambridge University Press, pp.193–212.
Keesing, Roger M., and Peter Corris. 1980. *Lightning Meets the West Wind: The Malaita Massacre*. Melbourne: Oxford University Press.
Keesing, Roger M., and Robert Tonkinson. 1982. "Reinventing Traditional Culture: The Politics of Kastom in Island Melanesia." *Mankind*, special issue, 13 (4).
Kelly, John D. 1989. "Fear of Culture: British Regulation of Indian Marriage in Post-Indenture Fiji." *Ethnohistory* 36 (4): 372–91.
———. 1991. *A Politics of Virtue: Hinduism, Sexuality, and Countercolonial Discourse in Fiji*. Chicago: University of Chicago Press.
Kettle, Eleanor. 2000. "A Description of the Verb Phrase in Ganoqa, an Austronesian Language of the Solomon Islands," BA dissertation. Canberra: Department of Linguistics, Australian National University.
Keza, Ghighiri. 1989. "The Maluku Tribe." In *Na Tututi Moa Pa Ganogga/Historical Tales of Ranongga Island*, ed. and trans. Kenneth Roga. Gizo: Western Province Government, pp.14–17.
Kirtley, Bacil F., and Samuel H. Elbert. 1973. "Animal Tales from Rennell and Bellona." *Journal of the Polynesian Society* 82 (3): 241–65.
Knauft, Bruce M. 1993. *South Coast New Guinea Cultures: History, Comparison, Dialectic*. Cambridge: Cambridge University Press.
Knudson, Kenneth. 1977. "Sydney Island, Titiana, and Kamaleai: Southern Gilbertese in the Phoenix and Solomon Islands." In *Exiles and Migrants in Oceania*, ed. Michael Lieber. Honolulu: University of Hawaii, pp.195–241.
Kolshus, Thorgeir S. 2014. "A House Upon Pacific Sand: W.H.R. Rivers and His 1908 Survey Work." In *The Ethnographic Experiment: A.M. Hocart and W.H.R. Rivers in Island Melanesia, 1908*, ed. Edvard Hviding and Cato Berg. New York: Berghahn Books, pp.155–78.

Kwa'ioloa, Michael, and Ben Burt. 1997. *Living Tradition: Changing Life in the Solomon Islands*. London: British Museum Press.
———. 2012. *The Chief's Country*. Brisbane: University of Queensland Press.
Lal, Brij V. 1992. *Broken Waves: A History of the Fiji Islands in the Twentieth Century*. Honolulu: University of Hawaii Press.
———. 2000. *Fiji before the Storm: Elections and the Politics of Development*. Canberra: Asia Pacific Press at the Australian National University.
Larmour, Peter, ed. 1983. *Solomon Islands Politics*. Suva: Institute of Pacific Studies, University of South Pacific.
Lanyon-Orgill, Peter A. 1969. *The Language of Eddystone Island (Western Solomon Islands)*. Balmains: Crichton Press.
Laracy, Hugh. 2000. "Niels Peter Sorensen: The Story of a Criminal Adventurer." *Journal of Pacific History* 35(2): 147–62.
Laracy, Hugh, and Eugenie Laracy. 1980. "Custom, Conjugality and Colonial Rule in the Solomon Islands." *Oceania* 51 (2): 133–47.
Lawrence, David Russel. 2014. *The Naturalist and His "Beautiful Islands": Charles Morris Woodford in the Western Pacific*. Canberra: ANU E-Press.
Laycock, Donald C. 1982. "Melanesian Linguistic Diversity: A Melanesian Choice." In *Melanesia: Beyond Diversity*, ed. Ronald James May and Hank Nelson. Canberra: Research School of Pacific Studies, Australian National University, pp.33–38.
Leach, James. 2003. *Creative Land: Place and Procreation on the Rai Coast of Papua New Guinea*. New York: Berghahn Books.
Lévi-Strauss, Claude. 1969 [1949]. *The Elementary Structures of Kinship*. Boston: Beacon Press.
Liloqula, Ruth, and Alice Aruhe'eta Pollard. 2000. "Understanding Conflict in Solomon Islands: A Practical Means to Peacemaking." State, Society and Governance in Melanesia Discussion Papers No. 2000/7. Retrieved 21 July 2008 from: http://ips.cap.anu.edu.au/publications/understanding-conflict-solomon-islands-practical-means-peacemaking.
Lindstrom, Lamont. 2008. "Melanesian Kastom and Its Transformations." *Anthropological Forum* 18 (2): 161–78.
Lindstrom, Lamont, and Geoffrey M. White. 1993. "Introduction: Custom Today." *Anthropological Forum* 6 (4): 467–74.
Luxton, C.T.J. 1955. *Isles of Solomon: A Tale of Missionary Adventure*. Auckland: Methodist Foreign Missionary Society of New Zealand.
Lyons, Kristen, et al. 2012. "Agro-forestry and Its Social Impacts: Social Science Research Final Report, 2012." Canberra: Australian Centre for International Agricultural Research. Retrieved 12 February 2015 from: http://aciar.gov.au/files/node/15439/fr2013_09_appendix_5_94018.pdf.
Macintyre, Martha. 1983. "Warfare and the Changing Context of 'Kune' on Tubetube." *Journal of Pacific History* 18 (1): 11–34.
———. 1989. "The Triumph of the *Susu*: Mortuary Exchanges on Tubetube." In *Death Rituals and Life in the Societies of the Kula Ring*, ed. Frederick H. Damon and Roy Wagner. Dekalb: Northern Illinois University Press, pp.133–52.
———. 1995. "Violent Bodies and Vicious Exchanges: Personification and Objectification in the Massim." *Social Analysis* 37: 29–43.
Macintyre, Martha, and Simon Foale. 2004. "Global Imperatives and Local Desires: Competing Economic and Environmental Interests in Melanesian Communities." In

*Globalization and Culture Change in the Pacific Islands*, ed. Victoria Lockwood. Upper Saddle River, NJ: Pearson Prentice Hall, pp.149–64.

———. 2007. "Land and Marine Tenure, Ownership, and New Forms of Entitlement on Lihir: Changing Notions of Property in the Context of a Goldmining Project." *Human Organization* 66 (1): 49–59.

Maddock, Kenneth. 1974. "Dangerous Proximities and Their Analogues." *Mankind* 9 (3): 206–17.

Maenu'u, Leonard. 1979. "Registering Clan Boundaries." In *Land in the Solomon Islands*, ed. Peter Larmour. Suva: Institute of Pacific Studies, University of the South Pacific/Solomon Islands Ministry of Agriculture and Lands, pp.226–31.

Makini, Jully, ed. 1991. *Na Buka Vivinei Malivi Pa Zinama Roviana/Roviana Custom Stories Book*. Gizo: Western Province Government.

Malinowski, Bronislaw. 1935. *Coral Gardens and Their Magic: A Study of the Methods of Tilling the Soil and of Agricultural Rites in the Trobriand Islands*. London: Allen and Unwin.

Malkki, Liisa. 1994. "Citizens of Humanity: Internationalism and the Imagined Community of Nations." *Diaspora* 3 (1): 41–68.

Mamdani, Mahmood. 1996. *Citizen and Subject: Contemporary Africa and the Legacy of Late Colonialism*. Princeton: Princeton University Press.

———. 2001. *When Victims Become Killers: Colonialism, Nativism, and the Genocide in Rwanda*. Princeton: Princeton University Press.

Marai, Leo, et al. 2010. "Remuneration Disparities in Oceania: Papua New Guinea and Solomon Islands." *International Journal of Psychology* 45 (5): 350–59.

Martin, Keir. 2013. *The Death of the Big Men and the Rise of the Big Shots: Custom and Conflict in East New Britain*. New York: Berghahn Books.

Marx, Karl. 1978a [1848]. "Manifesto of the Communist Party." In *The Marx–Engels Reader*, ed. Robert C. Tucker. New York: Norton, pp.469–500.

———. 1978a [1852]. "The Eighteeth Brumaire of Louis Bonaparte." In *The Marx–Engels Reader*, ed. Robert C. Tucker. New York: Norton, pp.594–617.

McDougall, Debra. 2000. "Paths of *Pinauzu*: Captivity and Social Reproduction in Ranongga." *Journal of the Polynesian Society* 109 (1): 99–113.

———. 2003. "Fellowship and Citizenship as Models of National Community: United Church Women's Fellowship in Ranongga, Solomon Islands." *Oceania* 74 (1/2): 61–80.

———. 2004. "The Shifting Ground of Moral Community: Christianity, Property, and Place in Ranongga (Solomon Islands)," PhD dissertation. Chicago: Department of Anthropology, University of Chicago.

———. 2005. "The Unintended Consequences of Clarification: Development, Disputing, and the Dynamics of Community in Ranongga, Solomon Islands." *Ethnohistory* 52 (1): 81–109.

———. 2006. "New Interventions, Old Asymmetries: Australia and the Solomon Islands." *The New Critic* 3. Retrieved 28 July 2013 from: http://www.ias.uwa.edu.au/new-critic/three.

———. 2008. "Religious Institutions as Alternative Structures in Post-Conflict Solomon Islands: Cases from the Western Province." State Society and Governance in Melanesia Project Discussion Paper No. 2008/5. Retrieved 28 July 2013 from: http://hdl.handle.net/1885/10083.

———. 2009a. "Becoming Sinless: Converting to Islam in the Christian Solomon Islands." *American Anthropologist* 111 (4): 480–91.

———. 2009b. "Christianity, Relationality and the Material Limits of Individualism: Reflections on Robbins's Becoming Sinners." *Asia Pacific Journal of Anthropology* 10 (1): 1–19.

———. 2012. "Stealing Foreign Words, Recovering Local Treasures: Bible Translation and Vernacular Literacy on Ranongga (Solomon Islands)." *Australian Journal of Anthropology* 23 (3): 318–39.

———. 2013. "Evangelical Public Culture: Making Stranger-Citizens in Solomon Islands." In *Christian Politics in Oceania*, ed. Matt Tomlinson and Debra McDougall. New York: Berghahn Books, pp.122–45.

———. 2014a. "Sub-national Governance in Post-RAMSI Solomon Islands." State Society and Governance in Melanesia Project Working Papers, No. 2014/3. Retrieved 1 Aug 2015 from: http://ips.cap.anu.edu.au/ssgm/working-papers.

———. 2014b. "Tired for Nothing? Women, Chiefs, and the Domestication of Customary Authority in Solomon Islands." In *Divine Domesticities: Paradoxes of Christianity in the Asia Pacific*, ed. Margaret Jolly and Hyaeweol Choi. Canberra: ANU E-Press, pp.199–224.

———. 2015. "Customary Authority and State Withdrawal in Solomon Islands: Resilience or Tenacity?" *Journal of Pacific History* (50) 4: 1-24. Retrieved 20 November 2015 from: http://dx.doi.org/10.1080/00223344.2015.1110102.

McDougall, Debra, Inia Barry, and Silas Pio. 2008. "Disaster and Recovery on Ranongga: Six Months after the Earthquake in the Western Solomons," unpublished independent report. Retrieved 28 July 2013 from: http://westernsolomons.uib.no/people/mcdougall.php.

McDougall, Debra, and Joy Kere. 2011. "Christianity, Custom, and Law: Conflict and Peacemaking in the Postconflict Solomon Islands." In *Mediating across Difference: Oceanic and Asian Approaches to Conflict Resolution*, ed. Morgan Brigg and Roland Bleiker. Honolulu: University of Hawaii Press, pp.141–62.

Meltzoff, Sarah Keene. 1983. "Custom Versus Civilization: A Japanese Fisheries Multinational in Solomon Islands Development: 1971–1981," PhD dissertation. New York: Columbia University.

Meltzoff, Sarah Keene, and Edward Lipuma. 1986. "Hunting for Tuna and Cash in the Solomons: A Rebirth of Artisanal Fishing in Malaita." *Human Organization* 45 (1): 53–62.

Merlan, Francesca. 1998. *Caging the Rainbow: Places, Politics, and Aborigines in a North Australian Town*. Honolulu: University of Hawaii Press.

———. 2005. "Explorations Towards Intercultural Accounts of Socio-cultural Reproduction and Change." *Oceania* 75 (3): 167–82.

Miyazaki, Hirokazu. 2004. *The Method of Hope: Anthropology, Philosophy, and Fijian Knowledge*. Stanford: Stanford University Press.

Moata, Izikeli. 2000. "Na Toa Pa Moa Beto Na Toa Kopira [Life in the past and life now]." In *Kutia Moko Pa Paranga Luqa* [Write it in Luqa language], ed. Alphaeus Graham Zobule. Honiara: SITAG, pp.23–24.

Monson, Rebecca. 2012. "Hu Nao Save Tok? Women, Men and Land: Negotiating Property and Authority in Solomon Islands," PhD dissertation. Canberra: Department of Law, Australian National University.

Moore, Clive. 2004. *Happy Isles in Crisis: The Historical Causes for a Failing State in Solomon Islands, 1998–2004*. Canberra: Asia Pacific Press.

———. 2007. "The Misappropriation of Malaitan Labour: Historical Origins of the Recent Solomon Islands Crisis." *Journal of Pacific History* 42 (2): 211–32.

———. 2008. "No More Walkabout Long Chinatown: Asian Involvement in the Economic and Political Process." In *Politics and State Building in Solomon Islands*, ed. Sinclair Dinnen and Stewart Firth. Canberra: ANU E-Press and Asia Pacific Press, pp.64–95.

———. 2013. Labour on Overseas Plantations. In *Solomon Islands Historical Encyclopaedia 1893-1978*. Queensland: University of Queensland. Retrieved 18 August 2014 from: http://www.solomonencyclopaedia.net/.

Morgan, Michael G., and Abby Mcleod. 2006. "Have We Failed Our Neighbour?" *Australian Journal of International Affairs* 60 (3): 412–28.

Munn, Nancy. 1986. *The Fame of Gawa: A Symbolic Study of Value Transformation in a Massim (Papua New Guinea) Society*. Durham, NC: Duke University Press.

———. 1990. "Constructing Regional Worlds in Experience: Kula Exchange, Witchcraft, and Gawan Local Events." *Man* 25 (1): 1–17.

———. 1996. "Excluded Spaces: The Figure in the Australian Aboriginal Landscape." *Critical Inquiry* 22 (3): 446–65.

Myers, Fred R., and Donald Brenneis. 1984. "Introduction: Language and Politics in the Pacific." In *Dangerous Words: Language and Politics in the Pacific*, ed. Donald Brenneis and Fred R. Myers. Prospect Heights, IL: Waveland Press.

Nanau, Gordon Leua. 2008. "Intervention and Nation-Bulding in Solomon Islands: Local Responses." In *Intervention and State-Building in the Pacific: The Legitimacy of "Cooperative Intervention"*, ed. Greg Fry and Tarcisius Tara Kabutaulaka. Manchester: Manchester University Press, pp.149–62.

Nash, Jill. 1984. "Women, Work, and Change in Nagovisi." In *Rethinking Women's Roles: Perspectives from the Pacific*, ed. Denise O'Brien and Sharon W. Tiffany. Berkeley: University of California Press, pp.94–119.

NDAJ (National Defense Academy of Japan). 2008. "Joint Report for Tsunami Field Survey for the Solomon Islands Earthquake of April 1, 2007." Yokosuka, Japan: National Defense Academy of Japan. Retrieved 27 December 2012 from: http://www.nda.ac.jp/cc/users/fujima/solomon-pdf/contents/Solomon2007_report.pdf.

Newland, Lynda. 2013. "Imagining Nationhood: Narratives of Belonging and the Question of a Christian State in Fiji." *Global Change, Peace and Security* 25 (2): 227–42.

Nguyen, Minh. 2005. "The Question of 'Failed States': Australia and the Notion of State Failure." View on Asia Briefing Series, March. Retrieved 16 January 2011 from: http://www.uniya.org/research/state_failure.pdf.

Nicholson, R.C. 1923. *Daniel Bula: From Barbarism to Christian Manhood*. Los Angeles: Robert Harkness.

Nourse, Jennifer W. 2008. "Rogue Kings and Divine Queens in Central Sulawesi and Guinea-Bissau." *Indonesia and the Malay World* 36 (105): 235–52.

Nowicka, Magdalena, and Maria Rovisco. 2009. *Cosmopolitanism in Practice*. Burlington, VT: Ashgate.

O'Callaghan, Mary-Louise. 2008. "RAMSI—The Way Ahead." In *Politics and State Building in Solomon Islands*, ed. Sinclair Dinnen and Stewart Firth. Canberra: ANU E-Press and Asia Pacific Press, pp.18593.

Ortner, Sherry B. 1973. "Key Symbols." *American Anthropologist* 75 (5): 1338–46.

———. 1984. "Theory in Anthropology since the Sixties." *Comparative Studies in Society and History* 26 (1): 126–66.
Paina, Dalcy Tovosia. 2000. "Peacemaking in Solomon Islands: The Experience of the Guadalcanal Women for Peace Movement." *Development Bulletin* 53 (October): 47–48.
Paini, Anna. 2003. "'The Kite Is Tied to You': Custom, Christianity, and Organization among Kanak Women of Drueulu, Lifou, New Caledonia." *Oceania* 74 (1/2): 81–97.
Panakera, Simeon. 1991. "*Butubutu Maluku*/The Maluku Tribe." In *Kaki Vavakato Pa Ganoqa/More Stories from Ranongga*, ed. and trans. Laurence Stubbs. Gizo: Western Province Government, pp.14–21.
Patterson, Mary. 2002. "Moving Histories: An Analysis of the Dynamics of Place in North Ambrym, Vanuatu." *Australian Journal of Anthropology* 13 (2): 200–18.
Pavukera, John. 1989. "*Na Vavakato Di Ka Vesu Iliganigani*/Story of Eight Giants." In *Manoga Maka Vavakato Pa Ganoqa/Eleven Stories from Ranongga*, ed. and trans. Laurence Stubbs. Gizo: Western Province Government, pp.8–15.
Piukera, Miranda. 1991. "*Vavakato Nana Temotemoko*/The Story of the Clam." In *Kaki Vavakato Pa Ganoqa/More Stories from Ranongga*, ed. and trans. Laurence Stubbs. Gizo: Western Province Government, pp.4–11.
Polanyi, Karl. 1944. *The Great Transformation: The Political and Economic Origins of Our Time*. Boston: Beacon Press.
Pollard, Alice A. 2000a. "Resolving Conflict in Solomon Islands: The Women for Peace Approach." *Development Bulletin* 53: 44–46.
———. 2000b. *Givers of Wisdom, Labourers without Gain: Essays on Women in the Solomon Islands*. Suva: Institute of Pacific Studies, University of the South Pacific.
———. 2003. "Women's Organization, Volunteerism, and Self-Financing in Solomon Islands." *Oceania* 74 (1/2): 44–60.
Povinelli, Elizabeth A. 1993. *Labor's Lot: The Power, History, and Culture of Aboriginal Action*. Chicago: University of Chicago Press.
Powdermaker, Hortense. 1966. *Stranger and Friend: The Way of an Anthropologist*. New York: Norton.
Premdas, Ralph, Jeffrey Steeves, and Peter Larmour. 1983. "The Western Breakaway Movement." In *Solomon Islands Politics*, ed. Peter Larmour. Suva: Institute of Pacific Studies of the University of the South Pacific, pp.164–96.
Rapport, Nigel. 2006. "Anthropology as Cosmopolitan Study." *Anthropology Today* 22 (1): 23–24.
Reilly, Ben. 2000. "The Africanisation of the South Pacific." *Australian Journal of International Affairs* 54 (3): 261–68.
Richards, Rhys. 2012. *Head Hunters Black and White: Three Collectors in the Western Solomon Islands, 1893 to 1914*. Wellington: Paremata Press.
Rivers, W.H.R.R. 1922. *Essays on the Depopulation of Melanesia*. Cambridge: Cambridge University Press.
Robbins, Joel. 1998. "On Reading 'World News': Apocalyptic Narrative, Negative Nationalism, and Transnational Christianity in a Papua New Guinea Society." *Social Analysis* 42 (2): 103–30.
———. 1999. "This Is Our Money: Modernism, Regionalism, and Dual Currencies in Urapmin." In *Money and Modernity: State and Local Currencies in Melanesia*, ed. David Akin and Joel Robbins. Pittsburgh: University of Pittsburgh Press, pp.82–102.

———. 2004. *Becoming Sinners: Christianity and Moral Torment in a Papua New Guinea Society*. Berkeley: University of California Press.

Robbins, Joel, and David Akin. 1999. "An Introduction to Melanesian Currencies: Agency, Identity, and Social Reproduction." In *Money and Modernity: State and Local Currencies in Melanesia*, ed. David Akin and Joel Robbins. Pittsburgh: University of Pittsburgh Press, pp.1–40.

Rosenblatt, Daniel. 2011. "Indigenizing the City and the Future of Maori Culture: The Construction of Community in Auckland as Representation, Experience, and Self-Making." *American Ethnologist* 38 (3): 411–29.

Ross, Harold M. 1978. "Competition for Baegu Souls: Mission Rivalry on Malaita, Solomon Islands." In *Mission, Church, and Sect in Oceania*, ed. James A. Boutilier, Daniel T. Hughes, and Sharon W. Tiffany. Lanham MD: University Press of America, pp.163–200.

Roughan, John. 2002. "Pacific First: A Failed State." *Solomon Star*, 13 February, p. 5.

———. 2006. "RAMSI Long on Muscle, Short on Respect in Solomons." *Pacific Islands Report*, 19 January. Retrieved 19 January 2006 from: http://archives.pireport.org/archive/2006/January/01-19-com.htm.

Roughan, Paul, B.K. Greener-Barcham, and Manuhuia Barcham. 2006. "Where to Now for RAMSI?" CIGAD Briefing Note. Palmerston North, NZ: Centre for Indigenous Governance and Development, Massey University.

Rumsey, Alan. 2000. "Agency, Personhood and the 'I' of Discourse in the Pacific and Beyond." *Journal of the Royal Anthropological Institute* 6 (1): 101–15.

———. 2004. "Christianity, Culture Change, and the Anthropology of Ethics." *Anthropological Quarterly* 77 (3): 581–93.

Rumsey, Alan, and James Weiner, eds. 2001. *Emplaced Myth: Space, Narrative, and Knowledge in Aboriginal Australia and Papua New Guinea*. Honolulu: University of Hawaii Press.

Rutherford, Danilyn. 2000. "The White Edge of the Margin: Textuality and Authority in Biak, Irian Jaya, Indonesia." *American Ethnologist* 27 (2): 312–39.

———. 2001. "Intimacy and Alienation: Money and the Foreign in Biak." *Public Culture* 13 (2): 299–324.

———. 2003. *Raiding the Land of the Foreigners: The Limits of the Nation on an Indonesian Frontier*. Princeton: Princeton University Press.

———. 2006a. "The Bible Meets the Idol: Writing and Conversion in Biak, Irian Jaya, Indonesia." In *The Anthropology of Christianity*, ed. Fenella Cannell. Durham, NC: Duke University Press, pp.240–72.

———. 2006b. "Nationalism and Millenarianism in West Papua: Institutional Power, Interpretive Practice, and the Pursuit of Christian Truth." In *The Limits of Meaning: Case Studies in the Anthropology of Christianity*, ed. Matthew Engelke and Matt Tomlinson. New York: Berghahn Books, pp.105–28.

Sahlins, Marshall. 1965. "On the Sociology of Primitive Exchange." In *The Relevance of Models for Social Anthropology*, ed. Michael Banton. London: Tavistock Publications, pp.139–236.

———. 1985. *Islands of History*. Chicago: University of Chicago Press.

———. 1992. *Anahulu: The Anthropology of History in the Kingdom of Hawaii*. Chicago: University of Chicago Press.

———. 2008. "The Stranger-King or, Elementary Forms of the Politics of Life." *Indonesia & the Malay World* 36 (105): 177–99.

———. 2013. *What Kinship Is—And Is Not*. Chicago: University of Chicago Press.
Scales, Ian. 2004. "The Social Forest: Landowners, Development Conflict and the State in Solomon Islands," PhD dissertation. Canberra: Department of Anthropology, Australian National University.
———. 2007. "The Coup Nobody Noticed: The Solomon Islands Western State Movement in 2000." *Journal of Pacific History* 42 (2): 187–209.
Scheffler, Harold. 1962. "Kindred and Kin Groups in Simbo Island Social Structure." *Ethnology* 1 (2): 135–57.
———. 1965. *Choiseul Island Social Structure*. Berkeley: University of California Press.
———. 1971. "Solomon Islands: Seeking a New Land Custom." In *Land Tenure in the Pacific*, ed. Ron Crocombe. Melbourne: Oxford University Press, pp.273–91.
———. 1985. "Filiation and Affiliation." *Man* 20 (1): 1–21.
Schneider, David M. 1965. "Some Muddles in the Models: Or, How the System Really Works." In *The Relevance of Models for Social Anthropology*, ed. Michael Banton. London: Tavistock Publications, pp.25–86.
———. 1984. *A Critique of the Study of Kinship*. Ann Arbor: University of Michigan Press.
Schneider, Gerhard. 1998. "Reinventing Identities: Redefining Cultural Concepts in the Struggle between Villagers in Munda, Roviana Lagoon, New Georgia Island, Solomon Islands, for the Control of Land." In *Pacific Answers to Western Hegemony: Cultural Practices of Identity Construction*, ed. Jeurg Wassmann. Oxford: Berg, pp.191–213.
Schram, Ryan. 2013. "One Mind: Enacting the Christian Congregation among the Auhelawa, Papua New Guinea." *Australian Journal of Anthropology* 24 (1): 30–47.
Schwartz, Theodore. 1993. "Kastom, 'Custom', and Culture: Conspicuous Culture and Culture-Constructs." *Anthropological Forum* 6 (4): 515–40.
Scott, Michael W. 1990. "Constitutions of Maasina Rule: Timothy George and the *Iora*." *Chicago Anthropology Exchange* 19: 41–65.
———. 2000. "Ignorance Is Cosmos; Knowledge Is Chaos: Articulating a Cosmological Polarity in the Solomon Islands." *Social Analysis* 44 (2): 56–83.
———. 2005a. "Hybridity, Vacuity, and Blockage: Visions of Chaos from Anthropological Theory, Island Melanesia, and Central Africa." *Comparative Studies in Society and History* 47 (1): 190–216.
———. 2005b. "'I Was Like Abraham': Notes on the Anthropology of Christianity from the Solomon Islands." *Ethnos* 70 (1): 101–25.
———. 2007a. "Neither 'New Melanesian History' nor 'New Melanesian Ethnography': Recovering Emplaced Matrilineages in South-East Solomon Islands." *Oceania* 77 (3): 337–54.
———. 2007b. *The Severed Snake: Matrilineages, Making Place, and a Melanesian Christianity in Southeast Solomon Islands*. Durham, NC: Carolina Academic Press.
———. 2008. "Proto-people and Precedence: Encompassing Euroamericans through Narratives of 'First Contact' in Solomon Islands." In *Exchange and Sacrifice*, ed. Pamela J. Stewart and Andrew Strathern. Durham, NC: Carolina Academic Press, pp.141–76.
———. 2012. "The Matter of Makira: Colonialism, Competition, and the Production of Gendered Peoples in Contemporary Solomon Islands and Medieval Britain." *History and Anthropology* 23 (1): 115–48.

———. 2013. "'Heaven on Earth' or Satan's 'Base' in the Pacific? Internal Christian Politics in the Dialogic Construction of the Makiran Underground Army." In *Christian Politics in Oceania*, ed. Matt Tomlinson and Debra McDougall. New York: Berghahn Books, pp.49–77.

Senft, Gunter, ed. 1997. *Referring to Space: Studies in Austronesian and Papuan Languages*. Oxford: Claredon Press.

Sheppard, Peter J., Richard Walter, and Takuya Nagaoka. 2000. "The Archaeology of Head-Hunting in Roviana Lagoon, New Georgia." *Journal of the Polynesian Society* 109 (1): 1–37.

Shryock, Andrew. 2009. "Hospitality Lessons: Learning the Shared Language of Derrida and the Balga Bedouin." *Paragraph* 32(1): 32–50.

———. 2012. "Breaking Hospitality Apart: Bad Hosts, Bad Guests, and the Problem of Sovereignty." *Journal of the Royal Anthropological Institute* 18: S20–S33.

Simmel, Georg. 1964 [1908]. *The Sociology of Georg Simmel*, ed. and trans. Kurt H. Wolff. New York: Macmillan.

SISO (Solomon Islands Statistics Office). 2012. "Report on 2009 Population and Housing Census: Basic Tables and Census Description," Vols. 1 and 2. Honiara: Solomon Islands Government. Retrieved 5 Feb 2015 from: http://www.spc.int/prism/solomons/.

Sissons, Jeffrey. 2011. "Anthropological Understandings of Hapuu and the Improvisation of Social Life." *Journal of the Royal Anthropological Institute* 17 (3): 628–31.

———. 2014. *The Polynesian Iconoclasm: Religious Revolution and the Seasonality of Power*. New York: Berghahn Books.

Spriggs, Matthew. 1997. *The Island Melanesians*. Oxford: Blackwell.

Stasch, Rupert. 2009. *Society of Others: Kinship and Mourning in a West Papuan Place*. Berkeley: University of California Press.

———. 2010. "The Category 'Village' in Melanesian Social Worlds: Some Theoretical and Methodological Possibilities." *Paideuma* 56: 41–62.

———. 2013. "The Poetics of Village Space When Villages Are New: Settlement Form as History-Making in West Papua." *American Ethnologist* 40 (3): 555–70.

Steeves, Jeffrey S. 1996. "'Unbounded Politics' in the Solomon Islands: Leadership and Party Alignments." *Pacific Studies* 19 (1): 115–38.

Steley, Dennis. 1983. "Juapa Rane: The Seventh-Day Adventist Mission in the Solomon Islands, 1914–1942," MA dissertation. Auckland: Department of History, University of Auckland.

———. 1989. "Unfinished: The Seventh-Day Adventist Mission in the South Pacific, Excluding Papua New Guinea, 1886–1986," PhD dissertation. Auckland: Department of History, University of Auckland.

Strathern, Marilyn. 1985. "The Disconcerting Tie: Attitudes of Hagen Migrants toward 'Home'." In *Circulation in Population Movement: Substance and Concepts from the Melanesian Case*, ed. Murray Chapman and R. Mansell Prothero. London: Kegan Paul, pp.360–76.

———. 1988. *The Gender of the Gift: Problems with Women and Problems with Society in Melanesia*. Berkeley: University of California Press.

Stritecky, Jolene Marie. 2001a. "Israel, America, and the Ancestors: Narratives of Spiritual Warfare in a Pentecostal Denomination in Solomon Islands." *Journal of Ritual Studies* 15 (2): 62–78.

———. 2001b. "Through a Moral Lens: Morality, Violence, and Empathy in Solomon Islands," PhD dissertation. Iowa City, IA: Department of Anthropology, University of Iowa.
Stubbs, Laurence, ed. 1989. *Manoga Maka Vavakato Pa Ganoqa/Eleven Stories from Ranongga*. Gizo: Western Province Government.
———, ed. 1991. *Kaki Vavakato Pa Ganoqa/More Stories from Ranongga*. Gizo: Western Province Government.
Sykes, Karen. 2007a. "Interrogating Individuals: The Theory of Possessive Individualism in the Western Pacific." *Anthropological Forum* 17 (3): 213–24.
———. 2007b. "The Moral Grounds of Critique: Between Possessive Individuals, Entrepreneurs and Big Men in New Ireland." *Anthropological Forum* 17 (3): 255–68.
Tambiah, Stanley Jeyaraja. 1986. *Sri Lanka: Ethnic Fratricide and the Dismantling of Democracy*. Chicago: University of Chicago Press.
Tausinga, Job D. 1992. "Logging in North New Georgia Timber Corporation." In *Independence, Dependence, Interdependence: The First 10 Years of Solomon Islands Independence*. Honiara: Institute of Pacific Studies, University of the South Pacific, pp.55–66.
Taussig-Rubbo, Mateo. 2012. "From the 'Stranger King' to the 'Stranger Constitution': Domesticating Sovereignty in Kenya." *Constellations* 19 (2): 248–66.
Taylor, Christopher C. 2001. *Sacrifice as Terror: The Rwandan Genocide of 1994*. Oxford: Berg.
Taylor, Frederick W., et al. 2008. "Rupture Across Arc Segment and Plate Boundaries in the 1 April 2007 Solomons Earthquake." *Nature Geoscience* 1 (4): 253–57.
Taylor, John Patrick. 2008. *The Other Side: Ways of Being and Place in Vanuatu*. Honolulu: University of Hawaii Press.
Thomas, Nicholas. 1994. *Colonialism's Culture: Anthropology, Travel and Government*. Princeton: Princeton University Press.
Thomas, Timothy. 2014. "Shrines in the Landscape of New Georgia." In *Monuments and People in the Pacific*, ed. Helene Martinsson-Wallin and Timothy Thomas. Uppsala: Uppsala Universitet, pp.47–76.
Thomas, Tim, Peter Sheppard, and Richard Walter. 2001. "Landscape, Violence and Social Bodies: Ritualized Architecture in a Solomon Islands Society." *Journal of the Royal Anthropological Institute* 7 (3): 545–72.
Tiffany, Sharon W. 1983. "Customary Land Disputes, Courts, and African Models in the Solomon Islands." *Oceania* 53 (3): 277–90.
Timmer, Jaap. 2008. "*Kastom* and Theocracy: A Reflection on Governance from the Uttermost Part of the World." In *Politics and State Building in Solomon Islands*, ed. Sinclair Dinnen and Steward Firth. Canberra: ANU E-Press and Asia Pacific Press, pp.194–212.
———. 2012. "Straightening the Path from the Ends of the Earth: The Deep Sea Canoe Movement in Solomon Islands." In *Flows of Faith: Religious Reach and Community in Asia and the Pacific*, ed. Lenore Manderson, Wendy Smith, and Matt Tomlinson. New York: Springer, pp.201–14.
Tomlinson, Matt. 2009. *In God's Image: The Metaculture of Fijian Christianity*. Berkeley: University of California Press.
Tomlinson, Matt, and Debra McDougall. 2013. "Christian Politics in Oceania." In *Christian Politics in Oceania*, ed. Matt Tomlinson and Debra McDougall. New York: Berghahn Books, pp.1–21.

Tonkinson, Robert. 1982. "National Identity and the Problem of Kastom in Vanuatu." *Mankind* 13 (4): 306–15.

———. 1993. "Understanding 'Tradition'—Ten Years On." *Anthropological Forum* 6 (4): 597–606.

Totorea, David. 1979a. "Development at Fiu Kelakwai." In *Land in the Solomon Islands*, ed. Peter Larmour. Suva: Institute of Pacific Studies, University of the South Pacific/Solomon Islands Ministry of Agriculture and Lands, pp.218–25.

———. 1979b. "Land Settlement." In *Land in the Solomon Islands*, ed. Peter Larmour. Suva, Fiji: Institute of Pacific Studies, University of the South Pacific/Solomon Islands Ministry of Agriculture and Lands, pp.201–7.

Trask, Haunani-Kay. 1991. "Natives and Anthropologists: The Colonial Struggle." *Contemporary Pacific* 3 (1): 159–77.

TRC (Truth and Reconciliation Commission). 2012. "Solomon Islands Truth and Reconciliation Commission: Final Report," ed. Terry Brown. Honiara: Solomon Islands Truth and Reconciliation Commission. Retrieved 12 Feb 2015 from: http://pacificpolitics.com/2013/01/solomon-islands-trc-final-report/.

Trnka, Susanna. 2008. *State of Suffering: Political Violence and Community Survival in Fiji*. Ithaca, NY: Cornell University Press.

Trouillot, Michel-Rolph. 1991. "Anthropology and the Savage Slot: The Poetics and Politics of Otherness." In *Recapturing Anthropology: Working in the Present*, ed. Richard Gabriel Fox. Santa Fe: School of American Research Press, pp.17–44.

Tryon, Darrell T., and Brian D. Hackman. 1983. *Solomon Islands Languages: An Internal Classification*. Canberra: Pacific Linguistics.

Tuza, Esau. 1975. "The Emergence of the Christian Fellowship Church: A Historical View of Silas Eto, Founder of the Christian Fellowship Church," MA dissertation. Port Morseby: University of Papua New Guinea.

———. 1977. "Silas Eto of New Georgia." In *Prophets of Melanesia: Six Essays*, ed. Garry Trompf. Suva: Institute of Pacific Studies, University of the South Pacific, pp.65–87.

Tuzin, Donald. 1997. *The Cassowary's Revenge: The Life and Death of Masculinity in a New Guinea Society*. Chicago: University of Chicago Press.

USGS (US Geological Survey). 2008. "Preliminary Analysis of the April 2007 Solomon Islands Tsunami, Southwest Pacific Ocean." Washington: US Geological Survey, Department of the Interior. Retrieved 12 February 2015 from: http://walrus.wr.usgs.gov/tsunami/solomon07/.

Valeri, Valerio. 1985. *Kingship and Sacrifice: Ritual and Society in Ancient Hawaii*. Chicago: University of Chicago Press.

———. 1994. "Buying Women but Not Selling Them: Gift and Commodity Exchange in Huaulu Alliance." *Man* 29 (1): 1–26.

Van Heekeren, Deborah. 2003. "Celebrating Mother's Day in a Melanesian Village Church." *Pacific Studies* 26 (3): 33–54.

———. 2004. "Feeding Relationship: Uncovering Cosmology in Christian Women's Fellowship in Papua New Guinea." *Oceania* 75 (2): 89–108.

Vischer, Michael P, ed. 2009. *Precedence: Social Differentiation in the Austronesian World*. Canberra: ANU E-Press.

Wagner, John, and Malia Talakai. 2007. "Customs, Commons, Property, and Ecology: Case Studies from Oceania." *Human Organization* 66 (1): 1–10.

Wagner, Roy. 1967. *The Curse of Souw: Principles of Daribi Clan Definition and Alliance.* Chicago: University of Chicago Press.

———. 1974. "Are There Groups in the New Guinea Highlands?" In *Frontiers of Anthropology: An Introduction to Anthropological Thinking,* ed. Murray J. Leaf. New York: Van Nostrand, pp.95–122.

Wainwright, Elsina. 2003. "Our Failing Neighbor: Australia and the Future of the Solomon Islands." Barton, ACT: Australian Strategic Policy Institute. Retrieved 20 November 2014 from: https://http://www.aspi.org.au/publications/our-failing-neighbour-australia-and-the-future-of-solomon-islands.

Walter, Richard, and Peter Sheppard. 2000. "Nusa Roviana: The Archaeology of a Melanesian Chiefdom." *Journal of Field Archaeology* 27 (3): 295–318.

———. 2006. "Archaeology in Melanesia: A Case Study from the Western Province of the Solomon Islands." In *Archaeology of Oceania: Australia and the Pacific Islands,* ed. Ian Lilley. Malden, MA: Blackwell, pp.137–59.

Walter, Richard, Tim Thomas, and Peter Sheppard. 2004. "Cult Assemblages and Ritual Practice in Roviana Lagoon, Solomon Islands." *World Archaeology* 36 (1): 142–57.

Wardel, Huon. 2010. "A Cosmopolitan Anthropology?" *Social Anthropology,* 18 (4): 381–88.

Watson-Gegeo, Karen Ann, and David Welchman Gegeo. 1991. "The Impact of Church Affiliation on Language Use in Kwara'ae (Solomon Islands)." *Language in Society* 20 (4): 533–55.

Weiner, Annette. 1980. "Stability in Banana Leaves: Colonization and Women in Kiriwana, Trobriand Islands." In *Women and Colonization: Anthropological Perspectives,* ed. Mona Etienne and Eleanor Leacock. New York: Praeger Publishers, pp.270–93.

———. 1988. *The Trobrianders of Papua New Guinea.* Fort Worth: Harcourt Brace Jovanovich.

Weiner, James F. 2013. "The Incorporated What Group: Ethnographic, Economic and Ideological Perspectives on Customary Land Ownership in Contemporary Papua New Guinea." *Anthropological Forum* 23 (1): 94–106.

Weiner, James F., and Katie Glaskin, eds. 2007. *Customary Land Tenure and Registration in Australia and Papua New Guinea: Anthropological Perspectives.* Canberra: ANU E-Press.

Werbner, Pnina, ed. 2008a. *Anthropology and the New Cosmopolitanism: Rooted, Feminist and Vernacular Perspectives.* New York: Berg.

———. 2008b. "Introduction: Towards a New Cosmopolitan Anthropology." In *Anthropology and the New Cosmopolitanism: Rooted, Feminist and Vernacular Perspectives,* ed. Pnina Werbner. New York: Berg, pp.1–32.

Wesley-Smith, Terence. 2008. "Altered States: The Politics of State Failure and Regional Intervention." In *Intervention and State-Building in the Pacific: The Legitimacy of "Cooperative Intervention",* ed. Greg Fry and Tarcisius Tara Kabutaulaka. Manchester: Manchester University Press, pp.37–53.

West, Paige. 2006. *Conservation Is Our Government Now: The Politics of Ecology in Papua New Guinea.* Durham, NC: Duke University Press.

White, Geoffrey M. 1983. "War, Peace, and Piety in Santa Isabel, Solomon Islands." In *The Pacification of Melanesia,* ed. Margaret Rodman and Matthew Cooper. Ann Arbor: University of Michigan Press, pp.109–40.

———. 1991. *Identity through History: Living Stories in a Solomon Islands Society*. Cambridge: Cambridge University Press.
———. 1993. "Three Discourses of Custom." *Anthropological Forum* 6 (4): 475–95.
———. 2013. "Chiefs, Church, and State in Santa Isabel, Solomon Islands." In *Christian Politics in Oceania*, ed. Matt Tomlinson and Debra McDougall. New York: Berghahn Books, pp.171–97.
White, Geoffrey M., and Lamont Lindstrom. 1989. *The Pacific Theater: Island Representations of World War II*. Honolulu: University of Hawaii Press.
White, Geoffrey M., et al., eds. 1988. *The Big Death: Solomon Islanders Remember World War II*. Suva: University of the South Pacific.
Williams, Raymond. 1973. *The Country and the City*. New York: Oxford University Press.
Williams, Shaun. 2011. "Public Land Governance in Solomon Islands." Justice for the Poor Briefing Note 6 (1). Washington: World Bank. Retrieved 25 June 2013 from: https://openknowledge.worldbank.org/handle/10986/10903.
Wolf, Eric R. 1982. *Europe and the People without History*. Berkeley: University of California Press.
Wood, Terence and Stephen Howes, eds. 2014. *Debating Ten Tears of RAMSI*. Canberra: Development Policy Center.
Woodburn, James. 1998. "'Sharing Is Not a Form of Exchange': An Analysis of Property-Sharing in Immediate-Return Hunter-Gatherer Societies." In *Property Relations: Renewing the Anthropological Tradition*, ed. Chris M. Hann. Cambridge: Cambridge University Press, pp.48–63.
Woodford, Charles Morris. 1890. *A Naturalist among the Headhunters*. New York: Longmans, Green.
Woodhead, Linda. 2004. *Christianity: A Very Short Introduction*. Oxford: Oxford University Press.
World Bank. 2010. "Solomon Islands Growth Prospects: Constraints and Policy Priorities." Honiara: World Bank. Retrieved 28 July 2013 from: http://hdl.handle.net/10986/2924.
WWFSPP (WWF South Pacific Program). 2003. "WWF Solomon Islands Country Programme: History of WWF in the Solomon Islands." Suva: WWF Pacific. Retrieved 10 March 2004 from: http://www.wwfpacific.org.fj/solomons_history.htm.
Yongjia, Liang. 2011. "Stranger-Kingship and Cosmocracy; or, Sahlins in Southwest China." *Asia Pacific Journal of Anthropology* 12 (3): 236–54.
Young, Michael W. 1997. "Commemorating Missionary Heroes: Local Christianity and Narratives of Nationalism." In *Narratives of Nation in the South Pacific*, ed. Ton Otto and Nicholas Thomas. Amsterdam: Harwood Academic, pp.92–132.
Zelenietz, Martin. 1983. "The End of Headhunting in New Georgia." In *The Pacification of Melanesia*, ed. Margaret Rodman and Matthew Cooper. Ann Arbor: University of Michigan Press, pp.91–108.

# Index

adultery, 135, 204
Adventist, see Seventh-day Adventist
Aena plantation, 41–42, 102, 198, 205, 217n8
affinal (in-law) relations, 6, 71, 76, 79, 127, 137, 146, 152, 156, 182
Akin, David, x, 37, 130, 164, 199–201, 203, 216
Alebua, Ezekiel, 231, 240n4
Alepio, Marina, viii, 52
Alepio, Mark, 52
Aleqeto, Edi, ix, 151
Aleqeto, Ego, 153
Aleqeto, Elison, 149, 151–53, 160
Allan, Colin, 166–67, 186n1
Allen, Matthew, 15, 20, 32n1, 37, 162, 201, 203, 221, 224, 227, 233
Alphaeus, Zobule, ix, 173–74
America or Americans, 4–8, 48, 54, 114, 127, 157, 178, 192, 230, 237
ancestors, 9, 11–12, 13, 14, 27, 28, 36–37, 41, 54, 56–57, 62n18, 64–65, 67, 70, 72, 78–80, 88, 94–96, 100, 103, 105, 115, 128, 138, 161, 176, 209, 216n1. *See also* land, ancestral
ancestors as proto-Christian, 119, 124, 128, 156
ancestral shrines (*tabuna*), 12, 40, 42, 45, 56, 68, 73–74, 78, 80, 82–84, 87, 90, 103, 106–12, 136–37, 145, 150, 155, 157, 160–61, 188
Anglican Church of Melanesia, 226
*aoro* (nut grove), 83, 128, 138. *See also* nut grove
Aqarao, Samu, 99–100
Aqolo, Voerini, ix, 100, 122n7
area of land cleared for settlement, 9, 10–11, 36, 79, 138–39, 143, 146, 149 151–54, 183, 210. *See also ia*
Armstrong, Herbert, 178

Arosi (of Makira), 30, 68, 70–71, 89n7, 157–58
Auki (capital of Malaita Province), 195
Australia, 1, 7, 18, 21–22, 39, 47, 109, 111, 119, 176, 197, 221, 228–31, 235, 240n6, 241n7, 241n13, 242n15
Australia, Aboriginal cosmology, 60
Australian foreign policy, 32n2, 229, 240n6, 241n7, 241n9, 242n15
Australian Strategic Policy Institute, 20, 229
Austronesian, 11, 22, 27, 30, 39, 56, 62n20–21, 103, 119, 192, 216n2
authority over land and people, 59, 65, 110, 113, 117, 135, 140, 144, 157, 166, 169, 170–72, 179–80, 185, 193, 201
Awana, 83–86, 188

Babata language (Choiseul), 192
Baga Island, 46, 110, 200
*bakia*, 8, 74, 79–80, 82, 90, 104, 130, 133, 135–37, 142–43, 145–47, 155–56, 178, 219. *See also* shell valuable
*bangara* (chief, leader), 56–58, 77, 109, 115, 121n1, 124. *See also* chief
Baniata, 149–52, 160–61, 173
baptism, 103, 111
bark cloth *(tapa)*, 103
base, ground, root *(kutana)*, 142, 149
beach, 6, 9, 29, 35, 39, 46, 77, 91, 94–98, 103
bêche-de-mer, 44, 181
Beck, H & C.P., 41, 198–99, 217n8
beer, 52
Bei, Apusae, 45, 109–10, 136
Beibangara, 108–10, 177
Bell, William R. (District officer), 200, 208
Bensley, Rev. A.A., 106
betel nut, 110–11, 114, 123n18, 125, 131
Betijama, 101–2

**276** *Index*

Beto, Simion, 9, 81–82, 131–32
Biak, 31, 103, 126
Bible, biblical, xiv, 68, 94, 99, 110, 114, 116, 120, 173
Bilua (Vella Lavella), 43, 46, 96, 102, 105–6, 114, 122n4, 123n11, 192
Binskin, Joseph, 46, 200
birthing, 95, 115, 209
birthing area (*sigu*), 103, 115
bodily practices, 71, 96, 98–100, 113, 121, 123n18
bonito, 106, 131, 150, 153
Bougainville, 4, 44, 190, 202
bridewealth, 159n15, 203–5, 214
British colonial administration, 19, 43–45, 47, 49, 62n12, 165, 178, 184, 201, 211, 216, 221, 223
British social anthropology, 25–26, 32n6, 162, 236–37, 242
British Solomon Islands Protectorate, 165, 197, 209, 221
brother-sister relationships. *See* sibling relationships
Bugotu (Santa Isabel), 81, 192
Bula, Daniel, 96
Buri village, 39, 41–42, 47–48, 109, 177
Burns, Philp and Company, 41, 165, 198
*butubutu* (clan, grouping), 12–13, 37–38, 54–60, 62–63nn21–23, 64–68, 70–72, 75–77, 79, 81–88, 90, 106–8, 122n1, 128, 132, 136–46, 149–50, 152, 155, 157–59, 161–62, 171, 173–74, 176–79, 183, 185, 187n8, 194, 219
*butubutu*, definition of, xii, 12, 54–60, 62n18, 106, 161
*buzabuza* (secondary forest), 52, 105, 138, 140–41, 145, 150, 209, 210. *See also* gardens

*Canarium* spp. trees and nuts (*ngari, neni*), 82, 83–84, 107, 128–29, 134, 138, 150, 196. *See also* nut grove
canoe houses, 3, 12, 40, 42, 45, 56, 73–74, 80, 85, 90
canoe landing places, 3, 39–42, 50
canoe travels, narratives of, 60, 91–100, 102, 110–11, 159n12, 219

canoes, 7, 39, 48, 52–53, 87, 89n7, 94, 101, 106, 107, 124, 126, 130–33, 226
canoes, building of, 44, 141, 178, 198
canoes, ghost, 76
canoes, motorized, 4, 39, 53, 116, 160, 193–94
canoes, war (*qeto*), 12, 44–46, 67, 73–74, 82–85, 86–87, 102, 150, 159n12, 193
capitalism, expansion of, 12, 20–21, 25, 38, 121, 126, 162, 164, 169, 197, 203, 221–23, 237, 243
captives (*pinauzu*), 1, 12, 46, 56, 64–65, 67, 73, 77–83, 86, 88, 88n2, 91, 102, 110, 135
care of elderly (*barozo*), 152
Carter, Marama, 115
carving, 51, 52, 111–12, 131
Cawa, Johnny, 231
cementing of graves, 76, 117, 145–46, 148. *See also* mortuary ritual
Central Province, 197
Chetwynd, Justice, 174–75
chiefs (*bangara*), 6, 14, 29–30, 33n11, 43–46, 54, 56, 58–60, 64, 67, 71, 73–79, 81–87, 89–90n12–13, 91, 95, 97–104, 108–10, 117, 121n1, 122n4, 124, 135–36, 144, 146, 151–53, 157, 159n12, 165, 170, 172, 179–81, 183, 185, 187n8, 193, 204–5, 209, 228, 232
chiefs, female or chiefly women, 85, 91, 101–2, 113, 117, 121n1. *See also* kalao bangara
Chiefs' Committee, Pienuna (also called Kubokota Chiefs' Committee), 136, 138, 174, 179–82, 184
Chiefs' Committee, Ranongga Island, 143–44, 181–82, 184
chiefly succession, 30, 87, 89n4, 90n13, 95, 176–80, 219
chiefs, respectful behavior toward, 71, 90, 158n6, 204
childbirth. *See* birthing
Choiseul, vii, 5, 32n4, 34, 43–46, 48, 62n12, 62n16, 64, 70, 74, 77, 81–84, 106–7, 109, 131, 140, 172, 179, 190, 192, 194, 201, 202, 217nn5–6
Christian conversion, 12–13, 30, 59, 77, 88, 95–97, 108, 113, 120, 124, 219, 230

Christian Fellowship Church (CFC), 168, 170, 202, 223
Christian universalism, 120, 236, 239
Christianity, 3, 12, 30, 54, 76, 84, 88, 91, 95–98, 100, 103, 114, 119, 134, 136, 138, 201, 219, 230–32
Christianity and ideas of freedom, 13, 112–13
Christian denominational rivalries, 31, 120–23, 178, 187n6, 202, 207, 220
Christmas. *See* holidays
clan, xii, 2–3, 8, 12–14, 21, 23, 36, 38, 40, 53–55, 58–60, 62n18, 68, 71, 78–79, 85, 118, 139, 142, 146, 160–61, 163, 167, 177, 182–83, 185, 194, 290. *See also butubutu*
coconut plantations, 49, 59, 76, 106, 140–41, 182–83
Cold War, 11, 18
colonial administrators, 164–5, 201, 216
Colonial Office, 48, 223
colonial state, 12, 19, 22, 46, 59, 119, 184, 190, 203, 215, 222, 235, 238
Commission of Inquiry into 2006 riots, 233, 242n15
Commissioner of Forests, 172–74
community, ideas about, 94, 125–26, 132, 176–80, 185–86, 237
community work, 51, 53, 106, 120, 126, 170–71, 179, 190, 192, 210, 215
compensation (*ira*), 18, 79, 135–36, 161, 172, 204–7, 214, 217n12, 225, 227, 232, 240
compensation, Malaitan practices of, 204–7, 214, 225, 240
conflict, 4, 10–11, 14–15, 17–22, 31–33, 37, 42, 50, 52, 157, 162, 168–69, 177, 179–80, 185–86, 189–90, 196, 201–7, 211–13, 215–16, 220–28, 232–35, 241n9, 241n13
conflict, class, 20, 212–13, 225–26
conflict, theories of 31–33
conservation 1–2, 14, 50, 136, 162, 164, 175–76, 179–81, 183–85
conversion. *See* Christian conversion
cooperative society, 41, 49, 61n9
Coppel, Nicholas, 234

copra, 11, 20, 45, 48–50, 62n14, 94, 101, 106, 109, 121, 125, 138, 141, 165, 169–70, 197–98, 208
corporatization, 163
cosmopolitanism, 23, 236–38, 242n17, 242n18
coup 2000, 18–19, 53, 169, 202, 222, 226, 241n7
crazy (*tuturu*), 12, 70, 87–88, 100, 106
cultural diversity, 27, 69, 70, 78, 191, 217n3
cuscus, 69, 107
customary, viii, 59, 112–13, 115–16, 130, 136, 141, 232. *See also kastom*
Customary Land Appeals Court, 172
customary land tenure, 2, 11, 13, 23, 36–38, 41, 50, 53, 60, 140–42, 161–69, 171, 173–75, 178, 186n1, 208–9, 215, 220, 235, 238

Daveta, Ezekiel, 173–74
death. *See* mortuary rituals, mourning practices
decolonization, 50, 176, 223
Degere (name of clan and territory), 36, 70, 149–51, 153–54, 159n11, 160, 164, 171–75, 185–86
Degere Development Company, 173
Dent, Rev. Tom, 99
descent theory, 25, 57, 63n21, 63n23, 162. *See also* British social anthropology
development, 2, 3, 10, 13–14, 20, 22, 41, 47–48, 61, 142, 160–65, 167, 170–71, 175–76, 179, 181–84, 187n5, 190, 198, 202–3, 210–12, 217n3, 221, 223–24, 228, 230, 234, 236, 240
"different person". *See* "other person"
Dimei, Pita, ix, 139
disease, epidemics, 40, 44, 100, 217n9
divination (*sabukai*), 107–8
Dovele (Vella Lavella), 43, 47, 109–10, 122n4
Downer, Alexander, 229
Dunateko, Joyce, 3, 9, 62n10, 114–18
Dureau, Christine, ix, 28, 85, 95, 98, 196, 200
Duvaha, 171, 186n3
dysentery, 44

earthquake, 8, 11, 34–36, 38–39, 41, 43, 49, 60n1, 74, 105, 143, 173, 183
Eddystone Island. *See* Simbo
Edge-Partington, Thomas, 200
education, 2, 59, 115, 120, 180, 183, 212, 214
Ekera, Liza, 3, 33n9, 51
Ekera, Rosie, viii, 3, 35, 129
Emu Harbour, 41, 48, 61–62. *See also* Koriovuku village
Enaduri, Helena, viii, 148
English language, 4, 25, 33n8, 44, 55, 109, 120, 154, 161, 208, 213, 216n1
Enoghae, 168
Ethnic Tension or "the Tension," 4, 11, 15, 17, 19, 190, 201–3, 206–7, 211, 215–16, 220, 222, 227, 231–34, 242n15
ethnicity and inter-ethnic relations, 17, 19–21, 23, 25, 27, 29, 31, 33n10, 188–89, 191, 193, 195, 197, 199, 201, 203, 205, 207, 209, 211, 213–15
ethno-nationalism, 21, 37, 162, 190, 211, 215, 223, 226
ethnography, 21–22, 30, 36, 56, 63n21, 66, 79, 236
Eto, Silas, 170–71
European Commission, 176
evangelists, 94, 96, 103, 109, 112, 178
exogamy, 54, 62n19, 71, 152, 177, 194

failed state, 4, 18, 20, 32n2, 229
Fallows Movement, 216, 223
Farland, Merle, 48
father's labor, 79, 117, 142, 145–46
Faukona, Justice, 173
feasts, 6–7, 26, 76, 79, 82–84, 100, 111–12, 120, 123n13, 132, 134, 149–50, 152, 155, 181, 192, 210
feasts, great *(vavolo)*, 77, 89n12, 109
fieldwork, 3–4, 16n1, 26, 31, 33n9, 54, 56, 64–65, 74, 126, 204–5
Fiji, 19, 30, 99, 108, 119, 122n2, 197
first contact, 40, 44, 95, 193
fishing, 7, 40, 69, 70, 71, 76–77, 86–87, 101, 106–7, 124, 125, 128, 131, 158n1, 181, 196, 234
Foale, Simon, ix, 141, 176, 181, 183, 187n5

folk tales *(vavakato iliganigani)*, 12, 66, 68–69, 86, 88
foreign, foreigners, 1, 3, 7, 10, 12–13, 15, 27, 30–2, 37, 50, 65, 67, 71–72, 79, 85–88, 91, 96, 98, 102–3, 108, 111, 117, 119–20, 137, 149, 165, 171–72, 178, 191–92, 222–24, 229–30, 235, 238, 240, 242n14
Forest Resources and Timber Utilisation Act 1996, 173
fundraising, 51, 117, 120, 126, 190
funerals. *See* mortuary rituals

Gaena'alu Movement. *See* Moro Movement
Galagala (name of clan and territory), 82, 177
Ganoqa language, xii. *See also* Kubokota language
Ganoqa region, 38, 41, 43, 48, 75, 82, 97, 105, 108–11, 177–79
gardens *(inuma)*, viii, 3–6, 10, 12, 36, 39–40, 42, 46, 51–53, 59–60, 62n17, 68–69, 76–77, 79, 82–83, 106, 111, 117, 120, 124–26, 131, 138, 140–42, 146, 150, 152, 158n7, 160, 162, 181, 183, 189, 193, 199, 209–10, 214. *See also buzabuza*
Gela, 216
gender relations, 2, 13, 26, 52, 86, 113–14, 117, 127, 203
genealogy, genealogical, xv, 3, 9, 21, 25, 55–58, 63n23, 139, 141, 162–63, 166–67, 171, 178–79, 185, 187n8, 188–89, 210
German, vi, 7–8, 43, 59, 192
German colonial administration, 62n12
Ghanoga, Ghanongga. *See* Ganoqa
Ghere, Rove, 42
giant. *See* ogre
Gilbert Camp, 17, 225
Gilbertese (Kiribati people), 192, 196, 209, 217n5
Girl's Brigade, 91
Gizo (capital of Western Province), ix, 2, 4, 6, 18, 36, 39, 43, 45, 47–49, 51–52, 101, 116, 125, 143, 173, 176, 180, 182, 186n4, 187n7, 192–93, 195, 202, 205, 209, 216n2, 217n5, 223, 227
Gizo market, 12, 52–53, 124, 126, 131

Gizo tax revolt, 223
Glengrow (SI) Company Limited, 173
globalization, 10, 23, 37, 50, 236
God, 1, 7, 31, 34, 59, 88, 94–96, 103, 105–7, 112, 117, 121, 125, 132, 136–37, 154, 156, 170–71, 178, 219, 230, 232
Goi Island, 123n15
Gold Ridge Mine, 224, 233, 241n13
Golden Springs, 168
Goldie, Rev. John F., 46, 98–99, 101–2, 105, 109, 122n6, 123n8, 201
Gospel, 88, 91, 93–99, 101, 103, 105, 107, 109, 111, 113–15, 117, 119, 121
Great Depression, 36, 41, 47, 197, 207, 217n8
Guadalcanal, 2, 4, 10–11, 14–15, 17–19, 22, 31, 37, 47–48, 69, 99, 107, 159n16, 189–90, 192–94, 197–98, 202–3, 206–11, 215–18, 220, 223–28, 230–32, 240–42
Guadalcanal Liberation Front (GLF), 227, 231
Guadalcanal Revolutionary Army (GRA), 17, 225. *See also* Isatabu Freedom Movement (IFM)
Guale (indigenous to Guadacanal), 15, 17–18, 31, 190, 207–8, 210–11, 218n14, 220, 224–25, 227–28, 232, 238
Guavoja, Emarine, viii, 6
guest. *See* host-guest relations
*guguzu* (inhabited place, village, hamlet), 2–3, 7–14, 18, 21, 24, 36, 40, 76, 94, 117, 120–21, 154, 170, 177–78, 184–85, 190–91, 207, 212, 230

hardship, fortress *(tapata)*, 40
Harrison, Simon, 18–19, 33n9, 66
Havea, Bishop David, ix, 92, 101
Havea, Marama, 92
headhunting, 12, 44, 67, 73, 77, 81, 85–88, 115. *See also* warfare
"heat the ground" ritual, 130, 149
High Court of Australia, 242n15
High Court of Solomon Islands, 14, 173–75, 186n4
Hilly, Francis Billy, 48, 169
Hilly, George, 41, 48–50, 61–62, 169, 194, 208

holidays, 7, 181, 190, 192, 195
Holy Mama, 170. *See also* Silas Eto
Honiara, 2, 4, 7, 14, 17–18, 20, 39, 53, 115, 125, 188–89, 191, 193, 195, 198, 202, 206, 210–14, 217n3, 219, 224–29, 231–33, 241n13, 241n14
hospitality, 1–11, 17, 19, 21, 23, 25, 27–29, 31, 33n9, 65, 115, 157, 199, 236, 238–39
host-guest relations, 1–10, 11, 29, 31, 65, 72, 91, 108, 126, 137, 140, 142, 144–45, 149, 155, 159n12, 174, 191, 195, 199, 206–7, 210, 216, 219–20, 233, 238–39
house, 10, 17, 71, 82, 120, 126, 143, 146–47, 150–51, 160, 170, 179, 195, 241–42n14
house society, 56, 156
household, 11, 52–53, 60, 115, 124–25, 153, 155, 169, 195, 238
Howard, John, 228–30, 240–41
Hviding, Edvard, x, 30, 32n4, 37, 44, 50, 54–55, 57–59, 62n10, 62n21, 65, 141, 167, 169, 170, 186n3

*ia* (area), 9, 138–39, 151
*iama* (ritual specialist or ancestral priest), 78, 83–85, 103, 105, 123n15
iconoclasm, 112
idol (*beku*), 106
in-married, 120, 179–80, 189, 192, 214, 217n3
inauguration, 73, 87
incest, 66, 71–72, 127–28, 135, 137, 143, 204
independence, 19, 167–68, 202, 240
individualism, 125, 237
Indo-Fijian, 19
influenza, Spanish, 199
Inuzauru Island, 5
Irapio, Luke, ix, 9–10, 35
Irivabika, 110
Isatabu Freedom Movement (IFM), 17, 226. *See also* Guadalcanal Revolutionary Army
Israel, Isrealite, 94, 119, 230
*Izizongo* 138–40, 142, 182. *See also* property

Japanese invasion, 36, 47
Jericho, 117

Jesus, 91, 103, 110, 114, 119–20, 171
Jijo, 107
Jiru, Derek Alekera, ix, 178
Jones, Rev. George F., 46, 109

Kadesi, John, ix, 7
*kalao bangara* (chiefly woman), 91, 95, 102, 115, 122n1
Kalena Timber Company, 172, 187n4
Kant, Immanuel, 11, 28–29, 238–39
Kaptain, 109
*kastom*, 12, 37, 54, 60n3, 107–8, 113, 164, 186n1, 201, 212, 219, 224–26, 232
Keara village, 6, 35, 39, 41–42, 83, 98, 105, 198
Keikoro villabe, 38
Keke, Harold, 227, 230–32
Kekoro community, committee, and women's association, 177, 179–82
Keleke (Vella Lavella), 109
Kemakeza, Allen, 228, 233, 241n7
Kennedy, Donald, 48
Kennedy, John F., 48
Kevin, Prudence, 103
kin-based love *(variroqu, vairoqu)*, 12, 57, 114, 126, 134, 156, 161
kin, kinship, kinsperson, xiv, xv, 2, 11, 13–15, 21, 23–32, 53, 56–58, 63n21, 63n23, 66, 69, 71, 75–76, 78, 81–82, 86, 88, 90, 96, 108, 114, 121, 126–28, 131, 133–35, 137, 139–40, 145–46, 148, 152–53, 155–56, 158n6, 160–61, 167, 171, 177, 188, 189, 193–95, 203, 205–7, 213–15, 239
Kiribati. *See* Gilbertese
Kobito, 2, 210
Kolomali village, 40, 42, 148, 208
Kolombangara Island, 4, 39, 44, 47, 56, 114, 165, 167, 205
Koqu village, 39, 42, 48, 116
Koribule, Matiu, 99, 108
Koriovuku village, 40–42, 48–49, 105, 194, 208–9
Kubokota language, 5, 32n8, 62n10, 88n2, 121, 216n2

Kubokota region, 2–5, 38–43, 45–46, 51, 54, 65, 97, 100–2, 105–8, 112, 127, 144, 164, 174, 177–78, 187n8, 194
Kubongava (name of clan originally from Choiseul), 8, 64, 106–8
Kudu village, 39, 41, 98, 105, 123n12, 217n8
Kukudu village (Kolombangara), 114
Kumana, Eroni, ix, 48
Kusage (North New Georgia), 170
Kwa'ioloa, Michael, 17, 20, 159n15, 188–89, 210–11, 214, 216n2, 217n12, 224–25
Kwaio (of Malaita), 77, 108, 123n16, 158, 191, 196, 198–201, 203, 205, 208
Kwara'ae (of Malaita), 121, 123n18, 188–89, 209–10, 214, 216n1, 225

Laena, Laela, 83
Lale village, 34, 39, 42, 97–100, 103, 113, 122n7, 145, 160, 174
land. *See* area, customary land, *ia, pezo*, territory
land alienation, 47, 125, 165–66, 222, 224
land, ancestral, 11–12, 36–37, 40–42, 54, 59, 67, 72–73, 86, 128, 138–39, 145, 149, 150, 153, 161–62, 164, 238–39
land, customary, 2, 11, 23, 38, 41, 50, 53, 59–60, 140, 142, 161, 163–69, 172–78, 186n1, 208–9, 215, 220, 232, 235, 238
land disputes, 31, 50, 72, 120, 157, 160, 162, 167, 183–84, 188, 202, 210
land tenure, 2, 12–13, 36, 52, 54–56, 59, 140–52, 164–67, 177, 183–84, 186n1, 188, 196
Land and Titles Ordinance (1959), 167
land transactions, 137, 155, 224
Langalanga (Malaita), 162, 205
Lapo, Giblin, viii, 2
Latavaki, Sito, 200
Lembu, 74–75
Leva Point (near Pienuna), 5, 90–91, 103
Lever Brothers, Levers Pacific Plantations Ltd, Levers Pacific Timbers, 165, 167, 207
Levi, Ben, 42
Liso, 7
local *(lokolo*, term of derision), 43

Index **281**

local area councils, 2
Local Court, 174
logging, 1–2, 11–12, 14, 37–38, 50–51, 60, 148, 158n1, 160–62, 164, 165–176, 181–82, 184–85, 187n4, 202, 223, 233, 234
logging license, 61–62, 169, 172–73, 175, 211
Lokasasa, 113, 145–47, 201
*lotu* (Christian faith or Christian services), 96, 99, 103, 110, 122n2. *See also* Christianity
love, 13, 28, 32n8, 77, 113–14, 124–25, 130, 133–34, 146, 148, 208, 232, 239
Luke, Glady, ix, 10
Luke, Ziosi, viii, 9–10, 35, 83, 124–26, 158n1
Luqa language, 32n8, 88n2, 89n3, 121, 216n2
Luqa region, 34, 38–39, 41–43, 51, 72, 85, 97–98, 100, 105, 108–10, 122n8, 124, 127, 148–49, 164, 174, 182, 192, 198
Lusibaea, Jimmy "Rasta," 231, 241n11
Lusibaea, Vika, 241n11

Maasina Rule, 48, 145, 186n1, 200–201, 208, 216, 218n15, 223, 226
Macintyre, Martha, 75, 86, 141
Madegusu. *See* Simbo
Maesatana, John, 210
Mahaffy, Arthur W., 45–46
Makapivo, Pastor, 102
Makira, 30, 68, 119, 157–58, 190, 197, 216, 218n15. *See also* Arosi
Malaita, 11, 14–15, 17–18, 32n4, 37, 47–48, 69, 77, 100, 119, 122n2, 122n3, 123n16, 138, 140, 145–46, 158n4, 159n15, 162, 186n1, 188–92, 195–98, 200–212, 214, 216, 216n1, 217n7, 217n12, 218n15, 220, 224–27, 231–32, 240
Malaita Eagle Force (MEF), 18, 226
Malaitans, relations with Ranonggans, 14, 138, 190, 199–200, 203–4, 211, 224, 236
malaria, 6, 9, 41, 53, 99, 122n8
Malinowski, Bronislaw, 16n1, 38, 69
Maluku (name of clan and territory), 70
Mamaloni, Solomon, 168–69
Mamdani, Mahmood, 19, 32n3, 104–5

Manning Straight, 83
market, 20, 53, 125–26, 172, 235
market gardening, 12, 51–53, 60, 125, 140, 193
market relations, 13, 126, 235
Marovo, 30, 39, 43–45, 47, 50–51, 54, 57–59, 62nn10–11, 62n21, 89n3, 99, 109, 114, 122n4, 141, 169, 176, 192
marriage, 7, 51, 54, 78, 134–35, 137, 139, 146, 155–56, 177, 192, 194, 203–5, 207, 216, 217n4, 228. *See also* wedding
Marx, Karl, 24–25
Matepitu, John, ix, 74, 123n14, 111–12
Matepitu, Matiu, viii, 3, 64–65, 106–7
matriliny, matrilineal kinship, 2, 12–14, 30, 37, 54–59, 62n18, 63n23, 68, 70, 78–79, 81, 90n14, 137, 139–40, 142, 144–46, 157, 162–63, 167, 178, 196, 204, 219
Meka, 6
Mekania, 43
Melanesia, 22, 25, 41, 61–63, 66–67, 79, 95, 102, 113, 115, 125, 128, 130, 134, 155, 162–65, 193, 213, 221, 224, 236, 241n12
Melanesian Brotherhood, 226
Melanesian relationality, 25, 32n5, 86, 90, 139, 142, 243n18
memorials *(merumeru)*, 73
menstrual taboos, 100
Mesia, 208–9
Methodist Mission, xii, 46, 48, 61n9, 62n14, 64, 91, 95–111, 114, 120–21, 122n4, 168, 170, 178, 187n6, 198, 200–202. *See also* United Church
Methodist Mission and language, xii–xiii, 109, 122n2
Methodist villages, 40–42. *See also* United Church villages
Methodist Women's Fellowship, 114–19. *See also* United Church Women's Fellowship
migrant laborers, 1, 19, 211, 228, 236, 240n2
migrant, migration, 1, 4, 10, 21–22, 27, 30, 40, 64–66, 108, 137, 140, 144, 154–55, 159n12, 182, 185, 188–89, 191, 197–98, 202–3, 211–12, 214, 216, 219–21, 224–25, 228, 236, 240n2

Ministry of Peace and Reconciliation, 232
missionaries, European, 41–42, 59, 91, 94–100, 103, 110, 113, 165, 230
missionaries, indigenous Solomon Islander, 84, 105–6, 109, 112, 114, 170
missionaries, Pacific Islander, 97, 99–100, 112, 122n2, 122n8
Moata, Pastor Izikeli, 124
mobility, 4, 18–19, 21, 23, 59, 120, 188–91, 193–95, 197, 199, 201, 203, 205, 207, 209, 211–13, 215, 217n3
modernists, 215
Modo village, 35–36, 38–39, 41–42, 45, 74, 77, 105–6, 109–12, 122n4, 123n14, 144, 177–78
Mokeru, 9, 35
Mondo. *See* Modo
money. *See also bakia*, 7, 10, 13, 33n9, 46, 49, 53, 60, 65, 72, 77, 82, 117, 124, 126, 131, 133–34, 136, 142–46, 148–49, 151, 156, 158n1, 168, 170–71, 175, 182, 195–96, 207, 212, 214, 219, 221, 227–28, 235, 240
Moro Movement, 218n15, 223, 232
mortuary ritual, 54, 67, 72–84, 97, 110, 117, 139. *See also* mourning practices
Moti, Julian, 233, 242n15
Mount Austin, 210
mourning practices, 8, 72, 75–79, 85, 90, 110, 177. *See also* mortuary ritual
Muma, Hatakiko, 43
Mumapitu, Ezi, ix, 108
Mumapitu, Paul, ix, 107–8
Munda village (Roviana), 98–99, 102, 105, 115–16, 122n4, 195, 202, 209
Munda Accord, 202

Nake, Amos, 77, 178
Nake, Timote, 178–79
Naorongo, Zinia, 116
nation-state, 11, 15, 20–21, 24, 28–29, 77, 119, 156, 165–66, 184, 188, 198, 202, 212–13, 215, 221–22, 224, 235–38
National Peace Council, 227, 234
National Referral Hospital, 195
nationalism, 162, 211–13. *See also* ethno-nationalism

Nduke. *See* Kolombangara
neoliberal, 15, 23, 235, 240n6
Neri, Timoli, ix, 82
New Bare village, 42
New Caledonia, 34
New Georgia, 1, 12, 30, 37, 39, 43–47, 50, 54–57, 61, 63n23, 65–68, 73, 76, 80, 88n2, 89n3, 106, 109, 122n5, 125, 131, 135, 141, 149, 156, 165, 167–68, 170–71, 190, 193, 197–98, 200–201, 216n2, 236
New Mala village, 61, 207–10
New Testament, xiii, 91, 94
New Year. *See* holiday
New Zealand, 1, 228
Ngaikeni village, 99–100
Ngopa, Levani, 99, 108, 122n8
Niami. *See* Vonga
Nicholson, Rev. R.C., 46, 56, 96, 123n11, 200
Niqu, Pastor Shem, 109–10
Niqusasa, 41, 48, 61–62, 110
non-Christian ancestralists, 100, 122n3, 123n16, 191, 196, 201
non-governmental organization (NGO), 14, 30, 164, 176, 184, 195, 227, 241n14
non-Ranonggans, 2, 216n2
non-state societies, 11
Nori, Andrew, 227
Noro, 18, 39, 51, 53, 195, 202, 209
North New Georgia, 168, 170–71
North New Georgia Timber Corporation (NNGTC), 171
Noso, 101
Nulu (name of clan and territory), 2, 70, 77, 82–83, 106, 144, 164, 176–84
Nunukujuku, Boazi, 106
nut groves (*aoro*), 41–42, 79, 83, 128, 138, 140–42, 150, 160–61
*nyete* (rotten *Canarium* nuts), 116, 196

Obobulu village, 42, 49, 51, 77, 89n10, 101, 134, 177–78, 180–81, 184
Oceania, 25, 27, 29–30, 33n11, 124, 239
Ofa, Devita, 100, 105
Officer, Graham, 63
ogre (*iliganigani*), 68–72, 86–89
Ole Lavata, 150, 160

Ole Tinoni, 106
Ole Tomete, 106
ontology, 30, 68, 138, 239
"other," 15, 88, 142, 156, 190
"other person" or "different person" (*goto tinoni*), 28, 56, 60, 70, 77, 78, 85, 128, 133, 137, 152, 157, 174, 182–83
Overseas Development Administration (UK), 176

Pacific Island Labourer's Act 1901, 197
Pacific Islander missionaries. *See* missionaries, Pacific Islander
Pacific Islands Forum, 228, 240
Pacific Islands region, 11, 29
pacification, 11–12, 36, 40, 47, 59, 73, 86, 88, 102, 131, 150, 165, 169, 193, 204, 238
Padaqeto, 46
*pajuku*, 9, 36, 79, 130, 142–45, 148–49, 154–59, 165, 224
Paleo, Costas, 43
Paleo, Dixon, viii, 43, 133
Paleo, Hazel Piqebakia (*also* Hazel Piqe), viii, 5–6, 93
Paleo, John Wesley (of Pienuna), viii, 64–65, 100–104, 110, 123n10, 123n11, 132
Pana, Barnabas, 109
Panakera, Charlie, ix, 48–49
Panakera, Geoffrey, viii, 3
Panakera, Simion, 3, 8, 48, 114, 169
Panakolo, viii, 149–54, 160
Papua New Guinea (PNG), 16n1, 26, 42, 66, 86, 140, 158n3, 162, 190, 193, 212, 240n6
Paqe village, 42, 149–50, 159n13, 160
Participating Police Force, 229, 242n15
Patu village (also called Patubolibolivi), 42
Patukango (name of clan and territory), 159n12
paternal nurture, 117, 139–40
path, 4–5, 7, 39, 43, 63n21, 68, 75, 90n15, 91, 100–1, 109, 112, 150, 161, 182, 193
patriliny, patrilineal kinship, 13, 37, 54–55, 58, 62n19, 79, 117, 139, 140, 142, 144–45, 156, 163, 167, 177, 196. *See also vinapodo*

Pavukera, John, viii, 2–3, 6, 8, 49, 64–65, 75, 106, 117, 122n1, 178, 181, 183
peace, 12, 17–18, 23, 29, 31, 88, 95, 119, 125, 203, 207, 219, 226–30, 232, 234, 238, 240
Peace Monitoring Committee, 227
Pejapeja hamlet, 101
Percy Sladen Trust Expedition, 30, 37, 55
personhood, 26, 31, 242n18
*pezo* (territory, land), 130, 137–40, 142, 149, 153, 182. *See also* territory
Phillips Commission (First Land Commission, 1919–1923), 166
Pienuna, evangelization of, 100–8, 120, 171–72
Pienuna residents, 42, 51–52, 64, 73, 75, 77, 83, 89n10, 106, 114, 132, 152, 188, 191–95, 206, 209
Pienuna school, viii, 2–3, 183, 191–92
Pienuna village, 1–3, 5–7, 9–10, 12, 17, 35, 39–40, 42–43, 48–49, 51–52, 62n10, 64, 73, 75, 77–78, 82–83, 89n10, 91–92, 94–97, 101–3, 105–8, 110, 112, 114–17, 120, 124–26, 129, 131–32, 134, 136, 138, 150, 152, 171–72, 177–84, 187n8, 188, 190–95, 205–6, 209, 217n3
pigs, pork, 7, 11, 79, 84, 11, 149–51, 153, 191–92, 211
Pijin. *See* Solomon Islands Pijin
*pinauzu*, 64–65, 67, 81–83, 88. *See also* captive
Pize of Rava, 82–83, 113
place names, xiv, 6–8, 68, 110, 217n13
Povana (name of clan and territory), 36, 42, 70, 83, 217n8
prayer, 102–3, 105, 136–37, 154, 207, 220, 226, 231–32
pre-Christian era, 12, 66, 83, 86, 88, 124
precedent, 28, 108, 240
priest, ancestral. *See iama*
property, 15, 18, 31, 41, 69, 76, 79, 86, 121, 124, 128, 130–31, 137–58, 158n10, 160, 163, 165–67, 182, 189, 196, 199, 202, 207, 211
property, Western understandings of, 23, 158n8, 185, 233, 235

Protectorate. *See* British Solomon Islands Protectorate
proto-human or quasi-human beings, 12, 66, 68–71, 86– 88, 89n7, 89n9, 95, 115
Puki village, 82

Qago, Evelyn, ix, 64, 89n10, 134, 209
Qeuru village, 41–42, 83, 105, 113, 123n12
Qiloe hamlet, 49, 178
Queensland (Australia), 47, 98–99, 122n5, 197, 227
quiet the adze *(moko temoko)*, 130, 132

Ragoso, Bruce, ix, 177, 179
Rama, Stephen, 64
Ranongga Island, xii-xiv, 1–4, 22, 71
Ranongga Island, alienated land on, 36, 41, 48, 102, 198, 208, 217n8
Ranongga Island, geography and terrain, 1, 8, 10–11, 34–36, 38–40, 126
Ranongga Island, languages of, xii, 216n2
Ranongga Island, relation to region, 17, 18, 22, 39, 43–44, 46, 59–60, 71, 189, 191–94
Ranongga Island, settlement patterns, 40–43, 72, 208–9
Rauru. *See* Choiseul
Rava village, 42, 82, 131–32
reconciliation, 136, 160, 231–32, 234
reforestation, 50, 171
refuge, 1, 17, 29, 65, 72, 239
Regional Assistance Mission to Solomon Islands (RAMSI), 15, 18, 20, 53, 221, 228–35, 242n15
Rendova Island, 149
*resana* (light rain, a sign of spirit presence), 9, 107
Resana, Manase, 98, 122n6
Resana, Mata, 98–99
resource capitalism, 38, 162, 164, 221–22
resource management, 180–83
return migration, 214, 225
Riringi, 109
ritual, 10, 56, 65, 86–88, 96, 130–32, 135–37, 151, 154–56, 185. *See also* mortuary ritual, marriage, compensation.
ritual, associated with fertility, 76–77
ritual, associated with warfare, 72–81, 84, 87, 88
ritual, Christian, 96, 99, 108, 119, 220, 231
ritual, function of, 96, 130, 151
ritual prostitute *(tugele)*, 82, 204
ritual transactions of property, 13, 130, 131–33, 141–54
ritual transmission of skills, 131
rituals, welcome, 86, 94–96, 102, 105, 219–20
Rivers, W.H.R. (William Halse Rivers), 37–38, 55–57, 61, 167
Roga, Lynette, 191
Rono, 109
Rooney, Rev. Stephen R., 98
Roughan, John, 38, 228
Rove, Gago, ix, 171
Rove Prison, 231
Rove, Rev. Ikan, ix, 170–71, 186n2
Roviana, 6, 43–47, 58, 62n11, 73, 78, 86–87, 97–99, 101–2, 106, 109–10, 114–15, 121, 122n4, 162, 170, 186n3, 192, 195–96, 202, 216n2
Roviana language, 89n8, 170
Royal Solomon Islands Police, 18, 242n15
*Royalist*, HMS, 45

Sabala village, 39, 41–42, 81, 105, 110, 113, 131
Sabana, 56, 188
sacrifice, 65, 67, 70, 79–80, 83, 87, 89n7, 94–95, 102, 112, 136, 210, 219
sacrificial victim *(vavaluna, kokomate)*, 73, 77–78, 83, 84–85, 90, 110
Sado, 98–99
Saevuke village, 39, 42, 150, 160
Sagela, 103, 105
Sagobabata, 103, 105, 187n8
Samata, Laela, 134
Samata, Manakera, ix, 134
Samata, Samuel, viii, 2–9, 62n10, 73, 77, 105, 122n1, 178–80, 183, 206–7, 209
Santa Isabel, 30, 43, 45, 56, 62n12, 73, 82–84, 95, 102, 122n5, 158n6, 188, 192, 194, 198, 201, 216n1
Sasala, Willy, viii, 62

Sasapitu, Grace Nose, 93, 131–33, 194
Sasapitu, Joseph, viii, 131, 194
"the savage slot," 27, 32
Scales, Ian, viii, 12, 43–44, 56, 59, 166, 202–3
school, schooling, 2–3, 39, 50, 53, 98–99, 101, 106, 114, 117, 120–21, 122n8, 126, 131, 160, 179, 183, 191–93, 198, 212–14, 221, 228, 240n4
school fees, 53, 131, 195, 214
Scott, Michael, x, 30, 63n21, 65, 68–71, 89n7, 157, 218n15
Sem, Jeffrey, iv, 192
Seventh-day Adventist Church, 38, 40–42, 78, 89n9, 91, 96, 105–12, 114–15, 120–21, 123n18, 136, 144, 168, 177–78, 187n6, 191–93, 196, 199, 202, 205
Seventh-day Adventist Dorcas Society, 97, 116. *See also* United Church Women's Fellowship
Seventh-day Adventists and language, xii–xiii, 109, 121, 122n2, 123n18
Seventh-day Adventist Mission, 41, 46, 91, 96, 108–12, 122n2, 122n4
Seventh-day Adventist treatment of ancestral shrines, 74, 78, 106, 108, 111–12, 136
Seventh-day Adventist villages, 40, 42, 48, 52, 61n9, 62n14, 74, 111–12, 120, 144, 168, 177–78, 187n6, 191–93
sexuality, premarital, 203–4
shell valuables, 6, 7, 10, 29, 65, 72, 80–82, 91, 100, 107, 111–12, 135–37, 158n4, 182, 219–20, 228
Shortland Islands, 44, 62n12, 76, 190, 216
shrines. *See* ancestral shrines
sibling relationships, 31, 71, 103, 113, 121, 124, 127–28, 146, 150–51, 156, 158n6, 163, 239
side (*kale*) of island, 38–40, 42, 82, 84, 177
side (*kale*) in ritual and kin relations, 7, 63n21, 54, 117, 135–36, 139, 146, 148, 172, 203, 206
*sigu* (birthing area), 105, 113
Silvester Rev. A.W.E., 48

Simbo, 6, 28, 34, 37, 39, 43–46, 55–57, 59, 61–63, 65, 67, 72–75, 77, 81, 86, 89n8, 95, 97–98, 121n1, 122n6, 122n8, 123n9, 158n6, 185, 192, 205
Sinalagu (Malaita), 200
slave, 67, 73, 75, 81–82, 113, 120, 135
Sogavare, Manasseh, 61, 227, 233, 241n7, 242n15
Solomon Islands Alliance for Change, 223
Solomon Islands Broadcasting Corporation, 61, 206
Solomon Islands Plantations Limited (SIPL), 224
Solomon Taiyo, 51, 53, 195
Solomon Western Islands Fair Trade (SWIFT) Trust, 172
Solomons Pijin language, xii, 4, 12, 37, 43, 121, 122n2, 158n1, 159n15, 161, 191–92, 212–13
sorcery, 44, 65, 72, 157
sovereignty, 19, 29–30, 84–85, 87, 91, 110, 219, 233, 238
Special Land Commission, 167
Speight, George, 19
spirits, 13, 60, 68, 70, 96, 105–8, 111–12, 119, 107, 121, 138, 149, 154, 157, 170
Spiritual Authority. *See* Rove, Rev Ikan
spiritual transformation, 13, 15, 46, 96, 121, 230–32
stranger, 1, 4, 6, 9–12, 15, 22–23, 27–31, 31, 33n11, 60, 66, 72, 83, 88, 91, 94–96, 119–21, 126–27, 133, 137–38, 149, 155, 185, 215, 219, 228, 236–39
stranger chief, stranger king, 30, 33n11, 87
stranger sociality, 11, 14, 28, 86, 184, 215
Strathern, Marilyn, 26, 32n5, 212
Stritecky, Jolene, ix, 9, 17, 225
stupid, stupidity (*tuturu*), 12, 66, 68–71, 87–88, 89n7, 95, 99
Suafo, James, 208–10
Suava village, 41–42, 82, 102, 198, 205, 217n8
Subolai (Vella), 145
Suluana, 115
synod, 91, 93–94, 101, 171–72

taboos, 13, 100, 111, 152, 181
tabu sites. *See* ancestral shrines
Tadi, 42
Takavoja, 95, 101–3, 113, 115, 117, 122, 187n8
*tamaza* (God, spirits), 107, 138, 149, 170. *See also* God, spirits
Tapurai (Simbo), 98, 122
Taqitaqi, 43
Taquaba village, 205
taro, 44, 87, 110, 134, 150, 182
Tausinga, Hon Job Dudley, 170–71, 186n2
territory, 23, 30–31, 36–37, 38, 41, 54–59, 60, 61n7, 65, 66, 68–69, 71, 74, 77–79, 84–86, 91, 136–40, 143–44, 146, 149–50, 152, 155, 164, 176–78, 182, 184, 188–89, 193, 219, 223, 238–39
Tetebule, Nyatakera, 101
Tevolo, Pastor, 105
Thurnwald, Richard, 59
Timber Control Unit, 168
"time before" or "time of darkness," 12, 66, 83, 86, 88, 124. *See also* pre-Christian era
Tiqi, 83, 102
Tiro (name of clan and territory), 159n12
Tirovuku, 107–8
To'ambaita (Malaita), 189, 198, 212, 214
Tobulu, 106–8
*tomete* (ancestors, the dead), 106–8, 138. *See also* ancestors, spirits
Tonili, 109–11, 123n14
Toribule, Jebede, viii, 3, 112, 194
Toribule, Marion, 171, 194
Toribule, Rev. Abraham, ix, 151
Townsville Peace Agreement (15 October 2000), 18, 207, 227, 229–30
trade goods, 45, 74, 197
tradition. *See kastom*
traditional money. *See* shell valuables
traditionalists, 100, 215
tribe, tribal, tribalism, 11, 13–15, 20–24, 54, 58, 60, 61n5, 117, 119, 138, 140, 160–86, 220, 236
*Tridacna* spp. (clam), 135

Trobriand islands, 69, 79
tsunami, 8–9, 34, 43
Tulagi, 45
tuna, 51, 125, 133, 195
Tutijama, 109
Tutty, Pastor R.H., 109–10
*tuturu* (forest spirits, also state of being stupid or senseless), 46, 70–71, 87, 89n7, 100

Ulufa'alu, Bartholomew, 169, 223, 227, 240–41
United Church, vi, 2–4, 38, 41, 89n9, 91–94, 109, 114, 116, 118–21, 123n18, 132, 135–36, 151, 171–72, 177, 182, 185, 193, 195, 226
United Church members and language, xii, 121, 123n18
United Church treatment of ancestral shrines, 74, 78, 106, 108, 111–12, 136
United Church villages, 41, 48, 52, 61n9, 62n14, 74, 111–12, 120, 144, 168, 177–78, 187n6, 191–93
United Church Women's Fellowship (UCWF), viii, 97, 112, 114–18, 192. *See also* Methodist Women's Fellowship, Adventist Dorcas Society
unity, 4, 24, 28, 31, 121, 125, 128, 192
urban life, 2, 14–15, 16n1, 17, 24–25, 28, 43, 53, 124–25, 189, 191, 194–95, 210–15, 233

Vanuatu, 30, 34, 113, 193, 242n15
*variroqu* or *vairoqu* (love), 28, 32n8, 114, 133–34, 146
*vavolo*, 77, 89n12, 109. *See also* feast
*vavuluna*, 77–78, 83, 90, 110. *See also* sacrificial victim
Vella Lavella, 4–5, 37, 39–40, 43–48, 55–56, 58–59, 62n15, 63n23, 67, 77, 82–83, 96, 102, 105–7, 110, 116, 122, 145, 177, 179, 192, 200
Vesu Gogoto, 40
village formation, 9, 48, 59, 78
*vinapodo* ("born of fathers" or patrilateral filiation), 58, 139, 145–46
Viru Harbour, 46, 51, 109, 122

Vitu (name of clan and territory), 64, 77, 95, 108, 144, 149–50, 152, 154, 159n13, 173–75, 177, 181–83
Voeta, Devita, 105
Vonga village, 42, 52, 107–8, 177, 184, 191
Vonunu, 96
Vori, 110

war raids, 44–45, 72–73, 77, 81, 84, 102, 108, 110
warfare, 1, 12, 30, 40, 44–46, 58, 65–67, 72–75, 77, 79–81, 84, 86–88, 120, 131, 226
warrior, 6–7, 13, 29, 40, 43–44, 46, 67, 77–78, 82–84, 86–87, 91, 94–95, 103, 110, 116, 177, 188, 193, 200, 206, 208, 219–20, 228
warrior welcome, 6–7, 29, 91, 94, 110, 219–20, 228
wastelands, 165–66
weapons, 44, 94, 197, 230, 234
Weather Coast (Guadalcanal), 18–19, 211, 217n7, 224, 227, 230, 240
wedding, 4, 7, 49, 139, 195
welcome. *See* warrior welcome
Wesley, John (of Lale), ix, 99–100, 122n7, 122n8
Wesley, Sera, viii, 93, 133
"West" or "Western" (Solomons) identity, 190, 196–203, 215

Western Province, 1–2, 4, 8, 11, 18, 37–38, 53, 62n16, 117, 120, 170–72, 181, 186n4, 190, 195–99, 202–3, 207–8, 210, 217nn5–6, 226, 240
Western Province Culture Office, 2
Western Provincial Government, 173, 175, 202
Wheatley, Kitchener, 61, 208–10
Wheatley, Norman, 109, 208
Wheeler, Gerald Camden, 61
White Australia Policy, 47, 197
White, Ellen G., 109
widow suicide, 75, 78
Women for Peace, 226
Woodford, Charles, 45, 165
Woodlark, 34
World War II, 25, 37, 41–42, 47, 50, 90, 114, 122n4, 144, 166, 169, 187n6, 201, 210, 217n8, 223, 238
World Wide Church of God, 178
worship, 34, 88, 96–97, 99, 103, 107, 110–12, 120, 122n2, 170
WWF (World Wide Fund for Nature), 2–3, 14, 136, 176–84, 187n5, 187n7

Zabana, 82
Zion (hamlet), 3, 105
Ziro, Edi, ix, 6
Zitabule, Pita, 105
Zobule, Alpheaus, ix, 173–75
Zodo, 76–77

www.ingramcontent.com/pod-product-compliance
Lightning Source LLC
Chambersburg PA
CBHW070911030426
42336CB00014BA/2369